World War II:
A Military and Social History

Thomas Childers, Ph.D.

PUBLISHED BY:

THE GREAT COURSES
Corporate Headquarters
4840 Westfields Boulevard, Suite 500
Chantilly, Virginia 20151-2299
Phone: 1-800-832-2412
Fax: 703-378-3819
www.thegreatcourses.com

Thomas Childers, Ph.D.

Professor of History
University of Pennsylvania

P rofessor Thomas Childers was born and raised in East Tennessee. He received his Bachelor's and Master's degrees from the University of Tennessee, and he earned his Ph.D. in History from Harvard University in 1976.

Since 1976, Professor Childers has taught in the Department of History at the University of Pennsylvania. He is a fellow of the Ford Foundation, term chair at the University of Pennsylvania and the recipient of several other fellowships and awards, including the Alexander von Humboldt Stiftung Research Grant, a fellowship in European Studies from the American Council of Learned Societies, and a West European Studies Research Grant from Harvard University.

In addition to teaching at University of Pennsylvania, Dr. Childers has held visiting professorships at Trinity Hall College, Cambridge, Smith College, and Swarthmore College, and he has lectured in London, Oxford, Berlin, Munich, and other universities in the United States and Europe.

Professor Childers is the author and editor of several books on modern German history and the Second World War. These include *The Nazi Voter* (Chapel Hill, 1983) and *Reevaluating the Third Reich: New Controversies, New Interpretations* (New York, 1993). He is currently completing a trilogy on the Second World War. The first volume of that history, *Wings of Morning: The Story of the Last American Bomber Shot Down Over Germany in World War II* (Reading, Mass: Addison-Wesley, 1995), was praised by Jonathan Yardley in *The Washington Post* as "a powerful and unselfconsciously beautiful book." The second volume, *We'll Meet Again* (New York: Henry Holt and Company) is set for publication in spring 1999. The final volume, *The Best Years of Their Lives*, will follow in due course. ∎

i

Table of Contents

Table of Contents

Table of Contents

World War II: A Military and Social History

Scope:

This set of thirty lectures examines the greatest conflict in human history, the Second World War. Between 1937 and 1945 approximately 55 million people perished in this series of interrelated conflicts. No continent was left untouched, no ocean or sea unaffected. The war fundamentally altered the international system, leading to the eclipse of Europe and the emergence of the United States and the Soviet Union as global superpowers. It ushered in the atomic age and produced, in Auschwitz and elsewhere, the most grisly crimes ever committed in the long course of Western civilization. It set the stage for the cold war, and it accelerated or, in some cases ignited, movements for national liberation around the world, prompting the rollback of Europe's colonial empires. In short, the Second World War has defined an entire epoch in human history, an epoch from which we are only now, in the final decade of the twentieth century, emerging.

The first four lectures are devoted to the origins of the war in Europe. They examine the relationship between the First World War, especially the way that conflict ended, and the Second. We examine the controversial Treaty of Versailles and the international security system that its framers envisioned, and we analyze the reasons for its failure. We dissect Adolf Hitler's conception of foreign policy, his domestic and international objectives, and the means he used to pursue his aims. We also address the failure of the Western powers—France, Great Britain, and the United States—to counter Hitler's attempts to destroy the Treaty of Versailles. This failure set the stage for overt Nazi aggression in 1939.

Lectures 5 through 11 focus on the war in Europe, from its outbreak in September 1939 to the failure of the German offensive before Moscow in December 1941. We examine the revolutionary German military strategy of Blitzkrieg and its dramatic success in Poland and in the West in 1939 and 1940. We explore the shocking collapse of France in the summer of 1940, the "Miracle of Dunkirk," and the German plans for an invasion of Great Britain. Two lectures are devoted to Britain's confrontation during 1940 and

1941—without allies and with only minimal aid from the United States—of a triumphant, seemingly invincible Nazi Germany, and its survival of that confrontation. Hitler's decision to attack the Soviet Union forms the point of departure for the final two lectures in this set. These lectures focus on the ideological background to Operation Barbarossa, the stunning successes of the opening phase of this gigantic military undertaking in the summer of 1941, and the reasons for its ultimate failure to achieve its goals. The German offensive bogged down in the snow before Moscow in December 1941, and the Blitzkrieg phase of the war came to an end.

In the next set of lectures—numbers 11 through 14—we turn to the war in Asia and the South Pacific. We examine the evolution of Japanese foreign policy and military thinking between the end of the First World War in 1918 and the invasion of China in 1937. The lectures provide an analysis of the dilemmas confronting Japanese policy makers in the years leading to their massive assault on European colonial possessions in Asia and on the American position in the South Pacific in 1941. We examine the planning for the attack on Pearl Harbor, the reasons for its success, and the American response. In the final lectures of this set, we examine Japanese strength at its high water mark and then turn to the two decisive American victories that signaled a major change of fortunes in the Pacific war: the naval battle at Midway and the long, bloody land campaign for Guadalcanal.

In Lectures 14 through 17 we return to the struggle against Germany, focusing on two major turning points in the war in Europe. We examine first the Anglo-American campaigns in North Africa between 1940 and 1942 and the invasions of Sicily and Italy in 1943. Allied victories in the Mediterranean Theater were highly controversial, provoking considerable disagreement between the British and American high commands. We will examine these differences over strategic priorities. Allied victories there marked a major turning point in the Western war against Germany, but, as Stalin complained and as the Americans agreed, even these successful campaigns seemed to delay the long-awaited invasion of northwestern Europe. Lecture 17 examines the battle of Stalingrad in 1942–1943, the turning point of the war on the Eastern Front. We examine the reasons for the failure of Hitler's plans in the Soviet Union and the remarkable rebound of the Red Army.

The next three lectures deal with Allied operations in Western Europe from the summer of 1944 to the spring of 1945. They focus on the planning for D-Day, the course of events on June 6, 1944, and the surprisingly long campaign in Normandy. We examine the German defensive schemes on the Western Front, the liberation of Paris, the controversy over Operation Market Garden, and finally the massive German counteroffensive in the Ardennes— the Battle of the Bulge—in December 1944. We also address the serious differences between Eisenhower and Montgomery over the Allied drive into Germany. The Supreme Commander insisted on a broad-based advance, while Montgomery advocated a "single thrust" toward the Ruhr and Berlin.

In the next set of three lectures, we shift our focus again to events in the Pacific Theater. We examine the American strategic decisions that would create a dual command structure and two axes of approach to Japan. The southwest Pacific would be dominated by General Douglas MacArthur and would be largely an Army theater, while operations in the central Pacific would be the responsibility of Admiral Chester Nimitz and hence the Navy. We will first examine the implications of this two-pronged strategy and then consider events in these two areas. We will analyze the Battle of Leyte Gulf, the gigantic naval engagement in the southwest in October 1944, and MacArthur's subsequent invasion of the Philippines. Next we follow Nimitz's relentless advance through the Central Pacific, the "island-hopping strategy," and the climactic battles of Iwo Jima and Okinawa.

After following the course of military events in Europe and the Pacific, the next two lectures interrupt the narrative to examine two features of the Second World War that distinguish it from all previous conflicts and place its terrifying stamp on the entire era. We will first consider the Nazis' efforts to create their "New Order" in Europe. We trace the role of anti-Semitism in Nazi ideology from the very beginning of the Third Reich and then analyze the steps that, after the outbreak of the war, led to the mass murder of European Jews. This "final solution to the Jewish question," as the Nazis euphemistically called their monstrous plans, is examined in detail. The use of strategic bombing, which would kill hundreds of thousands of civilians during the war, would fundamentally alter the nature of warfare in the modern age, and its effectiveness as well as its morality have remained among the most controversial issues of the war. We will examine the air war in both Europe and the Pacific, appraising its contribution to the Allied victory.

The next two lectures examine the creation of the U.S. Armed Forces (one of the most astonishing accomplishments of the Second World War) and social, economic, and cultural developments on the American home front during the war. We analyze how America's gigantic military machine, which hardly existed before 1940, was created. We will examine its organization, training, and social composition, and we will look at the day-to-day life of a new phenomenon—the GI, how he was fed, entertained, and equipped. In the same vein, we will examine the American economic miracle, the creation of the mammoth wartime economy, the influx of women into the labor market, and the social tensions that emerged during the war, especially the racial problems that led to riots in Detroit, Philadelphia, and other cities. We will also examine the hysteria that led to the internment of Japanese-Americans.

The final three lectures deal with the conclusion of the war in Europe and Asia, examining the "race" between the Red Army and the Western Allies to reach Berlin and the American air assault against Japan which culminated in the use of atomic weapons. We give special attention to Truman's decision to employ the bomb. The series concludes by assessing not only the historical significance and epochal political and economic impact of the war, but also its colossal human toll. ■

The Origins of the Second World War
Lecture 1

It was, like none before it, a total war, a people's war, leaving no element of society, regardless of which society, immune from its demands. It demanded the total immobilization of the nation's industrial, agricultural, financial, and human resources. And when it ended, it had brought fundamental economic and social changes in all of the combatant nations.

This course examines the historical importance of the Second World War, a conflict that was the single largest event in human history, stretching around the globe and consuming 55 million lives. It reshaped international politics, marked the emergence of the United States and Soviet Union as superpowers, and set the stage for the cold war.

World War II fundamentally altered the international system. It led to the decline of Europe in geopolitical and economic significance. It also led to the rollback of European colonial empires and the rise of national liberation movements in former colonies during the 1950s and 1960s. And it marked the origins of the welfare state in Europe.

These lectures will examine the macro-events of the war and its leading political and military figures, as well as how the war was actually experienced by workers, soldiers in the field, and the civilian population at home. In addition, we will explore the origins and consequences of the war, the role of economic factors in explaining its origins and development, and its impact on culture and society.

We will also explore the "psychic" dimension of the war, including its ability to evoke both the best and worst in human nature. The writer Studs Terkel called World War II the last "good war." Many have seen it as ennobling and as relatively free from the heavy emotional and psychological costs later associated with Vietnam. We have perhaps lost a sense of the grim realities of World War II, which we will try to recapture in these lectures by examining the full range of human experiences associated with the war, both those of its leaders and of the millions who suffered its consequences.

World War II had its origins in the conclusion of the First World War, with the sudden armistice of 1918 creating various problems. The German people had been led to believe that Germany's spring 1918 offensive would bring victory. The absence of

Interior of the Galerie des Glaces during the 1919 signing of the Treaty of Versailles.

foreign troops on German soil at the time of the armistice in October 1918 left many Germans convinced that the Army had been "stabbed in the back" by domestic enemies. The army blamed Germany's surrender on its republican government and leading political parties.

The victorious Allies were determined through the Treaty of Versailles (1919) to weaken Germany and provide a system of collective security for France and the new nations of Eastern Europe. Germany lost much of its territory: eastern territory (including mineral-rich Silesia) went to Poland; Memel was transferred to Lithuania; Alsace-Lorraine was returned to France; a Polish corridor was established between Germany proper and Prussia; and the Saar would be administered by the League of Nations for 15 years. Germany also lost many of its overseas colonies.

The United States would not become a member of the League of Nations. It was a preview of American isolationism that would dominate American policy in the 1930s.

The Allies required Germany to pay huge war reparations. The Versailles Treaty included a "war guilt clause" to justify these reparations. The Treaty included various clauses restricting Germany's armaments and troop levels.

It established a League of Nations and a system of collective security intended to keep the peace thereafter.

Problems with the Versailles Treaty and the collective security system arose almost immediately. The Treaty alienated the Germans, who saw it as a "dictated peace." They particularly resented the reparations and war guilt provisions. The German army shifted blame for the armistice toward the new republican government, thereby undermining its legitimacy. The U.S. Senate failed to ratify the Versailles Treaty or to approve the Anglo-American guarantees to France.

The United States began to withdraw into isolationism. Wary of being drawn into a new conflict on the continent, Britain distanced itself from France and sought accommodation with Germany. Italy was embittered because it had not been awarded new territories in the Adriatic region and in North Africa. Russia had not been invited to Versailles, and the new Bolshevik regime's distrust of the Western powers grew. ■

Suggested Reading

John Keegan, *The Second World War*, chapter 1.

A. J. P. Taylor, *The Origins of the Second World War*, Part I.

Gerhard L. Weinberg, *A World At Arms*, chapter 1.

Questions to Consider

1. Was the Treaty of Versailles too harsh? Not harsh enough?

2. Why were the victorious Allies unable to agree on enforcement of the Treaty?

The Origins of the Second World War
Lecture 1—Transcript

Hello, I'm Tom Childers. Welcome to this set of lectures on the Second World War. It's just over 50 years since the guns fell silent and the instruments of surrender were signed and the Second World War came, at last, to an end. Fifty years and yet we are still caught in its powerful thrall— books, films, magazines, museums are devoted to the war and assault us from all sides daily, whether we live in the United States, in Great Britain, in Germany, Japan, or Russia. They summon us to remember, to bear witness, to a momentous conflict that shaped the very contours of life in the twentieth century.

The complex of interrelated conflicts we call the Second World War is the most widely researched and exhaustively documented conflict in the modern era, and even so its sheer scope is staggering. Between 1937 and 1945, we estimate, no one knows for certain, 55 million lives were consumed by the war, dead. Millions more remained—wounded physically and mentally—or they simply vanished, or missing, never accounted for. The war was contested across all the world's oceans and seas, leaving few corners of the globe unscathed. It was fought in Europe, in Africa, in Asia, and drew combatants from North America, Australia, and South Asia. It was, quite simply, the single greatest, largest event in human history. Its political consequences were profound, yet fundamentally altered the balance of power in the world, leading to the eclipse of Europe and the emergence of the United States and the Soviet Union as superpowers. It ushered in the cold war, the ideological and strategic hangover from which we've suffered until this very decade. And it accelerated the retreat of European colonial empires throughout the world, intensifying and in some cases even generating movements of national liberation.

It was, like none before it, a total war, a people's war, leaving no element of society, regardless of which society, immune from its demands. It demanded the total immobilization of the nation's industrial, agricultural, financial, and human resources. And when it ended, it had brought fundamental economic and social changes in all of the combatant nations. After 1945, when the millions of veterans began returning home, people expected the States for which they had sacrificed and suffered to provide more in the way of health and homes and education. In Europe, the Second World War marks the real beginning of the welfare state, one of the most important social developments of the twentieth century. Historians have devoted a great deal of attention to, and can speak with some confidence about, the diplomatic origins, the underlying causes of the Second World War. We know a great deal about the economic mobilization for war and the social and political consequences of the war. We have numerous works—and very good ones—about the war's major statesmen, Franklin Roosevelt, Churchill, Stalin, Hitler, Tojo, and so on. We have great works about the leading military figures of the conflict, Eisenhower, Montgomery, Rommel, Yamamoto, Zhukov. These are important topics, key issues, in understanding the war, and we will certainly address them at some length in these lectures. But there is, for my money, more—another dimension that we ought to explore, and that we will explore. Until very recently, we've had surprisingly little about the actual experience of war—the soldiers, the workers, the loved ones left at home—how they experienced the conflict. And so, in these lectures we will examine the origins of the war, why was it fought, the politics and diplomacy of the participants, what were their goals, and what were the military strategies they employed to reach their objectives. We'll attempt to explain the war's outcome. What did the Allies win? Could the Germans and Japanese have prevailed?

We tend to overdetermine the outcomes of these things, but I think for anyone who lived through the war the outcome was anything but obvious, and certainly at the very beginning. We'll look at the role of economics. There's a growing tendency, I think, to believe that we simply out-produced—the Allies simply out-produced the Axis—that economic production doomed the Japanese and the Germans from the very outset. Is this the case? We'll also look at the changes in culture in society—primarily in the United States—but in the other combatant nations as well. But in all of this analysis, we don't want to lose sight of, indeed we will not lose sight of, the grim reality that war is about fighting and about dying. It confronts us with the most elemental human emotions and experiences—love, loss, fear, courage, sacrifice, cowardice, cruelty. It reveals humankind at its stunning best, ordinary men and women called upon to, and performing extraordinary feats of, bravery, of devotion to duty. And it also confronts us with humankind at its barbaric bestial worst; we think only of the great crimes of the Second World War to be reminded of that.

In this regard, it seems to me the Second World War confronts us with a peculiar irony; it is after all what Studs Terkel called the "good war," fought by the Allies to defeat the evil of Hitler's Third Reich and the militarism of Imperial Japan. But as time has passed, we seem to have come to the historical conclusion that the war, because it was fought for a good and just and even noble cause, that the fighting of the war was somehow itself ennobling, elevating, even glamorous, that the combat did not bring with it great agonies and sufferings—that post-traumatic stress syndrome, MIAs, POWs—were somehow unique features of the Vietnam experience. I think this is a view that subsequent generations of the war have, certainly not those men and women who actually lived through the war, but we had this kind of Vietnam syndrome, it seems to be, as we look back at the Second World War—and we have this sort of Mekong Delta-sized body of work about the Vietnam War—that the Second World War and the nature of it, what it meant in human terms, has somehow been lost. We want to address ourselves to that experience. And so in these lectures, we will try to probe the full range of wartime experiences—for the Second World War, for the meaning of the Second World War—to see it not simply from the perspective of those who directed the conflict, but from the perspective of those millions upon millions who did not make policy or formulate strategy, but found themselves and their families caught in the great and terrifying machinery of war.

Let's begin this odyssey then by turning our attention to the origins of the war in Europe, and especially the legacy of the First World War. A hundred years from now, if there are people still around watching films from The Teaching Company or reading books and thinking about the past—we hope that there will be—and they look back at our own troubled, star-crossed century, they may conclude that the two world wars of this century in fact constituted one great conflict—a kind of second Thirty Years War, like that of the seventeenth century, with a 20-year truce between the end of its first installment in 1918 and the beginning of its second in 1939. Now certainly there are differences, important differences, in motives, in objectives, in the nature of the regimes involved. The Soviet Union, after all, was not Czarist Russia; the Third Reich was not the Imperial Germany of the Kaiser, and so on.

There were differences in the means with which the war was fought—the nature of combat, the machinery, the technology, the weapons—and we will analyze those differences down the road in subsequent lectures. But it might be said, with some justice, that the origins of the Second World War in Europe are to be found actually in the Hall of Mirrors at the palace at Versailles, in the way the Great War, as the First World War was commonly called after 1918, was concluded. In the summer of 1918, the German public was led to believe that victory was within sight—there was light at the end of the tunnel. After four long years of suffering enormous casualties, immobilization of resources that had never been seen before in Europe, that the great offensive that the German army launched in the spring of 1918 was going to bring the long awaited and ultimate victory of German arms.

Information was tightly controlled, censorship was in place in Germany— as it was in all the combatant countries during the First World War—and that over and over through the course of the war the public, despite the long list of casualty figures in the papers underneath the black iron cross that appeared with frightening regularity, there was the sense that the war was going very well, that victory was within their grasp. And certainly this last great offensive in the spring of 1918 was to be that victory that was going to deliver the ultimate victory to Germany before the impact of the Americans could be felt on the war in Europe. Then in October, the high command made a startling announcement, an announcement that Germany had in fact surrendered; the country was in shock. How could this be? How could it be that the offensive that was going to bring Germany and the Kaiser its victory had led instead to an armistice, that the Germans had asked for an armistice? The sudden collapse left many in Germany believing that the army had, at the last moment, been stabbed in the back, that some sort of combination of domestic enemies—left-wing Social Democrats, the Catholic Center Party, the Liberal Parties dominated the right wing in Germany believed by Jews—had somehow stabbed the victorious army in the back at the crucial moment, just as victory was within their grasp. That was the only possible explanation, after all in 1918—in the fall of 1918—German troops were deep inside France, Russia had surrendered, the war on the Eastern Front had been won. We tend to think that Germany could not, and this is important as we think about the Second World War and the German invasion of the Soviet

Union, that the Germans could not have prevailed—that somehow this was a great folly.

But, of course, the German experience was they'd triumphed on the Eastern Front in the First World War—at great cost certainly. But in 1918, the war in the East had been won. The peace had not been won, the Bolsheviks were running amok in the East; the Germans didn't know what to do, but they had prevailed—the war there had ended successfully. German troops were still deep inside France—indeed Paris was still within marching distance of the German lines—and Germany itself was untouched. Its industries were still intact; there was no foreign soldier anywhere close to the German frontier. For the German public this was a triumphant Germany, and yet suddenly in November an armistice had been signed, asked for by the Germans. The Kaiser had passed into exile in Holland where he would be passed in 1940 by German troops on their way into Belgium.

The war was over and the proud German empire, the greatest military power in Europe, possibly in the world in 1914, had not only not seized their objectives but apparently lost the war. And a revolution had been proclaimed—overthrowing the old imperial regime—and a democratic republic had been established by a coalition of Social Democrats, Liberals, and the Catholic Center Party. The outsiders of the old empire were now the insiders; the world had been turned upside down. Then, in early 1919, the Germans were summoned to Versailles, to the ornate palace of the Bourbons just outside of Paris, for the peace Treaty. It was a convening of the diplomats of the combatant nations, along the lines of the Congress of Vienna, which had ended the Napoleonic Wars a century before. The German representatives were summoned to Versailles not to negotiate—this would be no negotiated settlement—but rather to hear the terms of the victorious Allies. For their part, the Allies, after suffering four long years of untold casualties, were determined to weaken Germany and to provide for some sort of international system of collective security. Woodrow Wilson, the American President, David Lloyd George of Great Britain, Clemenceau of France, Orlando of Italy—all came to the conference determined to make the world a safer place. This, after all, was "the war to end all wars," the war to make the world a safer democracy, and, for the Europeans certainly, what this meant above all else was to find a way to provide for collective security and to weaken Germany at the same time. Germany, after all, had held Europe at bay for four years, came very close to winning the Great War, and now something simply had to be done.

Woodrow Wilson arrived with the more idealistic agenda, certainly his idea that one of the causes of the Great War had been—was—frustrated nationalism. That what were needed was the national self-determination of peoples—allow the individual nations of Europe, the peoples of Europe, to have their own states, their own nation states—and that this would provide for some sort of stable peace. But they were all agreed that Germany somehow had to be weakened. They began with a series of actions; the first was to detach territory. The Germans simply had to lose something from the Great War, so a portion of German territory in the East was taken to create the new Polish state which came into existence, a state which hadn't existed at the outset of the war—a Polish corridor established between East Prussia and Germany proper to give this new Polish state access to the sea—meant that Germany had lost territory to this new "successor" state, as it was called, successor to the old Austro-Hungarian and German empires. Danzig, the largest German city in the area on the coast, the port city of Danzig, was to be given over to the League of Nations to administer. Memel, on the Baltic, was handed over to Lithuania. Alsace and Lorraine, the two provinces on the border of Germany and France, bounced back again to France in 1919; they had been taken from France by the Germans in 1871. So, that territory in the West was lost. The mineral-rich, industrial-rich Saar region on the German-French frontier was also to be administered by the League of Nations for a period of fifteen years. So these losses in Europe meant that the German state that would come out of the First World War had suffered significant territorial losses.

They also lost territory in Silesia, a coal mining area in Eastern Germany that was important to them. One doesn't usually think about this in terms of the First World War, the Treaty of Versailles, but Germany also lost overseas territories. The German colonies in Africa were distributed to the British and the French, while in the South Pacific, Japan would be the heir to Germany's South Pacific colonies. The Marshall, Gilbert, and Marianna Island chains were German—sort of always strikes one, I think, as somewhat odd to think about a place in the South Pacific called "Kaiser Wilhelm's Land," but it certainly existed. There's the Bismarck Archipelago, and these island chains—the Marshalls, the Gilberts, the Mariannas—went over to Japan as a result of the outcome of the Great War. In addition to these territorial losses, the Germans were also forced to pay reparations. All of the Allied victor states, particularly France and Great Britain, had begun the war as creditor states and ended the war as debtor nations. They had gone heavily into debt to the United States. We had loaned money to the Allies before our entry into the war, so that the British, the French, approached the Treaty of Versailles with the notion, and the Belgians as well, who had suffered under German occupation for the entire duration of the war, the Germans now were going to have to pay. Lloyd George had run a campaign just prior to, a domestic campaign in Britain just prior to the convening of the Versailles negotiations, in which he said they were going to make the Germans, he was going to squeeze Germany until the pips squeak. This was the so-called the Cacky Election, where Lloyd George talked a tough line about just exactly what they were going to extract from the Germans; the Germans were going to have to pay. There was no final amount set, it was in effect a blank check, but the Germans were going to be required to pay billions upon billions of dollars.

This reparations issue would become, I think, the most poisonous issue in European politics in the interwar years—at least down to the early 1930s, poisoning relations between France and Britain on the one hand, and Germany on the other, and also complicating relations between the United States and its former European partners. The Germans, what insult was added to injury, because not only was Germany forced now to pay reparations, but the Allies added a new clause to the Treaty, the so-called "war guilt clause." The war guilt clause was added as a justification for making Germany pay; Germany now was forced to accept full responsibility for the outbreak of hostilities in 1914. Now, there was a lot of difference of opinion about who was ultimately responsible and so on, but as far as the Treaty of Versailles was concerned, the Germans were responsible, there was a war guilt clause, and this was the basis for Germany's payment of reparations. So the loss of territory, payment of reparations, and then a series of military clauses were added to the Treaty, which also were meant to weaken Germany's position. The great German army—this German army which had been the pride of German society, which had fought successfully for four years during the course of the war—was now to be reduced to no more than 100,000 troops, just enough to maintain domestic stability in Germany. The Germans were not allowed to have an air force, at all. There were to be no tanks, no heavy artillery. The German army was to be stripped of its ability to make war; it was there to maintain domestic order, pure and simple. A German navy was certainly allowed to exist, but could have no more than six warships and, most important for the Allies, no submarines. The U-Boats had been one of the great problems for the Allies during the war and they were in no mood to tolerate the existence of this arm of the German military—so no submarines.

All of these aspects of the Treaty were bitterly resented by the Germans and would all become quite controversial during the course of the 1920s and early '30s. And many believed, in fact almost before the ink was dry, that the Treaty probably had been too harsh. And yet there's a curious thing about the Treaty, there was no occupation of Germany. After four years of bitter combat, on a scale that the Europeans had never experienced, the war ends, the Kaiser goes into exile, a new German government is declared, and there's no occupation. Allied troops were certainly sent into the Rhineland for a sort of temporary occupation and then the Rhineland, this area of Germany west of the Rhine River on the border of Belgium and France, was to be a demilitarized zone. But no real occupation. There were no Allied troops marching off to occupy Berlin and so on, one of the major differences between the outcome of the First War and the Second. Finally, a system of collective security, seen as absolutely crucial, was to be provided for by a new institution—and this was one of the brainchildren of Woodrow Wilson—and that's the League of Nations, an international organization which would help to negotiate differences between the nations of the world, which would hopefully prevent the outbreak of great tragedies such as the war that the world had just endured. So the League of Nations would be present to mitigate trouble, after the end of hostilities. But this wasn't going to be enough; the French in particular were concerned. After all the Germans were still just across the river. What were they going to do? The English could go back across the Channel, the Americans could drift off back across the Atlantic, but the French had the Rhine and that was it.

And so for the French, and this is the underlying story of French policy through the 1920s and into the 1930s, is they searched for security. There were still 20 million Germans too many, as far as the French were concerned, and so what were they going to do. Well at the meetings at Versailles, Wilson and Lloyd George pledged to the French a guarantee of French sovereignty and French territory; there was to be an Anglo-American guarantee. So when the conference came to an end, these attempts to weaken Germany and then to establish a system of collective security were all in place. And yet there was trouble, trouble almost instantly; indeed problems with the Treaty and the system of collective security emerged at once. Predictably, this was a surprise to absolutely nobody. The Germans, regardless of their political affiliation—whether they were in the radical left from the Communists, or on the radical right or the Conservatives, the Monarchists—all German political parties thought the Treaty was a dictated peace, that it was unfair, that it was an abomination. The Treaty alienated the Germans, they saw it as—a "diktat" was the German term, it means a "dictated peace." They resented all the provisions—not some of them but all of them—particularly, I think, the war guilt clause, and the reparations. Also, the way the war ended in this curious fashion, the German army was successful, remarkably successful, in diverting responsibility for the armistice away from the army itself. It had been the army that had called for the armistice, and yet the army managed to distance itself from the actual surrender and then certainly from the Treaty of Versailles. The responsibility for Versailles was the new republican government that had been established by the revolution. And so as the Germans came home from the Hall of Mirrors at Versailles where the Treaty was negotiated, the "stab in the back" legend had already taken root, a sense that the German army—there had to be some explanation—Germany had been sold out, the army stabbed in the back. The right wing, in particular, in Germany was convinced of this. And this stab in the back legend, the way the war ended, the Treaty of Versailles, served to delegitimize the new democratic government. The republican government in Germany was born with a heavy burden of responsibility for something that it had not, in fact, it had not been empowered during the war. Whereas the Kaiser, the army and so on, managed to sidestep that responsibility.

Although Germany, in the late 1920s, would try to fulfill the Treaty, it was never accepted in Germany. Its validity was always questioned; it became simply a mantra of all political parties. That was predictable. What was not predictable—and what came as a great shock and a blow to the Treaties and the international system of collective security—was that the United States Senate failed to ratify the Treaty of Versailles. The United States would not become a member of the League of Nations. It was a preview of American isolationism that would dominate American policy in the 1930s. So, that at the very outset one of the major pieces foreseen at Versailles of this great puzzle, this great system, was absent. The United States failed to participate, and, not only did we fail to enter the League of Nations, to ratify the Treaty of Versailles, the Senate also failed to approve the Anglo-American guarantee to France. It was an entangling alliance; we didn't want any part of being involved in European problems.

The upshot of this was that when the United States failed to ratify the guarantee to France, so did Great Britain. Britain was not going to do it without the United States and so at the very beginning, already by 1920, these key factors—in the international system, the anticipated international system—were absent. The anticipated collective security system was gravely weakened, if not utterly undone, almost from the beginning. The United States would remain heavily involved in European financial affairs in the 1920s, but resolutely refused to enter into any sort of collective security arrangement. Collective security was also further weakened by a growing British conviction in the 1920s that the Treaty of Versailles had been, as the Germans maintained, too harsh, and that the real problem for stability in Europe wasn't the Germans, who were defeated, but rather the French—the vindictiveness of the French. That the French were now going to use this opportunity to establish their hegemony on the continent. This is a theme we'll come back to in the future, but cooperation between Britain and France was not something that one could take for granted despite their cooperation during the Great War. And, with over a million dead and wounded in the First War, the British were extremely wary of being drawn into a new conflict. That was especially the case since the dominions—Canada, Australia, New Zealand, and South Africa—had become separate members of the League of Nations and were even more reluctant to be drawn into continental affairs.

Britain therefore favored accommodation with Germany; the British saw the League of Nations not as an instrument to enforce the Treaty, but as an instrument for reconciliation—to manage conflict, rather to enforce the Treaty. Italy was embittered because it had not been rewarded with territories in the Adriatic or in North Africa. The Italians wound up technically a victor state in the First War although they had suffered grievous losses fighting the Austrians in the south. Italy came away from the Treaty of Versailles also unhappy, unhappy that it hadn't gotten these former territories in North Africa or in the Adriatic. If republican Italy, which had fought the war, was disappointed with the outcome, fascist Italy—Mussolini would come to power in 1922—was infuriated by this turn of events.

There was also one other absentee at the Treaty of Versailles, and an important one; the new Bolshevik regime in Russia was not invited to the Treaty of Versailles, to the negotiations at Versailles. The Bolshevik regime in the new Soviet Union was a pariah state, an outsider—not invited. It's the beginning—along with the Allied intervention and the attempt to roll back the Bolshevik Revolution—to keep the Russians in the war. It's the beginning of a conviction on the part of the new Bolshevik leadership that the Western Allies couldn't be relied upon, that the West was not interested in real security with the Russians involved. What this meant then, at the conclusion of the decade, was that France was compelled to assume responsibility for enforcing the Treaty. What had begun as an attempt to weaken Germany and to provide for a system of collective security had already, even actually by the mid '20s, resulted in the situation in which France alone felt responsible for finding some sort of workable solution to what it saw as the ongoing German problem.

Hitler's Challenge to the International System, 1933–1936
Lecture 2

Hello, and welcome to our second lecture on the Second World War. In this lecture we're going to be examining the rise of Hitler's Nazi Party in Germany and the ideological and geopolitical wellsprings of his foreign policy. We will trace his step-by-step revision of the Treaty of Versailles, and also look at the rhetorical style—the way he presented his demands for change, both to the international community as well as to the German population at home.

The problems created by the Versailles settlement were present but manageable during the 1920s. Aware that it would have to maintain the Versailles settlement virtually alone, France established military alliances and agreements with East European "successor" states.

In 1924 Germany embarked on a "policy of fulfillment." By making a good-faith effort to fulfill the Versailles terms, Germany would demonstrate to the Allies that those terms were unreasonable. In 1924 Germany began to reintegrate itself into the European collective security system. It was among the states to sign the Kellogg-Briand Pact of 1928, a non-aggression pact that signaled the high-water

Courtesy National Archives, 165-GB-1000.

Paul von Hindenburg, president of Germany from 1925–1934; Kaiser Wilhelm; and General Ludendorff.

mark of postwar cooperation. The United States became somewhat more active in aiding Europe's economic recovery, becoming involved in the Dawes Plan, which extended financial aid from private sources to Germany.

The Great Depression imposed tremendous strains on Germany and on the European international system. The Wall Street Crash of 1929 brought massive unemployment and business failures in Germany. Growing resentment and political polarization fueled the rise of Hitler's Nazi Party (the NSDAP) between 1930 and 1933. The Nazis relentlessly attacked the Weimar government and the other political parties, promising to restore Germany to its rightful place in Europe and the world. Hitler demanded revision of the Treaty of Versailles.

Hitler pursued an aggressive foreign policy, which operated on two levels: geopolitical and ideological. His geopolitical goals were to destroy the Treaty of Versailles, attain *Lebensraum* (living space) in the east for the German *Volk* (people), ensure Germany's economic self-sufficiency, and create a Greater German *Reich* (Empire) to dominate the European continent. And his ideological goal was to unleash a crusade against "Judeo-Bolshevism" to ensure the racial purity of his *Reich*. Hitler knew that attainment of these goals would require war.

Hitler moved next to destroy the remnants of the Versailles Treaty. In 1933 he withdrew Germany from the Disarmament Conference and the League of Nations. In 1934 he signed a 10-year non-aggression pact with Poland, thereby undermining the French alliance system. In March 1935 Hitler announced that Germany was rebuilding its *Luftwaffe*, ostensibly as a defensive action. When the Western powers failed to react, he announced the following week that Germany would rebuild its army.

In March of 1936, Hitler sent troops into the Rhineland. It was German territory, but, as you'll recall from the Treaty of Versailles, had been a demilitarized zone.

The Anglo-German Naval Agreement of June 1935 horrified the French. This agreement demonstrated that the British had abandoned the Versailles settlement and reached their own accommodation with Hitler. Hitler's prestige in Germany and in the international community soared. Not only the remilitarization of the Rhineland in 1936, but also a great coup for Hitler's foreign policy was holding the Olympic Games in Berlin. ■

Suggested Reading

Eberhard Jackel, *Hitler's World View: A Blueprint For Power.*

Norman Rich, *Hitler's War Aims: Ideology, The Nazi State, and the Course of Expansion.*

A. J. P. Taylor, *The Origins of the Second World War*, Part II.

Questions to Consider

1. What were Hitler's basic goals in foreign policy?

2. To what extent were Hitler's moves in foreign policy determined by ideology?

Hitler's Challenge to the International System, 1933–1936

Lecture 2—Transcript

Hello, and welcome to our second lecture on the Second World War. In this lecture we're going to be examining the rise of Hitler's Nazi Party in Germany and the ideological and geopolitical wellsprings of his foreign policy. We will trace his step-by-step revision of the Treaty of Versailles, and also look at the rhetorical style—the way he presented his demands for change, both to the international community as well as to the German population at home.

We've been talking about the problems of the international system and the legacy of the First World War for the background of the Second. And I think what we need to emphasize even before Hitler's rise to power, is that already by the end of the 1920s the international system—as it had been envisioned by those diplomats who had framed the Treaty of Versailles—was already tattered. If not destroyed, certainly tattered. Without the steadfast support of the British and the United States' absence, France found itself in a position of having to—it felt—maintain, enforce, the Treaty of Versailles virtually alone.

The British had reneged on their guarantees to France when the United States had failed to ratify the Anglo-American guarantee. And without Russia, France was forced to rely on—it felt—in the new so-called "successor" states of Eastern Europe—those states that had been created, really, out of the collapse of the old Austro-Hungarian Empire and the German Empire. So that France had, in the 1920s, begun to establish a set of military alliances with Poland, with Czechoslovakia. Had made an agreement with Yugoslavia and with Romania in the East. And also with Belgium in the West. But these states, particularly those in the East, were hardly a substitute, hardly a replacement, for Russia.

The big problem for France was to find a counterbalance to German power in the East. The old Czarist Empire had provided this for the French in the prewar era and now the Soviet Union was not seen as a reliable alternative. So, France struggles all the way through the 1920s trying to find a way to manage this situation. In the '20s, and certainly after the mid 1920s, these problems were largely manageable. In 1924, the German government had embarked upon what was called the "policy of fulfillment." Gustav Stresemann was the chancellor, briefly, of Germany in 1923. He would become foreign minister of Germany in '24, and would dominate German foreign policy through the last portion of the 1920s. Stresemann was convinced, as were all German politicians, that the Treaty of Versailles was brutally unfair, that it had to be revised. But, he argued to his friends at home and to the international community, Germany's attempts to frustrate the Allies—the Germans from 1920 down to 1923—had tried not to pay reparations, to fudge this and that, complain certainly—just continued to argue that the Treaty was unfair and to be obstreperous. Stresemann argued that a new tact was now required. What Germany should do is to follow what he called the "policy of fulfillment." Erfuellungspolitik" is the German term.

What this meant was to make a good faith effort to fulfill all of the terms of the Treaty of Versailles, no matter how unfair they were seen as being. And by that good faith attempt, Germany would demonstrate, even to the French, that the Treaty had been, in fact, impossible; that its terms could not be fulfilled, and therefore a revision of the Treaty would take place, but through negotiation. Not confrontation, negotiation. In this sense, Germany, between 1924 and 1925, entered into a series of international agreements which reintegrated Germany into the community of nations. In 1925, Germany signed the Lacarno Treaty in which it basically recognized the frontiers that had been redrawn in the West. In 1926, Germany applied for membership and was received in the League of Nations, something that Germany had not been allowed to do previously. In 1928, Germany would be a signatory to the so-called Kellogg-Briand Pact, a non-aggression pact in which all states pledged themselves to resolve all of their differences amicably. I think one could find a similar non-aggression pact in almost every decade of the twentieth century and beyond, looking backward—one no more effective than the other.

The United States during this period was certainly active in economic matters. The United States had become involved in the so-called Dawes Plan, named for the American Charles Dawes, the vice president, to help Europe settle—to sort out its reparations problems, its war debt problems. But the

United States still remained on the sidelines. It was not a party to the various treaties that would be signed in Europe, other than this Kellogg-Briand Pact.

But, all of this attempt at negotiation on the part of Stresemann, this attempt to reintegrate Germany into the community of nations, which had taken up much of the last part of the 1920s, would all come to a crashing halt when the stock market crashed on Wall Street in the fall of 1929. The Great Depression would hit Germany like a steamroller. Germany, more than any other country—other than the United States—was powerfully affected by the Great Depression. Germany was quickly exposed, too, because Germany had taken many short-term loans from private sources in the United States; those loans were withdrawn, suddenly, in 1929 and early 1930, and the impact of the Depression was astounding.

Germany's unemployment rate would jump massively between 1928 and 1932. By 1932, one-third of the German workforce was either unemployed or working drastically reduced hours. A third. In addition, a tidal wave of failed businesses, especially of small shops, and farm foreclosures simply swamped the country. Businesses failed right and left. Those German businesses that had somehow managed to get through the turbulent post-war era up to 1924—a hyper-inflation in Germany of absolutely hyperbolic proportions—managed to get through a harsh period of stabilization in the latter part of the '20s, now found themselves swept away by the Great Depression between 1928 and 1933.

As a consequence, these economic problems fed what in Germany was called an "anti-system." Anti-republican sentiment. Anti-republican bitterness that held the democratic republic of Germany responsible for these failed economic problems. Now, not only was the German government—this republican government established by revolution in 1918 with a new constitution in 1919—not only was it held responsible for the loss of the Great War, and the Treaty of Versailles, it seemed to have delivered to the Germans one economic crisis after another, with the Great Depression being the final punctuation mark on that unhappy economic development.

Adolf Hitler's National Socialist German Worker's Party, the NSDAP, had less than three percent of the vote in 1928 before the effects of the Depression hit Germany. In 1930, the vote jumped to 18 percent. In the summer of 1932, the National Socialists, the Nazis, received about 37 percent of the vote. It was the most votes, the largest percentage of votes the Nazis would ever receive in anything like free elections. And in the elections at the end of the year, in November, the Nazi vote actually declined. This very difficult coalition that the Nazis had put together, of diverse social forces—put together largely on the basis of what we would think of as negative campaigning. "What are you opposed to? We're opposed to it, too. Are you unhappy? Well, we're unhappier than you are. We're going to solve your problems." Hitler was appointed chancellor on January 30, 1933 in one of, I think, the cruelest ironies of all of human history. At just the point when the Nazis themselves believed that their constituency was fragmenting, coming apart at the seams, Hitler was appointed chancellor—not on the shoulders of a groundswell of public support, but rather as a result of a back-door intrigue with President Hindenbourg, Paul von Hindenbourg, the great hero of the First World War.

There was nothing in the National Socialist approach to foreign policy during Hitler's rise to power that would necessarily have distinguished it from other German parties. It was a bit more radical, but it was opposed to Versailles. So were the Communists, so were the Conservatives, so were the Liberals, so were the Social Democrats that signed the Treaty. The Nazis, however, hammered away. They'd never been in power in Germany. As a consequence they were able to relentlessly attack the failures of the other parties. Relentlessly attacked the failed republican government. And, of course, the Nazis put forward a promise to restore Germany to its rightful position in the world. Now other parties had talked about this as well. But they were talking about compromise with the West. Could we see if we could get the reparations done away with? Just as in domestic politics, sober politicians would talk to their economic advisors and say, "Well, in order to pull Germany out of the Depression, we must do this, we must do that." And then there would be a huge debate, of course. "No, one can't do this. If you try to reduce prices, this will happen, that will happen."

The Nazi position to all of this was, when people pointed out the contradictions of their own economic policy, the Nazis would simply respond, "We will make it work! There will be a triumph of the will, over all the sort of nay-saying Liberals and Social Democrats, and so on. We will make it work!"

And that same forceful projection of determination was also there in foreign policy. They would not simply revise the Treaty, they would break the chains of Versailles. They would restore Germany to its rightful position in Europe and in the world.

Upon coming to power, for the first two years, really, of the National Socialist regime in 1933 and 1934, Hitler's attention was largely focused on domestic policy. Establishing the framework of the National Socialist dictatorship. Defeating his domestic enemies. Establishing really the foundations of what we would think of as a totalitarian regime. But Hitler would also have departures in foreign policy that were quite important. But before turning to the specifics of Nazi policy, I want to say a few words about Hitler's overall conception of the international system. His conception of international politics. How he wanted to operate, how he viewed the world, and how he hoped to see what his objectives were, and how he hoped to see those objectives realized.

There's a tendency, I think, to view Hitler as—especially in his foreign policy—as a madman. As a megalomaniac bent on world domination. There was a song within the Nazi Party that was sung during the rise to power, the lyrics of which were, "Heute da hort uns Deutschland und morgan die ganze Welt." That means, "Today Germany listens to us. Tomorrow the whole world." But, just a slight change of wording in German, they would sing, "Heute gehort uns Deutschland und morgan die ganze Welt." Which means, "Today Germany belongs to us. And tomorrow the whole world." I think there is a tendency to think that this is the way Hitler in his foreign policy operated. But, in fact, Hitler was far more cautious. He operated from a notion of the international system that was quite concise for him. He believed that the world would ultimately be divided into four major power blocks. A "multi-polar world"—he used the post-World War II terminology for it. Germany's rightful position would be to dominate the European continent. It would be the great hegemonic power of Europe. The British would be able to maintain their international empire, their global empire.

Hitler saw Britain in a very favorable light. I think he was obsessed with them in many ways. Frustrated with the British, as we will see. But in his overall thinking, Germany was to dominate the landmass of Europe. Britain was to have its international empire. The Japanese would be the dominant power in Asia. They were, Hitler liked to call them, the Aryans of the East. Japan would dominate Southeast Asia and the Pacific. And then finally, there would be the United States, which would dominate the Western Hemisphere. In the long run, Hitler believed that the United States was doomed. Too much racial mixture and so on. And this would ultimately bring the United States down. But in terms of the way he operated and thought, these were the four great blocks of power with which he had to deal.

For Germany his goals were also clear. He spelled them out in *Mein Kampf*, his political testament, autobiography, which he wrote in prison in 1924, published in 1925. And then in a second book, a book that was never published during his lifetime—appeared only after the Second World War, called sometimes "Hitler's Second Book" or "Hitler's Secret Book"—in which he dealt very specifically with foreign policy.

What were Germany's objectives? What did Hitler want for Germany? What was he trying to achieve? At one level, Hitler's goals were geopolitical, almost traditional. Germany, he felt, needed *Lebensraum,* or "living space." The German population needed to increase, to grow. And Germany, which already was not economically self-sufficient in 1914—it imported about 20 percent of its food, and hence was successfully blockaded, virtually starved, by the British after 1916—Hitler believed that Germany should be economically self-sufficient, capable of withstanding any sort of Allied blockade ala the First World War. *Lebensraum,* then. And where was that living space to come? Well, it was to come in the East. Germany would have to expand into the so-called successor states—Poland, Czechoslovakia, and of course, beyond, beckoned the Ukraine, the great agricultural areas of now the Soviet Union. So, living space. And what the Germans called economic autarchy; that is, economic self-sufficiency.

In addition, however, there was an ideological dimension to Hitler's foreign policy, an ideological level which saturated these geopolitical ideas. So far, in thinking about what he thought about for Germany, there was nothing really to distinguish terribly from some of the more radical framers or advisors to the Kaiser during the First World War. The idea of a "Gross Deutsch Reich," a "Greater German Reich," with territory in the East, was quite common among many on the German Reich during the First World War. But, for Hitler there was this second dimension. The new Greater German Reich—Greater German Empire that was to be created, that was to dominate the European continent—was to be a racially pure empire. He believed that Germany was what one might call the last best racial hope of mankind. He never, he didn't argue. This is a point that we will come back to when we see the terrible consequences of this ideology.

Hitler didn't believe that the Germans were a master race, and "Herrenvolk" is the term, in the 1920s, '30s, or '40s. But the historic goal of Germany was to concentrate as best it could to bring together the racial stock, the undiluted racial stock of the Aryans—these blonde-haired, blue-eyed types—and that the Germans were best able to do this. This meant creating a Reich, a Central European Empire that would be free of Slavs, the Polish, or Czech, or Slovak. Elements would have to be expelled or simply done away with. And of course, for Hitler, central to this, too, was the idea of the Jews. The Jews would have to go. They would have to be eliminated. He talked about this in general terms. The Jews would have to go. It was not simply, however, a racial notion. Hitler always talked, when he talked about foreign policy, or domestic policy in many cases as well, about what he called the threat of "Judeo-Bolshevism." Germany, indeed the world, was threatened by this Judeo-Bolshevik conspiracy, with its home, its center, in the Soviet Union. Therefore it was to be one of the great objectives of the National Socialist state of the Third Reich to conduct a crusade against Judeo-Bolshevism.

So, a war for living space in the East, which would obviously mean—and he didn't believe that these goals could be achieved peacefully. He believed—and this is much of what Nazi ideology was about in a kind of Social Darwinistic notion of the "survival of the fittest"—that life was struggle. That international politics was the struggle of nations. And it would be Germany's task to expand to the East and that did not mean through negotiation. It meant war. He calculated. He talked quite often about the prospect of war with Poland or with Czechoslovakia and then ultimately beyond that, a war against the Soviet Union—a war not only for living space, but also as seen as an ideological crusade against what he saw as Judeo-Bolshevism.

Needless to say, what this meant was not a revision of the Treaty of Versailles, this meant the destruction of the Treaty of Versailles. Removing all of the fetters of this hated Treaty. This is the set of concepts with which he worked. He was an opportunist. He was capable of making an alliance on Monday, breaking it on Tuesday. Making short-term agreements with, as we will see, the Soviet Union in 1939, when it suited his purposes. Only to shift a bit later on. But these concepts, these notions, were clearly behind Hitler's foreign policy from the beginning of his career down to the last days in the bunker in 1945. In 1933, when Hitler came to power, and really into 1934, he was in no position to embark upon an adventurous foreign policy. Instead, those years, as I said earlier, were devoted largely to a consolidation of his control over Germany itself. But one does see in 1933-34 some previews of Nazi foreign policy, and also his modus operandi—the way Hitler operated—none better, I think, than his handling of the disarmament conference of 1932-33 and the League of Nations.

When Hitler came into power in January of 1933, Germany was already a participant in an international disarmament conference. It'd begun in 1932. Hitler comes to power, and really his first initiative on the international scene had to do with this disarmament conference. Now you'll recall that the Treaty of Versailles had restricted Germany's armed forces considerably—100,000 troops was the maximum—no tanks, no artillery, no air force, and so on. At the disarmament conference Hitler instructed his representatives to make a daring proposal. Germany, he argued, would completely disarm. Give up all of its armaments, all 100,000, if France, Great Britain, Japan, the United States, and so on would do the same.

Well, this was an offer that he correctly assumed would be refused. And, in fact, France balked. And as soon as France did, Hitler had exactly what he wanted. He went back to the German population and said, "You see? The Treaty of Versailles? This disarmament, this is all a ruse. This is not about equality. This is not about disarmament. This is not about world peace. This is one more attempt to enforce this corrupt and miserable Treaty. We offered them complete disarmament. If that's what they wanted, they could've had it. But they didn't want it. All they wanted to do is to keep Germany in this oppressed condition." Hitler then withdrew from the conference with great fanfare, and withdrew from the League of Nations, also in 1933, which had sponsored and was involved with the conference.

This is absolutely quintessential Hitler. On the one hand, it's aggressive—he's withdrawing from this disarmament conference. On the other hand, Hitler always cloaked, always cloaked—right down to the time the first shots were fired on September 1, 1939—always cloaked his very aggressive policies in a rhetorical garb that emphasized Germany's demand for justice, Germany's demand for equality, Germany's demand to be treated as an equal in the international community. Germany should no longer be a second-class citizen. This played very, very well in Germany. And over time, it also had a corrosive effect on the resolve of the Allies. Especially in Great Britain. Those two—his withdrawal from the disarmament conference and his withdrawal from the League of Nations—then, really give us a glimpse of the way Hitler liked to operate.

In 1934, he surprised a great many people by signing a ten-year, non-aggression pact with Poland. Now, for those people who had been reading *Mein Kampf*, or had listened to Hitler's speeches, the discussion of *Lebensraum*, you think, "Well, *Lebensraum* is going to come to the East. It's got to be Poland! They've got to be Victim Number One." And yet, in 1934, the National Socialist regime signs a non-aggression pact with the Polish state. What this did was to strike a blow at the French alliance system. France, as you'll recall, had been trying to establish a series of alliances with the so-called successor states. Poland was the key to this, with its common frontier with Germany. And now the Germans had plucked Poland from this French alliance system with this non-aggression pact.

In 1935, Hitler was in a much stronger position domestically. Paul von Hindenbourg, the old Reich President, passed away in 1934. And Hitler was able to assume the position of Reich President, and also head of the armed forces. The German Army swore an oath of allegiance directly to Hitler. His position at home was very, very solid. Hitler had been—ever since his withdrawal from the non-aggression conference—Hitler had been making, I suppose we would say that now they would be called leaks of information. That Germany, having withdrawn from the disarmament conference, was also not going to abide by the disarmament clauses of the Treaty of Versailles.

That the Allies had already lost whatever justification they had for this. Then, in March of 1935, Hitler made a formal announcement. Germany had, in fact, he revealed, been building an air force. A *Luftwaffe*, as it was called. And would henceforth move on to do this in a formal, public way.

Germany was going to build an air force. Why? Britain had an air force. France had an air force. Poland had an air force. Germany needed an air force just for its own protection. This was not an act of aggression. This was not a provocative act. This was simply Germany declaring that it needed to defend itself. One week later when there had been no real outcry—there was a certain amount of blustering and complaint in the League of Nations in Paris and in London, but nothing more than that—one week later, Hitler announced his intention to introduce conscription. He was going to build an army, he announced, of half a million men, and then continue to expand it thereafter. Once again, the League protested. But there was no action taken. No action from Paris. No action from Britain. And now what Hitler had done by 1935 then, was he had completely destroyed the disarmament clauses of the Treaty of Versailles.

Then, then, in 1935, the cruelest blow of all for France. The two powers that were really seen by the French as, and the world as, the enforcers of the Treaty, France foremost, and more reluctantly Great Britain, now suffered a real split. In June of 1935, France was horrified to discover that Great Britain had entered into a naval agreement with Germany. The British had done this without consulting either the French or the Italians, who at this point were still seen as potential allies. And in this agreement, Great Britain recognized Germany's right—right—to build a navy up to 35 percent of Britain's surface tonnage and 60 percent of British submarine strength. In other words, what the British had done was to cut a deal with Hitler. In a sense, what this reveals is, the British had already given up on Versailles, they'd given up on disarmament, they'd given up on the enforcing any sort of military strictures on Germany, and opted to cut their own deal with Germany on the one thing that really mattered most to Britain, and that was the navy. So now, if Versailles had any breath left in it at all, this blow from Britain certainly was the end for Versailles.

In March of 1936, then, Hitler sent troops into the Rhineland. It was German territory, but, as you'll recall from the Treaty of Versailles, had been a demilitarized zone. It was crucial to the French position in Europe that that zone in Germany remain demilitarized, because this gave the French a clear avenue into the heartland of Germany directly to the Ruhr, the industrial heartland of the country, without any opposition. As soon as the Germans sent troops back into the Rhineland, as soon as they remilitarized the Rhineland, France's ability to influence events in Germany, not to mention to protect their alliance partners in the East, was gone. French military commanders urged caution, and the British opposed military intervention. The matter was referred to the League of Nations, which did nothing. The Germans, we now know, the German High Command, had not been in favor of this move at all. In fact, Hitler had been told by his military commanders that, "If the French send a regiment out there, we'll be humiliated. We couldn't possibly defend ourselves against the French"—who had the largest army in Europe at the time. Hitler gambled. He won.

The remilitarization of the Rhineland represents now, I think, this relentless pressure that Hitler was asserting. Pressure constantly. All in one direction. Revision, revision, revision of the Treaty. Or destruction of the Treaty. And his prestige in Germany and in the international community soared. Not only the remilitarization of the Rhineland in 1936, but also what was the great coup for Hitler's foreign policy—not in any power political way, but in terms of German prestige in 1936—was, of course, the holding of the Olympic Games in Berlin. We tend to think of this—there's one story that Americans seem to know about the 1936 Olympics and that's, of course, Jessie Owens's terrific performance there and the embarrassment it caused Hitler to have to acknowledge that here's a black man, an African-American—how does this fit with his racial notion of Aryans and so on? But from the German point of view, the Olympics were a terrific success. The world had come to Berlin. Germany was back. And not only that, the Germans won the 1936 Olympics on points—all of these obscure events, not the track and field things that the Americans dominated. But by 1936, the Treaty of Versailles, and the system of collective security that the framers of that Treaty had sought to create, was largely dead—largely dead.

The Failure of the International System
Lecture 3

In this lecture we're going to focus on the reasons for the failure of the international system to meet the threat of German foreign policy in the 1930s. We'll examine dilemmas of British, French, and Soviet foreign policy as well as the problem of isolationism confronted by Franklin Roosevelt in the United States.

Divided responses by the West European powers to the German challenge help to explain the failure of the post-Versailles international system during the 1920s and 1930s. In 1936 Hitler introduced a four-year plan to ensure German economic self-sufficiency. For the next two years he constantly asserted his desire for peace and justice while secretly preparing for war.

During the 1930s France was politically polarized and economically weakened. It cast about for allies with which to face a revived Germany, but it lacked a political consensus to confront the German challenge. It adopted an overly defensive, static, and reactive "Maginot mentality." For various reasons, French military planners failed to extend the Maginot line along the French-Belgian frontier.

France and Britain failed to respond effectively to signs of aggressive German intent. Distrusting Britain's reliability as an ally, France developed an uneasy relationship during the middle 1930s with the Soviet Union, which feared a possible German-Polish axis. In 1935 Stalin agreed to defend Czechoslovakia against external assault if France also honored its treaty obligations to Czechoslovakia. France also considered

Adolph Hitler (1889–1945).

an alliance with Italian dictator Mussolini, who feared German intentions regarding the Balkans. Possibilities for British and French cooperation with Italy against Germany were destroyed by Mussolini's invasion of Ethiopia in late 1935 and his intervention in the Spanish Civil War in 1936. The following year Italy allied with Germany.

As recounted in the 1937 Hossbach Memorandum, Hitler instructed his generals to prepare for a move into Eastern Europe that would bring Germany into conflict with France. Meanwhile, he removed top German officials who had expressed reservations about aggressive operations in the East, and he consolidated his own control over top positions in the German armed forces.

Crises involving Austria and Czechoslovakia during 1938 presaged war in Europe. The Austrian crisis arose in February and March 1938. In early 1938 Austrian chancellor Kurt von Schuschnigg sought British and French guarantees of Austria's sovereignty. These efforts upset Hitler when they eventually became known to him.

In 1938, Chamberlain was afraid that if a war came, any war, that it would lead to a decline of the British Empire and an emergence of real American power.

German ambassador to Austria Franz von Papen suggested a meeting between Schuschnigg and Hitler, which took place in Hitler's "Eagle's Nest" in the Bavarian Alps. Having sidestepped Hitler's demands that he cede to Germany the control of Austria's foreign policy, Schuschnigg returned to Vienna and announced plans for a plebiscite.

After Schuschnigg refused Hitler's demand to call off the plebiscite, Hitler announced Germany's annexation of Austria (the "*Anschluss*"), which he justified on the basis of the national self-determination of peoples. The international community issued only mild protests.

In summer 1938 a crisis arose regarding the Sudetenland region of Czechoslovakia. Ethnic Germans in the Sudetenland began to demand a "return to the Reich." The Czech government (with its well-equipped army) mobilized to resist the anticipated German assault. Mussolini and British premier Neville Chamberlain intervened in autumn 1938 to prolong the peace. Mussolini feared being dragged into war with the Allies over Sudetenland. French weakness and U.S. isolationism and unreliability convinced Chamberlain of the need to appease the Germans. Czechoslovakia's fate was sealed at the September 1938 Munich Conference, where Chamberlain, De Laudier of France, Mussolini, and Hitler presided over the annexation of the Sudetenland by Germany. ■

Suggested Reading

Telford Taylor, *Munich: The Price of Peace*.

Christopher Thorne, *The Approach of War, 1938–1939*.

Gerhard L. Weinberg, *The Foreign Policy of Hitler's Germany*.

Questions to Consider

1. In 1938 Prime Minister Neville Chamberlain was seen by most in Europe as a great hero, a savior of the peace. How did Chamberlain justify the Munich agreement and the policy of appeasement?

2. Why was France unable to play a more aggressive role in dealing with the threat of Hitler's Germany?

The Failure of the International System
Lecture 3—Transcript

Hello, and welcome to our third lecture on the Second World War. In this lecture we're going to focus on the reasons for the failure of the international system to meet the threat of German foreign policy in the 1930s. We'll examine dilemmas of British, French, and Soviet foreign policy as well as the problem of isolationism confronted by Franklin Roosevelt in the United States. Then, finally, we'll conclude with the treatment of the major international crises of 1938 and 1939 as Europe moved relentlessly toward the outbreak of war.

In 1936, with the Olympic Games, the remilitarization of the Rhineland, Germany had announced its return as a major power in Europe. In addition, in 1936 Hitler would introduce the so-called four-year plan, an economic plan to make Germany self-sufficient within four years—economically self-sufficient—to confront the dangers of an increasingly challenging international situation. And, as I said in the last lecture, I think it's extremely important to understand over and over and over again in 1936, '37, '38, Hitler would constantly emphasize his desire for peace. "Anyone who thinks that I want more," he would routinely say, "doesn't understand anything at all about me personally. After all, unlike some of the other states in the period I was a soldier at the front during the First World War, during the Great War, I know what it was like. I know what the suffering of the trenches was like and I don't want to plunge Europe back into anything like this. All I want is for Germany to be restored to its rightful place in the international community, for Germany once again to be the major power that it should be, and to be treated like an equal."

By 1936 he'd gone a long way toward restoring Germany—and with each of these steps, which certainly led to the piecemeal dismantling of the Treaty of Versailles—each was couched in this same defensive, reasonable, sort of demeanor of his. One tends to think of Hitler as this sort of ranting maniac. If we see the film clips, especially if one doesn't understand Germany, it just sounds sort of like this high-pitched shrieking where the point is to say "Deutschland" as many times in thirty seconds as he possibly can. But invariably Hitler had a set routine the way he would speak. It was always, he began, he would warm himself up and he would always begin, when he was talking about foreign policy there would be a long list of the various privations of Germany, the unfair treatment of Germany, and his very reasonable, peaceful determination to see justice prevail. By 1936, it was clear that the momentum was running all in Hitler's direction. The wartime alliance against Germany was badly fractured, and France especially found itself in an impossible situation.

Confronted by Hitler's relentless pressure, France cast about for allies, cast about for some sort of workable policy to confront this growing German threat. But France in the 1930s was paralyzed in very important ways. There was political polarization in France during the Depression. The Depression in France was not as dramatic as it was in the United States or Germany with massive unemployment, runs on the banks, failing businesses and so on. It was a long, protracted, economic agony. French political life fragmented in the 1930s, the popular front government had come to power in 1936 on the left; it was confronted by a right wing in France that was convinced that the Third Republic was simply corrupt, incapable of managing French affairs, and so on. And so while there was a clear perception of a German challenge, a fear of German revival, there was simply a lack of any kind of political consensus or political will to meet that challenge. No agreement about the necessity of rebuilding the armed forces or modernizing the armed forces, of adopting any sort of new strategy to meet changing times. In fact, it is in the 1930s that one sees what might be called the "Maginot mentality" really come to the fore.

The French in the late '20s had embarked upon a defensive scheme to protect the eastern frontier of France from German invasion; they had begun to erect extraordinary fortifications, a line of fortifications basically from the Swiss frontier up the borders of Alsace and Lorraine, over to the Dutch frontier. Enormous concrete pillboxes—it was state of the art, static, defensive positions that the French were creating. This Maginot Line, as it came to be known, was in fact symptomatic of French problems in the interwar years. French military thinking was fighting the First World War, was fighting the Great War of the trenches, a war in which he who occupied the defensive position had the advantage. There was no sense at all of the possibilities and mobility. There was a great deal of discussion in France, in Britain, and in

Germany about the use of armor, the use of aircraft, to create a more mobile, more flexible battlefield.

Charles De Gaulle, the young colonel in France, had already written and talked about this. He had been a tank commander in the Great War; had talked about the need to move beyond this defensive mentality that the French military seemed to be mired in. But, it was to no avail. France was simply unwilling, at this point, to embark upon any more ambitious military program to confront this German challenge. An interesting aspect of the Maginot Line of course, too, is that the Maginot Line runs up that frontier of Germany, over to the Ardennes Forest and then stops, but it does not continue all along the French frontier with Belgium. And one thinks, well, this is a kind of curious thing; after all, the Germans had invaded France twice since 1870, neither time had they tried to come where the Maginot Line was constructed, but instead had used this avenue through the Ardennes and then through Belgium during the First War. But the French did not build the Maginot Line, did not extend the Maginot Line across the Belgian frontier. There are several reasons for this, that are, I think, important. One is that France had an ambiguous relationship with Belgium. France had guaranteed Belgium sovereignty. It was not a military alliance in the sense that there was not an exchange of information, not an exchange of military, or a plan for a coordinated military response to a German invasion. France simply had proclaimed its determination to guarantee Belgium.

So for the French, politically, extending the Maginot Line across the frontier with Belgium was a problematic thing. What would your Belgian allies think if what you'd done was to build a fortification along their frontier so that you would simply withdraw behind it? So, politically, this was seen as a problematic thing for the French leadership. There were also engineering problems with it as well. As any soldier who had fought on the Western Front in the First World War understood from the experience of trench foot, the water table in northwestern Europe in this area of the Low Countries is very high; you dig down a little bit and you hit water. The idea of sinking these enormous concrete fortifications into that terrain was a problem. It was certainly solvable, they could've done it, but it was going to be an engineering feat to do it. It was going to be expensive to do it, and there simply was not, in France, the will or the determination to do it.

France had, in the 1930s, the largest army in Europe west of the Soviet Union. The French army still enjoyed a tremendous reputation as being the great military force on the continent. And the French, on the one hand, in their foreign policy, constantly strove to find some sort of collective security arrangement that we've been talking about—but militarily there's no follow-through. There is a sort of sense of, "Well, we know there's a threat, but what is one to do in the end?" They mistrusted the British. British-French relations from the '20s into the '30s were strained for a variety of reasons. The British, in particular, as we talked about in the last lecture, had become increasingly convinced that the Treaty of Versailles was too harsh, that it was unenforceable, and that the best thing to do was to meet legitimate demands of the Germans for change, for revision of the Treaty. But each one of those was one more nail in the coffin of the collective security arrangements that the French had hoped to see. The French, then, were looking for allies, someone they could trust, someone that they could rely upon in this context.

In 1935, a new opportunity presented itself; in 1935 the Soviet Union decided that it, too, was directly challenged by the revival of German power. Stalin was ready for some sort of arrangement with the Western powers, especially after 1934 when Germany had signed this ten-year, non-aggression pact with Poland. To the Soviets this looked like the Germans encroaching into Eastern Europe. Why were they making a deal with the Poles? Was this to be a spearhead for some sort of Polish-German alliance that could be directed against the Soviet Union? And in this sense, Stalin—and being trustful was not one of Stalin's great strong suits, I think—Stalin was convinced that something no good was afoot here. He saw this as a threat, and the Soviet Union would reverse its position, it would enter the League of Nations, it would seek to break its status as an outsider state, a pariah nation, and he named as his foreign secretary Maxim Litvinov, who became a major advocate of collective security. Litvinov, more than any other Soviet leader, was associated with building bridges to Western Europe, maintaining some sort of collective security arrangement that would protect the Soviet Union and Western Europe from German aggression.

The Soviet Union, also in the same spirit, in 1935 signed an agreement with Czechoslovakia in which the Soviets pledged to come to Czechoslovakia's aid if it were attacked by another party. Well, the other party was clearly

Germany. This is what everyone understood, but Stalin did not trust the French or the Czechs terribly about this. France had an agreement with Czechoslovakia, so Stalin wrote language into the agreement with the Czechs which said the Soviet Union would come to Czechoslovakia's aid if France first honored its obligations to the Czechs. Stalin was worried that what the West was trying to do was to channel German aggression eastward. And so what Stalin didn't want to do was to pledge to go to Czechoslovakia's aid along with the French only to have the French back out and leave them in the lurch.

There was another small problem for the Russians with this aid to Czechoslovakia, and that is, that in the 1930s, and until after the Second World War, there was no common frontier between Czechoslovakia and the Soviet Union. They were going to have to pass the Polish territory and the Poles were not terribly keen on the idea of the Red Army passing across Polish territory to aid the Czechs. Nonetheless, this agreement with Czechoslovakia in 1935 indicated that the Soviet Union was interested in becoming the counterweight in the East that France had been seeking. In addition, Stalin instructed the Comintern to urge Communist Parties in Western Europe to cooperate with Socialists and Liberals in forming popular front governments.

Up until this point, the official Comintern position—the official Soviet position—was that the greatest danger in the Western European states was not Fascism at all, but rather, corrupt Social Democracy. Now, in 1935 they reversed themselves on this and said, "Well, now what we need to do is to build bridges to the Socialists, even the Liberals, form popular fronts in order to meet this mounting fascist threat." So one has an uneasy, an uneasy Soviet-French relationship evolving in the mid 1930s as each—mistrustful of the other but concerned about Germany—tries to find some way through this thicket.

Italy was another possibility for the French. Italy had initially been a likely candidate to help France defend the Treaty. Mussolini—one would think ideologically certainly a brethren of Hitler—Mussolini was in many ways Hitler's model. Hitler was always very fond of him, respected him, but Mussolini in this period was concerned about German penetration of the Balkans. In 1934, the Nazis had attempted to overthrow the Austrian government. The Austrian Nazis had—whether Berlin was involved directly one doesn't know, but certainly the Germans weren't unhappy with this—it had led to the assassination of the Austrian dictator Dollfuss. It was a fiasco. The Austrian Nazis were put down, but the French, the Italians, and the British all rallied to Austria's support—that is, to support them against the possibility of German encroachment here.

So there was some real possibility that Italy could be seen as a counterweight. The Italians didn't want to see German influence extend down into the Balkans. But, in late 1935, Mussolini invaded Ethiopia, and when he did, England and France condemned his move and in the following year their opposition to his involvement in the Spanish Civil War. Mussolini came to the aid of Francisco Franco; when this occurred it simply drove a wedge between fascist Italy and the Western democracies. By 1936 Mussolini was already talking about a Rome-Berlin axis and in 1937 Italy would actually sign the anti-Comintern pact with Nazi Germany. So by the mid '30s, Italy has already removed itself as a possible counterweight to the Germans. The Soviets are a possibility, but still problematic.

The Germans, meanwhile, were hardly standing still. In November of 1937, Hitler called a top-secret meeting of his top foreign policy advisors and military men. It was a discussion about general aims and objectives of the regime in foreign policy. During what was a typical sort of Hitler rambling discussion that went on for some time, Hitler talked about the need for *Lebensraum*. He talked about the need for expansion to the East, that what his job would be, would be to isolate his opponents diplomatically, and that Germany should be prepared in the future to deal with a situation in the East—an attack on Poland—and also to face the possibility of a French attack in the West. In other words, what Hitler told his diplomats and his generals is at some point in the future, it's not clear exactly when, Germany ought to be prepared for a move into Eastern Europe, which would probably bring it into conflict with France—hopefully, not with Great Britain, but certainly with France. No notes were allowed to be taken at this meeting—it was top secret—but one colonel did keep notes, a man by the name of Friedrich Hossbach, and this has gone down into the record as the Hossbach Memorandum.

It's important because on the one hand it looks like in 1937, before the great turmoil of 1938 and 1939, that Hitler was already thinking very consistently about precise moves in foreign policy. The debate is whether or not this was sort of typical Hitlerian rhetoric where he's talking about taking a sort of tour of the rise in the possibilities, or, whether this really does represent a blueprint for action. But I think what's interesting about it is that within months, in fact within weeks, the minister of war, General Blomberg, was removed. The commander in chief of the army, General Fritsch was removed and the foreign minister, Baron von Neurath, was removed. All three men had voiced their—not opposition to Hitler's plans, this would've been too much—one simply didn't do this even in 1937—but had raised concerns, in effect saying, "Mein Führer, do you really mean to suggest that we're going to enter into the possibility of a two-front war or are you really talking about war against Poland and then possibly war with France, possibly Britain? What about the Soviet Union?" They raised all sorts of perfectly reasonable, legitimate sorts of concerns that you would expect foreign policy and military advisors to do. And within two months they were all gone, removed. Joachim von Ribbentrop, a Nazi with no real background in foreign policy, was named foreign minister. Hitler, himself, would move to consolidate the military positions in his own hands.

And so as 1938 began, Hitler was in exactly the position that he hoped to be in—the horizons seemed relatively clear; he had a potential friend in Mussolini; the West seemed to be in disarray. And then in February of 1938, a situation fell into his lap which was ideal for an opportunist like Hitler to deal with. The Austrian government since 1934 had been very nervous about Nazi intentions—this attempt to overthrow the Austrian government by Austrian Nazis as we've seen had been squashed by the Austrian government—but there was still concern that the Germans were funneling money to these Austrian Nazis—that they were fermenting trouble within Austria and that the Germans had designs on the Austrian state.

In early 1938, the Austrian chancellor, by the name of Schuschnigg, began taking feelers with the British and with the Italians about possibly guaranteeing Austrian sovereignty. This was leaked; Hitler interpreted this as a breach of any sort of relationship between Germany and Austria, inconsistent with their attempts to rebuild their relationship after the 1934 fiasco, and a crisis seemed to be in the offing. Now, the German ambassador in Austria at this time was a man by the name of Franz von Papen. Ironically enough, he'd been the last pre-Nazi chancellor of Germany. Hitler had earmarked him for assassination in 1934, but the guy had more lives than a cat and survived that, surfaces in 1938 as the ambassador to Austria, and suggests something that was quite rare, indeed almost unheard of at the time—we now take it for granted—it was, "What about a little summit diplomacy?" Why not have Chancellor Schuschnigg from Austria come up from Vienna while the furor is down at his home in the Bavarian Alps close to Salzburg? Have a face-to-face meeting, iron out these difficulties, and so on.

Schuschnigg departed from Vienna, traveling—it's remarkable thinking about this—with a very small entourage, arrives in Munich where he thinks he's going to meet with Hitler and instead is then taken in a large motorcade out through Bavaria, out to Berchtesgaden and then taken up to Hitler's house on this alp that overlooks this extraordinary scene in Bavaria, close to Salzburg. But they don't stop at the so-called "Berghof", which was Hitler's actual residence, but began winding their way around this very tiny typical alpine road, all the way into a parking lot right beside just the side of a mountain. Schuschnigg and just a handful of advisors climb out of the cars, look over, and are being escorted over to these two enormous doors that open into the side of the mountain. And they see stretching in front of them a long corridor with torches about every ten yards or so, beneath each torch a uniformed SS man, a Schutzstafel man—white gloves, black uniform, helmet, bayonet out. They walk down this long corridor into the mountain, climb into a small room—actually the room is well, it's about like this area here—gold-plated. Schuschnigg is standing there not knowing what's going on, hears a sort of odd humming noise in the background, and then suddenly realizes that the room is moving. The room was in fact an elevator and it was taking Schuschnigg, Ribbentrop, and company up. The doors swing open and there is Hitler standing in front of the elevator doorway and behind him is the entire general staff of the German army.

One can actually retrace these steps. All these things are still there— the road, this "Eagle's Nest," as it was called, at the top of this alp that literally is perched right on a peak of the Alps. One could not feel more isolated. I go into this detail, not simply for the sort of local color of it, but because it was the way that Hitler liked to do things; it put Schuschnigg in this position of vulnerability. He thought he was going for a discussion, a typical sort of diplomatic discussion that would take place in offices in Munich, suddenly discover he's going to Hitler's residence in Berchtesgaden. Only, it's not really that, and there he winds up on top of this mountain with Hitler and the German general staff. Hitler didn't waste much time. He demanded, absolutely insisted upon, Austrian acquiescence in freeing all of the Austrian Nazis, coordination of German foreign policy, military policy with Austria, and so on. In effect, what Hitler was talking about was the absorption of Austria by Germany. Schuschnigg managed to collect himself, to get off the alp without committing himself to anything. So they had to go back to Vienna obviously, went back, and then to Hitler's great astonishment Schuschnigg announced plans for a plebiscite to be held on March 13. This was too much. At this point Germany demanded that Schuschnigg call off the plebiscite or face war. Schuschnigg did call off the plebiscite. The German troops poured across the frontier into Austria and Hitler returned to the country of his birth—passing through Braunau where he was born, Linz where he grew up, and then into Vienna where he'd spent the unhappiest years of his life—to a cheering throng, and announced the annexation of Austria.

The international response was mild, to say the least. How did Hitler justify what he had done with Austria? It was clear, this was perfectly consistent with the principles espoused by Woodrow Wilson and the Allies at Versailles—national self-determination of peoples. In 1918, 1919, the Austrians, the sort of rump Austrian state, populated by ethnic Germans, had wanted to be part of the new German state, only the Allies had said no, this can't happen. France and Britain had not fought for four years in order to make Germany larger than it had been in 1914, and so that linkage—this union of Germany and Austria—had been forbidden. So what does Hitler do in 1938 in March? National self-determination of peoples—this is not an aggressive act, it is not a demand of German foreign policy run rampant; it is simply a justified act of national self-determination.

Hitler was not through in 1938. The summer would pass with a mounting crisis over Czechoslovakia, the Allies had been hamstrung in their response to the Austrian case, and now it seemed as if Austria was resolved. But now, Czechoslovakia had been moved onto the front burner. The mountainous area around Bohemia, this part of Czechoslovakia that extends into Germany in the east—the Sudetenland it was called—to a very large extent was populated by ethnic Germans. And in 1938, in the spring and summer of 1938, encouraged by the Nazis in Germany, Conrad Henlein and the Sudeten Germans began demanding autonomy for the ethnic Germans in Czechoslovakia, arguing that they were being repressed by the Czech state, that all they wanted was national self-determination of peoples. They wanted to come, as the term was, "Heim ins Reich", "To return to the Reich." This term, this policy, was clearly supported by the National Socialist regime. The Czechs, fearful of a replay of the "*Anschluss*"—this linkage of union of Germany and Austria— the Czech government mobilized its forces; they're going to fight.

Czechoslovakia, certainly Bohemia with its mountainous terrain, was a very tough area for an invasion. The German military was not keen on the possibility of an invasion at all, and the Czech army was well-trained and well-equipped. So Hitler was furious, he'd been shown up now by the Czechs, he wasn't ready to push the situation, and so the summer had elapsed without any sort of solution to this mounting, what was now being called the "Crisis of the Sudetenland." But in the fall—late summer, early fall— Hitler told his military people, "Prepare for an invasion of Czechoslovakia by October 1," while publicly stating all he wanted was to defend the rights of ethnic Germans in Czechoslovakia. At this point, in the fall of 1938, two people stepped in to save the day, to save the peace. One was Mussolini, who was nervous as a cat at this point, having rattled his saber—I suppose more appropriately for Mussolini it would be to pound his chest, since he was fond of ripping off his shirt there at the palazzo there in Rome. Despite all of this, despite his invasion of Ethiopia, his involvement in the Spanish Civil War, Mussolini was not at all keen on being dragged into war, possibly with France, maybe with the Soviet Union, maybe with Britain. Over what? The Sudetenland? No way. So he found an ally in the British Prime Minister by the name of Neville Chamberlain.

Chamberlain had become Prime Minister in May of 1937 and he would become the foremost exponent of a policy that we've come to know as appeasement. It was not his policy; he was not the originator of the term or of the policy. It had been in fact British policy almost since the end of the First World War, to meet reasonable German demands for revision of the Treaty, to deal with the Germans from a position of strength, yes, but to realize that the Treaty had probably been too harsh, and to therefore meet what could be argued were reasonable demands. As far as Chamberlain was concerned, this was the only alternative. The French, he viewed, were weak, unreliable. The French army might be huge, but he had no confidence whatsoever in its ability to actually pull off a defense of Czechoslovakia. The Americans were worse. The Americans were unreliable, we were wallowing in isolationism, and the other thing for Chamberlain—this is an important point that we'll come back to—Chamberlain was mistrustful of American interests in the long haul. This special relationship between the United States and Britain is largely a creation of Churchill and Roosevelt; it certainly was not Chamberlain's policy.

In 1938, Chamberlain was afraid that if a war came, any war, that it would lead to a decline of the British Empire and an emergence of real American power. So Britain would be reduced to the status of a second-class citizen behind the United States. And then, finally, Chamberlain had also learned his lessons from the summer of 1914. What would be worth another war? What issue? What problem would justify throwing Europe once again into this great cataclysm where millions of young men and women would die? The Sudetenland in Germany? In Czechoslovakia? You couldn't probably have found a room full of people in Britain who could've found it on a map, maybe even in the foreign office. And so, for Chamberlain the point was, meet reasonable demands. Deal with the Germans honestly, deal with Hitler from a position of strength certainly, but be ready to compromise. The result, as we all know, was the conference held on September 30 of 1938, in Munich, in which Chamberlain, De Laudier of France, Mussolini, and Hitler presided over the annexation of the Sudetenland by Germany. That conference was a major turning point in the prelude to the Second World War, and the implications of which we will take up in our next lecture.

The Coming of War
Lecture 4

In this lecture, we will focus on the implications of the Munich Conference. For Hitler's evaluation of the international situation, we'll examine his calculations about the Anglo-French responses to a possible invasion of Czechoslovakia—and Stalin's assessment of the Western powers in the last months of the war.

In late 1938 Europe stood on the brink of war. Chamberlain received a hero's welcome on his return from Munich. His efforts to save the peace in Europe were greeted by general relief. Intent on preserving peace in Europe, Chamberlain had made all allowable concessions to Hitler. He was convinced that the United States was unreliable, France was weak, and the British army could not undertake operations on the continent. He and many others believed that World War I had occurred because European leaders had not taken all possible steps to preserve peace and avert war. He feared that another war would subordinate Britain to the United States. And he sincerely believed Hitler's protestations of peaceful intent.

Hitler concluded from the Munich Conference that the Western powers were weak and lacked the will to fight. Stalin also concluded that the West was weak. He was angry that the Soviet Union had been excluded from the Munich deliberations. He was convinced that the West sought to channel Nazi expansionism eastward.

Until 1938, the German army acted to restrain Hitler's aggressive impulses. Nervous about fighting the well-equipped Czech army, certain members of the army high command conspired to overthrow Hitler if he ordered an invasion of Czechoslovakia. The conspiracy began to dissolve in the wake of Munich.

Asserting the need to quell Czech-Slovak ethnic tensions, Hitler invaded Czechoslovakia on March 15, 1939. This move could not be justified in terms of national self-determination; it was seen by all as naked aggression. In a dramatic policy reversal, Britain joined France in extending security guarantees to Poland. In March 1939 Hitler seized Memel; the veil had dropped.

The last prelude to war came in the summer of 1939. France and Britain delayed in bringing the Soviet Union into the European collective security system. Chamberlain and the British foreign policy establishment distrusted Stalin. Britain and France thought the Soviet Union was militarily weak due to Stalin's purging of the Red Army.

On August 23, 1939, the Germans and Soviets announced that they had signed the Molotov-Ribbentrop Pact, a non-aggression pact. The pact made no ideological sense; Germany and the Soviet Union were sworn ideological foes. However, the pact made a great deal of sense in terms of international politics at the time of its signing. Hitler hoped to avoid the threat of a two-front war following his anticipated invasion of Poland. He believed the pact would deter Britain from coming to Poland's defense. Stalin hoped that the pact would give him time to rebuild Soviet military strength.

The Molotov-Ribbentrop Pact made war in Europe inevitable.

Moreover, the secret annexes of the treaty provided for Soviet territorial gains in Poland and the Baltic states. The Soviet Union stood to acquire much of eastern Poland. The Hitler-Stalin Pact made war in Europe inevitable. Hitler had not intended to fight in the West in the autumn of 1939. After he refused Chamberlain's ultimatum to withdraw from Poland, however, the war was on. ∎

Suggested Reading

Jonathan Haslam, *The Soviet Union and the Struggle for Collective Security in Europe, 1933–1939.*

Klaus Hildebrand, *The Foreign Policy of the Third Reich.*

Williamson Murray, *The Change in the European Balance of Power, 1938–1939.*

1. Why was the Soviet Union so mistrustful of the West? Why did Stalin sign the non-aggression pact with Nazi Germany?

2. What were the implications of the Munich Agreement for Hitler's calculations?

The Coming of War
Lecture 4—Transcript

Hello, and welcome to the fourth in our series of lectures on the Second World War. We had concluded the third lecture with an examination of the *Anschluss*, the German *Anschluss* with Austria, the union with Austria in the spring of 1938, and then the evolving crisis over the Sudetenland in Czechoslovakia in the fall of that same year. In this lecture, we will focus on the implications of the Munich Conference. For Hitler's evaluation of the international situation, we'll examine his calculations about the Anglo-French responses to a possible invasion of Czechoslovakia—and Stalin's assessment of the Western powers in the last months of the war.

We'll also describe the impact of the Munich Conference on the German military conspiracy against Hitler, which had been gaining some momentum in the prelude to the conference. And the lecture will conclude by tracing the evolution of the Polish crisis in the summer of 1939, and especially the stunning ramifications of the Molotov-Ribbentrop Pact in August of that year. It's hard to talk about the Munich Conference or Chamberlain's policy of appeasement—it's simply, one thinks, if you want to discredit anyone politically at any time after 1938 all you have to do is say "appeasement." If you want to suggest that a political opponent has sold out something all you have to do is say "Munich," and the two things come together as an obvious condemnation of the myopic policies of Neville Chamberlain—and some would argue the criminally myopic policies of Chamberlain. But I think it's an important point to remember that in the aftermath, the immediate aftermath of the crisis in the fall of 1938, Neville Chamberlain was an international hero, wildly popular in Britain for having saved the peace. A huge sigh of relief passed across Europe that war had been averted, and Chamberlain enjoyed a brief period of great acclaim.

I'd like to come back and talk a bit about the actual conference itself. We saw in the previous lecture that at the last moment, as Hitler seemed intent on taking military action against the Czechoslovakian state, that Chamberlain, Mussolini, and De Laudier of France had agreed to meet with Hitler in late September—September 30 as it turned out—to see if war might indeed be forestalled. If one looks at the photographs of that conference and the negotiations—it all happens in an afternoon into the evening—there is this photograph of Chamberlain, De Laudier, Hitler, and Mussolini, all extraordinarily pleased with themselves; Goering, a rotund second in command of the Third Reich, head of the German Air Force, head of the four-year plan, bouncing around in the background—all terrifically pleased with their work that afternoon. Notable by their absence in that photograph are two people. One is, there is no representative of the Czechs at all; no Czechoslovakian representative was present at the actual discussions in Munich. The Czech delegation was standing outside the Führerbau, an administrative building for the Nazi Party in Munich, waiting to discover the fate of their country. There was another absence, a person missing from those discussions in Munich, and that, of course, was any sort of representative of the Soviet Union. Stalin was not present; no representative of the Soviet government had been a party to these negotiations.

What drove Neville Chamberlain to undertake this policy? We've talked about the fact that Chamberlain was determined to appease. It's hard to say the word without it just dripping with judgment. But appeasement at this point meant not caving in—not some sort of craven, weak, giving-in to the National Socialist regime, or to Hitler—but to make timely concessions on those points that could legitimately be granted to the Germans. There was a widespread feeling that Hitler might not have come to power had it not been for the vindictiveness of the Allies at the conclusion of the First World War. If one looks at Chamberlain's options in 1938, he was really determined to avoid war, not at all costs, but the breakout of war would be a real defeat for him. He wanted, he believed certainly that the United States was unreliable—the United States had retreated behind this veil of isolationism. Roosevelt would be reduced to being that of a spectator in 1938 and indeed into 1939, for reasons that we will certainly talk about. France, he believed, was weak. So, what were the real options for British policy? The British army was virtually non-existent in 1938; the navy certainly was strong. The British had been throwing a great deal of resources into the construction of an air force, but the British army was certainly in no position to undertake military operations on the continent—and France seemed not to be terribly inclined to do it.

Chamberlain therefore undertook this mission to Munich in an effort to save the peace. He had learned the lessons of the Great War, he believed. And this was a view that he shared with the other people in Europe—pundits, diplomats, politicians—as well as the proverbial man on the street. If only the leaders of Europe in that fateful summer of 1914 had been willing to walk the last mile—to leave no leaf unturned or whatever image one wants to use in that regard—to preserve the peace, then maybe Europe would not have slithered into the morass of war in the summer of 1914. So for Chamberlain, this going to Germany—first, when Chamberlain flew to Germany to meet Hitler in Munich he was treated to the same treatment as Schuschnigg; that is, taken up to the Eagle's Nest. The German general staff was not present so it wasn't quite the browbeating that Schuschnigg had received. Indeed, in his first encounter with Hitler, Hitler was—as he could frequently be when he certainly wanted to—he turned on the charm, he was sweetness and light itself; agreeable, ready to compromise, and so on. Chamberlain left that meeting believing that this was a man—certainly someone not to his taste—but a man with whom one could deal. So he flew, he took his first airplane trip, goes to Germany, begins the process of negotiation, returns back to Britain, negotiates with the French, brings the British cabinet into line so that everyone is in agreement—they will back this sort of agreement that Germany would ultimately basically receive the Sudetenland. He hoped that there would be some sort of plebiscite held in the future to ratify that decision. But, he was convinced that these were the sorts of necessary steps, and he also believed that he didn't have very many options.

It was important—it was absolutely essential—to maintain the peace. Britain would be a loser, Chamberlain believed, by any sort of new outbreak of war, even if Britain should win the war. If Britain had gone from being a creditor nation to a debtor nation between 1914 and 1918, another major conflict would really put Britain and the British Empire on the skids; make Britain a second-class citizen, as we talked about previously, to the United States. And, then there is the other, having said all of this, trying to give the rationale for Chamberlain's thinking. It is also apparent that he came away from his first encounter with Hitler and even a second one—he went back to Godesberg before the Munich Conference to try to negotiate a second time with Hitler. He actually seems to have trusted Hitler. He came away thinking, "Well, here's a man, I understand him, he's a nationalist, he's conservative, he's someone with whom we can deal. And if only Britain, France, and the other victorious Allies had treated Germany in a more equitable way after the First War, then maybe we wouldn't be in this position at the present time."

We all know, from the newsreels, the performance of Chamberlain upon his return to Britain, the standing outside the wing of the aircraft on that landing field, holding up—it's actually not the Munich agreement, but an auxiliary—an annex to that agreement in which Germany and Great Britain promise not to go to war with one another, not to use force. And suddenly he's holding up that sheet of paper, saying, "I believe this means peace in our time." I think that probably stands at the top of the list for famous last words in Western history. Again, it's extremely important to remember that Neville Chamberlain at that moment was probably the most popular man in Europe. He was seen as a real hero—the troublemakers, the warmongers, Churchill for example, and others in the British government, in the parliament, other pundits, who were saying, "No good will come of this, one can't make a deal with Hitler, with this National Socialist regime"—these men were largely isolated. Their voices could be heard, but in general the popular view was these people are troublemakers, they're warmongers, there is really a chance to save the peace and Neville Chamberlain has made an heroic attempt to do just that. Chamberlain came back indeed believing that the basis for peace in his time had been achieved.

Adolf Hitler drew rather different conclusions from his encounter with Chamberlain, De Laudier, and company at Munich. He drew the conclusion that the West was weak, that it would not fight—that when push came to shove, Britain would not intervene on the continent to undo German actions. He would later say, "I know how they will respond. I've met them, our opponents. I met them at Munich; they're worms."

Interestingly enough, someone else drew a similar conclusion to the Munich Conference, and that person was Joseph Stalin. Watching events from Moscow, in isolation, Stalin was furious. Furious that the Soviet Union had not been included, all the way through the crisis—the run-up to the Munich agreement, the Munich Conference. The Soviet Union hammered away in all of its public statements, "We stand prepared to come to the aid of the Czechoslovakian State. We will honor our obligations to Czechoslovakia, according to our Treaty." But of course, if you'll recall, the French would have to do so first. And the French showed no inclination to do that. As a consequence, Stalin believed that all Chamberlain wanted, all he was interested in, indeed all that the West was interested in, was funneling German aggression to the East, to point the Germans in the direction of the Soviet Union.

Behind the scenes there was also another reaction, and an extremely important one. The relationship between the National Socialist Party, this new Nazi regime, and the German army was a problematic one from the beginning. German military men were certainly very happy about Hitler's determination to restore the German army, to rebuild the German military machine, to restore German power and influence in the world. They had been very nervous, very worried, in 1933-34 about the SA, the Storm Troopers. In 1933-34, with the German army limited to 100,000 troops, the SA had between 400,000 and 500,000 men at its disposal. The German army, leaders of the German army, even those that were quite pro-Nazi, were worried that Hitler, when push came to shove, would side with the SA; that the SA would simply absorb the army, and that the old traditions of the Prusso-German army would be lost to this radical National Socialist Group. So—and in of course in 1934 the army swears allegiance. Why does it swear allegiance to Hitler? Because in 1934 Hitler had purged the SA, executed its leader. He seemed to have made peace with the army and to have said, "Given the choice now, what I need is the army, not the SA," even though the SA had been so instrumental in his rise to power and his consolidation of power in '33-'34.

All the way through the dramatic events that we've been describing—Hitler's revision of the Treaty—the German army, rather than encouraging Hitler, had acted as a restraint, had constantly said, "Well, are we really up to this?" In 1936, as you'll recall, they had been nervous about, indeed opposed, the remilitarization of the Rhineland, fearing any sort of French reaction would lead to an ignominious defeat on the part of Germany. They tried to convince Hitler in 1938 that the army was not even prepared to move unopposed into Austria. And as the Czech crisis began to develop, there was real concern in the army. The Czechs were well-armed, well-trained, they had good defensive positions. And within the high command of the army, voices were raised, quite secretly, of course, to say, "If we are given the order, if Hitler sends us on a suicidal mission to attack Czechoslovakia, then I think the time has come to put him under house arrest, to depose him, and to create a different sort of state." General Ludwig Beck was one of the leaders of this conspiracy. Discussions had taken place as the crisis mounted, and then, of course, comes Munich.

The German army, the leaders of the conspiracy, were absolutely flummoxed by this. They didn't believe that the West would cave in—here they had been once again arguing, "No, no, no, this is suicidal, we can't do it, this will lead to disaster." And once again Hitler had been proved correct. At the critical moment, when we're going to have to fight for the Sudetenland, the West had caved in. With that, with this Munich Conference, this conspiracy—military conspiracy—against Hitler began to dissolve. We'll see it resurface again; it would be many of the very same people, in the summer of 1944, on July 20, 1944, who would attempt to assassinate Hitler and to overthrow the National Socialist regime. But in 1938, the calling of the Munich Conference, Hitler's success at Munich, undercut this emerging military conspiracy against his regime.

At the end of this crisis, Hitler now felt that the horizon was open to him. In March of 1939, Hitler used ethnic conflicts between Czechs and Slovaks as a pretext to send German troops into what was left of Czechoslovakia. Robbed of the Sudetenland and the mountainous regions that guarded the entry into Czechoslovakia, there was very little that the Czech army now felt that it could do to defend itself against the Germans. German troops marched in, in the spring of 1939, on March 15. And now, with that invasion, although Hitler tried to dress it up, saying, "We're going in just to maintain order," the Czechoslovakian state was an illegitimate state. It was inherently unstable, and with ethnic violence there we're going to step in simply to preserve order. He sent troops in, in March of 1939, and this invasion of Czechoslovakia was unopposed. German troops marched in unopposed; this is the real turning point for the West. Whereas the *Anschluss* with Austria could be justified on the basis of national self-determination of peoples, the Sudeten crisis could be in some ways justified that way. One could talk about just demands on the part of the Germans. One could talk about legitimate compromise, but not this invasion of Czechoslovakia. The move into this rump Czechoslovakian state in March of 1939 was pure naked aggression—and that's the way it was perceived. Everyone knew it. It marks also, I might say, a major turning point in public opinion in Great Britain. Now those voices in the wilderness, people like Churchill—who had been arguing that Hitler was inherently untrustworthy, that one couldn't deal with him—now took on greater credibility, and Chamberlain's policy seemed to be, if not discredited, was certainly in deep trouble. At this point, Great Britain extended a guarantee to Poland—and France joined with the English in this guarantee.

Also, in March of 1939, the Germans seized Memel, this territory along the Baltic, which had been lost to Germany as a result of the Treaty of Versailles to Lithuania. So Czechoslovakia, now Memel— the Germans were moving over into a new phase of their foreign policy. The veil had dropped; although Hitler continued to make the usual sorts of introductions to his policies about justice for Germany, equality and so on, this was a tune that now had been played once too often. The extension of a guarantee to Poland by Great Britain was a startling reversal of British policy, but it didn't mean that Chamberlain had given completely up on the policy of appeasement. Chamberlain hangs on to this literally to the very last moment, because, in some ways for Chamberlain—even when the evidence began to come in that this policy had been misguided—there were too many chips on the table for him. Any war now was going to be a complete repudiation of all of his policies, all of the assumptions that he'd based his foreign policy on. He was so invested in this that he would continue, as we will see, to try to find some way to maintain the peace.

The key to peace in Europe in the summer of 1939, however, was not in London. Nor was it in Paris, nor it certainly wasn't in Washington across the ocean. It was in Moscow. The guarantees to Poland, the Franco-British guarantees to Poland, could only be effective—Chamberlain understood this, De Laudier understood this—could only be effective within the context of some sort of overall collective security structure, one which had eluded them, really, since 1919. And included in that collective security structure had to be the Soviet Union. The Soviet Union was really—now there was the sense that, well Poland is now going to be moved to the front burner of Nazi policy, so the Soviets have to be enlisted in this. The Soviets have to join in order to create a credible counterweight to the Germans in the East. Knowing this—as every policy maker, every newspaper reader in Europe understood in the summer of 1939—the British and French governments proceed in a most casual sort of way. They are supposed to send off representatives to talk to the Soviet Union. How do they do it? Do they fly them out to Moscow? No, they send them on a ship across the Baltic Sea in this kind of leisurely, almost Scandinavian tour arrangement. This didn't impress the Soviets very much at all. There was a sense, I think, on the part of certainly the Chamberlain government, that time was on their side. They didn't believe—Chamberlain just absolutely—and one can understand why he would think this—thought inconceivable that Stalin and Hitler could ever come to any sort of arrangement.

Stalin had to know, didn't he, that Hitler was his sworn enemy, that much of Nazi foreign policy was based on the destruction of the Soviet Union, the anti-Communist propaganda of the National Socialist regime? It was obvious, so as Chamberlain is reputed to have said, "The Bolshis and the Nazis will never be able to make a deal." In addition, Chamberlain and the policy-making circles in Great Britain at this point were very mistrustful of the Communist regime. There's no way around this. Stalin was certainly mistrustful of them, they didn't trust his intentions, and so there was no real community of interest here—certainly the threat of the Germans, of the Nazis—but no real community of interest here, of trust.

Also, there's another factor here that I think should be brought out—we'll talk about this again when we talk about the German calculations for an invasion of the Soviet Union in 1941. The Red Army, in the summer of 1939, was the largest army in Europe by a long shot. But, its status internationally was very low. In 1938, Stalin had begun a massive purge of the Red Army—we'll talk about this as I said in more detail a bit down the road. But we're not talking about just a purge at the very top levels of the Red Army, we're talking about a purge that goes all the way through the command down to company level. Thousands of Soviet officers and NCO's were purged in the course of 1938. There was a general sense in the West that the Soviet Union was weak, that it was a huge army certainly, but one that was riddled with political corruption—with this ideological sort of action on the part of Stalin—and that the purges simply had torn out the heart and soul of the Red Army.

Meanwhile, the Poles found themselves in an incredibly difficult position. The Germans, between the Munich Pact and the fall of 1939, had tendered a series of offers to the Poles asking them to join in the Anti-Comintern Pact aimed at the Soviet Union. The Poles, over and over again, reiterated their willingness to discuss a revision of the Treaty of Versailles. They would talk about Danzig, they would talk about the Polish corridor, nothing would be off the table. They were willing to compromise on these sort of territorial issues with the Germans, but the Poles absolutely refused to be reduced to the status of a puppet state. They didn't want to become simply a puppet of the Nazis and they also didn't want Soviet troops on Polish territory. The Germans made a number of offers to Poland in October of 1938 and January of 1939, and April of 1939, in the aftermath of the British and French guarantee, in each instance the Germans saying, "We can cooperate; we can do things." The Poles chose not to buy this offer. Poland refused each of these overtures, and with the last refusal the Poles set the stage for the conflict.

There was a growing sense in Europe, as the last days of summer arrived, that a real crisis was imminent, and then in late August the thunderbolt that sent shock waves throughout the diplomatic community. On August 23, 1939, the Germans and Soviets announced that they had signed a non-aggression pact. In fact, the Germans had begun talks with the Russians in May of 1939—economic talks with them—and instead of putting this on the more casual route that the British and the French had done, the Germans made a great deal of this. They sent high-ranking officials off to the Soviet Union, they emphasized the importance of these talks, and so they were taken seriously. On the one hand, what came to be known as the Molotov-Ribbentrop Pact—Molotov was the Soviet foreign minister, he replaced Litvinov—the Molotov-Ribbentrop Pact made no ideological sense whatsoever. Here were these two sworn ideological enemies of one another; they had spent most of their propaganda lives attacking one another. But, in the context of international politics in the summer of 1939, the Molotov-Ribbentrop Pact made a great deal of sense.

For Hitler, a pact with the Soviet Union in the summer of 1939 ended the prospect of a two-front war. Hitler was determined, by this point, to attack Poland. He was not going to be denied his war. As he said at one point in August, "I was cheated out of that war at Munich. Not again." He was determined; he was going to take what he wanted in Poland. He believed that the Molotov-Ribbentrop Pact would have a deterrent effect; that is, he counted on the Molotov-Ribbentrop Pact to restrain the British. The French he was not worried about; the French would do what the British wanted to do. The Molotov-Ribbentrop Pact, the Nazi-Soviet non-aggression pact, would, he believed, deter Britain from honoring its obligation to Poland.

For Stalin, whose intelligence people certainly knew all there was to know about Hitler's large ideological intentions—they've been able to read *Mein Kamph* and listen to the speeches; followed Nazi foreign policy—for Stalin, of course, this agreement made very little sense in an ideological way either. But again, within the context of the circumstances of 1939, it was extremely important. For one thing, it would allow Stalin to buy time. If the Germans were determined to attack in the East and if the West was unreliable—would not come to his aid—then at least some sort of agreement with Hitler would allow him to buy time; to rebuild the Red Army, to reduce the effects of the purges. And, there were secret annexes to this non-aggression pact. The Soviet Union and Nazi Germany had divided Eastern Europe into spheres of influences. They agreed it was clear the Germans were going to attack Poland in the immediate future and they agreed that the Soviets would move into the eastern part of Poland; that there would be a partition of Poland. Germany was to get Lithuania and Vilna; Russia was to get Latvia, Estonia, and Finland.

Both sides had interests in Romania and its oil fields—they couldn't come to any agreement about this. This didn't bode well for the long run. But, for Stalin, what these secret clauses did was to secure territorial and strategic advantages for the Soviet Union and Poland. Now, if the Germans were to attack, the Soviet border had been now moved hundreds of miles west. An attack against Poland, an attack against the Soviet Union would now encounter Soviet troops in Poland. The Molotov-Ribbentrop Pact made war in Europe inevitable. Hitler, as we said, counted on the pact to deter Britain and France from intervening. He did not believe Great Britain would honor its guarantee; he expected Mussolini to sign on. In May of 1939, Hitler and Mussolini had signed what was called the Pact of Steel, in which they both pledged full assistance to each other in the event of war, regardless of the circumstances, regardless of the situation. But in the last days before Hitler's planned attack on Poland, when he informed Mussolini that there'd been no coordination of policy between the two, it was an alliance largely in name only. When he informed Mussolini of his plans at the last moment, he was astonished with el Duce told him that Italy would not be able to help him out in the event of war, that in fact Italy would not be prepared for war until 1943.

Hitler proceeded without him. Hitler—and this is an extremely important point—did not anticipate or intend a war with the West in the fall of 1939. Germany was not prepared for war—a big war—in the fall of 1939. It had not made the economic preparations for a war, an extended or protracted conflict in 1939. The four-year plan had fallen far short of its goals—Germany was hardly economically independent. And when German troops marched into Poland, Hitler was convinced that Britain would see the light and that some sort of agreement would be made with Chamberlain. In fact, Chamberlain reluctantly issued an ultimatum that Germany had to withdraw from Poland and then they would talk. Hitler let that deadline lapse, and when it did, Europe was at war. We will take up the strategy employed by the Germans in September of 1939—the responses of the Allies—in our next lecture.

Blitzkrieg
Lecture 5

We are going to be dealing, in this lecture, with the actual outbreak of hostilities with the German assault on Poland in September of 1939, and with the Blitzkrieg—this new way of warfare that the Germans introduced to the world in Poland in September of 1939.

W e will examine the Blitzkrieg, or Lightning War, as a revolutionary military concept, tracing its origins in the thinking of the German high command during the 1930s. Blitzkrieg served Hitler as an economic and diplomatic strategy as well as a military one, since it would allow him, he believed, to conduct short wars against diplomatically isolated enemies without a full mobilization of the German economy.

The military elements of the Blitzkrieg included armored divisions, motorized infantry, and close air support. Its military goal was to avoid static trench warfare as Germany experienced between 1914 and 1918.

The Blitzkrieg also offered several political and economic advantages for Hitler. Lightning war against a diplomatically isolated adversary could be conducted without full mobilization of Germany's society and economy. A policy of armaments in breadth, not in depth, would allow Hitler rapidly to build up and deploy Germany's armed forces. Lightning campaigns would substitute for sustained military efforts, for which Germany in late 1939 was not yet prepared.

The Blitzkrieg strategy had the following components:

- It was an offensive operation in which tanks would lead the attack, followed by motorized infantry, tracked personnel carriers, and massed infantry.

- The Luftwaffe would first destroy enemy air forces and disrupt enemy communications, and then provide close air support to attacking ground units.

- This strategy was intended to provide the movement, speed, and flexibility that had been conspicuously lacking during the First World War.

The Blitzkrieg strategy was developed by General Heinz Guderian. Guderian had been appalled by the slaughter occasioned by the static warfare at Verdun during World War I. Guderian adopted his ideas about aggressive armored warfare from British military thinkers, especially Gen. J.F.C. Fuller and Capt. B.H. Liddell Hart. Hitler was impressed by Guderian's ideas, although the German military high command was dubious.

The assessment of the Red Army was low, and anti-Soviet sentiment was rampant in Britain and France and in the United States.

The first German Blitzkrieg was directed at Poland. Britain and France did not react as Hitler had anticipated to his aggression against Poland in September 1939. Their reaction raised the prospect of a two-front war for which Germany was not yet ready. Germans reacted with disappointment to news of the German invasion of Poland. Hitler's popularity had previously been based on his ability to achieve his foreign policy goals by means short of war.

The first Blitzkrieg against Poland—known as "Case White"—proceeded according to plan. Poland was vastly outmatched in troop strength and armaments. German troops reached Warsaw on September 8, 1939. The Polish army fought tenaciously in the face of a massive German aerial attack but was annihilated. Soviet troops crossed Poland's eastern frontier on September 17, 1939. Many escaping Poles traveled to Britain, where they formed Europe's largest army-in-exile.

The "Enigma machine" was used by the Germans to encipher their military communications. Polish mathematicians "broke" the mathematics behind Enigma and provided this information to the British after the fall of Poland. Britain and later the U.S. were able to successfully exploit German military communications as a result, particularly in the U-boat 'war' in the Atlantic in 1943–1944.

This war in the East ended by October 1939. It was followed in the West by a strange lull that lasted until the spring of 1940. Hitler launched a series of peace initiatives between November 1939 and February 1940 intended to prevent a two-front war.

In the East, the Russo-Finnish War was fought between November 1939 and March 1940. Afraid that Finland would fall under German influence and pose a threat to Leningrad, Stalin demanded that Finland cede part of the Karelian Peninsula to the Soviet Union. After the Finns refused this demand, Soviet forces attacked. The Finns resisted with great skill and tenacity despite being vastly outnumbered. The Red Army bogged down quickly and incurred heavy casualties. Although the Soviets ultimately prevailed, the fighting reinforced the poor combat reputation of the Red Army. ■

Suggested Reading

John Keegan, *The Second World War*, Chapter 3.

Gerhard Weinberg, *A World At Arms*, Chapter 2.

Questions to Consider

1. What objectives did the Blitzkrieg strategy serve for Nazi Germany? What were its main military components?

2. What considerations led Hitler to miscalculate the likely Allied reaction to his invasion of Poland? What were the consequences of this miscalculation?

Blitzkrieg
Lecture 5—Transcript

Hello, and welcome back to our series of discussions on the Second World War. We are going to be dealing, in this lecture, with the actual outbreak of hostilities with the German assault on Poland in September of 1939, and with the Blitzkrieg—this new way of warfare that the Germans introduced to the world in Poland in September of 1939. We'll look at Blitzkrieg not simply as a military policy, a military strategy, but also as a political and economic policy. It was all three. We'll look at what the components of that strategy were, why they were revolutionary. We'll talk about why Blitzkrieg was of a political and economic advantage to Hitler. And then we'll trace the campaign itself in Poland, what lessons were learned from it. And then, also, look—at the conclusion of the lecture—at the Russian invasion of Finland in the winter of 1939-1940.

So, let's begin with the Blitzkrieg. We certainly tend to think of the Blitzkrieg—it's a word that's now gone into the political lexicon of Blitz—Blitzkrieg—"Lightning War" is what it means. We all know this I think. What I think is less frequently known about Blitzkrieg was the extent to which it was not simply a military policy, but was part of a general approach of the Nazis—especially Hitler—to political and economic problems. The idea of Lightning Wars, quick wars, to be fought against diplomatically isolated states, was key to Hitler's thinking. Hitler's idea of knocking out an opponent, to destroy the opponent before it really had time to get itself mobilized, was important because Hitler wanted to be able to conduct business as usual. He had been tremendously impressed by his experiences during the First World War. At the end of the First World War, as you'll recall, the old regime, the Imperial German State, was overthrown by revolution at home. All the way through the war, and particularly after 1916, Germany was under tremendous economic pressure—pressure to provide food and housing, and so on, for its citizens.

Germans were forced to live with great privations in the last two years of the First War, and this had made a tremendous impression on Hitler. He believed that the regime had toppled in November of 1918 precisely because the old imperial regime had been unable to deal with the demands of its population. It had not been able to feed it, to clothe it, to provide fuel for warmth during those last two grisly years of the war. It sounds ironic in a sense, or almost counter-intuitive, but Hitler was very much attuned to public opinion. One thinks, here's this totalitarian dictator who certainly by 1939 can snap his fingers and get what he wants. But, in fact, Hitler was very, very sensitive to public opinion. The Gestapo, the secret police in Germany, had to submit reports every two weeks on what was called "Stimmung in der Bevolkerung". It's not public opinion, but opinion. They would go off and listen to—overhear—discussions in bars, on street corners, in the bakeries, and so on, and then write up reports. How did this policy play? How did that policy play? And these things were taken quite seriously at home. What Hitler wanted to be able to do was certainly to go to war, but against an opponent that he had carefully picked. They would be diplomatically isolated, so that that opponent could be knocked out in rapid fashion. What this would do would be to allow him to conduct military operations without a total mobilization of the economy, without the privations of the First World War, without the dislocations of moving from a peacetime to a wartime economy. And it allowed him to pursue a very rapid military buildup.

We're talking about a country that in 1935 had basically no armed forces. By 1939 Germany had extraordinarily well-trained and well-equipped armed forces. They did this by pursuing what was called a policy of armaments in breadth, but not in depth. That is, rather than mobilize the economy for full wartime production—rationing, allocation of scarce resources, and so on—armaments in breadth meant build armor, build aircraft, equip your infantry. But you don't do this as if you're planning to go to war for a year, two years, three years, four years, five years. These were to be lightning campaigns. You could do this, not on a shoestring, but certainly would not require the kind of full commitment of the society—the total mobilization of society—that the First World War had required. It was evident in 1939 that this was precisely the policy that Germany had pursued, despite the increasing awesome displays of military hardware and the four-year plan. Certainly in Nazi Germany by 1937-1938-39, Hitler would review at the grandstand there—on "Unter den Linden"—just across from the chancellery. Every year there would be the enormous display of military hardware. The German tanks, the new equipment, the heavy artillery, all rolled by; the soldiers goose-stepping proudly by.

Despite all of this—despite all of the talk in the four-year plan about putting Germany on a footing to be economically independent by 1940—Germany was certainly not prepared for any sort of protracted conflict in September of 1939. Much of the four-year plan had been devoted to developing synthetic materials, especially oil and rubber. But only 20 percent of Germany's oil needs were actually produced domestically. And less than 15 percent of its rubber could be produced by these synthetic methods. Germany also still imported about 20 percent of its food in 1939. So, Germany was hardly prepared to launch a major war against powerful enemies in the fall of 1939. What it could do, was to launch, Hitler believed, a surgical attack against an opponent like Poland. I said diplomatically isolated. Now, it's obvious that Poland has agreements with both Britain and France. But as you'll recall, Hitler was absolutely convinced that his agreement with the Soviet Union would act to deter British intervention. That France would fall into line. And so he would have his war against Poland. It would be over. No mobilization of the economy, no big international repercussions. The regime would move on. This would obviously not be the case. But the Blitzkrieg strategy that had been developed in Germany was ideal in a military sense for this type of thinking.

Well, what was that Blitzkrieg strategy? And how did it come about? First of all, it began with an emphasis in offensive operations. The great lesson of the First War had been that these massive battles, the first Battle of the Somme, in which the British lost 40,000 troops in a single morning. Charges across No-Man's Land. The pulverizing of positions at Verdun. Also, in the course of 1916, where heavy artillery, machine guns, automatic weapons of all sorts could be brought to bear against charging infantrymen. That this static war in which all the advantages seem to lie with those on the defense, could be avoided. How did one get around having another replay of the same kind of trench warfare, a war of attrition, which Germany could not win? The point was movement, was offensive operations. How to do this? Well, it was to take advantage of powerful armored forces. Tanks to smash border defenses and encircle large concentrations of enemy troops. Following the Panzers, the German term for tanks, would come motorized infantry, traveling in trucks and tracked personnel carriers. These highly mobile infantry forces would consolidate the gains made by armor, while the tanks would then move on deeper into enemy territory.

Next on the scene would come the mass of traditional infantry who would free the motorized units to pursue the advancing armors. And you have this big encircling movements by the armor, motorized infantry following it in, and then the traditional infantry following it. In the meantime, the Panzers would then be off and running again in another great pincer movement, moving deeper and deeper into enemy territory. All the while, these maneuvers would be supported by a massive application of tactical air power. The Luftwaffe, the German Air Force, was to be employed for close support of ground operations. Its first responsibilities in a Blitzkrieg operation would be to destroy the enemy air force, so that it would not be able to play a role, to disrupt enemy communications on the battlefield, and, of course, to provide close air support for the attacking units themselves. Massed armor, motorized infantry, and air power would deal a devastating blow to any sort of enemy, it was felt. The emphasis would be on movement, on speed, on flexibility—all of the things that one does not associate with the terrible operations of the First World War.

The man most responsible for developing the Blitzkrieg strategy in Germany was a general by the name of Heinz Guderian. He had become a general quite late, only in 1938. He was a veteran of the First War, an intelligence officer in that conflict, where he had witnessed firsthand the unbelievable slaughter at Verdun, the battle where the Germans had maintained, "Well, if we can't break through French lines, we'll simply bleed them white," so that this year-long battle was one of enormous attrition, unbelievable bloodshed. Guderian was powerfully affected by this that he was determined to avoid static warfare at all costs. Movement had to be the key. How did one break out of this dilemma? During the 1920s, Guderian was influenced by a number of British military thinkers. Guderian was himself not an original military mind, but he certainly picked up ideas from others and was able to develop them, to give them additional life. He was particularly influenced by General J.F.C. Fuller, who had been the commander of the Royal Tank Corp in 1918, a British officer who had made the very same arguments— basically, movements, use of armor, close air support—all of the sorts of basic elements of the Blitzkrieg. He'd also been influenced by Captain B.H. Liddell Hart, who also forcefully advocated aggressive armored warfare, and an offensive strategy using mass concentrations of tanks. Liddell Hart and Fuller had been largely ignored by the British High Command, but Guderian had taken these ideas on—as had a number of others within the German High Command.

The general staff in Germany, although it certainly had taken Guderian's ideas onboard to a certain extent, remained dubious—dubious about what they saw as a revolutionary move in strategic thinking—but Hitler was quite impressed. It was exactly the sort of thing that would appeal to him for any number of reasons—for the political and economic reasons that I've already mentioned, but also, I think, just the sense of daring, the sense of the unpredictable, the sense of the aggressive, the dynamic. All of these elements were present in Guderian's thinking, and all of them appealed, certainly, to Hitler. In 1937, Guderian published a book outlining what would amount to a blueprint for Blitzkrieg. Guderian would not only be a theoretical thinker, a military strategist in that sense, he would also become an operational commander of considerable skill executing the Blitzkrieg in Poland—particularly in the campaign against France and then also later in the Soviet Union.

So, as the war began, Germany was operating with this Blitzkrieg strategy at these different levels—political level, economic level, and military level—all based on the presumption of quick war, no full mobilization, and then one would move on to the next diplomatically isolated opponent—one after the other, after the other. The problem, of course, was that the British and the French had not played ball. They had not behaved the way Hitler anticipated that they would, and, as a result, Hitler found himself dealing with potentially a two-front war. We're going to talk in the next lecture about the attack in the West. Of course, one of the things that one discovers instantly about the war in September of 1939 was that although Britain and France surprised Hitler by honoring their obligations to Poland, there was nothing practical that Britain or France really was in a position to do to help Poland in the fall of 1939. British and French strategic thinking, as we will see, was still very much mired in defensive conceptions. There were no real plans for an attack on Germany—which would relieve the pressure on Poland—so the Poles were left to fend off the Germans by themselves. The period during which Germany is technically at war with Britain and France in September of 1939, all the way to the spring of 1940, would, of course, be known as the

"Phony War," the "Drôle de Guerre" in French, or the Germans call it the "Sitzkrieg," not the Blitzkrieg.

Hitler, aside from being astonished at the British response—he had supposedly turned to Ribbentrop, who had assured him that Britain would not honor its obligations to Poland—and when the announcement came in that they had, Hitler supposedly turned to Ribbentrop and said, "What now?" Completely caught off guard. Another reaction surprised him on that morning of September 1, 1939. Germans awoke that morning to a radio news bulletin in which they discovered, as their radio announcer told them, that Polish forces had attacked a radio station on the German-Polish frontier and that since daybreak German forces had been responding with force. I don't think very many people in Germany thought that Poland had attacked Germany on September 1, 1939, but there was considerable disappointment in Germany at this news. On that day in the morning of September 1, 1939, great convoys of troops began moving through the center of Berlin—tanks, trucks, and so on. Crowds gathered along Unter den Linden to watch the troops moving eastward. It was not a replay of the summer of 1914, when cheering throngs had tossed flowers at the departing troops. There was a sense of enormous depression. Hitler's popularity had been based to a very large extent on the fact that he had made great foreign policy victories, and he'd done it cheaply, no war. He'd managed to, not only revise, but destroy the Treaty of Versailles with not one drop of blood being spilled. The Gestapo reports were very clear about this. There was disappointment within the German people about this outbreak of hostilities. And Hitler himself commented later in the day how disappointed he was that as this convoy of German military vehicles moved eastward through the center of Berlin, that the crowd had stood not applauding, not cheering, but in stony silence watching the troops move east. The days of easy diplomatic victory were apparently over.

The campaign in Poland, on the other hand, was a terrific success. It was the first Blitzkrieg and it worked according to the blueprint, the game plan. It was called "Case White," and from the very beginning, of course, the Poles were frightfully overmatched. The Germans committed 52 divisions, one million men, into the assault on Poland. This from a military establishment that had 100,000 troops five years before. The Germans possessed a great advantage in armor—1,500 tanks to only 310 possessed by the Poles. Aircraft—the

Germans had 850 bombers, 400 fighters, versus 400 Polish aircraft, most of them the old World War I vintage double-winged planes, almost all of them obsolete. The German plan called for a two-pronged attack from Army Group North, and then one from the south. The one from the south was headed by a general who would play a very important role in the course of the Second World War. He was 64 years old at the time. His name was Gerd von Rundstedt, among the most distinguished and important of the German military commanders of the Second World War.

The plan was to smash into Poland in two great pincers, trap the Polish army west of Warsaw, and annihilate it. It wasn't to take territory. It was to destroy the Polish army in Western Poland, but for Warsaw. The plan had been drawn up by the German High Command, and it worked with even greater speed, and fewer problems, than its most wildly optimistic planners had believed it could. Warsaw was reached by September 8, a week after hostilities began. The city resisted—although there were calls the Germans had hoped that the Poles would surrender Warsaw, the Poles refused. And in what was to be an ominous preview of the conduct of the Second World War, and one of the things that would certainly distinguish it from its predecessors, the Germans launched a massive air attack against the civilian center of Warsaw. The Polish army fought tenaciously, but was, of course, overwhelmed. I'm sure that we've all seen still photographs, or even some of the footage of, at one point, Polish troops on horseback, the old Calvary units, charging across an open field, in some cases almost with lances, certainly with flags flying, into the teeth of these German armored units—cut down and annihilated. The Poles fought, and fought very tenaciously. But then on September 17, the other shoe dropped. The Soviet Union moved across the eastern frontier of Poland to occupy its slice of territory. Attacking from the east, this Soviet onslaught sealed Poland's doom.

In this confusion that prevailed on the battlefield in these weeks, about 90,000 Poles managed to escape from Poland, going through Romania, through Lithuania, and Hungary. Many ultimately reached Great Britain where the Poles—I think, this is also one of those things that one doesn't often hear very much about—the Poles would represent the largest army in exile of the Allied forces during the Second World War—far larger, for example, than the Free French units that would go ashore and participate in the Normandy invasion.

There was something else that—another contribution that—the Poles made in 1939. As the conflict broke out, the Poles had been working on something called the "Enigma machine," to break the German military code. It was a highly complicated piece of machinery and the Poles thought they'd done it. One of those Enigma machines made its way out of Poland and wound up in a place where it would not be used very effectively, unfortunately, and that was into the hands of the French High Command in the West. But that would be shared with the British. And although it had played no role in the operations in 1939, the Allies would take from the Enigma machine the beginning of the breaking of the German military codes, which would allow us over the course the Second World War, as we worked these things out—the British primarily—to anticipate German moves, to understand what the Germans were up to. And that, I think, has to be seen as a contribution of the Poles to the war effort.

Well, by the end of September the Blitzkrieg had done its job. Poland had been devastated, forced out of the war. Britain and France, as we've seen, were unable to do much of anything. Calls by the Poles for some sort of help—for the British, the French—to launch some sort of offensive into Western Germany, at least to pull the Germans back—they'd left the frontier virtually unguarded—went unheeded. The French, their entire strategic concept was defensive. It did not call for operations in Germany. And although there were a few exchanges, a few air attacks along the frontier, there were no operations launched by the British or the French to save Poland. By the end of September, then, Germany and the Soviet Union had completed yet another partition of Poland. The war in the East was over.

In the West, then, a strange lull would follow. Hitler would use this period from the end of the war in Poland in October, really down to the spring of 1940, to launch one peace initiative after another. Over and over again over the course of December of 1939; January, 1940; February, 1940, Hitler over and over again keeps trying to bring the British to their senses. He keeps believing that if can just—if he can just make the British understand that they have a place in his worldview, that they have a place, that he doesn't have any real issue with them; he doesn't want a war in the West. He's succeeded in what he wanted. He doesn't want to go to war in the West; he's not prepared for a war in the West. But, of course, the starting point, the "ausgangspunkt," as the Germans say, for any discussion with the British or the French, was that Germany keeps what it's gotten in the East. And, this, the British were absolutely unwilling to do. And so they waited. In the East, the war, however, didn't come to a complete standstill. Poland had fallen, but now came an odd interlude in a way—this Russo-Finnish War in November of 1939 that would go on to the middle of March 1940.

Stalin was concerned that Finland would fall under German influence; so much for the cooperation between Germany and the Soviet Union. Finland was too close; it was too dangerous; he was afraid that the Finns would fall under German influence. Leningrad, the Soviet Union's second largest city, was only 20 miles from the Finnish frontier. The Soviets demanded that the Finns cede territory on the Karelian Isthmus, which would put Leningrad out of range of potential attack from the north. A number of possibilities were open—exchanges of territory and so on—but ultimately the Finns refused all of these overtures from the Soviet Union, and the Soviet Union finally launched military operations on November 30, 1939, against Finland.

In all of the history of overmatched opponents in warfare, you probably could not find a better example than the Russo-Finnish War. The Soviet, the Red Army, outnumbered the Finns by 50 to one. Enormous advantages in equipment. The Finns, everyone believed, would be utterly unprepared—certainly not be able to deal with the Red Army. But, the Finns under Field Marshal von Mannerheim fought with great skill and tenacity. One always thinks about the winter being the ally of the Russians. In this instance, it was the Finns who made use of it, wearing white uniforms, outmaneuvering the Russians, fighting very well in very heavy bad weather. One of the things the Russians probably should've learned from this is that you don't want military operations in this part of the world in the wintertime. They would do it against the Germans later on with equally dubious results. They found themselves really surprised with the situation in Finland. The Red Army very quickly bogged down. The Finns fought with great tenacity. The Soviets were bogged down in the snow and the swamps and the dense forests of the area. They suffered humiliating defeats and heavy causalities all the way through this campaign, which was covered with great delight in the West. In the end, of course, the Soviets would prevail. But one of the upshots, and one of the most important ramifications of the Russo-Finnish War, was that it seemed to seal the bad reputation of the Red Army internationally. Everyone looking at this said, "Well, if the Soviets can't defeat the Finns—if it takes them this much time, this much energy with these advantages—then the purges of the Red Army have really been even more devastating than we thought." This was a lesson that was certainly not lost on Hitler and Berlin.

The Germans, when they approached the Soviets in 1941, would have this as a background to their thinking about Soviet military preparations and the status of the Red Army. One of the most astonishing aspects of this, at the time, is that the French and the British—particularly the British—actually considered sending aid, or even troops, across Scandinavia to help the Finns. Churchill was very keen on this idea. This was one of those ideas—he was not yet Prime Minister in Britain—but it was one of the ideas which also gave him the reputation of being a kind of loose cannon floating around. One can only think of how the war might have looked different if, for example, the British had been able to project power across Norway, Sweden, and into Finland. It was only really because the Swedes maintained their neutrality, refused to allow any sort of over-flight or passage, and because getting troops through the Baltic with the German Navy patrolling there was difficult, that the British were dissuaded from this.

But Churchill was very enthusiastic about this prospect. This, I think, along with his idea of attacking to the "soft underbelly of Europe," were military ideas whose time still has not come. At the conclusion of this campaign, in the middle of March 1940, Soviet standing in the West was at an all-time low. The assessment of the Red Army was low, and anti-Soviet sentiment was rampant in Britain and France and in the United States. Here was this bully nation, this bully state, this Communist state, which had now attacked small Finland, and the heroic Finns had fought with great skill to fend them off. The great question as March turned to April of 1940, was not what was going to happen, though, in Finland or in the East. The question was what was going to happen in the West. Would there be a campaign in Western Europe? Hitler still had not given up reaching some sort of accommodation with the British, with Chamberlain. And so one waited. Would the Phony War become a real war, a shooting war? Would the Drôle de Guerre be over? Would the Sitzkrieg turn into Blitzkrieg in the West? That answer would come in May of 1940. We'll take that up next time.

The German Offensive in the West
Lecture 6

We're going to be dealing with the German offensive in the West in the summer of 1940—the stunning attack of the Germans into Norway and Denmark; the Blitzkrieg through Holland, Belgium, and into France. We'll be examining the … rapid collapse of the French army and the French state in the spring of 1940 in the matter of 35 days.

The "Phony War" ended in April 1940. The new German offensive began with a preemptive assault on Denmark and Norway. Having secured his northern flank, Hitler prepared for an invasion of the Low Countries, where France had virtual parity with Germany in troops and armor.

British and French preparations for a German attack were inadequate. The Allies' military strategy remained defensive in orientation, in reaction to the high losses sustained as a consequence of their offensive posture during the Great War. The French adopted a "Maginot mentality" that emphasized static defense and fortifications.

Naval power remained the centerpiece of British military planning during the inter-war period. Having suffered economically during World War I, Britain was reluctant during the 1920s and 1930s to launch an extensive rearmament program. Britain devoted greater resources to its air force than to its army. It was among the first countries to develop a strategic bombing capability. Britain also developed new fighter aircraft to defend the country against attack from the continent.

Although the Allies' military strength was adequate in terms of numbers and technology, they faced certain problems. The French army lacked a unified command, and its divided leadership failed to respond speedily enough to the German Blitzkrieg. The government of the French Third Republic lacked political cohesion.

The French high command anticipated a German attack through Belgium. The "Gamelin Plan" called for the Allies to respond to a German advance by sending troops into Belgium. Gamelin ignored intelligence indicating that the Germans were massing in the Ardennes Forest. The Germans attacked Belgium and Holland simultaneously on May 10, 1940. As the Germans had hoped, British and French forces assumed defensive positions in Belgium. Then three German Panzer corps smashed through the Ardennes behind Allied lines, cutting off the Allied armies in Belgium. Led by Guderian and Erwin Rommel, German forces raced across northern France and Belgium during May 1940.

At the end of June 1940, Adolph Hitler was the master of the European continent.

Subsequent events became known as "the riddle of Dunkirk." Hitler ordered the advancing German forces to halt 15 miles from Dunkirk, where British forces were trapped.

The subsequent evacuation of more than 338,000 British troops from Dunkirk between May 26 and June 4, 1940, was a miraculous logistic feat.

Next the Germans turned south toward Paris. On June 10 the Weygand line north of Paris collapsed, and Mussolini's Italy declared war on France.

Why did the Germans halt?

- The marshy terrain was not suited to armor operations.
- German armored units needed maintenance.
- Perhaps Hitler wanted to let the British escape in order to placate their government.
- Perhaps he expected to destroy the British forces from the air without need for ground operations.

German troops entered Paris on June 13, 1940. Under the terms of the armistice signed on June 16, Germany would occupy coastal and northern France while the Vichy regime would administer the rest of the country. France would retain its empire and fleet. Charles DeGaulle escaped to London, where he established a free French government. ■

Suggested Reading

Winston Churchill, *The Second World War*; vol. 2: "Their Finest Hour," Book 1.

Alistair Horne, *To Lose A Battle: France 1940*.

Questions to Consider

1. Why were the Allies militarily unprepared for the German offensive of spring 1940?

2. Why did Hitler not press his advantage against the British forces in France following the success of his Ardennes offensive?

The German Offensive in the West
Lecture 6—Transcript

Hello. Welcome to our sixth lecture in the Teaching Company Series on the Second World War. In this sixth lecture, we're going to be dealing with the German offensive in the West in the summer of 1940—the stunning attack of the Germans into Norway and Denmark; the Blitzkrieg through Holland, Belgium, and into France. We'll be examining the conduct of the war in—on the Western front, what one, for instance, historian has called the strange defeat of France—this rapid collapse of the French army and the French state in the spring of 1940 in the matter of 35 days. We'll try to examine the reasons for the failure of France in this great moment, this traumatic moment, and the two visions of France that would emerge from these troubled days in the summer of 1940—a collaborationist France associated with the policies of the old Marshal, Petain, and the young lion, the colonel now, General De Gaulle.

We had stopped in our last lecture with the observation that as the war came to a close against Poland and then the Russians launched their attack on Finland in November of 1939, a campaign that bogged down and would carry on into March, the question was still unresolved about whether or not there would be a war in the West. Hitler had gambled, desperately hoping that there would be no campaign in Western Europe, had not counted on it, not wanted it. This was not the war he had planned; not the war he anticipated. But, his numerous overtures to Britain, in particular, had fallen on deaf ears. The British showed no inclination to bargain, now, with Hitler in 1940. And so, as the weather began to improve in the West, campaigning weather made its appearance and the anticipation was of the possible new German offensive in the West. That would come in April of 1940 as the Germans launched an attack in Scandinavia.

The Germans had become convinced through their intelligence reading that Great Britain and France were preparing to seize Norway, to seize ports in Norway, to forbid them to the Germans. And Hitler ordered a preemptive strike and an invasion of Denmark. The Germans launched their attack on April 9, 1940. They quickly overran Denmark with virtually no opposition. And then, despite some trouble, an invasion force of only 10,000 German troops seized Norway, the major ports of Norway. British and French troops arrived, only to suffer defeat, humiliation, and were evacuated in May of 1940. So, now Hitler had, with very little effort, secured his Northern flank— prevented what he was convinced was going to be a British attack there and now attention was focused on northwestern Europe, on the Low Countries and France.

Would there be an attack? On paper, France seemed to be prepared. On paper, the French position was, in fact, quite strong. The French army was able to match the Germans in terms of number of divisions in the field. In fact, on the eve of the German assault, the French and British together employed 81 divisions ready to confront the 75 German divisions that would be sent into battle. The French also possessed parity in armor. It is not true that the Germans had more tanks. The French were on virtually equal footing with the Germans in this regard. Nor was it a matter of technology. The great German tanks, which would be the terror of the Western front during the Battle of the Bulge and to match the Russian T-34 tanks in the East, the Panther and Tiger tanks of later day, were not available to the Germans at this time. And technologically these German tanks were not particularly superior to their British and French counterparts. In many ways the British Matilda tank was actually superior to the tanks available to the Germans.

We could say the same thing about air power, available air power. In May of 1940, the French actually possessed a numerical edge in aircraft: 4,360 to about 3,200 for the Germans. And the latest French models, especially the fighter aircraft, were not inferior to the best German planes. The ME-109, which would be in the early days of the war the best German fighter plane, was matched by French counterparts. So, as one thinks about the fall of France that would come in rapid order in May into June of 1940, it wasn't a matter of simply being overwhelmed by superior numbers or greater tanks, aircraft, and so on. The real key, I think, to the fall of France in 1940 was to lay in its military and political leadership. There were failures of military strategy, tactics, and organization on the part of the French that were key to understanding their failure to deal with the Germans.

British and French military thinking during the interwar years continued— and we've talked about this briefly—continued to be dominated by defensive considerations drawn largely from their experiences in the First World War. During that war, the French had been enthusiastic advocates of offensive warfare. All through the First World War, in fact, even when all the evidence was in and these charges across No Man's Land had been seen to be quite suicidal, the French continued to hold to the view that an army infused with fighting spirit could defeat any defensive force. The "elan vital" as the French called it, was the key to success. The effects, of course, during the Great War were a little short of devastation—suicidal charges, vast carnage in all of the major encounters during the war. So, after the war was over, the lessons had been drawn. French military planners, for the most part, were convinced that the emphasis in all future planning should be on defensive operations. How does one create a defensive position capable of withstanding a German onslaught? Petain himself, the great hero of Verdun in 1916, certainly emphasized this point. He would dominant military thinking after 1918 and his view was that the emphasis had to be on defense.

There was another problem for the French, another factor in French thinking. With a population of 42 million, France had suffered the highest per capita losses in the First World War. There was no French family, no French village, that did not have its grisly list of fallen heroes from that conflict. France could not afford casualties on the scale of the Great War. This had led in part to the construction of the Maginot Line, defensive positions, defensive fortifications, which would allow the French to maintain the defense of their country without the kind of mass slaughter they had suffered during the First War. Certainly, there had been voices in the French military. General Etienne, for example, had believed that the tank would revolutionize warfare and advocated offensive thinking in planning for a new conflict. He had found enthusiastic support from a young colonel, Charles De Gaulle, who would in the course of 1940 be promoted to the position of General and then enter the French Cabinet during the crisis days of 1940—both of whom believed in mobile offensive warfare. But the dominant strategic view of the interwar years in France had been on static defense and fortifications.

Now, the British had a slightly different set of emphases. We talked about General Fuller, about Liddell Hart, both men who had—were really pioneers in developing what would become the Blitzkrieg strategy, emphasizing the importance of offensive operations of mass armor. But, during interwar years,

Fuller and Liddell Hart were really voices in the wilderness. The army was the stepchild of British military policy. The navy was still the centerpiece of British strategic thinking. Britain—obviously, as an island nation, had to maintain high levels of exports and services, shipping insurance and so on, overseas investment. And so the navy was, as it had been literally for centuries, the centerpiece of British strategic thinking. All of those, the sea lanes and so on, had been disrupted by the First World War. Britain had suffered financially as well as in human terms during the war, and a new war, Chamberlain and others thought, would only make matters worse. As a result, Great Britain, during interwar years, was reluctant to launch any ambitious rearmament program. There was very little commitment. And, certainly, during the Great Depression in Britain it was not as intense as it was in the United States or in Germany, but it had the same effect of sapping the desire to undertake any ambitious rearmament program. On the other hand, if the navy was the centerpiece, the army the stepchild, the British were quite innovative in the interwar years in their emphasis on the air force.

The RAF, the Royal Air Force, had become an independent service during the First World War. It was not simply a part of the army. And the air force seemed to hold out the promise of a less painful solution to Britain's security needs. The British would be among the first to develop the idea of strategic bombing. The Germans, the Russians, the Japanese, the Italians, all certainly had talked about the use of air power in the interwar years. There was, through the 1920s and 1930s, in military strategic thinking, a great deal of discussion about the role of air power in the coming conflict. There were nightmare scenarios painted. The next war would be a war of the mass bombers raiding civilian centers—panic among the civilian population that would lead a civilian government to sue for peace. But, despite the emphasis on this sort of discussion in strategic circles, none of the great powers actually undertook to construct a strategic air force.

The Germans, with their Blitzkrieg concept, had used air power as—in a tactical way—for close support of ground operations. The Germans possessed two-engine bombers, nothing larger. The Soviets were the same. But Britain in the 1930s had begun, along with the United States—we'll talk about the Americans a bit later on—but in the 1930s the British had really begun to think quite systematically about strategic bombing; that is, the use of air power not for close support of military operations, but to strike at the capacity, the industrial capacity, of adversaries to make war—to attack their energy sources, to attack their transportation systems, to attack their industrial structures and their industrial workers. And had begun to develop, in the interwar years, the plans to construct big, four-engine bombers. They would come to be the Lancasters and others during the war. They would be able to fly long distances and to deliver, for the time, very large payloads against these sorts of targets. So, for the British, in the interwar years, the air force allowed them to be able to think about, "Well, this is a way to project British power. This is the navy, that's the traditional way to do it. But now, with the air force, we will be able to project our power around the globe using these large, strategic bombers."

The British, also in the interwar years, began to develop fighter defense—new kinds of fighter planes—high-tech fighter aircraft—the Hurricane, the Spitfire—planes that would certainly make their presence felt during the Battle of Britain in the late summer of 1940. These planes were developed as pursuit planes, planes to defend the British Isles—to defend the Kingdom against attack from the continent—and they had begun to think very creatively about this. We'll talk more next time, when we talk about the Battle of Britain and the possible German invasion of Great Britain in 1940; about the development of radar, which was certainly very important, tied to fighter command within the British armed forces. But, having said this, the land army of Great Britain was very weak despite the introduction of Britain's first peacetime conscription in the course of 1939.

The British would send off to France the British expeditionary force, a relatively small contingent of British troops, to support the French in their defensive positions against a German attack. And, in 1940, British troops had already departed for the continent to take up their positions in northwestern France, anticipating a possible German attack.

Well, numerically, then, the British and French position was not so bad. Technologically, it was not so bad. But, once one gets to looking at command and control, begins to look at organization, then one sees all sorts of problems for the Allies. For one thing, there was a lack of unified command within the French army, which was particularly damaging. The commander in chief of French forces was a man by the name of Maurice Gamelin. He was commander in chief, but he delegated operational control in northeastern France to another general—Alfonse Georges was his name. So if you think about what this means, you've got a commander in chief of the French forces, but he has a separate command for the northeast of France in exactly the area that virtually everyone anticipates a German onslaught to come. This made—to the British—made very little sense, but there were reasons, political reasons, within the French army for this. The division of authority created confusion within the French rank and file, within the French command structure. It was exacerbated by the fact that the two men disliked one another, indeed, disliked one another a great deal.

Communication between their headquarters was poor and Gamelin often lacked real knowledge of conditions at the front. This is actually one of the most surprising things about the war at this point. I don't think it's so much tanks and aircraft, it's the telephone that is something—a technological advance that the French don't seem to be on to at this point. Messages passed back and forth between Georges and Gamelin in the early stages of the war in the West by motorbike, by courier, rather than by telephone. There is no sense, and you see this over and over again at French headquarters as the crisis breaks on them on May 10, 1940—they constantly underestimate the impact of speed. They just don't have any sense of it. They think they're still working in 1914 and 1918. The Germans attack. There's a breakthrough. Okay. So, we have time, we pull back a little bit, send our mobile reserves up to the front, we have some time to get this done. But this is not the way the Blitzkrieg operates. They—it's speed. They don't understand how speed had revolutionized the nature of warfare, don't understand the nature of the Blitzkrieg, and with disastrous consequences.

This lack of command/control and unity of command was also reflected in a lack of political cohesion within the Third Republic of France. We've already alluded to the fact that French politics during the 1930s had been fractious, had been confrontational, polarized and, certainly, one sees this in the course of 1940 as well. De Laudier had resigned in March of 1940, succeeded by Paul Reynaud, who, like Churchill in England, had been a critic of appeasement and an advocate of serious military preparations for war for years on end. Reynaud had been one of the only French political figures to be an enthusiastic supporter of the idea of concentrated armor units, armor divisions, which would be the key to the Blitzkrieg. De Laudier he kept on as Minister of War for political reasons. Reynaud detested his predecessor, De Laudier, and that feeling was reciprocated. The two men didn't trust one another and communication was bad there. So, political consensus was also lacking. Reynaud held Gamelin in contempt, the general in charge of operations in France. He was too old, Reynaud believed. He was unimaginative. Reynaud was furious with the general over the inept conduct of French operations in Norway.

But, Gamelin still was the most influential military figure in France and he was in charge of the planning of the defense of France, for the Allied defense of France—really in Belgium, as well. He was certain that when the German attack came, it would come as it had during the First War, through Belgium. He had developed what was called the "Gamelin Plan" to deal with this. On the one hand, there was the Maginot Line along the German frontier, which would protect that front from the Germans. There was the Ardennes Forest, which would act as a block to German armored operations—and so the real key was the defense of the approaches through Belgium.

The plan called, then, for the Allies to send troops rushing into Belgium when the Germans launched their anticipated attack in the West. So, the plan was, "The Germans will attack, we will send troops rushing into Belgium, catch them before they are able to get very far, the Maginot Line will hold, the Ardennes is an anchor of our defense to the East—we don't have to worry about that—and we will take up our positions on the Meuse and Dial Rivers in Belgium."

A complicating factor for this was Belgium itself. Belgium—and we've alluded to this in a previous lecture—Belgium had received from Britain and France guarantees of Belgium sovereignty, but Belgium was not a military ally of either country. And what this meant was that Belgium, in the months leading up to the actual invasion in the West, Belgium had been at pains not to provoke the Germans. So, British and French military units had not been allowed to move into Belgium in 1939 to take up positions. The French and the British were going to have to wait for the Germans to strike first, and then they would rush their troops into Belgium. King Leopold of Belgium did not want Belgium to be occupied again, as it had been during the First War. Didn't want the Germans coming in, didn't completely trust the Allies. And what this meant was that the Western Allies, Britain and France, had to anticipate positions without actually having been there before—without having staked out their positions—and this was certainly a difficulty. Now, by this point, the Enigma machine was paying dividends. France was receiving information that suggested that there was going to be a German attack, that it was imminent. The information they received certainly suggested there was going to be an attack, as Gamelin thought there would be, through Belgium. But there was other information, too. The Germans seemed to be massing troops not simply along the Dutch and Belgian frontier, but also around the Ardennes. Gamelin simply ignored the intelligence and moved on with his plan. On May 9, Reynaud, the Premiere of France, was so fed up with his high command that he fired Gamelin—tried to fire him at any rate. He was blocked in the Cabinet—"You can't fire the commanding officer of the French Army," they said. And so, Reynaud himself resigned.

So, now, here you've got a situation with the Germans literally massing along the frontier. The French Premiere tries to fire his commander in chief. The Cabinet tells him he can't do it. The French Premiere resigns in a protest. Gamelin did, as well. So, at the very top, on May 10, France has no Premiere, has no commander in chief. Then on May 10, the Germans launch their attack. The attack came just as Gamelin thought it would. The Germans sent troops not exactly the way they had done it during the First War, where they had gone through Belgium, but not Holland. In this instance, the Germans launched a simultaneous attack on both countries. German infantry units move into the northern part of Holland, and German armored units move into Belgium with great, great speed.

This was exactly as Gamelin had expected. The French and British then rushed northward into Belgium to take up their prearranged positions on the Dial and Meuse Rivers, but this is exactly, of course, what the Germans wanted them to do. One of the troubling aspects—you talk about intelligence, and the problems of intelligence. The troops—the French and British troops moving into Belgium reported an odd thing: the Germans seemed to have virtually total air superiority, but they were not attacking British and French troops as they moved northward into Belgium.

Why were they not attacking? What were they doing? What was the point? Well, the point, of course, was that this is exactly what the Germans wanted them to do. They wanted them to rush to these positions in Belgium because then the second shoe would fall. A three-Panzer corps slammed through the Ardennes Forest into Luxembourg and Belgium—behind the British and French troops that had gone into Belgium—and began a drive westward across Belgium and northern France, dashing toward the English Channel. They cut off the Allied armies that had rushed to the north. By May 20, the Germans had reached the coast near the mouth of the Somme River. The general in charge of leading the Panzer—there were two, really, that distinguished themselves in this race across northern France and southern Belgium in 1941. One was Heinz Guderian, the father of the Blitzkrieg, and the other was a commander by the name of Erwin Rommel, who also would play a very important role in subsequent days in the war. At this point, Guderian now wheeled north. The French and British didn't quite know what the Germans were up to as the Germans moved more and more toward the coast. Would the Germans turn south, wheel around and head toward Paris? Would they go north? What would they do?

Well, Guderian now wheeled north toward the French Channel, ports of Bologna, Calais, and Dunkirk. He quickly seized the first two objectives and was less than 15 miles from Dunkirk when his commanding officer, General von Rundstedt, ordered him to halt on May 24. Guderian and others within the high command all protested directly to Hitler. Guderian was itching. The British expeditionary force was caught. They were sealed off with the Channel. The German forces had them basically surrounded. Guderian was absolutely adamant that he had to be given the authority to charge onto the beaches with his tanks and destroy the British who were trapped. Hitler, on the other hand, showing a rare burst of caution, sided with Rundstedt rather than Guderian, and gave the mission of seizing Dunkirk to the German infantry units who were moving down from the north from Holland.

It was a prophetic decision. Why? Well, there were military reasons that Hitler and Rundstedt could certainly cite. The terrain around Dunkirk was marshy. It was not good terrain for armored operations. There was concern—Rundstedt certainly had concern that the armor would get bogged down, that they'd be sitting ducks for British aircraft. There was another problem that they—he—also raised, which is that these armored units had dashed across northern France and Belgium without really stopping, and there were maintenance problems. They needed to be able to stop, regroup, tend to the tanks, and so on. Anyway, they felt, the British were finished. They were caught. There was no way for them to get off. So it was just a matter of who was going to do it. And they were also afraid of a counterattack from the south.

There's also another possibility that's often raised about this decision to stop the Panzers short of Dunkirk, and this is a political reason. An argument is frequently made that Hitler stopped the Panzers—in fact Hitler later indicated something of this sort. He stopped the Panzers because he wanted the British to be able to evacuate from the continent, to show the British that this was not a war to the finish with them. He had no quarrel with them. He was going to defeat France. This is not the war he wanted. He had no quarrel ultimately with Great Britain, and so he would allow British troops to escape this trap on the continent. I always find that giving Hitler credit for a kind heart, even with political calculation, is probably a big mistake, and I wouldn't put a great deal of faith in this. He certainly indicated it later on, but I think this is not a very serious consideration.

The other possibility, and one that he certainly—that was important to him—was that Hermann Goering, of the Luftwaffe, argued very forcefully that he and his pilots could destroy the British army without there having to be close combat along the beaches at Dunkirk. The British army was trapped. The Luftwaffe would establish air superiority over the beaches, cut the British to pieces, and there wouldn't have to be a military operation on the ground. And so, Hitler decided, in fact, to halt the tanks. While this was going on, the British commander of the expeditionary forces, General Lord Gort, began the evacuation of the beaches at Dunkirk. It really was—if Hitler's decision is often referred to as "the riddle of Dunkirk"—the evacuation of British troops off those beaches was really a miracle. It was an incredible logistical feat. The British began evacuating troops off the beaches on May 26. That evacuation went on until June 4. They saved over 338,000 troops, overwhelmingly British, though there were some French as well who were caught and evacuated. The British used all sorts of ships, everything from pleasure boats to tugboats, anything that would float, that could get across the

Channel to pull the troops off of the beaches. Meanwhile, the RAF, the Royal Air Force, the fighters, distinguished themselves in protecting the embarking troops and the naval craft. It was a momentous, momentous development.

Meanwhile, the Germans turned south. After the disaster at Dunkirk, the French had hoped to regroup. Reynaud hoped to rally the French people. Churchill made the extraordinary offer—knowing how little the British and French really care for one another in many respects—made an offer, an extraordinary offer, which was common Franco-British citizenship—trying to keep the French in the war, that the French would have all the rights of British citizens, and so on—subjects, I suppose one would say. Reynaud pledged to Churchill that he would make no separate peace. He brought Henri-Philippe Petain, the old hero of the First World War, into the government as vice premiere to buck up French resistance. Petain was 85 years old at the time. He replaced Gamelin with Maxim Vigon, another general who was in his 70s. Vigon hoped to hold a line just north of Paris, but he didn't have his heart in this operation much either. Then on June 10, Mussolini roused himself in Rome and declared war on France. With the French army collapsing everywhere—the roads of northern France absolutely choked with disintegrating army units, evacuees of all sorts—Mussolini declared war, though he didn't immediately open military operations against France. The so-called Weygand Line north of Paris collapsed and on June 14, 1940, German troops marched into Paris.

Reynaud and his followers wanted to continue the fight from French Colonial Africa, but Petain, whom he had brought into the government to buck up resistance, urged an armistice. And on June 16, 1940—in the same railroad car in which the Germans had surrendered in and signed the Armistice in 1918—Adolph Hitler accepted the surrender of France. France was allowed to keep its colonial empire and its fleet. The Germans occupied two-thirds of France—the coastal areas and northern France. A new French regime was set up in Vichy with Marshal Petain as the head of state. And Charles De Gaulle, now a general, refused to recognize the surrender or the collaboration of the Vichy regime, escaped to London, set up his own government, and began to organize Free French military forces for a—hopefully—liberation of France somewhere down the road.

At the end of June 1940, Adolph Hitler was the master of the European continent. The British had escaped with this miracle of Dunkirk, but there was no disguising the fact that Hitler and his allies completely dominated all of Europe. It was a victory on a scale that Hitler in his wildest dreams could not have anticipated. It was the high watermark of his popularity. The scene of German troops in Paris, something they had been denied for four years during the First War, they had now done in 35 days. The scene, and we'll close with this, of Hitler accepting the surrender at the Armistice where he—you've probably seen the film where he slaps his thigh in jubilation. The British propaganda people got hold of this, ran it backward and forward so Hitler looks like he's doing a little jig over the body of the recently deceased France. But it was a dark, dark day for Europe, for France, and for Western civilization.

"Their Finest Hour"—Britain Alone
Lecture 7

With this lecture, we're going to begin a set, really of two, to deal with the situation—the very perilous situation—of Britain in the summer of 1940 after the fall of France. It is the period when Britain stood alone against a Germany, which had become easily the dominant power in Europe—the masters of the continent—when Britain now faced the very real prospect of a German invasion of the British Isles.

We turn first to the precarious situation of Great Britain that summer after the collapse of France, when German troops stood poised for a cross-channel invasion of southern England. Hitler gave the order for an invasion—Operation Sea Lion—to be undertaken in the late summer or early fall. We will examine the scope of that plan, and Britain's preparations to repel the Germans. We will analyze British strategic thinking in these perilous weeks, as well as the military assets possessed by Churchill's government, especially the Royal Navy and the Royal Air Force (RAF).

Britain lacked allies at the time. France had been knocked out of the war, and the United States was not yet prepared to engage in hostilities with Germany. So Churchill and British military leaders hoped to prevail through strategic bombing, a naval blockade of Germany, and support for anti-German resistance movements on the continent.

British officials saw strategic bombing of Germany as their only viable offensive option. The Special Operations Executive (SOE) was set up in 1940 to establish and support anti-Nazi resistance movements and sabotage operations in occupied Europe. British hopes regarding a naval blockade of Germany were based on the success of a similar blockade between 1916 and 1918. Britain incurred lasting French resentment by destroying the French navy from the air in July 1940 in order to keep it from falling into German hands. The blockade remained largely ineffective while Germany continued to receive resources and economic assistance from the Soviet Union and elsewhere in Europe. The Royal Navy worked to prevent German U-boats from blockading Britain.

In July 1940 Britain was ill-prepared to withstand a German invasion. In June, Britain shipped its gold and negotiable securities to Canada, and it made plans for evacuating the government there as well. Britain's survival depended on the ability of the Royal Air Force to maintain air superiority.

So, for the Germans—thinking about this cross-channel invasion—there were very real problems to confront. Hitler, still, at this point, hoped that it would be possible to bring the British to their senses.

Following the failure of his peace feelers to Britain, Hitler had to confront the realities of a cross-channel invasion. Unlike the offensives against Poland and France, German operations against Britain were improvised. In July 1940 the German high command had made no plans for an invasion of Great Britain, yet Hitler set August 15 as the deadline for the invasion.

The German high command faced numerous problems in planning the invasion.

- The Army lacked faith in the Luftwaffe's ability to protect its troops from the RAF and thus planned to disperse its invasion force along a 200-mile coastal front in England.

- The German Navy was ill-equipped to ferry the invasion force across the channel and protect it from the British navy.

- The success of the invasion depended on the Luftwaffe, but this air force was tactical and not equipped for sustained strategic bombing.

- Hitler still hoped to avert the need for an invasion.

Panic prevailed in Britain in mid-1940, but a sense of confidence slowly emerged as the difficulties facing the Germans became clearer. ■

Suggested Reading

Winston Churchill, *The Second World War*; vol. 2: "Their Finest Hour," Book 2.

John Lukacs, *The Duel*.

Gerhard Weinberg, *A World At Arms*, Chapter 3.

Questions to Consider

1. Describe Britain's strategic position in the summer of 1940. How did Britain hope to hold out against the expected German assault?

2. What problems did the German high command confront as it prepared for a cross-channel invasion of Britain?

"Their Finest Hour"—Britain Alone

Lecture 7—Transcript

Hello. Welcome to our seventh lecture in this history of the Second World War. With this lecture, we're going to begin a set, really of two, to deal with the situation—the very perilous situation—of Britain in the summer of 1940 after the fall of France. It is the period when Britain stood alone against a Germany, which had become easily the dominant power in Europe—the masters of the continent—when Britain now faced the very real prospect of a German invasion of the British Isles. In this first hour—the first lecture devoted to this set of topics, we're going to deal with the German plans for the invasion of England, "Operation Sea Lion" as it was called.

What did the Germans think they were doing? How were they going to go about planning this invasion? We're going to look at the British situation. And certainly there was a sense that this was a dire and very, very dangerous set of circumstances in which the British found themselves. But they also had some assets, strategic assets, with which to confront the Germans. So we want to examine Britain in this period, which Winston Churchill would refer to as "their finest hour."

With the fall of France suddenly in the summer of 1940, the shock of this was just overwhelming. Probably no other surprise was greater in the entire history of the Second World War than this sudden collapse of France between May and June of 1940. It had been anticipated that France would be able to maintain its defenses against the Germans. The French had the largest army in Western Europe. Certainly there was a sense that, well, France would be able to defend itself with British help. It might be something of a replay of the First War, which had certainly dragged out for some time. No sense at all—no one was prepared—for the utter collapse of France after 35 days of combat. Churchill, addressing the British public in the summer of 1940 after the fall of France, would say the following words, words which would become hallmarks of this period of British resistance, and I quote, "What General Weygand called the Battle of France is over. I suspect that the Battle of Britain is about to begin. Upon this battle depends the survival of Christian civilization; upon it depends our own British life and the long continuity of our institutions and our Empire. The whole fury and might of the enemy must very soon be turned on us. Hitler knows that he will have to break us in this Island or lose the War. If we can stand up to him, all Europe may be free and the life of the world may move forward into broad, sunlit uplands. But if we fail, then the whole world, including the United States, including all we have known and cared for, will sink into the abyss of a new, dark age, made more sinister and perhaps more protracted by the lights of perverted science. Let us therefore brace ourselves to our duties and so bear ourselves that if the British Empire and its Commonwealth last for a thousand years, men will say, 'This was their finest hour.'"

For the British in June, July, August of 1940, there was no aid to be expected. They were without allies, the United States still on the sideline with a Roosevelt administration chafing to find ways to send material aid to Britain. But Britain—indeed, as Churchill suggested—now stood alone to confront the German menace. The British chiefs of staff, in this situation, were in utter agreement that Britain could not win the war; indeed, could not even continue the war, without considerable support from the United States. It was too much to expect that the United States would actually enter the conflict, but certainly material support, which was already flowing to some degree to Great Britain. Still, they believed victory could be attained by a combination of certain factors.

On the one hand, the British believed in the policy of strategic bombing that we talked about in a previous lecture. So a bombing offensive against Germany, a naval blockade of Germany, was something that was still considered a possibility. And—Churchill was very keen on this option— was the support of resistance movements in occupied Europe, leading to insurrection all over the continent. The first of these instruments, weapons to be used against Germany: strategic bombing. We've already talked about the systematic destruction of Germany's capacity to make war—attacks upon its industries, on its transportation system, on its sources of energy. This policy of strategic bombing was recognized as the only practical way for the British in 1940 to hit the Germans—and indeed for the foreseeable future. The British army was still extraordinarily weak—in no position, especially after Dunkirk, to think about any sort of offensive operations but the bomber. Strategic air power was one way to bring the War home to the Germans. The RAF, as we've seen, had been independent since 1918 and had begun already to plan for such a campaign. Churchill would give great impetus to Bomber Command, as it was called in 1940. The construction of heavy bombers—large, four-engine planes capable of taking significant bomb loads as far as Berlin—were already under construction and some already operational. The Stirlings, the Blenheims, and then, finally—as we will see a bit later on—the gigantic Lancasters, which would wreak so much havoc over occupied Europe in the coming years. So strategic bombing was the one offensive option that Britain had—this offensive arrow in the quiver of the British government at this point.

Another element was what Churchill had called insurrection—setting Europe ablaze. In 1940 he would organize what was called SOE, Special Operations Executive. Special Operations Executive was to be a covert operation. It was to send agents into all of occupied Europe. It was organized according to national sections. There was an F section for France; a section for each of the occupied countries, including Germany. Agents would be sent into these individual countries, arms would be delivered to these agents and resistance forces, which they would organize. And then these resistance forces would carry out sabotage, espionage, anything to cause trouble for the Germans.

These operations began very early on. Really, by 1941 they were in full swing. They would continue on very effectively all the way through the war. The important thing about SOE—this was not an intelligence-gathering organization. This was an organization for sabotage. This was to conduct covert operations against the Germans everywhere, to cause them trouble. To recruit resistance fighters in all of occupied Europe, to organize them, and then to provide them with the weapons necessary to carry out their operations. And already, in 1940, the British had begun to plan—sending small aircraft to deliver these agents. They were delivered by submarine; they were delivered by parachute dropping into occupied Europe, to cause trouble for the Germans. Now, at this point, of course—SOE—this is a pinprick. This is something that will cause the Germans irritation at this point. In the long run, of course, Churchill had far greater hopes for this organization.

The last option for the British, one more element of their policy at this point, was naval blockade. This had been extremely effective during the Great War from 1916 onward. Britain had slowly starved Germany to death in the Great

War and this was still seen as an option for Britain. The British navy was still very strong and Germany's was quite weak. There were some worries about what would happen if the Italian and French navies were to be brought under German control, particularly the French navy. So this was of some concern. And indeed, in July 1940, the British took the extraordinary step of issuing the French—there was a call for the French to send their ships to British ports, or to French North Africa away from the Germans. Churchill did not want the French fleet to fall into German hands. When the French, in July, wavered on this a bit, an ultimatum was issued to the French fleet at Mers-El-Kebir in North Africa, the British saying, "sail these ships out, or scuttle them yourselves, or we're going to have to take drastic action." And indeed, in July 1940, British planes attacked the French fleet outside Oran, Mers-El-Kebir—killing over 1,500 French sailors. What had begun of two allies fighting the Germans, now by July of 1940, the British had launched an air attack against the French fleet. It was the low point of Anglo-French relations, obviously, in this troubled period.

The problem about this for Churchill was that the effects of a naval blockade would be negligible as long as the Soviet Union and Germany continued to cooperate economically. Part of the deal that Hitler had struck with Stalin, the Molotov-Ribbentrop Pact, was an economic agreement that the Soviet Union would provide Germany with raw materials and other necessities needed for the German war effort. And indeed, Stalin was very, very scrupulous about this. Regular supply trains arrived across the frontier into Germany. It was considered essential. So the idea is, somehow, that Britain would be able to blockade Germany. This was a long shot, I think. It could not be a replay of the First War. The German position was far stronger economically in this instance. They had now, really in 1940, the Germans had the resources of all of continental Europe at their disposal. So a naval blockade didn't strike anyone as really particularly effective, but the British navy was Churchill's strongest weapon and he needed to be able to find a way to use it. In fact, in 1940, the Royal Navy had to devote considerable energy simply to preserve—to maintain—the sea lanes to Britain so that Britain would not be blockaded or starved by German U-boat activity.

More pressing than ways that Britain might win the war in 1940, was the stark problem of how was Britain going to survive. It's one thing to talk about war-winning strategies, another—in the summer of 1940—to talk about survival. Because now—as Churchill had said in the address that I quoted at the outset—a German invasion of Britain seemed imminent. In July of 1940, the Germans seemed poised for a cross-channel invasion and Britain was woefully unprepared. The army was small and it was still reeling from the disaster on the continent. Three hundred thousand British troops had managed to escape from Dunkirk, but all of the heavy equipment—all the heavy artillery, the tanks, vehicles—had all been left behind, so that the British army—certainly the soldiers—had survived, but the British expeditionary force had come back in complete disarray.

In the summer of 1940, there was no real fighting force—organized fighting force—that would be capable of dealing with a triumph at Wehrmacht. Local defense volunteers were organized, but they were under-equipped. Weapons from the First War, muskets, all sorts of things drawn out—pitchforks issued to British farmers to be prepared for a parachute invasion, and so on. The government publicly exhorted the population to stand firm—Churchill talking that, "We will fight on the beaches, we will fight in the streets, we will fight, we will never surrender." Defiant language, certainly, but at the same time, privately, the British government began shipping Britain's gold, foreign exchange reserves, and negotiable foreign securities to Canada. In June and July 1940, over $5 billion in gold, bonds, and securities crossed the Atlantic and the British war effort could now be financed from North America if necessary. In other words, the British government had already begun dealing with the very real prospect that the Germans could launch a successful invasion and the war would have to be continued from abroad. Indeed, evacuation of the government to Canada was already discussed and plans were made, secretly, to organize guerilla resistance inside Britain in the event of a successful German invasion.

Meanwhile, feverish work was done along the coast. Beaches were mined, tank traps set, all sorts of civil defense arrangements made, paramilitary training conducted. The British government—at this point, the British cabinet—secretly entertained plans for the use of poison gas, if necessary, to thwart the German invasion. That decision was OK'd by the cabinet. The British were prepared to use poison gas, if necessary, in an extreme situation, to prevent a successful invasion.

It was clear to everyone in the summer of 1940 that the future of Britain would be decided in the next few weeks, possibly months, and it would largely be decided in the air. It was the ability of the RAF, the Royal Air Force, to deny German superiority over the Channel in the invasion beaches, that was going to be the key. And everyone certainly recognized it. In order for the Germans to launch this cross-channel invasion, they were going to have to maintain air superiority—establish and maintain air superiority—something they had been unable to do at Dunkirk.

The Germans, for their part—now looking at the prospect of a cross-channel invasion—on the one hand were enormously confident. The Wehrmacht was at the high point, the apex of its reputation. There is hardly any way to describe the euphoria in Germany as a result of the victory over France. It was the high watermark of Hitler's popularity, for Germans who had spent four years during the First War attempting to subdue the French, to take French territory, to reach Paris, and had been denied. This was, finally, the complete reversal of fortunes that the Germans in the interwar years had sought. The plan, the invasion of France, had succeeded beyond the high command's greatest hopes, and now they had to confront the possibility of a cross-channel invasion of Great Britain.

Hitler had largely assured his high command that after the fall of France that Britain would finally see the light and make a deal. That even Churchill, "that great warmonger," as Hitler liked to call him, would have to be brought to his senses and realize that there was no point in Britain continuing the struggle. When this did not happen, however, the high command was given the responsibility of planning—to think about an invasion of Great Britain. And for the first time the Germans confronted the realities of what that would mean; what an invasion across this body of water would actually entail. Unlike the German operational plans for the invasion of France, or the invasion of Poland—both of which had been the result of months of staff planning—very careful planning, logistical calculations and so on, Operation Sea Lion, as the German plan for the invasion of Great Britain would be called, was from the very beginning an improvisation.

Not even the most rudimentary plan for an invasion of Britain had been drafted when France fell in June of 1940. High command had no contingency plans for this. And then on July 16, after numerous peace feelers to Britain had been rejected, Hitler authorized the high command of the army to begin plans for a cross-channel invasion. He gave them a target date. That target date was August 15. One month. One month for an operation whose success would require extraordinary coordination between the army, the navy, the air force; which would require logistical planning—logistical feats—that the Germans had as yet not accomplished. These were the problems confronted, then, by the German high command. Their original draft, the army's original draft—and it was the army that did the planning. What's interesting about this, one sees, one thinks about the Germans as being terrifically organized. But the way Hitler approached this was he gave the chief of staff of the army, Halder, the order to begin planning. The army did this without consultation with the navy, without consultation with the air force. They simply began to plan. "How would we, looking at the map of Britain, how would we like to proceed?"

So the plan was drawn up by the army and called for 500,000 German troops to land along a 200-mile coastal front in the south and southeastern parts of England. This plan, when you think about this, a 200-mile wide invasion beach, in effect, front, revealed the army completely lacked faith in the German Luftwaffe. They'd seen Dunkirk. They had no real desire for a more compact landing area because they were afraid that Goering's air force would not be able to achieve the necessary air superiority there, and so this dispersal of forces would protect them a bit more from the RAF.

When this plan was presented to Admiral Raeder, the head of the German navy, he was mortified, absolutely mortified. First of all, he pointed out that he lacked the ships necessary to transport troops. There were not adequate naval forces to deal with the Royal Navy. How was he going to protect a cross-channel invasion force against the largest navy in Europe? And the question of transporting troops—how are these 500,000 troops going to get across the Channel? The Germans had no real landing craft; no amphibious craft had been developed—nothing like the Higgins boats that the United States would develop and employ in the war against the Japanese in 1942. They'd been giving no thought to this whatsoever—no logistical planning, no technological planning for this. Raeder initially came up with the idea, well, they wouldn't try to transport troops across. Well, they obviously weren't going to take ports, they weren't just going to allow them to sail into ports and unload. So without amphibious craft, what were they going to do?

Raeder came up with the idea of using tugboats to tow barges that had been used on the Rhine and Moselle canals in Germany—literally to pull German troops across the Channel. This, of course, was not something that the German army was very happy about. I think anybody who's had any adventure or any experience at all with going across the English Channel realizes that this is not a terribly calm or tranquil body of water. So one can only imagine what it would be like to tow barges—these long, Rhine barges—across the Channel. General Halder, of the army, when confronted with Raeder's objections, believed that an invasion on a more concentrated area would simply be suicidal. And although he never directly confronted Goering, it was perfectly obvious that he believed that the air force simply couldn't do its job.

But, the army could not budge Admiral Raeder. He said, "It can't be done. It simply can't. We don't have the ships, we don't have the landing craft. If you want an invasion front over 200 miles, this is beyond our capacity to do this." Raeder convinced Hitler, then, to postpone the invasion to September 15 to give him a little more time—another month, by which time Raeder hoped somehow to scrape together enough landing craft to ferry the army across the Channel. When one considers the amount of planning—minute planning that went on for months and months and months—by the Allied forces for the cross-channel invasion going in the other direction in 1943-44, one sees just exactly how slapdash this thing was. This was an improvisation. This was something that Hitler never had intended to be confronted with. He didn't want an invasion of Britain. If Churchill wouldn't come to his senses, well then, all right, there was this belief—I think a general belief—that the momentum of German arms would simply carry them across the Channel—until of course they actually stopped and began looking at what this meant operationally.

All agreed that the key to success was the Luftwaffe; Hermann Goering's forces would have to establish air superiority over the Channel. Raeder and Halder both agreed about this. The Luftwaffe would be charged with driving the Royal Navy from the scene and destroying the RAF. It was also called on to break the initial resistance of British land forces and annihilate reserves behind the lines. This was a fairly tall order. Goering believed, however, that the Luftwaffe would be able to subdue the RAF—as he confidently told Hitler—within five weeks. This after his failure at Dunkirk. Indeed, I think his failure at Dunkirk spurred Goering to probably promise more than he could deliver.

Goering, with his usual bluster, was quite confident, but the Luftwaffe was going to confront some very daunting problems—problems every bit as daunting as that confronted by the navy and the army. We talked about this a bit briefly in a previous lecture, but it's important to underscore it again at this juncture. The German Air Force, the Luftwaffe, was essentially a tactical air force. It was built, it was constructed, its planes were there for tactical ground support. It had built a fleet of fighters—dive bombers and medium bombers—that were very well-designed for that mission, but not for strategic bombing, not for long-range operations, not to attack industrial centers, not for a sustained campaign of bombing. Its pilots, their training, their equipment, were all geared for close support of ground operations and not for the sort of task that it was now being asked to do.

The German bombers were two-engine planes; they had limited range, limited bomb loads. And I think the Luftwaffe personnel—who were actually charged with thinking of how to deal with this—believed that this was going to be a difficult job for them. The Stuka, used with such terrifying effect in Poland and in France—this German dive bomber, which roared out of the skies with its landing gear down—there was an air vent underneath it so that as it dove down toward the ground, wind howled through that vent, shrieking, so that as one after the other, after the other, came down, it had a terrifying effect on ground troops—it had worked remarkably well in the Polish campaign, where it didn't have to confront an air force. On the Western Front against France, the Stuka still sounded terrifying, but they were shot out of the air by faster British planes with terrifying regularity for the Germans. So now the Stuka was slow, it had little armament, and would be terrifically vulnerable in the skies over Great Britain. The top German fighter aircraft, the Messerschmitt-109, a very good aircraft indeed, had an effective range of about 125 miles.

So, for the Germans—thinking about this cross-channel invasion—there were very real problems to confront. Hitler, still, at this point, hoped that it would be possible to bring the British to their senses. This invasion would not be necessary. One sees, I think, in his thinking, his operational planning—if one can call it that for the invasion of Britain—that we see the fruit of this improvisation. We see the Germans had not planned for this war in the West. This had come as a shock. The fall of France—which had a terrific psychological effect, terrifying psychological effect—it's the fall of France that finally jumpstarts the United States, for example, into drastic production schedules and so on. Everybody had thought that France would hold out for a long time; that there would be time to gear up and so on. But now this was not going to be the case.

The Germans stood at the Channel, and yet, I think as one reads through the British documents and through the German documents in the summer of 1940, it's a fascinating thing to see. It really is this duel, as the historian John Lukacs has called it, between Churchill and Hitler. As you begin to read through the British documents, there's a real sense of panic. Panic. The French have let them down. They've signed a separate peace with the Germans. The Germans seem absolutely unstoppable. The Wehrmacht was at the height of its prestige and Britain seemed absolutely vulnerable, its army basically destroyed, largely defenseless. And this is when one begins to get the British beginning to send their gold reserves and so on abroad to Canada.

And yet, as Churchill begins to look at the situation more closely, they begin to think about the prospects of how to defend Britain against a German invasion, and they think about it in reverse. What would the Germans do? How are they going to approach this? Then suddenly you begin to see, it's almost a day-to-day thing. After about two, three weeks, even in this desperate situation, there's a growing confidence coming out of Downing Street. A growing confidence from the British government that even with this unbelievable juggernaut that the Germans have created, that that Channel is a very big barrier indeed. And that Britain did enjoy certain great assets of geography—and of training and technology—that could be used against the Germans.

The flipside of that is with the Germans—who after the fall of France, in this euphoria of thinking, "Europe is at our feet," as it certainly was—they now have to confront the operational realities of this cross-channel invasion. And the initial enthusiasm, there's a song that was sung in the German military in the summer of 1940. I don't think it was heard very often after that. It's called Wir Fahren Gegen England. Don't worry, I'm not going to sing it. But it was filled with this confidence, this jaunty, "Goodbye my dear, today, wir fahren gegen England"—"We're going against England." But then, when one looks at Admiral Raeder, when one looks at Franz Halder, the chief of staff of the army, when one looks at Goering, it's only Goering who's talking very confidently at this point and no one was taking him terribly seriously.

For the Germans, the operational realities of an invasion of Britain were daunting, and, as we will see, would prove to be impossible to overcome. We'll take this up in the next section in the next lecture when we look at the Battle of Britain, one of the major turning points of the Second World War.

The Battle of Britain
Lecture 8

We'll examine [in this lecture] the course of the air war over Britain from July to October of 1940, the period that is usually referred to, officially, as the Battle of Britain. [We'll] look at the objectives of the German air campaign, the Luftwaffe's plan to establish air superiority. We'll look at the British countermeasures, some of the British advantages.

Establishing air superiority over the Channel and the planned landing zones in southern England was the prerequisite for a successful German invasion of Great Britain, and in July 1940 the Luftwaffe began its air assault against targets in Britain. This colossal air battle was ultimately won by the RAF.

Aircraft spotter in London.

Digital Stock World War II CD.

The British enjoyed some important advantages. The RAF had capable commanders and a range of aircraft—including the Spitfire and Hurricane—which were superior to German aircraft. The British had a high rate of production for fighter aircraft. Radar gave the British advance warning of enemy air attacks. The "Ultra" machine allowed Britain to read German coded messages.

The German air campaign went through several phases and had several objectives. The first phase began on July 10, 1940. During July and August, the Luftwaffe attempted to establish air superiority over the Channel and landing beaches.

German attacks on RAF airfields began on August 8. "Operation Eagle"— an effort to destroy RAF airfields, flying units, supply, and the aircraft industry—was launched on August 13. The Germans both inflicted and suffered tremendous casualties. The British government was genuinely worried that German attacks on the airfields would destroy the RAF.

On September 7, however, Hitler shifted the focus of the Luftwaffe attacks to London, probably in an effort to concentrate the RAF fighters so they could be more easily downed and to erode British will to resist. Hitler ordered the "postponement" of Operation Sea Lion on September 17, after the attacks on London had failed to achieve their strategic objective. Churchill said of the RAF pilots: "Never in the field of human conflict was so much owed by so many to so few." In all, the Germans lost 1,882 aircraft and the RAF lost 1,265 in the Battle of Britain.

> **"Never in the field of human conflict was so much owed by so many to so few [RAF pilots]."**
> **—Winston Churchill**

The Germans' nighttime terror bombing of London and other British cities between September 1940 and May 1941 was known as the Blitz. It began when the Luftwaffe tried to minimize their own losses by shifting to nighttime terror raids rather than daytime precision bombing. In November the raids were expanded to other cities, including Coventry.

The bombing became a regular feature of British life in late 1940 and early 1941. A written report on activities in the Smithy Street bomb shelter in East London in September 1940 dramatizes the psychological impact of the Blitz on Londoners. London was bombed for 57 consecutive nights beginning in September 1940. It resumed again in March and April 1941 and lasted until the end of May. ■

Suggested Reading

John Keegan, *The Second World War*, Chapter 4.

John Terraine, *A Time For Courage: The Royal Air Force in World War II*.

1. Describe the phases and objectives of the German air campaign against Britain.

2. What considerations led the Germans to switch from daytime precision bombing of Britain to nighttime terror bombing?

The Battle of Britain
Lecture 8—Transcript

In our last lecture, we dealt with the German preparations for the invasion of Great Britain. Germany, Britain—everyone understood that an invasion was being planned, that the Germans were attempting to, would be attempting to, launch a cross-channel invasion of the British Isles. The prerequisite, the point of departure for this, was air superiority over the Channel, over the landing beaches in southern England. Anticipated then, by everyone, was an air battle. That battle would come in the summer and early fall of 1940. It came to be known as the Battle of Britain, and that is what we will take up in this, our eighth lecture.

We'll examine the course of the air war over Britain from July to October of 1940, the period that is usually referred to, officially, as the Battle of Britain. Look at the objectives of the German air campaign; the Luftwaffe's plan to establish air superiority. We'll look at the British countermeasures, some of the British advantages—technological advantages, planning advantages— they had. And then we will conclude with a description of life in Britain under the bombs, living through the Blitz. The Blitz is the period, not so much in reference to the Battle of Britain itself, but to this longer phase of bombing that Britain was forced to endure through the fall and winter of 1940 and into 1941, when the Germans shifted their bombing objectives from airfields to the civilian population and to major urban centers.

As the Germans and British both confronted the problems involved with a cross-channel invasion, the British held some significant advantages. We've talked about some of those in the last lecture, but let me emphasize in this lecture the role of fighter command, the RAF. Fighter command was led by Air Marshal Hugh Dowding, who had led this element of the Royal Air Force for some time. The fighter command possessed two excellent fighters, both of which Dowding had helped to develop—the Spitfire and the Hurricane, which flew at speeds in excess of 300 miles per hour. They were well-armed, they were highly effective operational aircraft—certainly the match for anything the Germans had at their disposal.

Aircraft production for fighters had jumped dramatically in the summer of 1940 under the leadership of Lord Beaverbrook, appointed by Churchill to a new post created during the war—the post for the Ministry for Air Craft Production. Beaverbrook assumed that position on May 14 and began an extraordinary campaign for aircraft construction. Indeed, throughout the crucial months of 1940, when aircraft would be at such a premium, the British would actually produce more fighters than would Germany; in fact, by a ratio of almost four to one in the course of this crucial Battle of Britain. Throughout the battle, the RAF was able to put up approximately 600 fighters daily to the Germans 800. This—part of the production issue here, and I will say this parenthetically—Hitler constantly, even during the Battle of Britain, certainly after the fall of France, desperately wanted to shift the German economy back to a complete peacetime footing. He was always talking about this. This was always on his mind. We will see this come into play later on in more extraordinary circumstances in October of 1941 with the Germans deep inside the Soviet Union. He was eager to move back to a peacetime economic schedule of production.

As a consequence, the British, who were desperate in the summer of 1940, are producing like mad, factories going at 24 hours a day. Something the Germans, incidentally, never got around to doing during the entire course of the Second World War, running factories on a 24-hour basis. So the British were, I think, driven, obviously, by desperation, driven by fear of this imminent German invasion, producing at a quite extraordinary rate in the summer of 1940.

Britain also possessed a technological asset of inestimable value, and that was radar. It had been developed in Great Britain by Robert Watson Watt and a team of government scientists. Its use for air defense was quickly perceived before the war, and by 1937, a series of some 50 radar installations—the so-called home chain—covered the British East Coast to the north, providing early warning against approaching aircraft from the continent. Reports from these radar stations or from the ground observer corps were flashed to fighter command headquarters outside London at Uxbridge. The country was divided into four defense sectors, each with its own fighter group. Using the early warning provided by radar, fighter command could vector squadrons to the anticipated target area to intercept the enemy planes or to reinforce the sector under attack. The way the system worked was—radar was effective in picking up the approaching German formations. That information would then be flashed back to Uxbridge, but at the same time this extraordinary network of civilian observers was also employed. They would then follow the approach. The communication between these ground observers and fighter command was also extremely important.

The Germans never quite, I think, appreciated the role of radar when it mattered during the Battle of Britain. We'll see this in just a moment. And, extraordinarily, never, I think with one exception, actually launched a systematic attack on the radar installations. Also of some value to the British was Ultra, the ability to read German coded communications that we've talked about in the past. Reports from Ultra indicated, certainly, that Germany was having some logistical problems. British high command was informed about difficulties with the tugs, with the barges, the movement of troops to the coast. This sort of discussion we talked about in the last lecture about the problems of transporting troops across the Channel. Ultra was also important in that it was able—the British were able—to determine the location of German airfields in France and in Holland, and also had some sense of Luftwaffe strength. What Ultra could not do was to help, really, to be very useful in determining targets, or operational objectives of the German Air Force. In other words, it didn't—the British weren't able to follow literally orders coming down from above to projected targets for a particular day or night. Nonetheless, with radar and with Ultra in place, these were advantages—assets—that the British had and were certainly very thankful for as they prepared for this Battle of Britain.

The first phase of the long anticipated German air offensive against England would come in July. German bombers began to appear over coastal England on July 10, attacking several port cities—Plymouth, Dover, Portsmouth, and others. For almost three weeks, German planes attacked coastal defenses and shipping, sinking over 40,000 tons, but never really denting Royal Navy strength in the Channel. The British, of course, tried to disburse the fleet to keep it at the periphery. It didn't want to be caught in the Channel where it would be really vulnerable to German attack, but it was always lurking just off scene as it were. Attacks on RAF airfields began on August 8, but there was surprisingly little contact between the Luftwaffe and the RAF in this initial phase of the Battle of Britain. The great air battles that one sees so much about were still waiting to occur. Still, by the beginning of August, even after these initial raids, which were nowhere nearly as intense as what was about to fall on Britain, the Germans had already lost over 100 bombers.

With the invasion of Britain set for September 15, the Germans launched "Operation Eagle" on August 13th with the objective of breaking the English Air Force in, as the order read, the shortest possible time. The targets were airfields, flying units, and supply—as well as the aircraft industry. It is—I indicated this a moment ago, but what's remarkable, is the Germans, even after their first experience flying over these British radar installations, which were quite substantial edifices along the coast—as the Germans planned their attack on the Royal Air Force and all of the installations associated with it, they never actually targeted these radar stations. There was no plan to destroy them. So, I think we see right away the underestimation, the lack of understanding of exactly how important these radar installations were at this point.

The Germans inflicted terrific casualties on the British, shooting down over 100 British planes. But they also absorbed great casualties themselves. Moreover, British pilots were able to bail out; fly again. Whereas a German pilot lost—shot down over Britain—was lost. One sees already beginning in this phase of the Battle of Britain that, I think, romantic stereotype that one has from the Battle of Britain of the RAF pilots sitting slumped in their leather chairs looking like sort of a Cambridge or Oxford College—their silk scarves. They're alerted, they race out to their Hurricanes—or to their Spitfires—with the grass airfields, zoom off to confront the wave of German bombers coming in, fight, are shot down, bail out, are back in time for tea. Another alert comes later in the afternoon; they're up in the plane and off again.

This is the stereotype. It was sort of the stuff of Errol Flynn films in the Second World War—the dashing RAF pilots during the Battle of Britain. It's one of those cases where the stereotype actually, I think, is quite true. British pilots did—there were any, over and over again one saw, if one reads through the RAF reports from the Battle of Britain, of British pilots who were shot down, bailed out, came down, were transported back to their units in the afternoon, and then were up in operations again later on the same day, or certainly the next day. So, Germans found themselves confronting English farmers' pitchforks when they came down if they bailed out, and so, therefore, were lost to the Luftwaffe.

On August 24, with the losses mounting on both sides, the Luftwaffe shifted its objective to the airfields themselves, to concentrate on the airfields, the RAF airfields. It would be the crucial phase of the Battle. During the last week of August the RAF lost so many planes and pilots that replacements could not keep pace. Concentrated German attacks, for the first time, left fighter command in a desperate position and alarm swept the government. At this point, in the last part of August, there was for the first time, I think—in British ruling circles, government circles—a real fear, and certainly within the RAF, that the Germans had now found the key. If they continued—these systematic attacks on the airfields continued—the RAF was not going to be able to rebound. No matter how much "elan vital" the RAF pilots possessed, no matter how many planes were being produced by Lord Beaverbrook, if the Germans continued this pointed attack, the Battle of Britain would be lost.

Fighter command lost almost 300 aircraft between August 24 and September 6, far more than German fighter losses in the same period. But, on September 7, the Luftwaffe miraculously, from the British point of view, shifted its priorities once again, redirecting its attacks away from airfields to focus on the city of London. It was a drastic change in targets and its timing was absolutely critical. This shift in priorities—this is probably the critical element in the Battle of Britain—was favored by Goering and approved by Hitler. It's often seen as a reflection of this sort of Hitlerian obsession for vengeance. The RAF had launched a surprise attack—I'm talking—it was a real surprise on the level virtually of Jimmy Doolittle's surprise attack on Tokyo in early 1942. The British, when they seemed to be down, out, the war lost and so on, launched an air raid on Berlin. The Germans—Goering at one point had said, "If an Allied bomb falls on a German city, you can call me Meyer." There were jokes already by the end of 1940 that Field Marshal, Air Marshal Meyer has made a mistake once again.

The first British raid on Berlin coincided with a visit to the German capital by the Soviet Foreign Minister Molotov. And as Molotov and Ribbentrop were discussing matters in the Foreign Ministry, air raid sirens began to peal—to wail over the city—and Ribbentrop and Molotov and company had to adjourn to the bomb shelters down beneath the Foreign Ministry. It was a somewhat embarrassing moment for the Germans. According to Molotov's recollections of this, Ribbentrop had just been saying, "Well, the British are finished. We need to—now we need to be making plans about how the world is going to look after the fall of Great Britain." And having said, "Britain is finished," Molotov responded, "Well, if they're finished, what—who's that up there and why are we down here in the air raid shelter?"

It was not vengeance for this attack on Berlin. I'm sure that may have played a role. I'm sure it gave Hitler a great deal of satisfaction to be able to then bomb the capital of Britain—to move away from this strictly military target to extract some vengeance for this raid on Berlin. But, more important in German calculations than this, was a belief that the attacks on the airfields had succeeded, were going well. But now what the Germans wanted to do was to lure the RAF up into the sky. That an attack on London, that a series of attacks on London, would bring—would concentrate—British fighters in this one area. And if they could be shot down, this would work—be to Germany's double advantage. They would be able to bomb the capital city, cause damage, perhaps damage British morale seriously and, at the same time, shoot down large numbers of RAF planes.

That shift, however, was of decisive importance. London was heavily defended and for 10 days in mid September, bright clear days, the skies over southeastern England were filled with formations of black German bombers droning toward London where 2,000 antiaircraft guns awaited them. Vectoring fighters to intercept, the RAF relentlessly attacked these formations of German fighters, and the losses were astronomically high for both. But, by mid September, the result was clear—the Germans had failed to attain their strategic objectives. The RAF had not been broken, British morale had not cracked, and the Luftwaffe had been unable to secure the necessary air superiority for a cross-channel invasion.

On September 17, Hitler ordered the postponement of Operation Sea Lion. It was a postponement technically, but everyone understood that this was it. This was not going to be revived. Hitler was quite—actually quite eager to do it. One senses almost relief on his part. This had never been part of the plan, this war with Britain. He still hoped that there might be some way out of it. He'd largely given up on Churchill. The idea that they could break British morale with bombing would still linger. It's one of the great, unlearned lessons, I think, of the Second World War—and bombing in the Second World War—is you don't break civilian morale with bombing. The British morale was not broken during the Battle of Britain or during the Blitz which followed, nor would German or Japanese morale be broken by Allied bombing during the war either. At the conclusion, then, this period, the Battle of Britain—usually is seen as lasting from July 10 till the end of October because the raids continued on into the end of October—German losses during this period were 1,882 aircraft. A disproportionate number of those were bombers. RAF losses were 1,265. So, huge losses on both sides. During the war itself—and even in Churchill's otherwise, I think, really remarkably good and useful history of the Second World War—there's enormously inflated numbers on both sides. The Germans claim this—well, this is just sort of standard operating procedure for wartime claims. What is clear is that both sides had suffered terrifically.

Up to this point, all of these air operations had taken place in the daytime. The availability of any sort of sophisticated aiming devices for aircraft, well, there really was no availability. It was crude. Bombing techniques were crude, air crews had to be able to see what they were aiming at. There was no sort of radar bombing and this sort of thing at this point in the war obviously. And daylight operations were enormously costly. Both the British and the Germans would draw this conclusion, and it was that you could not conduct major air operations, certainly strategic operations, in the daylight. You were simply asking for trouble. It was at this point—at the conclusion of the Battle of Britain—when it was obvious that the RAF had done its job. September had come and gone, the German invasion had not come, Operation Sea Lion was clearly on hold or ultimately abandoned. The British had made it. They had survived through this summer of 1940 and as fall approached and the bad weather over the Channel approached, the British had what they needed, which was breathing space. They had, indeed, survived, and they had survived alone.

It was at this juncture that Churchill would utter those famous lines, and I think it's in this period when Churchill delivers virtually all of these great speeches that he is so well known for during the Second World War. The "we'll fight on the beaches, fight on the streets" speech. The "their finest hour" speech. But also the line, "Never in the field of human conflict was so much owed by so many to so few"—his reference to the RAF pilots who had done such a remarkable job in defending Britain during the German onslaught. I have to say, at this point, that this,—this comment, "Never in the field of human conflict was so much owed by so many to so few," was paraphrased a bit later on in North Africa when hundreds of thousands, literally hundreds of thousands of battalion troops surrendered to a very small British garrison in the East. I believe it was Anthony Eden who said, "Never in the field of human endeavor have so many surrendered so much to so few."

The Battle of Britain was over, but the German attacks continued. There was no longer a danger of a German invasion, but this didn't mean that Britain was out of trouble. In September, the Germans shifted to nighttime raids. Nighttime meant—this was a reflection of their own mounting losses and their concern about those losses, and it also indicated that they had largely given up on any sort of precision bombing. This was not—they were not after airfields bombing in the dark. They now shifted not only to nighttime, but also to attack London and other major urban centers in Britain. Indeed, the raids now became largely terror raids, either to break British morale or simply to continue pressure on Britain. In November, Germany expanded the raids to other cities. The Coventry Raid, which destroyed—was an industrial town, but destroyed the old fourteenth-century gothic cathedral in Coventry, which was, I think for British morale, the sense of, you know, "The Germans are barbarians. How can they be bombing—how can they be bombing these great cultural treasures?" And so on. Life in London during this period—this was the period after the Battle of Britain, when the nighttime raids began, that is usually referred to as the Blitz.

I'd like to read you a lengthy report of life as Londoners began to live it in the fall of 1940. It would be a life that would continue on with different levels of intensity off and on for the remainder of the war as the raids would continue. But certainly nothing like the intensity of these nighttime terror raids in the fall of 1940 as Londoners were sent to bomb shelters, basements, the tubes, the undergrounds, the subways of London, to escape the bombardment. This is from a public record of a report on the activities in the Smithy Street shelter in East London in September of 1940. "This record begins at 8:15 p.m., September 7 inside a street shelter at Smithy Street, Stepney, East London. Already about 35 people have crowded in. Some are sitting on stools or deck chairs, some standing. At 8:15 a colossal crash, as if the whole street was collapsing, the shelter itself shaking. Immediately, an ARP, air raid patrol helper, a nurse, began singing lustily in an attempt to drown out the noise, 'Roll out the barrel,' while Mrs. Smith, wife of a cleaner screams, 'My house! It's come on my house! My house is blown to bits!' Her daughter, 25, begins to cry, 'Is it true? Is it true? Is our house really down?' There are three more tremendous crashes. Women scream and there is a drawing together physically. Two sisters clasp one another, women huddle together, there is a feeling of breath being held, everyone waiting for more. No more. People stir, shift their positions, make themselves more comfortable.

"Then, suddenly, a woman of 25 shouts at a younger girl, 'Stop leaning against that wall, you bloody fool! Like a bleating lot of children! Get off it, you bastard! Do you hear? Come off it! My God, we're all going mad!' People begin shouting at one another. Sophie, 30, screams at her mother, 'You get on my nerves, you do. You get on my nerves. Shut up! Shut up! You get on my nerves.' Here, the ARP helper, the air raid patrol helper, tries once again to start some singing: 'Roll out the barrel,' she begins. 'Shut up your bleeding row!' shouts a man of 50. 'That's enough noise out of you.' Outside the gunfire bursts forth again. It grows louder and now the ARP girl begins walking up and down the shelter between the rows of people, singing and waggling her shoulders, a fine looking girl, tall and handsome with a lovely husky voice. 'There is a good time a'comin, though it's ever so far away.' An older woman to a young girl sitting beside her says, 'Why don't you sing?' 'I can't. I don't want to. I can't,' cries the girl. 'I can't. Oh, God.' The singer tries to get people to join in, but they won't. She gives up and sits down.

"Around midnight, a few people in this shelter are asleep, but every time a bomb goes off, it wakes them up. Several women are crying. At each explosion there is a burst of singing from the next shelter. Two men are arguing about the whereabouts of the last bomb. Suddenly, a girl cries out, 'I wish they'd bloody well stop talking and let me sleep. They talk such a lot of rot. It's such rot. That man, just listen to him. He's got such a horrible voice. Tell him to stop. Tell him I said he's got to stop. He's got a horrible voice!' The girl's neighbor tries to calm her, urges her to try to sleep. 'No!' she screams. 'It's no good. I'm ill. I think I'm going to die.' By now, the women with the deck chairs are lying back in them wearily, rocking and groaning. A woman of 60 says, 'If we ever live through this night, we have the good God to thank for that.' A friend says to her, 'I don't know if there is a God, for he shouldn't let us suffer like this.'

"When the all clear goes at about 4:30 a.m., there is a groan of relief. But soon, as the first people go outside the shelter, there are screams of horror at the sight of the damage. Smashed windows and roofs everywhere, smoke screaming across the sky from the direction of the docks. People push and scramble out of the shelter doorway and there's a wild clamor of shouting, weeping, and calling for absent relatives. 'Where? Where'd she go? Oh, we never should have—' shrieks a woman incoherent with anxiety. Others sob and cry and cling to one another. One man throws a fit. Another is sick. Later that day in the windowless front room of one of the shattered Smithy Street houses, a young woman sits among the remains of her possessions crying her heart out. It's her birthday. 'I'm 26,' she sobbed. 'I'm more than halfway to 30, and I wish I was dead.' "

London would endure these attacks for 57 consecutive nights, running from the beginning of September on deeper into the fall, nor did they stop then. After a lull in the winter, they were resumed in March and April of 1941 as the Germans again began a series of terror attacks on the center of London and other cities. It was to become a regular feature of British life and it was a preview, a dreadful preview, of what the air war would bring, not simply to England, but with far greater impact to the cities of Germany and, later on, to Japan as well. In late April of 1941, and into early May, the attacks on Britain, the air attacks on Britain began to subside. And then, at the end of May, they stopped altogether. The planes, the German planes that had been such a—had made such regular appearances in the skies over Britain were simply no longer there. Where were they? Well, they had begun to move across the continent and were massing in what had previously been Poland.

Hitler had given up on any sort of sustained attack on Great Britain and was preparing now for what was to be the main event. The largest military operation in human history was being planned by the Germans. It was not Operation Sea Lion, but Operation Barbarossa, the invasion of the Soviet Union, and this is where the aircraft had gone. At the end of this period, then, of the Battle of Britain—and then the Blitz through the fall and winter of 1940 and into 1941—Britain had stood alone and Britain had survived. It was a major turning point in the Second World War.

Hitler Moves East
Lecture 9

We will now follow the planning of what came to be known as Operation Barbarossa—Hitler's decision to invade the Soviet Union—the factors that he weighed as he made this momentous decision, and the planning for what was to be the largest military operation in human history.

Operation Barbarossa in fact did turn out to be the largest military operation in human history. Both ideological and practical considerations shaped Hitler's decision to invade the Soviet Union. He believed that the "civilized" world was destined to clash with the Soviet Union as the center of Judeo-Bolshevism. He sought *Lebensraum* for Germans via eastward expansion into the successor states of the old Austro-Hungarian Empire and ultimately into the Soviet Union. He assumed that Great Britain had essentially been defeated by 1940 and was no longer a factor on the continent. Thus he did not risk a two-front war. He questioned the leadership, organization, and morale of the Red Army, and he assumed that it had been gravely weakened by the purges of 1938.

The planning for Operation Barbarossa began in the summer of 1940. The invasion was planned for spring 1941. After some debate, it was decided that the goal of the operation should not be the capture of Moscow or other specific cities, but instead the destruction of the Red Army in western Russia. Three army groups were assembled. Army Group North would advance toward Leningrad through the Baltic states; Army Group Center would advance toward Moscow; and Army Group South would invade the Ukraine.

Why was the invasion postponed from its initial starting date of May 15 until late June 1941? Some have attributed this delay to Hitler's need to invade the Balkans in April 1941 to restore order there following Mussolini's disastrous invasion of Greece in October 1940. In fact, unusually wet weather in eastern Europe in spring 1941 was responsible for the postponement of Barbarossa. Stalin discounted intelligence reports of the German invasion plans. He suspected Churchill of trying to foment trouble between the Germans and Soviets.

The invasion was to be an ideological crusade against "Asiatic Bolshevism." Invading troops were ordered to eliminate all resistance without regard to international law. The infamous "Commissar Order" required the summary execution of all captured Bolshevik agitators, guerrillas, saboteurs, and Jews, and it ordered the army to eliminate all active or passive opposition. The German Army—not the Nazi Party—issued directives requiring its troops to assault "Jewish sub-humanity" without regard to the Geneva accords.

The invasion began on June 22, 1941. The Germans caught the Russian troops completely unprepared. During the first 24 hours, the Germans inflicted tens of thousands of casualties, took almost 10,000 prisoners, and destroyed 1,200 Soviet aircraft, almost all on the ground. ∎

Suggested Reading

Alan Clark, *Barbarossa: The Russian-German Conflict, 1941–1945*.

John Keegan, *The Second World War*, Chapters 6–9.

Gerhard Weinberg, *A World At Arms*, Chapter 4.

Questions to Consider

1. What considerations motivated the German invasion of the Soviet Union in 1941?

2. How did the invasion serve Nazi ideological objectives?

Hitler Moves East

Lecture 9—Transcript

In the fall of 1940, with Great Britain still unsubdued, Hitler began to shift his attention away from this campaign against Great Britain—which he'd never intended, never wanted—and to focus on what for him had always been, throughout his political career, the primary objective. And that was to be a crusade against the Soviet Union. In this, our ninth lecture in the series on the Second World War, this ninth lecture, we will now follow the planning of what came to be known as Operation Barbarossa—Hitler's decision to invade the Soviet Union—the factors that he weighed as he made this momentous decision, and the planning for what was to be the largest military operation in human history. We also, we're going to look at the ways in which this was not to be a traditional military campaign. This was not simply going to be a campaign for geopolitical reasons to establish *Lebensraum* for the Germans in the East. This was an ideological campaign, a war to the death between ideological systems—a crusade against "Judeo-Bolshevism," as Hitler frequently put it.

So, let's begin by looking at the background of what came to be known as Operation Barbarossa. We've talked about Hitler's ideological orientation. Certainly the Soviet Union played a major role in Hitler's thinking, his ideological thinking. He had in his earliest speeches, and certainly in *Mein Kampf* and later public addresses, talked about what he saw as an inevitable confrontation between the forces of civilization, which he saw as National Socialist Germany, and "Asiatic Bolshevism," or Judeo-Bolshevism. Hitler used these terms interchangeably. We've seen how Hitler was determined to establish *Lebensraum*, living space, for the Germans. That meant expansion to the East. He had originally hoped that this could be done by Blitzkrieg against diplomatically isolated opponents—Poland. It certainly meant expansion toward the successor states of Eastern Europe and, ultimately, towards Russia—the Ukraine, and the—with its great breadbasket of Russia and the great mineral resources offered by the Soviet Union.

These ideas represented the very core of National Socialist ideology and for Hitler the war against the Soviet Union was the main event toward which the regime had been pointing from the very beginning. A war in Eastern Europe was a virtual inevitability from the time that Hitler came to power. It was what his policies were aimed toward, and now having secured, he believed, his position in Western Europe, he was impatient to turn to the East. And yet, there's something of an irony involved in this. Hitler, in *Mein Kampf,* had written extensively—and certainly spoken extensively—about the failures and mistakes of the old imperial regime Germany. That it had lost the First War because it had engaged in a two-front war. That it allowed itself to be bogged down in this two-front war. That this was the great era of the Kaiser and his advisors, his military; and that a National Socialist regime would avoid this situation. So why now? Why, with Great Britain still unsubdued, turn to the Soviet Union in the fall of 1940 and begin to give an order for his generals to begin planning an invasion for the spring of 1941?

In the fall of 1940, Hitler was increasingly impatient. One sees this in a lot of his utterances to advisors, to close confidants within the National Socialist Party, to his military men. Hitler had a—there was a growing concern. He had a growing concern about his own health. One sees this in his—the so-called table talk, the "tischgespraeche." He had sort of sycophantic followers who were close to him, and, as he would go on in these long monologues over dinner, over lunch, would take down religiously what the Führer had to say. We have these now in a series of things called "Hitler's Table Talk." And in this one sees that in 1940 Hitler was afraid and talked about, "Well, what happens if I die before my life's work is completed?" He'd originally thought about the war that he now was enmeshed in, was a war that he had thought would probably come at some point in 1942, maybe 1943, but now here it was in 1940. He wanted to get this life's work accomplished. The attack on the Soviet Union, the destruction of the Soviet Union was much of what that life's work was about. And he could actually argue that the time was right.

It is true that Great Britain was not defeated, but it was certainly eliminated as a factor on the continent. Despite Germany's setback in the battle of Britain, England was extremely weak. It had survived, but it was certainly unable to intervene on the continent in any meaningful way. It certainly could not reverse the great tide of events that had swept across Europe in 1939, 1940. It was hanging on and hanging on by its fingernails. So in this sense, Hitler could convince himself, and with some plausibility, that an attack on the

Soviet Union would not mean enmeshing in Germany in a two-front war. There was not a real front in the West. And, he believed that the Soviet Union was particularly vulnerable at just this junction. That the longer he waited for an attack on the Soviet Union, the stronger the Soviets would become.

Part of the reason for this calculation was the effect of the purges of 1937 and 1938—the purges of the Red Army that we've talked about. We've alluded to those purges, but I think one really needs to understand the scale, the scope, of these purges, to have some sense of how they might affect military operations. The numbers, the extent, of Stalin's purges, these were staggering. Of the 80 members of the Military Soviet in 1934, only five were still alive in 1940. All 11 Deputy Commissars were eliminated. Every commander of a military district, including their replacements for the first wave of victims, had been executed by the summer of 1938. Thirteen of the 15 army commanders, 57 of the 85 corps commanders, 220 of the 446 Brigade commanders, had been executed by 1940.

But the losses didn't stop there. In fact, the greatest number of victims were among the officers from the rank of colonel down, extending all the way to the level of company commander. The army, the Red Army, was now under the thumb of the political commissars of the Bolshevik Party. The Soviet Union possessed an army of 200 effective divisions, German intelligence estimated, organized around infantry divisions. Although the Soviets had begun to reorganize and to create armored units, armored divisions like the Germans—learning their lessons from the German Blitzkrieg against Poland and in the West—the process was only just beginning in 1941. The equipment of the Red Army was lavish. The Soviets possessed more tanks and as many aircraft as the rest of the world put together. And its manpower reserves seemed virtually inexhaustible.

But Hitler and the German military doubted the quality of the Red Army and its equipment. Mass, which the Russians had in excess, Hitler thought, was useless without leadership and without the proper sort of technology. It had been a truism of the old Czarist armies that the Czarist armies arrived too late with too much. The sense about the Red Army in 1940, '41, was that it was true. It was enormous. And in that sense it was a terrifying prospect to think about this enormous military organization. On the other hand, Hitler viewed the Red Army as disorganized, its morale destroyed by the purges, and riddled with communism.

The winter war against Finland hadn't done anything to restore his faith in the strength of the Red Army. Indeed, the winter war reflected that just exactly how far the disintegration of the Red Army had become, how weak it actually was, having been bogged down in this campaign against Finland. "You only have to kick in the door," Hitler told General Rundstedt, "and the whole rotten structure will come crashing down." Hitler would say variations—would dilate on variations of this theme—over the course of the spring of 1941 and into 1942—that the Soviet regime was unpopular at home; it was corrupt; it was hated by its own subjects. And that all one had to do was to smash into the Soviet Union and the whole political structure would come apart at the seams.

General Halder, who had been mastermind at the campaigns in Poland and in Western Europe, was put in charge of Barbarossa. He estimated that the Soviets would be unable to resist a German invasion for more than eight to ten weeks. The military planning for this operation began in the summer of 1940, and by the end of July the decision had been made to attack the Soviet Union in the spring of 1941. The operation was code named Barbarossa, named for the medieval German emperor who had driven to the East—famous for his "*Drang nach Osten*," this Drive to the East. In December —December 18, 1940—Hitler had issued a general directive with more specific orders, and then followed those up again in January. There was some debate within the high command and with Hitler over objectives. Hitler originally had favored an attack, which would focus on Leningrad in the north and another prong of the attack moving into the Ukraine toward Kiev. Most of the military men favored some sort of more concentrated drive toward Moscow—seize the political nerve center of the Soviet Empire and destroy it that way. All agreed that the destruction of the Red Army in Western Russia was key to either one of these objectives.

Finally, as planning reached its final stages, agreement was reached that the objective of the operation should not be cities, specific geographic points—not necessarily Moscow or Leningrad, or Kiev in the Ukraine. But rather—the key objective, the central objective, the mission stated for the German army with its invasion of the Soviet Union—was the destruction of the Red Army in Western Russia. This, both Halder and Hitler were convinced, could be accomplished within two months, maybe a little longer, maybe a little less if things broke their way. In one sense, the Germans—there was a geographic notion to this—the Germans didn't have any intention of occupying all of the Soviet Union, or driving to the Urals and so on. A general line, a line running from Arkhangel on the Arctic Ocean in the North to Astrakhan on the Caspian Sea in the South. This is a—geographically speaking—a line of extraordinary length and required a military operation of extraordinary proportions to achieve. It would, in short, be the most ambitious military operation in human history.

Three army groups were assembled for this operation, Army Group North. Now, that said, these groups don't necessarily have geographic objectives to destroy the Red army in Western Russia. But, for general purposes, Army Group North was directed through the Baltic states with a general direction toward Leningrad. Army Group Center would be focused on a drive headed largely toward Moscow. And Army Group South was aimed toward Kiev and into the agriculture-rich Ukraine. The Germans assembled 145 divisions. 102 of those were infantry units, 19 were armored divisions, 14 motorized infantry units were all assembled—2,500 tanks, 2,700 airplanes, and over a million troops assembled for this operation. It was an extraordinary logistical feet. These troops were moved from Western Europe to the East, assembled, and prepared to launch this invasion in May of 1941.

There was one other aspect of the logistical organization for the invasion, which as the invasion began didn't so much strike Europeans, but when American military people got hold of the information—and the data from the invasion—there was one striking aspect of it—of German preparations—that General Marshall and others in Washington saw as more striking than the 2,700 tanks, more striking than the million troops, the 2,700 airplanes: the German army moving to the Soviet Union requisitioned 10,000 horses. For American military there was a sense of, well, where are the trucks? How—what are these horses for? What are the horses to be used for? We will come back to this in a bit.

The original invasion date was set for May 15, 1941. At that time, the high command calculated that the spring rains would've subsided and that the turf on the terrain in the Soviet Union would be firm enough to support the Blitzkrieg operation that the Germans planned to unleash. But in October of 1940, Mussolini, against Hitler's fervent pleas to the contrary, had invaded Greece. It was one more ill advised military operation on the part of the Italians. Hitler had tried to convince Mussolini not to do this. He thought it would be a terrific blunder. He didn't need his Southern flank in the Balkans to be in question and didn't want British involvement in the Balkans at this sensitive moment when Germany was preparing for this enormous, colossal attack on the Soviet Union.

The Italian operations in Greece were a fiasco from the word go. The Italians had jumped off from Italian-occupied Albania—attacked into Greece. The Greeks—like the Finns before them in the Russo-Finish War—fought with great tenacity; not only defeated the Italians in Greece but drove them back into Albania, and then followed them into Albania. The Greeks had become, in the spring of 1941, the same sort of heroes around the world that the Finns had become—had been—a bit earlier. Finally, Hitler decided that the situation in the Balkans had become so unstable that he needed to send troops in to stabilize it. Therefore, in April of 1941, the Germans launched an invasion of both Greece and Yugoslavia.

This is usually cited as a key variable in explaining subsequent events, particularly the postponement of Operation Barbarossa. Hitler postpones it until late June in order to bail Mussolini out in the Balkans. Since, as we know, the snows would come in the late fall in the Soviet Union and German troops would become bogged down in the snow west of Moscow, this lost month of campaigning in the spring is often seen as being really crucial. And so this diversion of German troops into the Balkans, a key explanatory variable in the failure of the Germans to take Moscow or drive the Soviet Union out of the war in 1941.

But, I don't think this holds up very well. It is true that involvement in the Balkans did divert German attention. There was a postponement of Operation Barbarossa, but I think probably more than Mussolini's misadventures in Greece, the weather in Eastern Europe was far more important. The spring of

1941 was unusually wet. In fact, I think, just looking at the weather in Eastern Europe over the past, last spring—where there was enormous flooding in Poland and in Eastern Europe—it was the wettest spring since 1941. It was unusually wet and the rivers in Poland were flooded until early June. So tanks needed hard terrain, the roads in the Soviet Union were primitive, and Hitler decided to postpone the attack until June. The new date for the invasion was June 22, 1941. It was 129 years to the day after Napoleon had launched his disastrous invasion of imperial Russia in 1812. It's interesting that as the Germans began to mass troops along their frontier—now remember the German Russian frontier is in Poland now. Poland is basically vanished. So Russian troops have moved west. Soviet intelligence was very good. The Soviets possessed the best spy system in the world at this point, and Stalin had been receiving intelligence reports from a spy ring in Japan—Soviet spy ring in Japan—which indicated that the Germans were moving troops to the East and planning an attack.

Churchill's information from the breaking of the German code—the British and the United States were providing the Soviets with information—suggests that the Germans were up to no good. In fact, they were planning an invasion of the Soviet Union. And Stalin steadfastly refused to heed these warnings. Among other things, Stalin was quite concerned that what Churchill, in his desperation, was trying to do, was simply stir up trouble between the Soviet Union and its ally, Germany. He didn't want—he was afraid that this was—that Churchill was simply being wily and shrewd and trying to provoke some sort of incident between Germany and the Soviet Union to break that alliance to save Britain. And, as a consequence, he did not inform his military commanders in Western Poland about German troop movements. Even they, the local commanders, began receiving reports—indications of German fly-overs that were clearly unusual. There was a case of a German deserter who had gone across the lines and reported to the local Soviet commanders that a huge military operation was in the offing, but to no avail. As the Germans began their preparations—the huge logistical preparations for this invasion—they also began preparations of another sort—preparations to indoctrinate their troops for the campaign against the Red Army.

This was to be a war unlike the war against Poland. It was going to be a war radically different from the war that had just been conducted in Western

Europe. This was going to be an ideological conflict, a war to the finish. A decree had been issued by Hitler in the late days of May indicating to the high command that they should prepare the troops for the sort of war they were about to embark upon. And, in the last days before the invasion, a series of directives were drafted by the high command and National Socialist officials to be read to German troops—all German troops going into the Soviet Union.

I'd like to quote from them. They give us a chilling preview of what this war in the East would be. "In the struggle against Bolshevism," one of these directives read, "we must not assume that the enemy's conduct will be based on principles of humanity or of international law. In particular, hateful, cruel, and inhuman treatment of our prisoners is to be expected from political commissars of all kinds as the real carriers of resistance. The troops must be advised: 1) In this struggle, consideration and respect for international law with regard to these elements are wrong. They are a danger for our own security and for the rapid pacification of the conquered territory. 2) The originators of barbaric, Asiatic methods of warfare are the political commissars of the Bolshevik Party. Accordingly, measures must be taken against them immediately and with full severity. Accordingly, whether they're captured in battle or offering resistance, they are in principle to be disposed of by arms." This was the infamous "Commissar Order" issued to the, by the high command, by Hitler actually in the high command of the troops.

On June 4 that order was elaborated in another fashion before troops going into the Soviet Union. It stated, "Bolshevism is the mortal enemy of the National Socialist German people. Germany's struggle is directed against this destructive ideology and its carriers. This struggle demands ruthless and energetic measures against Bolshevik agitators, guerillas, saboteurs, Jews, in the complete elimination of every active or passive resistance." The wording of that is very important. Troops going into the Soviet Union were told, therefore, you're going to encounter an addition to the Red Army, for other sources of resistance, Bolshevik agitators, guerillas, saboteurs, and Jews. Well, Bolshevik agitators didn't exactly show up and register themselves with the oncoming German army. Saboteurs obviously don't. Guerillas don't, but the one group in that list that proved to be extraordinarily vulnerable was the Jewish community of Eastern Poland and the Soviet Union. And they now become targets.

A few days after the invasion began, these directives were followed up by a series of others. General—Marshal—Field Marshal Walter von Reichenau, commander of the sixth army, issued another statement to elaborate on this, which Hitler saw as being—capturing particularly the essence of combat against the Soviets. "With respect to the conduct of troops toward the Bolshevik system, vague ideas are still widely prevalent," Reichenau wrote. "The most essential aim of this campaign against the Jewish-Bolshevik system is the complete crushing of its means of power and the extermination of Asiatic influence in the European region. This poses tasks for the troops that go beyond the one-sided routine of conventional soldiering. In the Eastern region, the soldier is not merely a fighter according to the rules of the art of war, but also the bearer of an inexorable national idea and the avenger of all bestialities inflicted upon the German people and its racial kin. Therefore the soldier must have full understanding of the necessity of a severe, but just, atonement on Jewish sub-humanity. An additional aim in this is to nip in the bud any revolts in the rear of the army, which as experience proves, have always been instigated by Jews."

Now these—what I've just quoted—these are not internal National Socialist documents. These are directives issued by the German army for the conduct of its troops in the Soviet Union, acting on what they thought was the will of the Führer. The Soviet Union had not signed the Geneva accords, and so in one sense the rules of war, of international law, were not going to apply. But what the German army was being told, heading into the Soviet Union, was this is basically going to be war without rules. That this is a fight to the finish—an utter, complete, ideological conflict in which no quarter will be given. Don't anticipate one and don't give one yourself.

Just a little after daybreak on June 22, 1941, a train traveling west from Soviet occupied territory crossed a bridge. It was a delivery of raw materials to the Germans. The German troops that were crouching on the other side of the river watched as the train came across the bridge, making sure that this last delivery of raw materials was made. They crossed the bridge and just after sunup, the Germans launched Operation Barbarossa. They caught the

Russians utterly by surprise, utterly unprepared. By pushing the frontier to the West, Stalin may have bought time, but he exposed those units to exactly the sort of large-scale pincer movements that the Germans had perfected.

Within the first 24 hours, the Germans would inflict tens of thousands of casualties on the Russians—would take close to 100,000 prisoners. And the Red Air Force, the Soviet air force, which was the largest in the world, was caught almost entirely on the ground. Twelve hundred Soviet aircraft were destroyed in less than 24 hours, almost all of them on the ground. When, on the following day, the Soviet air force ordered a counterattack with Soviet bombers, they took off from positions that the Germans already knew, and they were annihilated in the air.

The Soviets would now confront a German army with terrific materiel, with a plan that they believed was—they were convinced would work—now without air cover and without the sort of political support they believed was necessary, without the intelligence that was crucial. Within 24 hours, the German army had inflicted upon the Soviets a bigger defeat than the Germans had inflicted upon any of their opponents in the West. Everything had gone exactly as Hitler had anticipated. The Red Army appeared to be exactly the sort of weak, politically corrupt, inefficient organization that his military had suggested that it would be. "You only have to kick in the door," Hitler had said," and the whole rotten structure will come crumbling down."

There was one other thing that Hitler had said though that was also very prophetic. Convinced as he was of victory, he also added, "In war, any time when you launch an operation, you go to war, it's like opening the door into a dark room. You think you know what's there. You think you know where the furniture is arranged, but you never really know until you step inside." The Germans had just stepped inside Soviet occupied territory on June 22, and the Soviets were not to be the only ones who were surprised. We'll take this up in our next lecture.

The Germans Before Moscow
Lecture 10

We're going to examine the German campaign in the Soviet Union in the summer and fall of 1941, to try to determine whether or not the Nazis could have won in the Soviet Union in this initial phase of the campaign, whether their failure to take Moscow in this summer and fall campaign would prove to be fatal for the regime, whether it marks a terrific turning point in the war.

The Germans drove deep into the Soviet Union in the summer of 1941, as Operation Barbarossa proceeded according to plan, exceeding even the German high command's expectations. Yet, even as the Germans took hundreds of thousands of prisoners and inflicted ghastly casualties on the Red Army—and civilians—the invaders began encountering unsettling logistical and weather problems that slowed the offensive by late summer.

Initially, the German invasion of the Soviet Union proceeded according to plan and achieved its objectives.

> ### The Germans made spectacular gains in June and July:
>
> • Army Group North captured the Baltics.
>
> • Army Group Center encircled Smolensk.
>
> • Army Group South met fierce resistance in Ukraine.
>
> • The Red Army incurred enormous casualties. German General Franz Halder commented: "The Russians lost the war in the first two weeks."

Despite their impressive victories, the Germans faced problems. The rapidly advancing Army Groups North and Center began to outdistance their supplies. Terrain and weather proved more difficult than anticipated.

The Red Army resisted tenaciously and inflicted huge casualties on the Germans. The Germans' brutality prompted the Russian defenders to fight heroically even in the face of hopeless odds. Advancing behind the German forces, the *Einsatzgruppen* murdered one million Soviets (mainly Jews) during the early months of the invasion. Stalin's order that all Soviet deserters would be shot also motivated the troops to stand and fight. Soviet partisan troops behind the advancing German lines created constant problems for the German armies. The Soviets' new T-34 tank worried the German high command.

Germany was now in for precisely the long, protracted conflict that Hitler had hoped to avoid.

A new strategic debate over objectives arose within the German high command in mid-July. Hitler sought to divert units from Army Group Center to Army Groups North and South. He favored a drive on Leningrad. Guderian and other generals sought to concentrate German forces for an assault on Moscow. The panzers paused in late July as this debate took place. They did not resume their advance until late August.

Hitler had several reasons for wanting to maintain the Germans' broad front strategy:

- Logistical and supply problems were imposing a severe burden on the Wehrmacht.

- The German forces had nearly exhausted their manpower reserves.

- The Soviets were redeploying new reserves to meet the Germans.

The existence of this debate over objectives showed that the Germans had failed to achieve their goal of destroying the Red Army in the West.

The German offensive resumed in September. Two hundred thousand civilians died during the siege of Leningrad. Kiev was encircled and eventually capitulated. On September 30, 1941, Army Group Center moved toward Moscow. Panic ensued in Moscow as the government pondered whether to evacuate. The Soviets began to dismantle industrial enterprises and reconstruct them far to the east. Heavy rainfall during October forced the Germans to postpone the final offensive until early November, after the onset of cold weather. The German forces were unprepared for the Russian winter; the troops lacked winter uniforms and their vehicles lacked antifreeze.

The Soviets responded by redeploying troops from the Far East for the defense of Moscow. On December 5/6, the Soviets launched a massive surprise counter-offensive under the command of Marshal Zhukov. The German offensive halted, and the Blitzkrieg phase of the war came to an end. Why did Barbarossa fail? Could it have succeeded? ■

Suggested Reading

Alan Clark, *Barbarossa*, Chapters 4–9.

John Erickson, *The Road to Stalingrad*.

Gerhard Weinberg, *A World At Arms*, Chapter 5.

Questions to Consider

1. Evaluate the strategic debate within the German high command during mid-1941 over the objectives of the Soviet campaign.

2. What factors contributed to the eventual failure of Operation Barbarossa?

The Germans Before Moscow
Lecture 10—Transcript

On June 22, 1941, the Germans launched Operation Barbarossa against the Soviet Union. It was the largest military operation in human history. It was, without question, Hitler's greatest gamble of the Second World War. For 24 hours, the National Socialist plan, the Nazi plan, worked to perfection, capturing over tens of thousands of Russian prisoners, inflicting terrific casualties on the Soviets. And the operation—this great three-pronged attack in the Soviet Union—was off to a tremendous start. In this, our tenth lecture of the series on the Second World War, we're going to examine the German campaign in the Soviet Union in the summer and fall of 1941, to try to determine whether or not the Nazis could have won in the Soviet Union in this initial phase of the campaign, whether their failure to take Moscow in this summer and fall campaign would prove to be fatal for the regime, whether it marks a terrific turning point in the war.

Certainly in those first days, the campaign went spectacularly for the Germans. Army Group North drove 155 miles through Lithuania and into Latvia in five days alone, movement on a scale unprecedented in European history. By July 10, German armor was within 80 miles of Leningrad in the North. Army Group Center cured up two gigantic encirclements of large Russian forces, one near Minsk, the second near Smolensk, 200 miles farther east, in mid July, capturing almost 500,000 Russian prisoners and inflicting horrendous casualties. On August 5, the last resistance in the city of Smolensk came to an end. The Germans in Army Group Center had covered 440 miles in 23 days and were only 200 miles from Moscow. Army Group South found the going a bit slower, encountering fierce resistance in the Ukraine—but still German units were moving steadily forward. General Franz Halder, the Army chief of staff and the man most responsible for the planning of the campaign, wrote on his birthday, June 30, "The Russians lost this war in the first eight days." And just a few days later, on July 3, he noted in his diary, and I quote again, "On the whole, one can say that the task of smashing the mass of the Russian army has been fulfilled. It is probably not too much to say when I assert that the campaign against Russia has been won within two weeks."

But the Germans, despite their astonishing gains, were confronting some disquieting problems. The groups, army groups, particularly Army Groups Center and North, had begun to outdistance their supplies and were encountering mechanical difficulties, especially the armored units. The roads and the terrain in the Soviet Union were not exactly what they had expected. Looking at the map, the Germans had done reconnaissance; they thought they understood what they were getting themselves into. But, looking at the map of the Soviet Union, they had what seemed to be major roadways, modern roadways—upon encountering them they discovered in many cases were nothing more than sort of dirt tracks, sometimes gravel. Hardly the super highways, the autobahns, that the Germans had been building in Germany since the early 30s. The terrain was much more difficult, the transportation more difficult, the roads far cruder than the Germans had anticipated.

Nor was the Red Army behaving quite the way the Germans thought. The Russians had been roundly defeated, routed. The Blitzkrieg was working as if by textbook and yet the Russians didn't seem to understand that they were defeated; they hadn't read the text. One gets, on the one hand, this tremendous sense of euphoria. The Blitzkrieg—hundreds of miles, hundreds of thousands of prisoners, terrific casualties inflicted on the Red Army—and yet, the Russians aren't behaving the way, for example, the French or the Belgians had before them—or the Poles. You can imagine the frustration back at army headquarters—Hitler's headquarters—looking as one looks as the pins move in the map, the lines are drawn in the map. Each day the army groups move deeper and deeper into the Soviet Union. Each day the after-action reports disclose hundreds of thousands of Russian prisoners of war, Russians surrendering in incredible numbers, terrific casualties, unbelievable casualties inflicted on the Soviets.

And yet, the Russians fought tenaciously, even when there was little or no hope of prevailing, and they were inflicting terrific casualties on the Germans as well. One of the problems that the Germans encountered was a problem of their own making. We discussed in the last lecture these extraordinary orders—directives—given to the German troops entering the Soviet Union, about this was a war without quarter, a fight to the finish, don't expect humane treatment if you are captured, therefore don't necessarily take prisoners yourself. The German behavior in the Soviet Union was so brutal from the very outset that Russians, despite the fact that the Germans captured hundreds of thousands of them—other Russians, if there was any option of fighting on, they did, even when there was little chance of survival, in part, because they didn't want to fall into German hands. Moving along, this is not a topic for this lecture's discussion, but we will certainly come to it. Moving along, almost with the troops in the Soviet Union, were special SS commando units called *Einsatzgruppen*. These SS units were given "special" orders, special tasks. They were to move against the saboteurs, guerrillas, and Jews in the Soviet Union. And so all across the Eastern Front, along with the military operations, which were going swimmingly for the Germans, these *Einsatzgruppen*, these special SS commando units, were conducting a bloodbath all over the Soviet Union. Wherever the German troops moved, were killing—we estimate, no one knows for certain—but it is estimated that these *Einsatzgruppen* would kill almost a million Soviets within the first few months of the war, mostly Jews.

But it was a distinction, that for, if you were on the receiving end of this, was not an easy one to make. The Germans were behaving in the Soviet Union like the barbarians they maintained that the Soviets were, and, as a consequence, these Russian units, if there was any hope—falling into German hands was death, they assumed—and so they fought with incredible tenacity against the Germans.

There was a second reason, too. Stalin, who—as the invasion had broken on his Western frontier, had gone almost into seclusion for about 48 hours, afraid of assassination because he had ignored so much of the intelligence suggesting a German attack—Stalin rallied and the NKVD, the Soviet secret police, and the political commissars in these army units, were also instructed—given very clear instructions—if people break ranks and begin to run, to retreat, this is desertion and these people are to be shot instantly. So if you're a soldier in the Red Army, you've got the Germans in front of you behaving in one barbarous fashion; you've got the NKVD behind you acting in another.

There's a particularly chilling description of this, this comes a bit later on in this first attack into the Soviet Union, actually from the siege against Kiev, but I think is worth reading to get some sense of the position these troops found themselves in. Talking about a Russian unit, as the Germans advance on this Russian unit in around Kiev, a German watching this wrote, "Stalin presided over their death, for specially trained electricians had rigged up apparatus and played recordings of his speeches to the defenders of key positions." This is around Kiev. "During the fighting, the words of Stalin, magnified to gigantic proportions by the loudspeakers, rained down on the men kneeling in holes behind the tripods of their machine guns, din in the ears of the soldiers lying amid the shrubs of the wounded writhing in agony upon the ground. The loudspeaker imbues that voice with a harsh, brutal, metallic quality. There is something diabolical and, at the same time, terribly naive about these soldiers who fight to the death, spurred on by Stalin's speech on the Soviet constitution. By the slow, deliberate recital of the moral, social, political, and military precepts of the Party, about these soldiers who never surrender, about these dead scattered all around me. About the final gestures, the stubborn violent gestures of these men who died so terribly lonely a death on this battlefield amid the deafening roar of the cannon and the ceaseless braying of the loudspeaker."

The Russians, then, would extract a very high price from the Germans as the Germans moved deeper and deeper into the Soviet Union. Even the lack of coordination confused and perplexed the Germans. Communications between Moscow and top military headquarters in the front had broken down as the Germans made these great advances into the Soviet Union. As a consequence, a great many military units—cut off from the rear by this breakdown in communication—confronting the Germans—simply fought on in their own way. Uncoordinated military activity along the front, and this confused the Germans. They couldn't figure out what was going on. Was there a plan to this? Why was this unit moving here or there? Was this part of an overall plan? It wasn't, but the Germans certainly did not know that.

What one sees, already at the end of the first month of the campaign—that is by the end of July—is that the Panzer leaders in these three German army groups are still wildly enthusiastic about the campaign. This is going, to them, absolutely according to the book. Huge pincer movements, they break through these Russian lines, roar across this flat Soviet terrain, moving quickly, closing the pincers on these Germans. So the Panzer leaders remain tremendously optimistic, very keen on the operation. But the infantry units

135

that were following them in—the motorized infantry and then behind them, what I often refer to as the bottom of the food chain—the infantry men who are walking their way in to this, who are having to clean up the final resistance. The infantry officers had begun to have a very different view of what the war in the East was all about. For the Panzer leaders it was movement, close the encirclement, move on for another one. For the infantry units, these were the people who were closing with and fighting with the Russians at close quarters, and this was a war that they hadn't anticipated. It's true that the Russians were being pushed back, they were surrendering, they were being killed, wounded in massive numbers. And yet, as one German wrote home, "This is not like France, this is not," which was, he suggested, "maneuvers with live ammunition."

This was real combat and of a sort that was unnerving, especially as the Germans drove deeper into Russia. They left behind thousands of enemy troops, stragglers, partisans who snipped at them, who made hit and run attacks on them. Small units, platoons, companies of Red Army units that now became partisans—who simply lived off the land far behind German lines. And certainly the Germans didn't know where they would show up or how they would behave. One sees in the letters written home by German soldiers and also the entries into the German war diaries, many instances where far, far, far behind what the Germans thought were the front lines, a company-size Red Army unit would show up and launch an attack. This was something that made life behind the lines difficult for the Germans. And that the Soviets were fighting with everything they had available to them. German intelligence had led the high command to believe that Soviet military technology was crude, and in these early days it certainly seemed as if that were the case, the Russian air force and so on. But, even the crudeness of the way with which the Russians fought proved to be unnerving to the ordinary soldier who found himself confronted with the Red Army and its remnants in the East.

One instance of this, which I'd like to read you, an entry from one German who survived an attack far behind German lines on the main highway from Korosten to Kiev—the map depot of the sixth army, who had just taken up a bivouac in a village, far, as I said, behind the German lines. "We had no proper sentries," the man wrote, "just a few men strolling about with their rifles slung over their shoulders as the whole of the sixteenth motorized was meant to be between us and the Russians. There was quite a lot of fraternization with the villagers; I remember that some of them had never seen a lemon before. Then the inhabitants began to withdraw to their homes. We thought that seemed a little peculiar, and soon the village was completely empty of Russians. A short time afterward there was the sound of horses and a dust cloud to the south. Some people said that it was a supply column from one of the Hungarian divisions." There was a Hungarian division fighting alongside the Germans in the invasion. "Then they were upon us, like an American film of the Wild West, sturdy little horses riding at a gallop through our camp. Some of the Russians were using submachine guns, others were swinging sabers. I saw two men killed by the sword less than ten meters from me." Think of that, 80 years after the Austro-Prussian war. "They had towed up a number of those heavy two-wheeled machine guns. After a few minutes whistles began to blow and the horsemen faded away. The machine gunners started blasting us at very close ranges with infilade fire. Soon, tents and lorries were ablaze, and through it all the screams of the wounded men caught in the flames."

This kind of behind-the-lines attack was something that the Germans in their planning simply hadn't calculated. The French, the Belgians, the Dutch— all of the other combatants that the Germans had confronted—when the situation required it, simply surrendered. This was it; you made a logical choice, a rational calculation, and surrendered. One gets the sense with the Germans, even as things are going extremely well for them, there is this growing sense of what they've got, they have a tiger by the neck, they're winning, they've got it down. They're holding it, but they can't possibly relax, even for a second. There's no way to relax because if they do then it will be upon them.

In addition to the fact that the Russians seemed to be beaten, but didn't know it, and were fighting against all odds, one begins to see in the "Kriegstagebuch," the war diary of the high command, some other disturbing revelations. A new weapon had appeared on the front. The Germans were convinced that they had the best tanks in the world. There had been some advances since the summer of 1940 and they were also convinced that although the Soviets apparently had more tanks than anybody else, that these were technologically crude, hardly a match for German technology. But the tank that they began to discover, a week, two weeks, three weeks into the campaign, was the T-34 tank, which was certainly more than a match for anything the Germans could put into the field; in fact it was the most technologically advanced tank of its time.

This was very disturbing news to the German High Command. Franz Halder, who as you'll recall had been writing in his diary on his birthday and shortly thereafter that the Russians had lost the war within eight days—then he revised it to say two weeks—now there's this sort of sense of, well now, wait a minute, where did this come from? Why didn't intelligence tell us that this was out there? And it wasn't just the prototype. The French also had had good tanks, they'd had good airplanes, but they hadn't developed them; they weren't there in numbers. The T-34 began showing up in surprising numbers already in the campaign in 1941, and this was a great concern. So the war, the war was already a source of some frustration. On the whole things were going better than they could have anticipated, tremendous gains. And, again, the perspective from back at headquarters, just looking at the map—and especially if one is from a German perspective where the distances are quite small— now to be thinking in hundred-mile breakthroughs and so on—this was quite amazing. But, these problems had also begun to surface. They were only problems, disquieting problems at this point; they would come to be major problems a bit later on.

At the strategic level, then, as the Blitzkrieg continues to work, and to work according to clockwork, at the strategic level, a debate erupts and it erupts in mid July about a month into the campaign. Hitler proposed, at this point, diverting Panzer groups from Army Group Center to Army Group North for a drive on Leningrad. Hitler had always favored a drive to the north through the Baltics with Leningrad as its main objective, and he revives this at this point. He also wanted to divert another armored division from Army Group Center to take Guderian's division and send it to Army Group South, where another great encircling movement seemed to be possible.

Halder, Guderian, the other German commanders—most of the other German commanders—were quite unhappy with this. They wanted to concentrate as much as possible, their forces, for a drive on Moscow. Moscow seemed to be there for the taking. Meanwhile, the Panzers halted. The German advance into the Soviet Union halted as this debate was sorted out. Where were the Germans going to concentrate their forces? Not until August 20 were the Panzer divisions finally diverted as Hitler desired, that is the weakening of Army Group Center, and the offensive began to move again.

One of the questions that has certainly surfaced—continues to be debated— is whether or not the Germans could have taken Moscow if they had concentrated their forces, if they hadn't wasted this time in late July early August. This was good campaigning weather— perfect campaigning weather for them—but at this point the operation didn't so much stall as simply stop while the Germans tried to decide exactly what their strategic position ought to be.

One factor that has to be considered, in making up one's mind about this, has to do with logistics. The Germans were having all sorts of problems with supply. They had outrun their supplies. The road conditions that we've described were very bad, the rail lines in the Soviet Union were difficult for them to use, the Russians continued to harass them; partisans were blowing up the railroad tracks behind the lines, and so on. So there were strains, very serious strains in supply for the Wehrmacht at this point.

The other problem for the Germans, too, was that the Germans had stretched their own manpower to the absolute limit. The Germans were operating at this point, really, without reserves. They were at the end of their reserves. There hadn't yet been a total mobilization of Germany for the war and they were largely at the end of their reserves. And, and, there were some troubling indications that the Russians were beginning to move troops from elsewhere toward the West, that there were Russian reserves of manpower available that were being brought to bear on the situation.

So, one of the arguments that Hitler used was, if we made a spearhead directly for Moscow we're likely to outrun our supplies, sure enough. And, if these Russian reserves are, in fact, out there, what if they cut off this spearhead? We would be opening our flanks—this would be disastrous— better to move in the way we are moving in this broad front. Regardless of how one evaluates this, the very debate within the German high command is itself symptomatic of the Germans' biggest problems.

What the debate revealed is that Operation Barbarossa had already failed in its original objective. It had not destroyed the Red Army in Western Russia. The Germans had attempted too much, they couldn't proceed on all of the objectives at once, and they were still 200 miles from Moscow. Their anticipation that if they inflicted devastating enough casualties on the Russians that they would surrender or just completely break down had failed to materialize. And, as a consequence, this very debate—Do we concentrate on Moscow? Do we move toward Leningrad? To Kiev?—already reveals that this original objective, the stated mission of Barbarossa, had not been attained.

In September, the offensive resumed. The city of Leningrad was put under siege, a cruel siege indeed, in that winter of 1941-1942—200,000 inhabitants of Leningrad would die as a result of starvation and malnutrition-related diseases; would freeze to death in this city in the north. In the south, Kiev fell to a gigantic encirclement and 600,000 more Russians would go into German captivity, and Kiev finally fell on September 26. On September 30, Army Group Center finally moved on Moscow. The drive, once again textbook perfect—600,000 more Russian prisoners of war. A general panic in Moscow broke out.

Stalin ordered tank traps to be dug, trenches to be dug around the city. There were rumors abroad in Moscow that the government was abandoning the city and moving east. Panic began to break out among the civilian population. It looked as if, at this point, that indeed the unraveling of Soviet society, of the Soviet regime, which the Nazis had anticipated, was finally going to happen. One of the most extraordinary achievements of the entire Second World War, in fact a miraculous achievement, also took place in this very same period, and that was the dismantling of Russian factories. About 1,500 Russian industrial facilities were dismantled, bolt by bolt, as the Germans bore down upon them—the Germans with complete air superiority, attacking all across the range of the Western Soviet Union. The Russians dismantle 1,500 factories, put them on railroad cars, take them east, move over a million workers to the east and begin to build new industrial cities beyond the Urals and in Siberia, away from the Germans. It was an extraordinary achievement by any standard, an amazing achievement, something the Germans certainly hadn't anticipated.

At the same time that the Russians are doing this, Adolf Hitler gives an order to put the German economy back on a peacetime footing. The war in the Soviet Union was over, it had been won, Hitler did not want to strain relations at home. He wanted to keep business as usual, not a full mobilization of Germany's economic resources, and so the German economy was to be put back on a peacetime footing. The offensive which had been launched at the end of September—this final move toward Moscow—ran into trouble with weather. Not the snow that one usually thinks about with the Soviet Union, but rain. It fell steadily through much of October, and in many places the tanks and trucks mired in the mud could not move, and the offensive bogged down—in fact, stopped—until November. When the frost finally came, when the weather began to get cold, then the Germans were able to move again and resume the offensive, the move toward Moscow, at the beginning of November.

This final drive for Moscow began on November 15 when the ground had finally frozen enough for the tanks to have the necessary foundation they needed. But German forces, at this point, were badly weakened by losses. Their supplies were inadequate, the tanks were having mechanical troubles, and the weather—which had been a problem from the beginning—not snow up until this point, but rain—now turned genuinely ugly. The first snow in October, a dusting, had been a mere preview. In late November the temperature simply dropped like a stone. Temperatures by late November reached ten below zero Fahrenheit.

German troops had been issued no winter clothing, not even overcoats. They were operating in the Soviet Union in cotton uniforms and denim. The vehicles had either little or no antifreeze available; they were supposed to be already out of this theater by the time winter set in and progress was agonizingly slow. The tank engines had to have fires lit under them so the engines wouldn't freeze. If you opened a can of rations, if you didn't eat it immediately, it would freeze within 30 seconds, at the end of November. The Russians, meanwhile, were not only preparing a defense of Moscow, but planning a major counter-offensive. Georgi Zhukov, who was placed in charge of the defense of Moscow, a general who had earned his stars out fighting the Japanese along the Manchurian frontier—something we'll talk about in a subsequent lecture—was put in charge of the defense of Moscow. He began moving reinforcements from the Far East, assured that the Japanese would not attack. These movements the Germans had very little knowledge of. Troops from Siberia, from the Far East, began arriving east of Moscow, reinforcing the Red Army position. And then, on December 5, 1941, Zhukov launched a massive counterattack north and south of Moscow, catching the Germans completely by surprise. It halted the German offensive—not only halted it, it threatened to turn the German position into a complete rout, a catastrophe for the Germans.

This counter-offensive would stall in January and February and the Germans would resume their offensive operations in the spring of 1942. The war wasn't over; the Germans hadn't been defeated. It would be the Germans who would launch a new offensive in the spring of 1942, not the Russians. But there was no disguising the fact that the Blitzkrieg phase of the war had come to an end. Germany was now in for precisely the long, protracted conflict that Hitler had hoped to avoid. He had not been able to either destroy the Red Army or seize Moscow. And now—having just ordered the economy to go back on a peacetime footing—he was now forced to make the reluctant admission that this was a war with no end in sight. Not only that, events all the way across the globe—at Pearl Harbor two days later—would transform what, until this point, had been a European war, into a genuine global conflict. And four days after that, Adolf Hitler would declare war on the United States, so that a global conflict was now at last a reality. That's a story that we will take up down the road.

The War in Asia

Lecture 11

In this lecture, we want to shift our attention to Asia—to the diplomatic background to the conflict in Asia, to a discussion of the Sino-Japanese conflict, which had begun in many ways in 1931 and certainly become a major war by 1937.

The roots of the conflict in Asia lay in the diplomatic context of the end of World War I. The Japanese emerged from the First World War as the leading power in the Far East. Japan seized the Marshall, Mariana, and Caroline Islands in the Pacific, all of which were former German possessions. At Versailles, Japan was awarded former German concessions in China despite protests from the United States and China.

Japanese naval officers resented the restrictions imposed on the Japanese fleet at the Washington Naval Conference of 1921–1922. Many in the Japanese armed forces were convinced that Japan's only salvation lay in expansion, particularly on the Asian mainland. Expansionists sought access to food, oil, and other raw materials through military conquest. Many Japanese military officers were increasingly disgusted with their country's corrupt civilian government. China was an especially inviting target for Japan. Manchuria was rich in natural resources and appeared ripe for the taking. Since 1905, influence in Manchuria had been split between Japan and Russia.

The Mukden "Incident" of 1931 led to the Japanese seizure of Manchuria and the creation in 1932 of the Japanese puppet state of Manchukuo. This operation underscored the strong influence of the military over the civilian government in Tokyo. Condemned by the League of Nations, Japan withdrew in 1932. The Chinese central government was weak and divided. The Nanking government could not respond effectively to Japanese aggression.

Japan engaged in full war with China in July 1937. In July 1937 the Japanese Kwantung Army invaded northern China from Manchukuo. The Soviet Union signed a non-aggression pact with China. The Soviets and the Chinese Communists announced their intention to support Chiang Kai-shek's forces, which were defending China against the Japanese. In November 1937, Japanese forces besieged the new Chinese capital, Nanking, which fell on December 12.

The "Rape of Nanking" in December 1937 and January 1938 provoked widespread condemnation of Japan, especially in the United States where the "China Lobby" was particularly strong. Some 200,000 Chinese civilians died in the attack. The capital was moved to Chungking. Canton fell in October 1938. In December 1938, the United States extended a $25 million loan to China. But armed clashes with the Red Army on the Mongolian border in August 1939 sobered Japanese military commanders about prospects for expansion to the north.

Tokyo faced a strategic dilemma. The Japanese army favored expansion to the north against the Soviet Union, while the navy advocated expansion southward through Southeast Asia and the Pacific and seizure of the colonial possessions of the western European powers.

Crying baby after Japanese bombing of Shanghai.

A compromise solution was reached, as outlined in the "Fundamental Principles of National Policy" of August 1936. Japan should extend its influence in China and the South Seas gradually and by peaceful means. Both the army and navy would be strengthened so that they could better resist the Russian army and the U.S. Navy. This policy committed Japan to an arms race with the Soviet Union and the United States, and it called for expansion into China.

The triumph of Germany in the west in 1940 had a dramatic effect on Japanese strategic thinking. In July 1940 the civilian government was replaced by a more aggressive cabinet that pursued an alliance with Germany and the Axis powers. The new government was determined to crush China. It decided to push southward into Southeast Asia. The new cabinet sought to silence domestic opposition.

Japan faced continued resistance in China during 1940 from Chiang and the Chinese Communists. Tojo reasoned that a move to the south against Western colonial possessions would help Japan subdue China by cutting off Chiang's external supplies. It would also provide needed raw materials for Japan. This planned push to the south required Japan to reach a non-aggression pact with the Soviets and to prepare for conflict with the United States. War games conducted in May 1940 showed that Japan could prevail in a short conflict with the United States but might lose a long one. The war would be a great strategic gamble.

The situation in East Asia deteriorated during 1941. Japan felt threatened by U.S. economic sanctions and aid to China. Following Japan's demand in July 1940 that Britain close the Burma Road, the United States imposed a limited embargo on the sale of certain key goods to Japan. In late 1940, Tojo linked Japan with the Axis powers in the "Tripartite Pact." Each member pledged to support the others in a war against the United States. The United States offered to assist the Dutch if they would cut off oil shipments to Japan, and it provided $70 million in new loans to China.

In March 1941 the U.S. Congress passed Lend-Lease and provided additional support for Chiang. In April 1941 Japan and the Soviet Union signed a non-aggression pact, indicating that Japan had chosen the southern strategy.

Japan and the United States inched closer to conflict. Roosevelt rejected the proposal but prolonged negotiations in spring 1941 in order to prevent Japan from attacking. Japan hoped to resolve its differences with the United States through negotiation but was prepared to use force if necessary.

Japanese threats to French Indochina, the Dutch East Indies, British Malaya, and the American Philippines in July 1941 led the United States to freeze Japanese assets. Great Britain and the Netherlands followed, and Japan found itself cut off from 90 percent of its oil supplies.

What everyone understood was that some sort of military action would be undertaken by imperial Japan.

Events moved rapidly toward war in late 1941. In early September 1941 the Japanese government decided that it would be ready for war by late October. Minister of War Tojo assumed power in October 1941. Diplomatic overtures continued. Japan offered to withdraw from Indochina and parts of China if the United States would not interfere with Sino-Japanese peace negotiations and if it would normalize trade relations with Japan and support Japanese acquisition of the Dutch East Indies.

The Japanese government set a secret deadline of November 25, 1941, for progress in the talks. Roosevelt knew that this was an important date. Because the U.S. government expected an attack, it was less interested in negotiating.

Although the American military position was weak, Roosevelt rejected the Japanese proposals and demanded Japanese withdrawal from China. On November 26, 1941, a large Japanese carrier force set sail in the northern Pacific. Its objective was the U.S. naval base at Pearl Harbor. ∎

Suggested Reading

Suburo Ienaga, *The Pacific War, 1931–1945*, Chapters 1–6.

Akira Iriye, *The Origins of the Second World War in Asia and the Pacific.*

John Keegan, *The Second World War*, Chapter 12.

1. What factors explain the resurgence of Japanese expansionism during the 1930s?

2. What developments and strategic considerations led the Japanese government to choose the "southern strategy" of expanding into Southeast Asia and the southwest Pacific? What were the consequences of this choice?

The War in Asia
Lecture 11—Transcript

In our first ten sessions, we focused exclusively on the background to the war and the actual combat in the European Theater. In the winter of 1941, the nature of war would change from a European war into a global conflict.

In this lecture, we want to shift our attention to Asia—to the diplomatic background to the conflict in Asia; to a discussion of the Sino-Japanese conflict, which had begun in many ways in 1931 and certainly become a major war by 1937, so in advance of events in Europe; to analyze the strategic dilemma of the Japanese leadership in this period, the late '30s, and in the final period before the decision to attack Pearl Harbor; and then, finally, the deterioration of relations between the United States and Japan in 1941.

We'll begin with some background about the strategic position of Japan. The Japanese had emerged from the First War as a victor state, having helped to capture German concessions in China and having seized the Marshall, Mariana, and Caroline islands in the Pacific, all of which had been German possessions. At the negotiations at Versailles, Japan was rewarded with the former German concessions in the Shantung area and on the Yellow Sea, despite vehement Chinese protests and expressions of disgust from the United States.

At the Washington Naval Conference in 1921-1922, Japan had agreed to limits on naval construction, which left it in an inferior position to the United States and Great Britain. The Japanese had agreed to limit the size of its fleet to three-fifths the size of the British and American fleets, and the Japanese also appeared to recognize Chinese territorial integrity.

These concessions rankled many junior naval and army officers in Japan, who were resentful of what they considered to be Western arrogance, and were increasingly influenced by extreme nationalist ideas that were sweeping the country. Many were convinced that Japan's future security could be assured only through the seizure of raw materials—food, and oil in particular—and that such seizures would ultimately have to come through military conquest.

Japan was also experiencing at this time a population explosion, which exacerbated problems of overcrowding, of unemployment and poverty in Japan; and a growing disgust with the civilian government, which military leaders saw, at any rate, as wracked with scandal and corruption. These military leaders believed that Japan's salvation lay in expansion, particularly on the Asian mainland, where China, but especially Manchuria, offered a particularly enticing target. Manchuria was rich in natural resources, and since 1905 influence over this northern region of China had been split between Russia and Japan. Japan had military garrisons in the southern part of Manchuria, but the region was largely regarded as a virtual wilderness where a Chinese warlord claimed control. It was seen as territory ripe for the taking by the Japanese.

Then, in 1931, middle-grade officers of the Kwantung army, the Japanese military force stationed in Manchuria, manufactured what they called an "Incident" on the South Manchurian Railway near Mukden. Within hours, a full-scale attack on Manchuria was underway. While the civilian government in Tokyo vacillated, the Kwantung army seized Manchuria in a few months, establishing the puppet state of Manchukuo under Japanese protection in 1932. The Japanese civilian government was unable to restrain the army and was forced to defend its actions in the international community.

The League of Nations, for its part, condemned Japanese actions in Manchuria, and the Japanese, for their part, withdrew from the League of Nations. Condemnation of Japanese actions in Manchuria attracted worldwide disapproval, but that disapproval was particularly sharp in the United States, where a strong interest in China had traditional roots.

The nominally sovereign Nanking government—Chinese government— was unable to master the situation. Torn by battles between rival warlords, especially since 1927, and a civil war also against the Communist Chinese under Mao, China seemed to be coming apart at the seams. Not only did it offer rich mineral resources, food also, for the Japanese, but China itself in this period seemed to be something of a crazy quilt of territories held together by warlords who fought with one another—ideal for the taking. It was a situation that the Japanese hoped to exploit.

In 1937, the Japanese asked China to join a "Tripartite Pact" with Japan and Manchukuo aimed at the Soviet Union and to allow five of its northern provinces to be transformed by the Japanese into a buffer zone against potential Soviet expansion. The Japanese were quite concerned about Russian influence in Manchuria and in the Far East, and this is exactly where these two great powers, the Soviet Union and Japan, would come into potential conflict. The Chinese refused to sign on to this Japanese alliance plan, and after a series of incidents, full-fledged war broke out in July of 1937.

Although the Japanese government continued to refer to its actions there as the "China incident," the Japanese had, in fact, embarked upon an aggressive, expansionist war. In July 1937, Japanese units, army units, moved into Northern China from Manchukuo. The Soviet Union signed at the same time an agreement, the Sino-Soviet non-aggression pact, with the Chinese, and the Chinese Communists announced in September that they would support Generalissimo Chiang Kai-shek in his war now against the Japanese.

So Soviet intervention—you have a Chinese civil war going on, which now is put in abeyance, a situation that verges on the chaotic—but with the Japanese certainly attempting to exploit this. By November 1937, Japan occupied Shanghai, and in December besieged the new capital city of Nanking. In six weeks, the city of Nanking would finally fall on December 12, and in the following period, into January of 1938, Japanese troops engaged in widespread executions, rape, and the random murder of civilians, in what came to be known as the "Rape of Nanking."

These Japanese atrocities, which were widely documented, widely covered in the press, marked a dramatic escalation in the massacre of civilians which had accompanied the Japanese military operations in China. The totals are vague, but the conservative estimates are that about 200,000 people died—Chinese civilians died—in this Rape of Nanking. Some of those famous photographs of the Second World War stem from precisely this period. There's that famous photograph of a small child, almost an infant, sitting alone in the middle of a railroad track with smoldering buildings and wrecked railroad cars behind it, the child almost itself smoking. It's from this period, and it attracted tremendous attention, particularly in the United States. Reports from China, photographs of burning cities, of dead children, startled the international community, but, as I said, especially here in the United States, where the "China Lobby" was particularly strong and vocal. Outrage at Japan was widespread.

At this point, Chiang Kai-shek moved the capital to Chungking, in the interior, and then in October of 1938, Canton fell. In December of 1938, the United States—in a desperate attempt to shore up Chiang Kai-shek's regime, to maintain Chinese resistance to the Japanese—the United States extended a loan of $25 million to the Chinese government. This is a fairly remarkable thing at the time, actually, if you think about it—where the Europeans were very much concerned about American isolationism—that the United States seems readier to become involved in the Far East than in Europe itself.

Japanese policy between 1936 and 1940 was dominated by a compromise agreement between the army and the navy and embodied in a document entitled, "Fundamental Principles of National Policy." This document was drafted in August of 1936. There had been a debate within the Japanese military, and the military by this point had clearly come to dominate the civilian government in Japan. The Japanese army saw Japan's great nemesis, its great enemy, as the Soviet Union, and constantly pressed for new appropriations to reinforce the position of the army, to build up the army to fight a land war against the Soviet Union in Manchuria or in the north. The Japanese navy, on the other hand, tended to emphasize the ripe fruits to be taken by an expansion to the south, through Southeast Asia, the colonial possessions of Europe, Indochina, Malaya, the Dutch East Indies, possibly the Philippines.

And hence, the debate tended to focus around this notion of a northern strategy or a southern strategy. The north tended to be emphasized by the army, the southern by the navy. But this Fundamental Principles of National Policy which was drafted in August of 1936 was a compromise. It called for Japan to secure "a firm diplomatic and defensive position on the East Asiatic continent." What did that mean? It meant China—to establish itself in China; and "the extension of national influences to the South Seas"—this is the bow to the navy.

The document insisted that advances in the south were to be accomplished "gradually and by peaceful means" and that in the north, caution should be exercised to avoid confrontation with the Soviet Union. At the same time, both the army and navy were to be greatly strengthened to a level at which they could "resist the forces of the Soviet Union, and the navy should be expanded to a level sufficient to secure command of the Western Pacific against the U.S. Navy."

Although stated cautiously, this program, in 1936, was quite dangerous. It saddled Japan—it committed Japan—to an arms race with the Soviet Union and the United States. It called for—no matter how mildly it was stated—for an expansion into China. It was going to bring Japan into conflict with the Soviet Union if Japan moved to the north, and the southern route would certainly lead to trouble with Great Britain, France, and the United States.

The German victory in the West in the summer of 1940 had a dramatic effect on Japanese strategic thinking. The moderate government—civilian government—was finally toppled and replaced in July of 1940 with a far more aggressive cabinet whose goals were first of all to establish some sort of alliance with the Axis powers. Japan and Germany clearly were the wave of the future, and some sort of alliance with Germany would be the key foreign connection for the Japanese. This new Japanese government in July of 1940 also was determined simply to crush China. There would be no compromise on this. Now it was the question of seizing what one wanted in China, pursuing the war to its ultimate conclusion, and third was a push to the south. The collapse of France, the occupation of Holland by the Germans, the defeat of Britain—it was clear, wasn't it, that England was defeated?—all of these things made the southern strategy, this move into Southeast Asia, very, very attractive to Japanese policy makers. French Indochina, British Malaya, the Dutch East Indies—all the Dutch East Indies with their tremendous oil deposits, rubber in Indochina, rice—all of these things were important for the Japanese, and now, with the defeat of precisely these powers in Europe, this was clearly the way to go.

In addition, this new Japanese cabinet wanted domestically to install "a new political structure" as they called it, to silence the opposition. The leading figure in this new cabinet was the minister of war, a military man by the name of Tojo. So in July of 1940, the Japanese government sees opportunities and is determined to take a more aggressive tack in its foreign policy.

The most important feature of Japanese foreign policy was the situation in China. Despite the great victories over the Chinese since 1937—Japan, for example, held most of coastal China and the most important inland cities already by 1940—the Japanese continued to face resistance from Chiang Kai-shek, supported by Britain, France, and the United States. We were sending financial support, material, and so on. And of course there were the Chinese Communist guerillas, who, when they weren't fighting Chiang Kai-shek, decided to fight the Japanese.

There was a strange situation that was already emerging, that would remain all the way through the war, which is that one was never quite sure exactly what the fronts were. I don't mean the geographical fronts, but the political fronts. We support Chiang Kai-shek so that he will fight the Japanese. But Chiang Kai-shek is just as interested in fighting the Chinese Communists under Mao as he is the Japanese. The Japanese want to defeat Chiang Kai-shek but they also have the Chinese Communists to deal with. And so this was the situation, the diplomatic situation, that one found oneself in, in 1940.

A move to the south against French, Dutch, and English colonies would help resolve the Chinese conflict for the Japanese, Tojo felt. Japan estimated that in 1940 about 41 percent of the outside supplies reaching China came via Haiphong Harbor in French Indochina. Thirty-one percent came from India across the Burma Road; 19 percent by coastal waters, that is, Hong Kong; and two percent over the land route from the Soviet Union. So the seizure of the Dutch East Indies—Indonesia today—would provide needed oil that would be lost if the United States, as anticipated, imposed economic sanctions. So a move to the south would not only provide new raw materials for Japan— much needed raw materials—but would also help to cut the Chinese knot, as they sometimes put it—that it would close off the supply routes to Chiang Kai-shek and the Chinese.

What this required was some sort of arrangement with the Soviet Union— the Japanese now became interested in the non-aggression pact with the Soviets—but what it really required was preparation for a conflict with the

United States. The Japanese hoped to avoid it, but they were unwilling to give up a push to the south. The Japanese by this point are already very seriously contemplating, and begin to plan, a strategic offensive that would take them into Indochina, Malaysia, the Dutch East Indies. Of course, just to the east of those, if one visualizes the map, is the Philippines, with the American position in the Philippines. And so one option was to move through Southeast Asia and leave the American position alone; don't attack the Philippines. But if you do that, you're exposing all of your operations to the potential attack from the United States from its Philippine bases.

It's interesting, and I think prophetic: Naval map exercises were held in Japan in May of 1940—war games, conducted by the naval chief of operations. Those map exercises revealed that, for a very short time—a matter of months, possibly even a year—in a potential conflict with the United States, Japan would be tremendously successful. But if the conflict went beyond that—if the United States were not knocked out of a conflict within a matter of months—then over the long haul there were grave potential difficulties for Japan. In other words, those map exercises suggested that war with the United States was a great strategic gamble.

Nonetheless, the decision to pursue this course was officially approved at a conference—a Japanese government conference—in July of 1940; that is, to pursue this southern strategy, even if it ran the risk of conflict with the United States. The Japanese were determined to cut off supplies reaching Chiang Kai-shek. This was a major goal, and in July 1940 the Japanese demanded for the British to close down the Burma Road. The British didn't want to do this; they wanted to continue to support Chiang Kai-shek, but now it's July 1940; the British have bigger worries on their mind than what's going on out in Burma and on the frontier with China. And so the British looked to us, looked to the United States: Would the United States support Great Britain if Britain resisted this Japanese demand to close off the Burma Road? The Roosevelt administration reluctantly had to say, well, no, we won't support you, we can't do that. This would run the administration into trouble with Congress. We wouldn't support Great Britain in an act of defiance, but, the United States, in response to this Japanese demand, announced a limited embargo on the export of scrap iron, steel, and certain grades of aviation fuel to Japan.

Then, in September of 1940, the Japanese formally entered the so-called Tripartite Pact with Germany and Italy. This was the link to the Axis in Europe. Tojo believed that this linkage of Japan with the Axis in Europe would deter American interference; that the Americans wouldn't want to be drawn into conflict with Japan, especially if it meant a linkage to the Italians and the Germans. This agreement, this Tripartite Pact, called on each signatory to come to the aid of any other signatory involved in war with a power not currently at war in Europe. This is clumsy diplomatic language, but what this really basically meant was, the United States. It could have meant the Soviet Union when the pact was signed, but it certainly meant the United States.

If Tojo hoped that what this would do was deter the United States, he was disappointed. It produced exactly the opposite effect in Washington. The United States offered support to the Dutch if the Dutch would refuse to enter into long-term contracts to supply Japan with oil from the Dutch East Indies, and FDR pushed through additional loans to China amounting to $70 million.

In October, the British reopened the Burma Road, and Great Britain, the Netherlands, and Australia began talks—mutual defense talks—about possible reactions to Japanese aggression in Asia. In March of 1941, the United States passed the Lend-Lease Act and made provisions which would allow us to provide additional support to Chiang Kai-shek in China.

In April of 1941 then, Japan entered into an agreement with the Soviet Union, the Japanese-Soviet non-aggression pact. This pact, this Japanese-Soviet non-aggression pact, is interesting. What it did was to show that Japan and the United States were inching toward a real military confrontation. The Japanese had clearly decided on a southern strategy—not confrontation of the Soviet Union, but a push into Southeast Asia.

In 1941, Japanese-American relations continued to deteriorate. One could see the storm clouds forming. Japan felt threatened by American economic sanctions and unhappy about American aid to China. In May, the Japanese government made new proposals to the United States for improving relations. If the United States would halt its aid to the Chinese and resume normal American-Japanese trade, the Japanese would vacate China within 25 years. This was an offer that the Americans felt they had to refuse, but President Roosevelt kept the negotiations going. He wanted to continue to engage the Japanese in discussions, hoping to avert forcing the Japanese into aggression—to continue to talk, to continue to negotiate.

While these negotiations were under way, of course, Germany launched Operation Barbarossa, its invasion of the Soviet Union, without, I might add, Japanese foreknowledge. The Japanese-German connection is just that. It's a connection; it is not a military alliance; it is not even really much of a political alliance. They act independently, and the Japanese were certainly not privy to German calculations about invasion of the Soviet Union. Like virtually everyone else, the Japanese assumed a quick German victory. They reinforced Japanese troops in the north in Manchuria but clearly had decided to move south. Still, the Japanese government hoped to acquire what it wanted by diplomatic means. But if the United States or the West could not be brought to reason, then so be it. Japan would be prepared for war; it would seize what it had to have.

When the Japanese sought and received permission to send troops into Indochina from the French, who were in no position to resist at this point—the French still had their empires, something the Germans had allowed them—it put Japan within easy striking distance of the Dutch East Indies, Malaya, Singapore, and the Philippines. President Roosevelt knew also, because of the American breaking of the Japanese code—this was called "Magic" in the Pacific—the United States knew that military preparations were already under way; that is, the Japanese, while continuing to negotiate, were making military preparations for a move into Southeast Asia. If the negotiations came to nothing, then Japan wanted to be ready. The civilian government in the United States, the American military authorities—everyone knew this. We had broken the Japanese code on September 25, 1941; it was the diplomatic code, not the military code, although that would come a bit later on.

The United States responded by freezing all Japanese assets. Great Britain and the Netherlands followed suit, and now Japan found itself, in the fall of 1941, cut off from 90 percent of its oil supplies. If this situation weren't reversed, Japan would be reduced to impotence. A proposed meeting between heads of state, Japan and the United States, was rebuffed by the United States. Cordell Hull, the American secretary of state, was not interested in pursuing this. Neither was Franklin Roosevelt, and the drift toward war began to gather momentum. In early September, Japan decided to be fully prepared for war by the end of October. Then, in October, Minister of War Tojo, the general Tojo, assumed power in Japan. Still, while Japan prepared for a drive to the south and possible war with the United States, the diplomatic traffic intensified. All through the fall of 1941, as the Japanese are pretty clear about what they want to do; that is, they know what their military strategy is going to be—it's going to be to launch a major assault into Southeast Asia; it's going to bring it into war with France, Great Britain, Holland, and undoubtedly the United States—there's still the hope that somehow this can be negotiated, that some sort of diplomatic solution can be achieved. The Japanese offered withdrawal from Indochina and parts of China if the United States would not interfere in Sino-Japanese peace negotiations, and would agree to normalize trade relations between the United States and Japan, and, that the United States would support Japanese acquisition of the Dutch East Indies. This would give Japan the oil that it needed. The Japanese framed it in such a way that this would be the maximum set of demands; this would put limits on Japanese demands in Asia.

Secretly, the Japanese government had set a deadline of November 25 for progress in the talks. The Roosevelt Administration knew this; that is, while we were negotiating with the Japanese, Cordell Hull, Franklin Roosevelt understood that November 25 was an important date for the Japanese. They didn't know exactly what this meant; they didn't know that this would automatically trigger an attack—certainly didn't—if it was going to trigger an attack, where that attack would come. But they understood that the diplomats—the Japanese diplomats in Washington had been given to understand—that if nothing had happened, if no substantive progress had been made by November 25, then a new situation, a radically new situation, would apply.

What everyone understood was that some sort of military action would be undertaken by imperial Japan. This made it very difficult, I think, for the Roosevelt administration to negotiate in good faith. Everything that the Japanese seemed to be offering on the table was interpreted as being, well, they're not serious about this; they're really just setting us up; they're really planning a military attack. And of course it made the United States a lot less interested, I think, in negotiation. Although the United States military position was stunningly weak in the fall of 1941—staggeringly weak, astonishingly weak—the Roosevelt administration rejected the Japanese proposals on November 26 and demanded outright Japanese withdrawal from China, period. Not only was this a breakdown of the negotiation, this was, as far as the Japanese were concerned, an absolutely irresponsible slap in the face on the part of the Americans. On that same day, November 26, 1941, a large Japanese carrier force set sail in the northern Pacific. Its objective was the U.S. naval base at Pearl Harbor in Hawaii.

The Japanese Gamble
Lecture 12

In this lecture ... we're going to examine Japanese thinking behind their assault on Pearl Harbor; the planning for war against the United States, their options; [and] the role of Admiral Yamamoto, the man, the architect of the Japanese planning for the attack.

The Japanese leadership faced important decisions as they planned for war against the United States. Japan's leaders believed their country had three options:

- It could abandon its ambitions in the Pacific, Southeast Asia, and China.

- It could attempt a compromise with the United States and hope for concessions.

- It could take military action.

Japan had two principal military options. First, it could strike the European colonial possessions in Southeast Asia but spare the Philippines in order to preserve peace with the United States. Or Japan could strike American positions in the Pacific, notably the Philippines and Pearl Harbor. Eventually Japan's leaders decided that military action in Southeast Asia would require an attack on the United States.

Admiral Yamamoto argued that if Japan chose to fight the United States, it must strike a crippling blow against the U.S. Pacific fleet at Pearl Harbor. This attack would allow Japan to "run wild" for six months and secure control of Southeast Asia and the western Pacific. Yamamoto's plan assumed that the United States would negotiate peace terms following the loss of its fleet, and that it would accept Japanese dominance in East Asia. Yamamoto did not believe that Japan would prevail in a protracted conflict with the United States.

The Japanese chose to attack the U.S. Pacific fleet at Pearl Harbor. Admiral Yamamoto's plan had several components. Japan would launch simultaneous attacks on the U.S. islands of Wake and Guam; British Malaya, Burma, and Hong Kong; the Dutch East Indies; and the American Philippines. The centerpiece of the operation would be a surprise attack on the U.S. Pacific fleet at Pearl Harbor.

And then on December 7, when a message was transmitted — a new alert transmitted to Pearl Harbor — it would come on December 7, and it was too late to do any good.

The assault force would be centered on Japan's aircraft carrier fleet. Japan had a very well-trained and -equipped naval air force. The element of surprise was essential. The attack force maintained strict radio silence and followed a northern course well away from the standard sea lanes.

The Japanese forces attacked Pearl Harbor on the morning of December 7, 1941. The attackers achieved complete surprise. They destroyed much of the U.S. fleet and U.S. air power. Japanese losses were minuscule. However, the victory was not complete. The three American aircraft carriers were not at Pearl. Seven heavy cruisers were also at sea. Only two battleships were wholly destroyed. The attackers failed to hit American fuel depots. They did not destroy the U.S. submarine base. Admiral Nagumo, who commanded the attack, was concerned to protect the Japanese carriers and thus did not order a follow-up air assault. The United States declared war on Japan on December 8, 1941.

There were several reasons for the American defeat at Pearl Harbor and in the

Courtesy National Archives.

President Roosevelt in an address to Congress just before U.S. declaration of war on Japan.

Philippines. Some of these reasons involved intelligence failures. Some historians have suggested that FDR had advance knowledge of the attack, which he saw as an opportunity to involve the United States actively in the war. There is no evidence that the U.S. government knew that Pearl Harbor had been targeted for attack.

The U.S. government had not yet broken the Japanese military code. It anticipated a Japanese attack in Southeast Asia but not at Pearl Harbor. It was confident that Hawaii was secure.

Security breakdowns in the Pacific were also important. The initial alert message was not taken seriously; the ships had no torpedo nets; and there was no general alert. The conduct of Admiral Husband Kimmel and General Walter Short was later criticized. However, the Japanese success was mainly attributable to a brilliant plan that was carried out to perfection. ■

Suggested Reading

John Keegan, *The Second World War*, Chapter 12.

Gordon W. Prangle, *At Dawn We Slept: The Untold Story of Pearl Harbor*.

Ronald H. Spector, *Eagle Against the Sun: The American War With Japan*, Chapters 1–5.

Questions to Consider

1. What were the components of Admiral Yamamoto's plan for victory over the United States in the Pacific?

2. What factors account for the devastating U.S. defeat at Pearl Harbor?

The Japanese Gamble
Lecture 12—Transcript

On November 26, 1941, a Japanese carrier force—a large fleet, an attack fleet—set sail across the northern Pacific headed toward Pearl Harbor. Their departure was cloaked in secrecy; their trip cloaked in radio silence. The Japanese had decided to undertake the great gamble. Just as Hitler had rolled the dice with his invasion of the Soviet Union in the summer of 1941, the Japanese would take an equally enormous gamble in the fall of 1941.

In this, our twelfth lecture on the Second World War, we're going to examine Japanese thinking behind their assault on Pearl Harbor; the planning for war against the United States, their options; the role of Admiral Yamamoto, the man, the architect of the Japanese planning for the attack. We'll examine this daring military venture against the American installation at Pearl Harbor; examine the reasons for Japanese success and the American defeat at Pearl Harbor.

The Japanese, in the fall of 1941, as we've seen in the previous lecture, were increasingly convinced that the Americans had left them with no viable options. They, in this situation, felt, well, there were three possibilities that they could entertain. One was to abandon their ambitions in the Pacific—simply take a step back—abandon their ambitions in the Pacific, in Southeast Asia, perhaps even China, which was the centerpiece, always the centerpiece, for Japanese thinking during the war. They could attempt to compromise with the United States, lead the Americans to resume trade in exchange for some sort of concession in Indochina or possibly even China. Or they could take military action; they could resolve this dilemma simply by smashing the European allies in the South Pacific, in Southeast Asia, and the United States.

The military options that the Japanese high command considered as they confronted these possibilities was to strike at the European colonial possessions in Southeast Asia. This was a very attractive option in the summer and fall of 1941. French Indochina—France was in no position to do anything about a Japanese attack; Malaya and Singapore, British possessions—equally, Britain at this point, not in much of a position to act;

the Dutch East Indies. All of these were keys to Japanese strategy on largely the Asian mainland, the Dutch East Indies important because of its oil.

What would the American reaction be if Japan attacked these European colonial possessions but did not attack the American position at the Philippines? Could Franklin Roosevelt bring the United States into war against Japan? If the Japanese took a gamble, they would be leaving their military flank open by ignoring the Americans in the Philippines—but would it work? Could they attack through Southeast Asia, avoid confrontation with the United States, and emerge triumphant? Would Franklin Roosevelt be able to bring his isolationist population in the United States into the war?

These options were ruled out, largely because of what one could think of as the worst-case scenario. Japanese military commanders looking at the map said, well, if we attacked only through Southeast Asia, our supply lines would be vulnerable to an air attack from American planes stationed in the Philippines on Luzon—that there would be the Philippines sitting right in the middle of this avenue of approach—this avenue of attack—through Southeast Asia. And what would happen if, the United States at the last moment or in the midst of these Japanese operations, simply went to war and attacked Japanese forces? This would be a military disaster. So the worst-case scenario was employed here. Perhaps the U.S. Pacific fleet stationed at Pearl Harbor, almost 4,000 miles away—could the Americans employ this?

For the most part, the Japanese decided—it became clear to the Japanese military leadership that the military option—if the Japanese decided to go with the military option, it was going to mean an attack on the United States; that there was no way simply to go into Southeast Asia and avoid an attack on the United States. The key obviously would be the Philippines, but there was another possibility as well, and that was the Pacific fleet stationed at Pearl Harbor. If the American Pacific fleet were to be attacked, the Japanese felt that they had two options on this score. One was an old plan of battle in the Western Pacific, which was to draw the Americans out, attack in the open sea, and so on. But this was an older plan they thought was really antiquated—didn't want to engage in that.

Admiral Yamamoto, the commander in chief of the Japanese combined fleet, had come up with his own idea about the prospect of a war with the United States. Yamamoto had good reason to be familiar with the United States. He had attended Harvard; he had been naval attaché in Washington. He was an opponent, and had long been an opponent, of war with the United States. He had seen American industrial potential. He was quite clear about this: that if war were to come and it were to be a protracted war that Japan would have a very difficult time indeed.

He also was among the first to recognize the importance of air power for naval operations. He had been instrumental in the formation of the Japanese carrier strategy. The Japanese in the 1930s would really pioneer the use of the aircraft carrier; Yamamoto had been key in that.

He believed that if Japan were determined to follow a military path and determined on war with the United States, then Japan would have to take bold action. The only way Japan could prevail in a war with the United States was to strike a crippling blow at the American fleet—the Pacific fleet—stationed at Pearl Harbor. If the Pacific fleet were neutralized, he said, Japan would, to use his words, "run wild" for six months—maybe a little longer, maybe as much as a year, but certainly for six months—securing Southeast Asia and the Western Pacific. Perhaps then the United States would be discouraged from the prospect of a long, bloody struggle and would recognize Japanese domination in East Asia.

So, for Yamamoto, it's a roll of the dice. It has to be a short conflict; there has to be some devastating blow; the Pacific fleet has to really be laid waste. And then to count on—a very common view among the Japanese leadership—that the Americans were soft; that the Americans were interested in material things; that the United States, confronted with a defeated fleet and no real obvious means of reversing the situation in the Pacific or in Asia, would simply say, "Well, we're not going to throw bad money after good. We're not going to do more about this," and simply make some sort of negotiated peace with Japan.

His plan called for simultaneous attacks against the American islands, American-controlled islands, of Wake and Guam; against British Malaya and

Hong Kong on the Asian mainland; with additional attacks on Burma, the Dutch East Indies, and the Philippines. But the centerpiece—the centerpiece of Yamamoto's plan—was to be a surprise attack on the U.S. Pacific fleet at Pearl Harbor.

There were several keys to the plan. Japan had pioneered the aircraft carrier, especially the use of carrier fleets that would mass over 300 aircraft against enemy targets. In some ways this was almost the equivalent of the German armored divisions, the use of armored divisions on the ground—not simply having aircraft carriers spread out across different naval formations, but to concentrate them, to bring to bear great air power—naval air power—on the situation.

The United States in the 1930s had also been interested in carrier operations—it had also begun to develop the aircraft carrier, along with Japan—the United States and Japan are the two powers which do take seriously the prospect and really begin to build and think in operational terms about use of the aircraft carrier. Great Britain possessed an aircraft carrier, an operational aircraft carrier, as did Italy, both operational in the Mediterranean. But it was really the Japanese and the Americans who saw the real possibilities of naval air power.

Although the Japanese had built the world's largest battleship, the *Yamato*, and had another under construction, the aircraft carrier had become the nucleus of Japanese naval forces. The Japanese fleet really built around the aircraft carrier. In 1941, the imperial Japanese navy had ten aircraft carriers in operation; their potential opponent, the United States, only three in the Pacific, based at Pearl Harbor.

Although the combined strength of the British, Dutch, and American fleets in the Pacific and East Asia was roughly equivalent to Japan's, there was no unity of command among those potential allied nations, so that their forces were not bound together; there was no real coordination of planning by the British, Americans, and the Dutch in this theater.

The largest of these forces was by far the Pacific fleet. There were about 100 ships, 96 actually present, in the Pacific fleet at Pearl Harbor: eight battleships; seven heavy cruisers; three aircraft carriers; and, of course, numerous smaller vessels. Also in the Hawaiian islands, the Army Air Corps and naval land-based planes at Hickam Field gave the United States—not only made Pearl Harbor and the Hawaiian position a major naval center, but also an air center for the United States as well.

So for Yamamoto, it wouldn't be the Philippines, where the Americans anticipated an attack; but rather, Pearl Harbor, 4,000 miles away, that would be the key target in his planning. The plan was an extraordinarily daring military plan. A carrier strike force of six aircraft carriers, accompanied by two battleships, eight destroyers, and three cruisers, would launch a surprise attack against the U.S. fleet at Pearl Harbor. The air fleet that the Japanese would launch against these American targets consisted of 360 planes: high-level bombers, dive bombers, torpedo bombers, and fighters, all to be launched against the American ships at anchor at Pearl Harbor. The ships were also—these Japanese planes were equipped with special torpedoes. This was a surprise to the Americans.

One of the reasons that at Pearl Harbor—the concern about security of the ships being close together—there was a conviction on part of the naval commanders there, naval intelligence, that the Japanese did not have the technological capacity to deliver torpedoes by air; that they would need a different setting, they weren't able to do it. But the Japanese had been working on this, and they were equipped with special torpedoes that they could launch from aircraft. The Japanese also had available to them the best equipped, best trained, naval air force in the world, and an aircraft that was highly effective in these early stages of the war. This was the Mitsubishi A6M fighter, better known as the Zero. It was a very efficient, very capable aircraft, and although it would be later rendered less effective by American advances in technology, in 1941 it was state of the art.

Surprise was essential for the success of Yamamoto's plan. When you think about what he was talking about—a surprise attack by Japanese naval forces traveling thousands of miles across the Pacific to attack an American installation—it required a vast armada to sail 3,500 miles without detection, to catch the Americans by surprise. This meant strict radio silence would have to be enforced throughout the cruise. The fleet would then have to adhere to a precise timetable so the ships arrived exactly where they were supposed to be at the right time. He had charted a northern course across the Pacific, across a vast expanse of water well off the usual sea lanes. In October of 1941, a Japanese ocean liner had tested the route to see what it encountered. It did not see another ship at all on its voyage, nor did it see an airplane.

Although Yamamoto was to be in charge of the operation—to be in charge of the planning for the operation—the man that was actually going to lead the attack fleet on Pearl Harbor was Admiral Nagumo. He was placed in charge of the Pearl Harbor attack force. This may have been a fateful decision on the part of the Japanese. Nagumo was a very, very capable commander, a man with a very strong record in the Japanese navy, but he was a battleship man; he was not a naval aviator. And although he was certainly adept at using naval air power, this was not, I think, his natural response to things, and this has implications, as we will see.

So while negotiations in Washington were grinding to an unsuccessful halt, this Japanese attack force had set sail across the northern Pacific, bearing down on Pearl Harbor. On December 7, 1941, the Americans at Pearl Harbor—it was a Sunday morning—a few Catalina flying boats, scout boats, had been sent out. None of the Army or Navy fighters were on alert or flying patrol that morning.

At 7:02 the two radar operators on duty phoned in to the Army aircraft warning service information center at Oahu and told them that they had picked up some aircraft about 137 miles away. This was about an hour's flying time, one estimated. At the Army aircraft warning service information center, the duty officer in charge that morning told them not to worry. There were planes coming in, a flight of B-17s on their way to the Philippines. They were scheduled to come in from the West Coast of the United States that morning. That's probably what these were.

One can only think the worst possible job in the world, I think, in the military in peacetime is to be duty officer on a Sunday morning. One can only imagine what happened to this lieutenant, after telling him not to worry.

Radar itself, the radar installations at Pearl Harbor, were operating at a very crude level at this point. They had only been set up in August of 1941, and they were on—they were operational—from 4:00 to 7:00 a.m. This was it. So, in fact, the radar was about to be switched off when this phone call came in, alerting them that there were unidentified aircraft being picked up on the radar screen.

Nonetheless, additional phone calls were made. At approximately 6:53, the harbor control post in the operations office of the 14th Naval District received a message from the USS Ward, the duty destroyer patrolling the entrance to Pearl Harbor. The Ward had discovered and attacked a submarine operating just outside the harbor entrance. The duty officer had orders to contact higher authorities if he received a message such as this. But, to give you some indication of what his responsibilities were—this is a different duty officer, fortunately, I suppose—he had to phone six different offices in order to make a report that something—that the Ward had in fact seen a submarine, attacked the submarine, just outside the harbor. At 7:00 a.m. he began making calls. At 7:41, the first wave of Japanese planes roared in over the tropical hills in Oahu, and 181 dive bombers, torpedo planes, and fighters began their assault on the American positions there, on the American ships.

At 12,000 feet above Oahu, Commander Mitsuo Fuchida, looking down at what he saw, was absolutely astonished. He saw the American battleships moored together in groups of two. As he said later on, and I quote: "I had seen all German warships assembled in Kiel Harbor. I have also seen the French battleships in Brest, and finally I have seen our own battleships assembled for review before the emperor. But I have never seen ships, even in the deepest peace, anchored at the distance of less than 500 to 1,000 yards from each other." The picture down there was hard to comprehend. At 7:53, Fuchida radioed back to the waiting Japanese task force and simply said three words, "Tora, Tora, Tora," the code word indicating that complete surprise had been achieved. The Japanese began their attack with devastating success. They had achieved complete surprise.

Japanese planes had been launched from a point 220 miles northwest of Oahu, and their attacks were devastating. They sank four of eight battleships and inflicted severe damage on the others. They sank three destroyers, four smaller ships; damaged three cruisers. Twenty-four hundred American service personnel were killed. At Hickam Field, the Japanese air attack destroyed 160 American aircraft; disabled 128 others. Equally astonishing to the Japanese flyers who were on this mission, as astonishing as the position of the fleet moored at Pearl Harbor, were the position of the American aircraft at Hickam Field—because instead of being distributed around the airfield on their revetments, they found them, almost wingtip to wingtip, stacked in the center of the airfield, away from potential Japanese saboteurs. But it was like shooting fish in a barrel.

The shock for the Americans was devastating, and Admiral Nagumo had reason to exult. His own losses had been absolutely minuscule. For all of the damage that the Japanese inflicted on the American forces at Pearl Harbor, 29 aircraft had been lost. One of the reasons that more planes were not lost by the Japanese is that a great many of the anti-aircraft positions did not have live ammunition. The Americans hadn't distributed live ammunition despite the fact that there had been a general alert called some time before.

But, while the attack had gone far better and certainly smoother than he had dared hope, the destruction caused by the Japanese attack was also not as complete as it might have been. His greatest disappointment was that the three American aircraft carriers which had been the major object of the Japanese attack were not present. They'd escaped. Seven heavy cruisers were also at sea, and only two of the battleships that were hit were really beyond repair. The Japanese attack also failed to destroy the submarine base, or the fuel storage tanks, or the repair and maintenance facilities at Pearl Harbor.

In short, what the Japanese had managed to do was to achieve a major tactical victory, but not the strategic knockout punch that Yamamoto had envisioned. Nagumo's air commander, and a very competent one he was, a man by the name of Ginda, urged the admiral to launch a second wave of attacks against Hawaii and to locate the American carriers and destroy them. He was beside himself in dealing with Nagumo. They'd achieved complete surprise, the Americans were virtually defenseless, and yet Nagumo hesitated to launch the second attack—in fact, he refused. He had scored a great military victory and at minimal cost, and he did not want to endanger the carrier fleet of Japan. He ordered a return to base.

As a consequence, Japan had achieved a tremendous victory, but it certainly fell far short of the stunning victory that Yamamoto needed. And on December 8, 1941, Franklin Roosevelt, addressing Congress, talking about the attack, would refer to it as "a date that will live in infamy," and the United States, rather than deciding that its position in the Pacific and in East Asia was untenable, responded with outrage and with fury at this Japanese surprise attack.

The failure of the United States at Pearl Harbor—the fact that we had succumbed to a surprise attack—certainly has been investigated, discussed, and will continue to be investigated and discussed, one assumes. There is, and I'm not going to spend much time about this, the so-called Roosevelt conspiracy theory: that Franklin Roosevelt, knowing and understanding that the United States sooner or later was going to be drawn into conflict, was looking for an opportunity to do it; that American intelligence had received information, especially through the breaking of the Japanese code, that an attack was coming; and that Roosevelt had suppressed this information so that we would, in fact, be attacked and drawn into the war, not anticipating the enormity of the attack on Pearl Harbor. I don't think there's very much to this.

I think the most extensive evidence we have suggests that the Roosevelt administration did not—certainly knew after November 25 that the Japanese were planning some sort of action—but certainly not an attack on Pearl Harbor. An alert had been issued to the American installation at Pearl Harbor, but here one can talk about failures of communication, but not about conspiracy. The breaking of the Japanese code at this point, the Magic intercepts as they were called—the United States had been able to break the diplomatic but not yet the military code.

And, of course, one of the key aspects of Yamamoto's plan was that this carrier task force would maintain radio silence as it moved across the northern Pacific, and the Japanese exercised great radio discipline in this regard. Had they not, by the way, Yamamoto would have known that the carriers weren't at Pearl Harbor. That's one of the prices they paid for this, because the Japanese submarines had been able to pick up the fact that they weren't.

170

American naval intelligence had begun to penetrate the Japanese navy code, that's certain, but at this point could really interpret only about 10 percent of the intercepted messages, and this was a long and complicated process. There was certainly an anticipation of an attack in Southeast Asia—probably the Philippines, but not Pearl Harbor.

Here, I think, one can talk about certain problems in American thinking about this. In March of 1941, an American aviator and a naval airman had completed a report on the defense of Hawaii, and it specifically pointed out that a surprise attack from the air was "the most likely and dangerous form of attack against the fleet base at Oahu." It also said that, if it came, that one of the places it might very well come would be from the northwestern route, which was not really guarded. Still, Hawaii, many felt, was the strong point of the American position in the Pacific and in Asia, and no less a realist than Army chief of staff George Marshall described it to Franklin Roosevelt in May of 1941, and I quote from this report, talking about Pearl Harbor: "This is the strongest fortress in the world. Enemy carriers, naval escorts, and transports will begin to come under air attack at a distance of approximately 750 miles. This attack will increase in intensity until within 200 miles of the objective. The enemy forces will then be subject to all types of bombardment closely supported by our most modern pursuit aircraft. An invader will face more than 3,500 troops backed by coast defense guns and anti-aircraft artillery." Hawaii seemed quite secure.

In the aftermath, and finally, let me say this as well, there were security breakdowns both at Pearl Harbor and in Washington—that's quite obvious. Washington had ordered the Pacific fleet on alert, but there had been so many false alarms since October that one more, one more alert.... This was not backed up, incidentally, by the information that we knew from the diplomatic code that something was going to happen after November 25; if that information had gone to the commanders at Pearl Harbor, both Army and Navy, then it might have added a little more teeth to this new alert. As it was, this was seen as one more. The last warning had come on November 27; there had been no follow-up from this coming from Washington.

And then on December 7, when a message was transmitted—a new alert transmitted to Pearl Harbor—it would come on December 7, and it was too late to do any good. There were no torpedo nets for ships at Pearl Harbor. And a general alert had not been issued after the destroyer reported sinking a Japanese ship near the entrance to Pearl on the morning of December 7. All of these would have been too late, I think, anyway. The man who paid the price for this, of course, was Admiral Husband Kimmel.

There were long-range reconnaissance flights off of Oahu, but mostly to the west-southwest; recon to the north was not done on a daily basis and it was not done on December 7, 1941. General Walter Short, the American army commander there, had to pay the price for having understaffed radar group. There was conflict between the signal corps and the Army Air Corps so that even the radar operators were not Army Air Corps operators, but Army signal corps. There were, if you'll pardon the allusion, wires were crossed in the communication between signal corps and Army Air Corps, and, of course, the fact that Short had lined his aircraft up in the center of the airfield at Hickam Field to guard against sabotage by fifth-column Japanese inhabitants of the Hawaiian Islands. All meant that severe security breaches had occurred.

But the real reason, I think, for the success of the Japanese attack on Pearl Harbor doesn't have to do with breaches in American security or any sort of conspiracy having to do with Franklin Roosevelt. It has to do with the fact, I think, that this was an absolutely brilliant plan carried out to virtual perfection by Admiral Yamamoto and the Japanese imperial fleet. It was an extraordinary military accomplishment to sail across the northern Pacific in secrecy and to catch their opponents completely by surprise.

The Pearl Harbor attack would mark the beginning of American entry into the war, quite obviously, and, of course, the Japanese would launch further attacks all across Southeast Asia. What had begun first as a Sino-Japanese war in the Far East had now become a war linked to the war in Europe with the United States. Several days later, Hitler would declare war on the United States. This was now truly a world war.

The Height of Japanese Power
Lecture 13

In this lecture [I'd like] to examine the Japanese move across Southeast Asia, to look at the Axis at the high point of its power around the globe, and then to look at Japanese strategic options in the spring of 1942, concluding with the first real engagement between American and Japanese naval forces in combat, and that would be the Battle of the Coral Sea, which marks something of a—possibly one thought at the time—a turning point.

In the wake of victory at Pearl Harbor, the Japanese rolled forth to an unbroken series of triumphs that established their dominance in Southeast Asia and across the South Pacific. Admiral Yamamoto had predicted that the Japanese could "run wild" for three or four months following the Pearl Harbor attack.

The Japanese steamrolled throughout the western Pacific and Southeast Asia. Guam and Wake fell in December 1941. Hong Kong was taken by Christmas. The sinking of the HMS *Prince of Wales* and HMS *Repulse* on December 10, 1941, gave Japan naval superiority in Southeast Asia. The loss of Malaya and of Singapore in February 1942 was a huge blow to Western morale. The Japanese began to speak of creating a Greater East Asia Co-Prosperity Sphere.

Burma and the Netherlands East Indies fell in March 1942. Britain had been pushed out of Southeast Asia, and its position in India was threatened. The Japanese also attacked the Philippines, destroying U.S. air power at Clark Field.

MacArthur underestimated the Japanese and overestimated the local Allied force. U.S. troops on Corregidor surrendered on May 5, 1942. U.S. troops on Bataan held out until April 1942. In the Bataan "death march," 75,000 troops from the U.S. garrison were marched 55 miles to a railhead. More than 7,000 died along the way.

Japan was dominant throughout Southeast Asia and the western Pacific in the spring of 1942. The Allies feared that Japan would move east toward India or east toward U.S. possessions in the Pacific. Meanwhile in Europe, the Russian counteroffensive before Moscow was stalled. German U-boats operated with near-impunity off the U.S. coast. The German Navy sank many U.S. merchant ships during the winter of 1941–1942.

Japan faced several strategic options in the spring of 1942. Their leadership considered three competing offensive strategies. One involved a thrust westward into the Indian Ocean and perhaps onward to link up with German forces in the Middle East. This option most frightened the Allied leadership in early 1942. Another option was a continued push to the south to seize New Guinea and perhaps Australia. A third option was a strike against the last American outpost in the Pacific—Midway, followed perhaps by an invasion of the Hawaiian Islands. Yamamoto argued that Japan had to engage the U.S. fleet as early as possible, destroy U.S. naval power in the Pacific, and force the United States into a negotiated settlement.

Instead of adopting one strategy, Japan sampled from each. Japan considered seizing Madagascar from France. Britain seized the island to keep Japan from taking it. Japan's advance into the Indian Ocean—Churchill's and Roosevelt's nightmare—came to naught in April 1942. Jimmy Doolittle's raid on Tokyo on April 18, 1942, underscored the vulnerability of the home islands and prompted Yamamoto to plan a "ribbon defense" across the Pacific by driving U.S. forces out of Midway and Hawaii. The Japanese plan called for attacks in New Guinea and the Solomon Islands to disrupt the supply flow to MacArthur in Australia.

U.S. and Japanese naval forces clashed at the Battle of the Coral Sea on May 7–8, 1942. This was the first great naval battle between aircraft carriers and the first in which carrier-based airplanes inflicted all damage. The battle ended in a draw. Japan withdrew without attempting a landing at Port Moresby. The United States achieved its strategic goal of blocking the Japanese advance. The battle seemed to end in an Allied victory.

Yamamoto hoped to destroy the U.S. Pacific fleet in order to protect the home islands and prevent a repetition of Doolittle's raid. Japanese forces would attack Midway in order to lure the U.S. fleet out of Hawaii. The Japanese would follow up the Midway attack with a major invasion front. They had huge superiority over the United States in ships and aircraft.

Here, however, Magic came into play. Not black magic, not sleight of hand, but the breaking of the Japanese naval code.

Due to intelligence provided by "Magic," the U.S. carriers secretly relocated from Pearl Harbor to Midway. The stakes were very high. If the Japanese succeeded, the U.S. position in the Pacific would be untenable. Admiral Nagumo launched his air attack against Midway on June 4, 1942. Initially, the attack proceeded according to plan. But as the Japanese returned for a second strike, U.S. aircraft arrived. ■

Suggested Reading

Saburo Ienaga, *The Pacific War*, Chapters 7–8.

Ronald Spector, *Eagle Against the Sun*.

Gerhard Weinberg, *A World At Arms*, Chapter 6.

Questions to Consider

1. How did the Japanese leadership resolve the strategic decision that it faced in early 1942?

2. What was the strategic significance of the U.S. victory in the Battle of the Coral Sea?

The Height of Japanese Power
Lecture 13—Transcript

At the conclusion of our last lecture, the Japanese had just attacked Pearl Harbor. The United States had been caught by surprise, and the Japanese were on the move, not only against the Americans at Pearl Harbor but all over Southeast Asia.

In this, our thirteenth lecture, we're going to examine what I would call the "Japanese steamroller." You'll recall that Admiral Yamamoto had said that for 100 days, maybe longer, he could run wild—that if surprise were achieved at Pearl Harbor, the Japanese forces would have an open hand for two, three, maybe four months; after that, he would not be willing to say. And so what I'd like to do in this lecture is to examine the Japanese move across Southeast Asia, to look at the Axis at the high point of its power around the globe, and then to look at Japanese strategic options in the spring of 1942, concluding with the first real engagement between American and Japanese naval forces in combat, and that would be the Battle of the Coral Sea, which marks something of a—possibly one thought at the time—a turning point.

You'll recall that on December 7, 1941, the Japanese had struck, with devastating effect, the American installation at Pearl Harbor. Japanese forces also attacked Guam and Wake, 1,100 miles to the east. Further, the failure of the relief expedition to Wake Island was another blow to American morale; American troops were left there to deal with the situation.

Hong Kong had surrendered by Christmas. Malaya, and Singapore at its southern tip—the Gibraltar of Asia, the English had called it—had fallen to the Japanese. British forces, under the command of General Arthur Percival, had fought a long campaign which was disastrous for the British. The two British ships, the battleship *Prince of Wales* and the battle cruiser *Repulse*, were sunk by aircraft on December 10, and the Japanese achieved, at one blow, naval superiority in Southeast Asia. On February 15, the British garrison at Singapore surrendered, a humiliating blow to the British and to Western prestige in Asia. Singapore was seen, as I said, as the Gibraltar of the East, this absolutely impregnable fortress of the British. It was a symbol, not simply of British power, but of the West in Asia. The Japanese certainly would make a great deal of propaganda capital out of this, seeing this as the beginning of a Japanese liberation of Asia from European colonialism. It is at this point that the Japanese begin to talk quite expansively about a Greater Asian Co-Prosperity Sphere, Asia for the Asians, and so on.

For the British, of course, coming when this does, it's a double whammy in a sense, with all of the bad news from Europe and now this. Burma, first attacked on December 10, also was invaded in January; Rangoon fell on March 6. Chinese forces arrived to help hold the line south of Mandalay, but the Allies began a 1,000-mile retreat back into India. Ceylon was threatened but not attacked, but there was no way to avoid the terrifying truth for the British that Great Britain had been pushed out of Southeast Asia, and India itself, the jewel in the crown of the British Empire, was threatened.

The other major target, of course, for Japanese forces in December of 1941, had been the Philippines. American forces there were commanded by General Douglas MacArthur. MacArthur had been chief of staff of the Army from 1930 to 1935. From 1935 to 1941, he had been the adviser to the Philippine government, helping to build a Philippine defense force; and since 1941—earlier in '41 he'd gone back on active service as American commanding general in charge of U.S. forces in the Philippines.

The Philippines would prove as much a debacle as Pearl Harbor, in some ways even more so. The Japanese were able to destroy American air power at Clark Field, despite advance radio warning that the Japanese had attacked Pearl Harbor; destroy much of the American naval installation in Manila, forcing naval units to evacuate to Australia. General MacArthur's strategy for dealing with the possibility of invasion was one that we'll see again with Rommel, thinking about the German defense of fortress Europe—which was to halt the invaders at the beaches. "Halt them at the beach" strategy, it was called.

This reversed a longstanding American plan to withdraw to the Bataan Peninsula, which was flanked by Manila Bay on the west. MacArthur insisted on engaging the enemy at the coast, and he certainly expected to have considerable relief—reinforcements— arriving from Washington. He underestimated both the strength of his own troops, anticipating that there would be a quick reinforcement of his forces—I don't know how it was possible to think in these terms under the circumstances—but at the same time he also drastically underestimated the quality of Japanese troops that he was going to be confronting. And he overestimated considerably—the numerically strong Allied force in the Philippines was largely Filipino—certainly overestimated their strength at this moment.

The Japanese attack came from the north and south. The Americans fought a fighting retreat back to Bataan, but with disastrous consequences. It was a logistical nightmare. Troops with low supplies were forced back to Bataan, fell victim to disease, to beginnings of malnutrition. They couldn't hold out without relief. The situation was going to be desperate. Everything about the defense in the Philippines, insofar as we'd given it very much thought, really was based on the idea that there would be a steady flow of reinforcements, supplies, and so on, from Hawaii.

While American and Allied forces were being soundly beaten, Bataan held out. The American forces held out against tremendous odds at this point. MacArthur, who might very well have been sacked or been in considerable trouble, just as Kimmel and Short had been at Pearl Harbor, became, ironically, a national hero. Roosevelt and General Marshall, back in the United States, even thought about a congressional medal of honor. There were those in the armed forces who thought a court-martial might be more in line with MacArthur's performance. But MacArthur was ordered to escape from the Philippines to Australia, something that he was not keen on doing. He did in March, vowing—of course, leaving with those famous words, "I shall return." American forces were left under the command of General Wainwright. Bataan fell in April of 1942, but General Wainwright and the American garrison on the fortified island of Corregidor would hold out until May 5, 1942, an astonishing siege which was in many respects seen as kind of the Alamo in the Second World War.

Finally, at the conclusion, of course, of the siege of Corregidor, came the Bataan "Death March." The American garrison would be marched 55 miles to a railhead. Part of this was Japanese miscalculation. The Japanese had anticipated there being about 25,000 American POWs—prisoners of war. There turned out to be 75,000. There wasn't transportation for them, and so the Japanese, under this incredibly hot sun, began marching the American garrison toward a railhead for removal. Along the way, there were acts of cruelty, of torture. Over 7,000 men died on what came to be known as the Bataan Death March, the details of which were kept from the American public until much later on in the war. Four thousand of the 700 who died were Filipino soldiers. The Philippines, then, had fallen to the Japanese.

All over Southeast Asia, the Japanese were dominant—and this really does represent the Axis at its height. Winter and spring of 1941-42 seemed to bring one disaster after another. In the Pacific it was Pearl Harbor, the Philippines, the humiliation of Singapore, and the fall of all of Southeast Asia. By the early spring of 1942, the Japanese dominated all of Southeast Asia and the Western Pacific. There was fear that they would attack west, threatening India, or move against the United States at Midway and Pearl Harbor again to seize the Hawaiian Islands, seeking a knockout blow that had eluded them in this first attack on Pearl Harbor.

Across the globe in Europe, Nazi domination of all of Central and Western Europe was utterly secure. The Germans had obviously just run into a severe setback before Moscow in December of 1941—and yet I think it would be a mistake to assume, as so many people frequently do, that somehow not taking Moscow in that winter meant that the German offensive in the East was over, that somehow the Russians had prevailed. It would be the Germans, in the spring of 1942, who would launch another massive offensive on the Eastern Front. Hitler's New Order would be set in place at this time. On the Eastern Front the Russian counteroffensive before Moscow would run out of steam by spring. The Russians proved to be tremendously adept at defensive operations early on in the war but had difficulty organizing large mass offensives—attempted a winter offensive against the Germans in January-February with horrendous losses for the Red Army.

On the seas, it was a period known as the "second happy time," as German U-boats operated with near impunity off the coast of the United States and in the Gulf of Mexico. It took some time before cities on the East Coast began to—actually—we had blackouts. Up until this time, the German U-boats were active up and down the coast. This was exactly what the German naval forces had talked about and one of the reasons that they had pressed Hitler to declare war on the United States, which he had done on December 11. His generals, who at this point in December, were up to here in trouble in Russia, certainly weren't happy with this news—were in shock that now they not only had to fight the Red Army but there was the potential strength of the United States to deal with as well. But the navy, the German navy, Admiral Doenitz in particular, Admiral Raeder, both had repeatedly emphasized to Hitler, "The Americans are already at war with us. They are shipping things to Britain. If you allow us to strike now we can sink so much American tonnage they will not be able to be a serious logistical factor for the foreseeable future." So for the German navy, the declaration of war was exactly what the doctor ordered. And in this winter of 1941-42, the German navy would sink tons upon tons of American shipping.

So '42 began with the Axis powers, including now Japan, on a roll, and yet the year would end with stunning Allied victories on all fronts—at Midway and Guadalcanal in the Pacific, at Stalingrad in the Soviet Union, and at El Alamein in North Africa.

The war by early 1942 had become a genuine World War, linking Bataan to Baghdad, Mandalay to Morocco. It was fought from Leningrad to Basra; from the snows of Stalingrad to the sweltering jungles of Guadalcanal; fought in T-34 tanks, the height of armored technology; and fought by men riding on camels in the desert.

In the Pacific, the Japanese were beginning to suffer already. There was concern—both elation and concern. Elation because things had gone well beyond what the Japanese had hoped; they had been so successful on all fronts. There were some voices within the Japanese military that argued, well, one has to be careful and not suffer from what they began to call "victory disease," that is, an overconfidence.

And yet the Japanese had a number of strategic options in the spring of 1942 that they had to evaluate. In the full flush of its victories in December, January, and February, this 100 days of relentless triumphs, the Japanese had come to dominate all of Southeast Asia, the Western Pacific. Everywhere, its forces had crushed its enemies on land and on the sea. It seemed to be a reinforcement of all of those Japanese notions about the quality of their troops, their equipment, and so on.

Now, the Japanese leadership faced crucial choices, and three competing offensive strategies came to the fore. One would be a thrust into the Indian Ocean to move west, where the Japanese navy would wrest control of the sea lanes from Great Britain and the army might even link up with the Germans in the Middle East. The Japanese would foment revolution, rebellion in India, anti-British sentiment there on the rise; could block the Suez Canal; and would bring a greatly weakened Great Britain to its knees.

This was the option that most frightened the Allies in early 1943. Roosevelt and Churchill realized that there was little, in fact virtually nothing, that could be done to prevent a major Japanese assault in the Indian Ocean. And the possibility of a link-up between Nazi Germany—forces coming across North Africa—and the Japanese, coming up through the Indian Ocean, was a nightmare scenario indeed.

Others within the Japanese military, however, were urging instead a continued push to the south, including either an invasion of Australia or at least the seizure of the south coast of New Guinea, especially Port Moresby, and the capture of a number of islands in the South Pacific, such as Fiji and New Caledonia. Such an offensive would serve the great purpose for the Japanese of severing communications between the United States and Australia, making it impossible for the Americans to use Australia as a forward military base for another attack and for an attack on the Japanese new empire.

Finally, as another option, some, especially in the imperial navy and especially Admiral Yamamoto, advocated a strike against the last American outpost in the Pacific. Midway, approximately 600 miles west of Oahu, would be the first target, and then, subsequently, an invasion of the Hawaiian Islands. The Japanese push here would force the American Pacific fleet to come out and fight at a time when it was still weak, and reeling from Pearl Harbor. Yamamoto argued very forcefully in the councils of government that what needed to be done now was to engage the American fleet—engage the Pacific fleet before it could be rebuilt.

Here one also sees the tension between the army—the Japanese army, which was very much in favor of this push south toward New Guinea and Australia—and the Japanese navy. These are tensions that would remain part of a problem for the Japanese high command, the Japanese leadership, throughout the war. Yamamoto argued that an attack against the remaining naval positions of the United States, especially Midway and the Hawaiian Islands, would deal a death blow to America's ability to act in the Pacific and probably force the Americans into some sort of negotiated settlement. What had not been achieved at Pearl Harbor, in other words, would now be made good.

In fact, everything looked ripe for the taking for the Japanese in early 1942, with both the United States and Great Britain very, very much on the ropes. With these options being debated within the high military circles in Japan, no one solution was arrived at; instead, the Japanese sampled, one might say, from each.

First, they toyed with the idea of taking the French colony of Madagascar, off the southeast coast of Africa. The French government, the Vichy government, the collaborationist government, wanted to invite the Japanese to seize the colony so that the British wouldn't take it. The British beat them to it, British troops landing in May. Those British troops encountered fierce resistance from the French. This is, I think one sees now, the legacy of that British attack on the French fleet in North Africa in 1940. It took until November— the British troops landed in May—it took until November before Madagascar was finally in British hands.

The Japanese, meanwhile, had dispatched their main carrier force to the Indian Ocean off Ceylon and only recalled it in April. It was never actually used. They steamed the fleet out—the main carrier fleet out—into the Indian Ocean, threatened the Middle East, threatened India, but then seemed to not know exactly where to proceed with it, and so it was withdrawn.

While considering Yamamoto's plan, thinking about the possibility of a Japanese assault on the Hawaiian Islands, Japanese leaders were jolted by a very, very dramatic and unpleasant surprise. On April 18, 1942, sixteen B-25s, two-engine light bombers, took off from the aircraft carrier Hornet, commanded by Jimmy Doolittle, and attacked Tokyo. It was a daring mission. The planes took off 700 miles from Tokyo. Flying these two-engine light bombers off of a carrier deck was an extraordinary feat, something that I think not only the Japanese didn't think was possible, but I think most American airmen didn't think was possible either. They took off 700 miles from Tokyo; bombed the city and a number of other targets along the way.

The physical damage inflicted by the so-called Doolittle raid was inconsequential, but its psychological impact was profound— profound both in the United States and, of course, in Japan. In its immediate aftermath, Yamamoto called for the development of plans to invade Hawaii and Australia, creating what he called a "ribbon of defense" across the Pacific. If the Americans could launch an attack against the Japanese home islands in this situation in the spring of 1942 when American power was at its absolute low point, what would it be like if the Japanese allowed the Americans to build up their forces? This of course—Yamamoto was constantly emphasizing this in discussions—we must defeat the Americans now, we must defeat the Americans now.

The main objective, then, was to remove the American military presence in the Pacific, and that meant an attack on the Hawaiian Islands and Midway Island, 600 miles to the west. The Japanese plan called for attacks in New Guinea and the Solomon Islands in the South Pacific, in order to cut the flow of men and material to Australia. This was a vital link in the supply lines to Australia, where Douglas MacArthur was building up a significant military force.

The Japanese first thought about putting—seizing—the island of Tulagi, and did so without opposition in May, and then began operations in New Guinea. But on May 7 and May 8, Japanese naval forces encountered American naval units in the Coral Sea. For the Japanese, this was something of a surprise. The U.S. Navy had begun to use the intercepts; we were understanding more and more of the Japanese naval codes, so that we had some indication that the Japanese were moving forces into the Solomon Islands. If they seized— if they were able to establish an air base in—the Solomons, Tulagi, or one of the other islands there, then this was going to really imperil this lifeline to Australia. And so we began to move naval forces there to contest this Japanese action.

The Coral Sea, where these two great naval forces would collide, is a stunningly beautiful body of water—tranquil, strikingly beautiful, more used to seeing trading schooners or Melanesian war canoes than the gray steel of modern warships. Japanese naval forces encountered the Americans on May 7-May 8 of 1942. It would be like no other battle in naval history, for both sides possessed aircraft carriers. The Battle of the Coral Sea became the first great naval action between aircraft carriers; and, revolutionary in what this meant in one sense for naval operations, it was the first naval battle in which no ship actually sighted one from the other side. It was all done with fighter aircraft—aircraft-carrier-based planes. They would inflict all the damage in the engagement. The Japanese lost one heavy and one light carrier; the United States, the heavy carrier the Lexington, and another suffered serious damage, the Yorktown. The battle, in a tactical sense, was pretty much a draw. Both sides took losses, but at the end the Japanese withdrew without attempting a landing at Port Moresby. This was extremely important. Without inflicting a devastating defeat on the Japanese, the strategic goal of blocking the Japanese at this point had been achieved.

May 6 represented the nadir of the American war in the Pacific. At dawn on that date the American garrison at Corregidor had surrendered, and the agonies of the Bataan Death March had begun. But the Battle of the Coral Sea, as it came to be known, on May 7-May 8, seemed like a victory against a foe that until this point had seemed almost invincible. Did it signal a shift in momentum, or a mere detour on Japanese's victory tour of the South Pacific?

The answer to that question would come just one month later, at the Battle of Midway in June of 1942. The Japanese plan was to destroy the U.S. Pacific fleet, especially the carriers that had escaped the Japanese at Pearl Harbor. Only when the Pacific fleet had been eliminated would Japan be really secure. No more Doolittle raids, no more attacks on the home islands; only then would the Japanese position in the South Pacific be secure. The plan, then, was to lure the U.S. fleet out of Pearl Harbor by launching an offensive against the island of Midway. An air fleet of six carriers under Admiral Nagumo, the admiral who had been in charge of the attack on Pearl Harbor, would be followed by the main body, an enormous Japanese fleet that would bear down first on Midway and then on Pearl Harbor and the Hawaiian Islands. Yamamoto's plan called for attacks on Midway, and then, a major invasion front indeed. Submarines would alert the air fleet when the U.S. ships had set sail, then the carriers would jump them, and the main body, the Japanese fleet, would then close and finish off the Americans.

Two light carriers and other ships were sent as a diversion to the Aleutians in the north, in a move that Yamamoto thought the Americans would think, "Ah, here is the end run that we've been worried about. The Japanese are going to take this northern route and then come down the coast, from Alaska down the West Coast." This, I think, made a certain amount of sense at the time, when one considers the hysteria that had broken like a massive wave on the West Coast of the United States after Pearl Harbor—the fear of a Japanese invasion, sightings of Japanese ships, aircraft, and so on. So this force was to be sent into the Aleutians.

The Americans didn't buy this at all. This was in one sense, I think, Yamamoto being too clever by half. It was—and later he would say that he thought this sending of this diversionary group to the Aleutians was a symptom of the victory disease that had inflicted the Japanese high command.

Still, even with this diversionary force headed to the Aleutians, the Japanese possessed enormous superiority in ships and in aircraft. Six aircraft carriers ultimately would be brought to bear by the Japanese in this big fleet against the Americans, versus three for the United States; it would turn out to be one more. 272 aircraft to 180—272 Japanese planes to about 180 American, not to mention the battleships, destroyers, and cruisers of the accompanying force, the main body. That would mean 162 Japanese warships to 76 at the disposal of the United States.

Here, however, Magic came into play. Not black magic, not sleight of hand, but the breaking of the Japanese naval code. Despite the very light radio traffic which had been ordered by Yamamoto, that radio traffic alerted the United States to his plans. It allowed the American carriers to leave Pearl and set up station, out of Midway, undetected by Japanese submarines or by Japanese aircraft.

Still, this was going to be a desperate battle. Even if the code had been broken and we were aware of the Japanese battle plan, this was an enormous Japanese fleet. The stakes could not be higher. If the Japanese succeeded—and even with this intelligence, this was going to be a touchy matter—if the Japanese succeeded, the American position in the Pacific would be untenable indeed.

On June 4, Admiral Nagumo launched his air attack against the island of Midway. They inflicted terrific damage on American forces there. All was going very well. The Japanese fleet had maneuvered into position exactly as it should; the Japanese aircraft carriers dispersed exactly as they should. The first attack had hit poorly defended American positions at Midway. There was a sense as the word came back from the attacking planes to the carrier, and then flashed by code to the main body, that the attack was going just as indeed it was anticipated that it would.

As his bombers were returning from a second strike, which had been ordered—you'll recall the great mistake, and one of the things that Nagumo had been in trouble for with Pearl Harbor—was that there had been this one great launching of the attack, and had not been followed up. Ginda, his air adviser, had pressed for Nagumo to launch a second attack on Pearl Harbor, and he had resisted that temptation. On this day, he would not make the same mistake. He would launch a second strike on the American positions there.

So as his bombers were returning from a second strike against Midway at about 8:45 a.m., positions were picked up. Suddenly, the Japanese spotters began to see aircraft, and they weren't simply the returning aircraft from the Japanese fleet. Unanticipated aircraft. Those aircraft would be the flights from the American carriers, and the Battle of Midway was about to take a very unexpected turn.

Turning the Tide in the Pacific—
Midway and Guadalcanal
Lecture 14

In this lecture, we will proceed to talk about the battle at Midway and then another turning point in the Pacific war, a major one—the first great land battle between Japanese forces and American forces, and that would be the Battle of Guadalcanal.

We will focus first on the crushing defeat of the Imperial Navy at Midway in June 1942, which saved the American position in the Hawaiian Islands and severely damaged Japanese carrier forces. The fortuitous U.S. victory at Midway Island became known as the "Miracle of Midway."

The Japanese planes were preparing for a second assault on Midway on June 4, 1942, when a U.S. air squadron appeared. The U.S. planes were shot down and the Japanese carriers suffered no significant damage. One group of U.S. dive bombers had gotten lost looking for the Japanese carriers. It later found and attacked them at the worst possible moment for the Japanese; three of the four carriers were sunk and the fourth severely damaged. Without the carriers and air cover, the main Japanese force could not press the attack on Midway.

The victory over the Japanese on Guadalcanal was the first land defeat for Japan in the war, and the first serious defeat of the Japanese army.

The Battle of Midway marked a key turning point in the U.S.-Japanese struggle. The outcome shifted the naval balance in the Pacific. It marked the end of Japan's initiative on the high seas. Henceforth the Imperial Navy would be on the defensive. Pearl Harbor was secured for the United States.

The major turning point on land came with the Battle of Guadalcanal, August 1942-February 1943. U.S. forces attacked the Japanese airfield on

Guadalcanal on August 7, beginning a six-month epic struggle that proved to be the longest in the Pacific war.

The U.S. attack was intended to keep the Japanese from securing a foothold in the Solomon Islands, located northeast of Australia. The fighting involved seven naval battles and ten land battles.

The brutal and vicious fighting at Guadalcanal shaped the nature of combat between Japanese and Americans in the Pacific. It marked the first U.S. experience of Japanese suicide attacks. The jungle environment underscored the distinctiveness of warfare in the Pacific theater. Japanese and American propaganda helped to enhance the brutality of the conflict.

Sea battles off the coast—notably at Savo Island in the central Solomons—were extremely costly to both sides. Admiral Halsey took charge of the U.S. fleet. Guadalcanal represented the first defeat for Japan on land and marked a shift in momentum and initiative to the United States. ∎

Suggested Reading

John Costello, *The Pacific War*, Chapters 15–20.

Walter Lord, *Incredible Victory: The Battle of Midway*.

Ronald H. Spector, *Eagle Against the Sun*, Chapters 6–10.

Questions to Consider

1. Why was the Battle of Midway a key turning point in the war in the Pacific?

2. What was new or different about the nature of the fighting on Guadalcanal? How did it affect subsequent U.S.-Japanese warfare in the Pacific?

Turning the Tide in the Pacific—
Midway and Guadalcanal
Lecture 14—Transcript

Hello. Welcome to the fourteenth lecture in our series on the history of the Second World War. We'd concluded our last lecture with the Japanese plans for, and their launching of, their attack on the American installation at Midway.

It was the plan of Admiral Yamamoto—as usual with the admiral, a highly complex plan and a controversial one within the Japanese high command itself. Yamamoto's plan in brief, to recapitulate, was to draw the American fleet out of Pearl Harbor, to engage the Americans at sea—the Americans taking the bait of a Japanese naval assault on the island of Midway—to engage the Americans and finish off the fleet, a job which had not been accomplished as planned at the attack on Pearl Harbor.

This, Yamamoto believed, would drive the Americans out of the war in the Pacific, that it would not be necessary—this was a debate within the Japanese high command, about whether or not it was, it would be—necessary to actually occupy Midway or the Hawaiian Islands. This was not part of the plan for the operation at Midway at this time, but something to be discussed possibly for the future. The real goal was the destruction of the Pacific fleet, at this point, and then hopefully a negotiated settlement with the United States.

In this hour, this lecture, we will proceed to talk about this battle at Midway and then another turning point in the Pacific war, a major one—the first great land battle between Japanese forces and American forces, and that would be the Battle of Guadalcanal.

On June 4, we had stopped with the Japanese Admiral Nagumo launching an air assault against the American installation at Midway. His planes were just returning from that strike and preparing for a second, when, out of the blue, American planes were spotted—enemy planes spotted. They were not supposed to be there. Yamamoto certainly had believed that the carrier

189

Yorktown had been sunk at the Battle of the Coral Sea; he expected at most two aircraft carriers.

Although the planning had been meticulous for this operation, the Japanese submarines that were supposed to monitor the movements of the American fleet had been slow to take up their stations. The assumption on Yamamoto's part and everyone else's—Nagumo's and the others' within the Japanese admiralty—was that the American fleet would venture out of Pearl Harbor only after the attack on Midway. It was the attack on Midway that was to draw the American ships out. Certainly, the Japanese had dispatched spotter planes to search for any movement of the American fleet, but, by the time those planes actually saw evidence that the Pacific fleet had left Pearl Harbor, it was hours after the planes were aloft, and, as we will see, it proved to be too late.

This first attack on Midway—air attack—had been tremendously successful, bringing devastation to the American position there, and the planes were loading up for a second assault. Out of the blue, as we said earlier, suddenly appeared a squadron of American planes. Just where they had come from was not at all obvious. They made one diving pass after another at the Japanese carriers and were simply shot out of the sky. They—it was, for the Japanese, almost like target practice. The American planes were slow, they were vulnerable, they came down in these sort of dive-bombing runs, and were literally shot out of the sky. There were almost no hits. The Japanese, having been surprised, heaved an enormous sigh of relief as these American planes were shot down. Their carriers had not really been hit, not taken any significant damage, but the Japanese fighters that had gone after them had also dropped lower in order to follow the dive bombers; and then what often is referred to as the "Miracle of Midway" occurred.

The American planes had been launched earlier in the day to find the Japanese carriers. One group of dive bombers had gotten lost; had wandered around in the skies over the Pacific looking for the carriers; had been unable to locate them. This was a group from the carrier *Enterprise*.

At just this moment, after this first wave of American—first wave of the attack—had ended in failure but had drawn what Japanese planes were aloft down lower, suddenly the group that had gotten lost suddenly broke into the clear through the clouds, and there was the Japanese naval fleet below them—the carrier fleet below them. They then began to dive onto the Japanese carriers. The decks of the Japanese carriers were cluttered at this point with bombs, gasoline, and planes, stacked up one after the other preparing for takeoff. When the 37 dauntless dive bombers dropped out of the sky and began their attack, it was the absolute worst possible moment for the Japanese position; the worst position to be caught in. And within five minutes, three of the four Japanese carriers were burning and in deep trouble. These planes did not miss their targets, were not shot out of the sky, and the devastation now on the Japanese carrier fleet was unspeakable. The fourth of the Japanese carriers would suffer tremendous damage and would be sunk later on during the course of the day.

It was a catastrophe for the Japanese—an utter catastrophe. The American admiral, Raymond Spruance, had managed his operation with great skill, with great daring himself. He had taken on what was a much larger force, counting on the intelligence of Magic intercepts, and then his own pilots to do their job. It was a remarkable victory.

When the word was passed back to Yamamoto about this disaster, he at this point decided, well, maybe the thing to do was simply to try to make the best of a terrible situation and rush the main force of the fleet forward to encounter the Americans, to go ahead with that part of the operation. But without the air cover, without the carriers, this would have been very, very dangerous indeed. He did press forward a bit, but Admiral Spruance wasn't about to take the bait. Having himself suffered severe damage to one of the carriers, he withdrew. There would be no follow-up.

The great plan of Admiral Yamamoto had come not, as Pearl Harbor had been, to a tactical victory but a strategic—not the strategic knockout blow—now the situation had been reversed. At the end of the Battle of Midway, the Japanese fleet had suffered a terrible loss. The Battle of Midway would shift the naval balance in the Pacific in a single day; in fact, in a five-minute period. It marked the end of Japan's initiative in the high seas. Henceforth, though there would be—the Japanese fleet was still enormously powerful, still a tremendous threat to the United States and its allies—henceforth, the Japanese navy would be largely on the defensive, would be fighting major naval engagements, but at this point the momentum begins to shift, and shift in a very dramatic way—almost exactly in the kind of nightmarish scenario that Yamamoto had himself predicted.

For the Americans, it was a tremendously uplifting victory. Pearl Harbor was now secure. The Japanese had lost four heavy carriers, and they had lost 253 aircraft and their pilots. It was truly a devastating victory, and one in which a numerically much smaller force had defeated a much larger.

If the Battle of Midway marks a major turning point in the naval war in the South Pacific, the Battle of Guadalcanal, coming later in 1942, would be a major turning point of strategic significance fought on land—a battle that would be fought between August of 1942 and February of 1943. This battle would mark the first major engagement between American soldiers and Japanese soldiers. It would have strategic implications. It would have psychological implications as well, as Japanese and American troops encountered one another at close quarters for the first time.

We had discussed, when we were talking about Japanese strategic options, one of the major options endorsed by the Japanese army had been a move south into New Guinea, and possibly toward Australia, to cut off American access to Australia, so that Australia could not be a forward post for American operations in the Pacific. Japanese attention had turned to New Guinea, to Port Moresby in particular. The Japanese wanted airfields, particularly in the Solomon Islands, an obscure chain of islands just off to the east, northeast of Australia. Tulagi had been judged by the Japanese to be unsuitable for the sort of airfield that they needed, but another island, a larger island in the Solomons, one with the unlikely name of Guadalcanal, did seem to be—to offer the possibilities for a major air base.

On July 5, 1942, an American reconnaissance plane reported seeing something unusual. The Japanese were on Guadalcanal, and they were beginning work on what was clearly an airfield. For Admiral King, who was following this—the Americans had been anticipating this, and in fact there was a sort of, there was a race afoot to see who could establish themselves in the Solomons first.

Just looking at the map, this chain of islands, I think when one thinks about the Pacific Theater of operations, you're really talking, for the United States, and for the Japanese, about how does one project power literally across thousands of miles of ocean? How does one do this? We've been talking about these great battles, this great conflict in Europe itself, with the invasion of the Soviet Union by the Germans and this largest military operation in history, with this enormous front that was to go literally from virtually the Baltic down to the Caspian Sea. But here we're talking about distance on a scale unmatched in the history of warfare. How does one actually project power? How do you bring power to bear on a situation 2,000, 3,000, 4,000 miles away?

Looking at the map, a whole series of islands, chains of islands, islands that I suspect virtually nobody could have really knew anything about, very much about, except military planners in the interwar years, suddenly now would become key steppingstones, key strategic positions, which had to be taken.

The Japanese understood what these were; so did we. And as we began to jockey for position to maintain the routes or—from our point of view maintain the routes—or to block them from the Japanese to Australia, the Solomon Islands now become—loom very, very large.

Admiral King, looking at the map, was convinced that we had to do everything possible to prevent the Japanese from establishing this foothold and creating an airfield in the Solomons. He had already begun plans for an assault on Tulagi, but now with the reports from Guadalcanal coming in, all preparations had to be speeded up. An invasion had to take place before the Japanese could complete the airfield. If the airfield on Guadalcanal became operational, then the situation was going to—could—become desperate. The planning, then, for the attack, it was not an improvisation, but this was done in a much more speeded up way than had been anticipated.

The attack was set for August 7, 1942. When the Marines went ashore then, it would begin a six-month-long struggle that comprised seven major naval engagements; at least 10 pitched land battles, skirmishes, and air attacks, that seemed never to stop. When American troops stormed ashore on August 7, 1942, it was the first amphibious assault since 1898 for American forces.

The Battle of Guadalcanal turned into an epic struggle. Fought alongside the great battles of Stalingrad in the East and the battles in North Africa, it marked a major turning point in the war. It was the longest battle in the Pacific conflict, one that would not only have enormous strategic implications, but one that shaped the nature—the nature of combat—and offered a grisly preview of what war in these islands would be like. It would be a struggle of such sheer brutality and viciousness that it rivaled the Russo-German war on the Eastern Front. A war—from the American point of view—a war against an enemy already demonized by coverage of Japanese atrocities in China, a view of—sort of word of mouth. The Bataan Death March did not, as we indicated in an earlier lecture, had not become common knowledge; the details of it were certainly repressed by the American government, but things come out.

The American troops embarking on that invasion of Guadalcanal were already primed; already believed that they were going to face an enemy that was vicious—an enemy that had of course brought on Pearl Harbor, an enemy that was adept in jungle fighting—the Japanese had been fighting in Southeast Asia and so on. These were the evil Japanese, the butchers of Nanking, the masters of jungle warfare—an enemy infamous for atrocities. And, American troops would confront this terrifying enemy in the strange, alien environment of steamy jungles all across the South Pacific.

I want to read you a description of that terrain in the Solomons: "The jungle of the Solomons is the type known as rainforest, indigenous to the larger islands of that general area of the Pacific, notably New Guinea and the Bismarck Archipelago. It is characterized by giant hardwoods, which tower well over a hundred feet into the sky, with boles six and eight feet in diameter flared out at the base by great buttress roots. Among and beneath the trees thrives a fantastic tangle of vines, creepers, ferns, and brush, impenetrable even to the eye for more than a few feet. Exotic birds inhabit its upper regions. The insect world permeates the whole in extraordinary sizes and varieties: ants whose bite feels like a live cigarette against the flesh, improbable spiders, wasps three inches long, scorpions, and centipedes. The animal kingdom is less numerous, represented by species of rats, some distant relatives of the possum, lizards ranging in length from three inches to three feet, a few snakes—mostly of the constrictor type—and some voracious leeches, peculiar in that they live in trees and drop onto the unwary passerby from above. No air stirs here, and the hot humidity is beyond the imagining of anyone who has not lived in it. Rot lies everywhere just underneath the exotic lushness. The ground is porous with decaying vegetation, emitting a sour, unpleasant odor. Substantial-looking trees, rotten to the core, likely to topple over when leaned against, and great forest giants, crash down unpredictably in every windstorm. Freshly killed flesh begins to decompose in a few hours. Dampness, thick and heavy, is everywhere, result of the rains which give the forest its name, unbelievably torrential in season, never ceasing altogether for more than a few days at a time. Mosquitoes, bearers of malaria and a dozen lesser-known fevers, inhabit the broad, deep swamps, which are drained inadequately by sluggish rivers, where dwell giant crocodiles, the most deadly creature of this particular region."

This dramatic description of the conditions understates the case. For the Americans, as well as the Japanese, these conditions were unprecedented. To fight in this—this a theme we're going to return to on a number of occasions as we talk about the war in the Pacific, because we want to talk about why the war in the Pacific seems different. It's almost—it is not only a geographically different war from an American point of view, but the war in the Pacific is fought in a different way than the war in Europe would be fought. One historian has called it a war without rules, as opposed to a war fought in Europe with rules. And part of the reason, one suspects, for this, has to do with the nature of the terrain, this absolutely alien, different, exotic—and I don't mean exotic-interesting but exotic-threatening, terrifying in many ways—environment contributed to it.

That and the fact that so many of these conflicts in these islands in the South Pacific took place literally away from civilization; this is not a sort of culturally value-laden sort of observation, but we're talking about islands where there were very few—maybe a few—scattered villages, no towns, no cities, very little in the way of roads, so that somehow away from civilization, away from anything that the Japanese would recognize as civilization, away from anything the Americans would recognize, put onto an island where you were simply there with your enemy, created—helped to create—an environment in which this desperate sort of struggle would take place.

Some of the most ferocious fighting in the entire Second World War would take place on Guadalcanal. Constant shelling from ships, which ran down what was called the slot, the strip of water between the islands; from aircraft that flew above; from mortars; from snipers; and so on.

The objective of the First Marine Division was to seize the airstrip and hold it. The airstrip was the key. In the attempt to take that airstrip and then to manage it, the American troops would come into conflict with Japanese troops—this we saw for the first time—and their experience was unforgettable.

The enemy, if one reads through—there was a very popular book that was published during the war called *Guadalcanal Diary*, published after the battle, obviously, before the war was over—what's striking about it is, as one reads through the discussions between these young Marines, as they prepare to go into battle with the Japanese, is that they're already primed, they're already primed for a desperate struggle, already thinking that this is an enemy that will give no quarter. They, I think, had, not so much had been, victim of American propaganda about this but a general worldwide sense of the atrocities of the Japanese that we've talked about, that had been covered by the worldwide media—in China, the Rape of Nanking, and so on—and they were ready, they thought, to deal with the Japanese.

But encountering snipers hidden in the jungle, encountering the usual sorts of combat—mortar fire, artillery fire, heavy artillery assaults, only this time naval gunfire—these things were terrifying and horrible, but it was another aspect of the way the Japanese fought. It wasn't just snipers, but we would encounter there the fanatical suicide charges of Japanese troops—the banzai charges—and this made an enormous impression on those Marines who were present. And I would like to read you an account of one.

"The battle"—this is a battle for Bloody Ridge, which was key to defending the airstrip; there's some proper names here; don't worry about them; it's the impression of this conflict that I think one wants to come away with— "Edson's raiders and his troops, American troops, were well placed in their foxholes with machine gun posts covering the ridge on September 12 when the first wave of Kawaguchi's troops came screaming out of the jungle in front of them, just after 9 p.m., in an attack that was timed to coincide with the arrival of supporting fire from the destroyers on the Sound. It was a combined sea and land attack, with Japanese naval units standing off the coast and lobbing shells directly over the ridge and into the jungle beyond, in the general direction of Colonel Edson's outfit." This was written by William McKinnon, another American soldier who was there. From his battalion's position covering the river flank of the airfield, he saw the opening night's battle of what came to be called Bloody Ridge.

The Marines, holding the front line, knew that with the Japanese withdrawal into the jungle at dawn, the night attack had "been nothing but a prelude." They had made only a limited counterattack which merely flushed a few snipers out of the trees. As the sun went down that evening, the stirrings of new activity could be heard over the course of jungle insects and the screech of cockatoos. Ordered to move forward because the situation up front was threatening, McKinnon advanced toward the ridge. His outfit, which had had no sleep for nearly two days, stumbled, groping their way forward to a new position in the darkness. The crunch of mortar shells heralded the beginning of that night's assault.

Suddenly, the jungle came alive with the Japanese yelling obscenities and banzais, and hurling firecrackers. This was "a special brand of terrorism," as the colonel described it. The sky and the jungle were blazing with fireworks and a hellish bedlam of howls. Firecrackers, a cheap imitation of machine guns, exploded in front of, in, and behind their position. Parachute flares that burned brightly for an instant, bobbed along, then went out—lighted the scene intermittently. From the jungle below came the rhythmic accompaniment of the slapping of gun butts and the chant, "U.S. Marines be dead tomorrow. U.S. Marines be dead tomorrow." The chanting became a mad religious rite, which heralded a series of frenzied banzai charges through the pouring rain, as the darkness was broken by the flashes of gunfire and the eerie green glare of the Japanese flares.

For a time, Edson's battalion holding out on the top of Bloody Ridge was cut off, until McKinnon's men drove back assaults with machine guns. When one wave was mowed down—and I mean mowed down—another one followed it into death.

These—this sort of behavior in combat, the chanting in the darkness of the jungle, followed by these banzai charges across the terrain, where their enemies would just be mowed down; the Japanese soldiers didn't seem to have any real hope of actually overwhelming the American position—left the Marines staggered, just completely bewildered, and utterly convinced that they were fighting an enemy of such fanaticism that they weren't quite human; that there was no explanation for this sort of thing, that the attack on the airfield, which would come—another attack on the airstrip the next day, after the little scene we've just described, led once again to, in the following morning—literally of the American troops going out and finding Japanese bodies stacked up where they had fallen during the course of the evening. It didn't seem to some of the Marines as if the point for the Japanese was actually to take the airstrip at this point, but rather it was the attack itself that seemed to be of importance. For American troops, it was to be the beginning of the long, agonizing encounter with the Japanese—the beginning of this epic struggle between American forces in the Pacific and the Japanese.

Not only on land was Guadalcanal important. There were a number of naval battles that took place off the coast: Savo Island in August, which was a Japanese victory; the Battle of the Central Solomons; Cape Esperance in October, fought at night—the Japanese navy was very adept at nighttime operations, had really pioneered them—the naval Battle of Guadalcanal itself, November 13 to November 15; and a number of others. So many ships were sunk in the close waterways off Guadalcanal that the area was dubbed "Iron Bottom Sound."

Finally, in February, unable to dislodge the Americans or to retake the airfield, the Japanese effected a very skillful evacuation of the island, and by February 9, Guadalcanal was entirely in American hands. This conflict—and actually taking these two conflicts together, the battle at Midway and this epic struggle at Guadalcanal—mark a major turning point in the Second World War in the Pacific.

The victory over the Japanese on Guadalcanal was the first land defeat for Japan in the war, and the first serious defeat of the Japanese army. It marks the beginning of—certainly not so much a Japanese withdrawal; their position is still very strong in the Pacific and they would fight to defend it tenaciously over the next months and years—but just as Midway marked the beginning of a shift in momentum of initiative to the United States, so too did Guadalcanal. This, then, was not—as Churchill said about the situation in Europe, one could also say about the South Pacific—this wasn't the beginning of the end, but perhaps the end of the beginning.

The War in North Africa
Lecture 15

In this lecture, what I would like to do is to talk about Axis strategy—German and Italian strategy in North Africa—what the Mediterranean Theater meant to Mussolini, to Hitler; to pose the question that is often raised when one analyzes German policy during the war is—was the Mediterranean Theater an opportunity, the Middle East an opportunity, lost for the Germans, a strategic opportunity that Hitler did not fully appreciate?

The Mediterranean Theater was a sideshow for Hitler, who was mainly concerned with subduing the Soviet Union. Hitler sought alliances with Spain, Vichy France, and Italy to put pressure on British positions in the Mediterranean, but without success. Neither Franco nor the Vichy regime nor Mussolini was a reliable German military ally. Hitler avoided direct military involvement in the Mediterranean.

Mussolini, by contrast, had important ambitions in the Mediterranean. Perceiving British weakness, he was determined to conquer Egypt and Greece and reestablish the Roman Empire. He did not coordinate his actions with Hitler.

Mussolini's disastrous Egyptian campaign (1940) prompted Hitler's intervention and the creation of the Afrika Korps under the command of General Erwin Rommel. Rommel forced the British back into Egypt but failed to dislodge them from Tobruk. By late May the German offensive bogged down. Meanwhile, a pro-German coup in Iraq led to British intervention in April 1941. British and Free French troops moved into Syria in June 1941, where they fought Vichy troops.

Hitler's vision was European rather than global. Even if he had been inclined to seize available opportunities in North Africa and the Middle East, any effort to assert German power there would have faced significant obstacles. Tripoli was very far from Alexandria and had limited port facilities, both of which posed logistical problems. Because only one east-west road ran along the North African coast, it would have been hard to engage in broad flanking movements or move supplies. Logistical and supply problems made it hard to sustain huge military operations; much of the fighting went back and forth over the same territory. Britain's ability to resupply its troops in Egypt swung the tide in its favor during 1942.

Montgomery and Rommel fought a desert war during 1941 and 1942. Rommel pushed the British forces westward toward Egypt, but the fighting deadlocked along the Egyptian border in May 1942. By late June, German forces had pushed deep into Egypt. Victory in the first battle of El Alamein (July 1942) seemed to be within Rommel's reach, but he failed to sustain the offensive due to supply problems. Meanwhile, British supplies poured into Egypt.

In August 1942 Churchill appointed Gen. Harold Alexander to command British forces in the North African theater, and he chose Gen. Bernard Montgomery to command the British Eighth Army. At the second battle of El Alamein (October 23, 1942), Montgomery attacked with huge superiority. Although the British suffered extensive casualties, Hitler refused to reinforce Rommel. Finally, in November 1942 Rommel retreated back into Libya.

Having suffered such colossal casualties in the First War, the British commanders … did not want to see another bloodbath on that scale.

The Allied camp was divided by conflicts over strategy. The Americans pressed for a cross-channel invasion in 1942 or 1943 at the latest, and for strategic and political reasons they resisted British interest in a Mediterranean strategy. American officials feared that a North Africa operation would divert Allied strength from the cross-channel invasion. They were wary of supporting British colonial interests. They were concerned about a possible Russian collapse and heedful of Stalin's demands for a second front. In March 1942 the Americans proposed Operation Roundup to build up forces in Britain for the cross-channel invasion, and Operation Sledgehammer (a smaller landing in France during 1942) to mollify the Russians.

The British supported a cross-channel operation in principle but sought to delay it past 1942. They raised various practical objections to the U.S. plans. The logistical base for the invasion was not yet prepared. Churchill was convinced that Britain could not survive another major defeat. The British questioned the battle-worthiness of American troops, who had not yet engaged in armed conflict.

The disastrous outcome of the small British raid at Dieppe in August 1942 convinced the British that they were not yet ready for a large-scale invasion of the continent. Churchill advocated an invasion of French North Africa while the buildup for the cross-channel operation moved forward. Churchill and his staff

Gen. Dwight D. Eisenhower, supreme commander of Allied forces in western Europe during World War II (and U.S. president from 1953 to 1961).

emphasized the need to stretch German resources by attacking around the periphery of Hitler's Fortress Europe—North Africa, Greece, and Italy.

Churchill convinced FDR that French North Africa was the only reasonable area for action during 1942. This operation, begun in November 1942, was code-named Operation Torch. The British position carried the day and the Allied invasion of French North Africa was launched. General Eisenhower was placed in command of Operation Torch, but General Alexander and the British staff dominated planning. The Allied forces would land in the west and then march eastward to Tunisia. Mistrustful of DeGaulle, the Allies turned to Gen. Henri Giraud to led the Free French forces.

Although Allied forces bogged down in Tunisia, squabbled among themselves, and suffered a serious defeat at the Kassirene Pass, they amassed great strength by early 1943. Meanwhile, Hitler failed to reinforce Rommel until it was too late. By March 1943 the Allies had driven the Germans from North Africa. As the Americans had feared, however, the success of Torch caused a delay in the cross-channel invasion of northern Europe. ∎

Suggested Reading

Carlo D'Este, *World War II in the Mediterranean, 1942–1945*.

John Keegan, *The Second World War*, Chapters 17–18.

Questions to Consider

1. Why did North Africa and the Middle East represent a missed opportunity for Hitler? What factors militated against German military success in that region?

2. Describe the Anglo-American debate over Allied strategy in 1942 and 1943, and evaluate its outcome.

The War in North Africa
Lecture 15—Transcript

The year 1942 and the beginning of 1943 mark, as we've seen, in the Pacific, a major turning point in the war. We've talked about the German halt before Moscow. I'd like to turn our attention in this, our fifteenth lecture, to the war in North Africa. It is a complicated and, I think for Americans in particular, particularly puzzling theater of operations to understand, especially from 1940 down to Operation Torch in 1942, when the United States enters the war, because of the back and forth nature of the war between the Italians first, Germans, and then the British.

In this lecture, what I would like to do is to talk about Axis strategy—German and Italian strategy in North Africa—what the Mediterranean Theater meant to Mussolini, to Hitler; to pose the question that is often raised when one analyzes German policy during the war is—was the Mediterranean Theater an opportunity, the Middle East an opportunity, lost for the Germans, a strategic opportunity that Hitler did not fully appreciate? We want to examine, too, the British view of the Middle East and the centrality of a Mediterranean strategy for Churchill and the British high command; the conflicts that this brought the British into with the United States, their new allies in 1942; and the implications of Operation Torch and our involvement, the Western Allies' involvement, in the Mediterranean.

Hitler's original strategy after the fall of France had been to bring pressure on Britain from a number of different angles. He had hoped that he would be able to lure Franco's Spain, Vichy France, and Italy into a firm alliance which could then put pressure on the British in the Mediterranean.

Hitler himself did not want to commit significant resources in the Mediterranean. He never thought it was a terribly important theater for Germany. For him, as we've seen, the Soviet Union was the major target, and anything that distracted him from that was a mistake. But, he hoped that some combination of the Spanish, the Vichy French, the Italians, would be able to put pressure on British colonial possessions, the British position in the Middle East and the Mediterranean.

He certainly tried to craft some sort of workable strategic alliance with these Mediterranean powers, but without success. Franco was a great source of frustration to Hitler. The Nazis had supported Franco during the Spanish Civil War. Franco certainly talked the game of solidarity with Mussolini and with Hitler, but Hitler made a trip to the Spanish frontier to negotiate with Franco in 1940, and, as Hitler would later say, "It was like chewing rocks to deal with Franco." Franco would agree with everything in principle, but then raise so many practical objections that Hitler was completely frustrated. Franco, for example, wanted German support for the seizure of Gibraltar. He wanted French colonies in North Africa, Morocco, Algeria, and French West Africa. Hitler was completely unwilling to enter into this, because this would run him afoul of the French, whose support he also wanted, with Petain and so on. Hitler was reluctant to agree to Spanish designs on French colonies, and the negotiations ended without result.

Hitler still hoped to—for some sort of cooperation from—the French, some sort of German-Vichy alliance, but the French were not at this point prepared for any sort of genuine military alliance with Germany. Mussolini certainly was, but he was surprisingly uncooperative when it came to the details. He had the unpleasant habit of springing surprises on his alliance partner, something that Hitler reciprocated with far greater implications. But the Axis, the pact of steel, the Mussolini-Hitler alliance was—this was largely a public relations relationship rather than a strong, well-crafted, military alliance. Indeed, Mussolini would ultimately draw Hitler into the Mediterranean, but not to achieve German objectives, but rather to help Mussolini achieve his in the area. In the end, the Germans committed far more energy in Africa than Hitler ever anticipated, but it still would fall short of strategic decisiveness.

Italy's African policy deserves a certain amount of attention here. Mussolini was determined in 1940 to take advantage of what he perceived to be British weakness. He believed, as did Hitler, that Britain was finished, so he decided that what he wanted to do was to conquer both Egypt and Greece. We've talked about the implications of his invasion of Greece. His Egyptian campaign was launched in 1940. Mussolini was enthusiastic about it; tried to drum up support domestically for it. His military high command was not at all enthusiastic about going to war in 1940 against Great Britain. And the British—although the Italians were talking about invasion, the British caught the Italians by surprise in December of 1940, and disaster would follow disaster. The British took 45,000 prisoners in one operation in December. In January, in another, they took 45,000 Italian prisoners. Later in the month, they encircled Tobruk, an important port city, and another 30,000 Italians surrendered. Twenty thousand more followed in February. Over 130,000 Italians surrendered, while Great Britain suffered fewer than 2,000 casualties in the course of 1940 and into 1941 in their operations against the Italians. This is what prompted that famous quote that we've already mentioned before of Anthony Eden's, about, "Never has so much been surrendered by so many to so few."

At this juncture, with the British on the offensive against the Italians, what was supposed to be an Italian operation to seize the initiative in the Mediterranean, of course, backfires. The British now, unable to move anywhere else, go onto the offensive themselves, and Hitler now feels compelled to draw—to enter—the fray. By the end of May 1941, Britain controlled virtually all of Italian East Africa, while reconquering French and British Somaliland. At this point, Hitler decided to intervene. He dispatched Erwin Rommel in February of 1941 to save the situation—in '42 rather—to save the situation. He was reluctant to throw significant resources into North Africa, but the Italian fiasco had to be brought under control.

Rommel was sent to Libya in charge of a small armored force—it was actually one armored division and one mechanized division—and that force, which was called the Afrika Korps, would dramatically change the complexion of the North African campaign. Rommel had barely arrived, all his troops weren't even yet in place, when he lashed out at the British, forcing them all the way back into Egypt; actually capturing the British General O'Connor. He was unable to dislodge the British from Tobruk, whose port he needed for supplies, and so by late May the offensive had ground to a halt. A deadlock now existed along the Egyptian frontier, and there was a pause in the hostilities.

But even as the hostilities slowed along that front, the war would spread across the Middle East like a desert sandstorm. In Iraq, a pro-German coup led to British intervention in April of 1941. The British sent troops, forced the new—pro-German Rashid Ali to flee to Iran, and restored a friendly, pro-

British government in Baghdad. Britain also was concerned that the Germans might land troops in Syria, and so British and Free French troops—troops loyal not to Vichy but to the government of Charles De Gaulle in London—moved into Syria in June, where they fought against stiff resistance from French troops loyal to Vichy. By the end of the month, all of the eastern Mediterranean was in British hands, but Rommel, with his understaffed and underequipped Afrika Korps, continued to be a serious concern.

The dilemma for German strategy was that for Hitler the Mediterranean had always been intended to be a sideshow. The main preparations being made militarily were for the invasion of the Soviet Union. He was not interested in North Africa or in the Mediterranean. This is where, I think, one sees in Hitler his limitations. One always thinks about Hitler being this sort of megalomaniac determined to dominate the world, constantly seeking ways to expand. His policies were certainly very radical, and the New Order that he hoped to achieve in Europe was certainly very radical. But in the way he deals in the Mediterranean, I think one sees in Hitler a traditional European, and particularly German, statesman. He simply, I think, never fully appreciated the strategic implications of the Middle East and was very reluctant to seize the opportunities presented to him.

One of the debates raised frequently by German generals after the war, thinking back about mistakes from the war, was to pose the question, could Germany have prevailed if Hitler had been willing to devote the necessary forces to North Africa? Seize the Suez Canal, for example, and take the Middle Eastern oil fields. Part of—the whole last part of the war, Germany would be desperate to find sources of oil, to secure sources of oil. This would have cut the British off from their links to the empire—made the linkages between the war in Asia and Europe tenuous at best for the British—and so these were real possible opportunities.

However, while it is quite true that Hitler's perspective, his vision, was continental and European, rather than thinking in larger global terms, or even in this theater of the Mediterranean close to Europe, there were other problems, I think, that would have made it extremely difficult for Germany to have asserted itself in the Middle East. One was the very real problem of logistics. The logistical problems make it doubtful whether any sort of

German strategy in the Middle East would have been successful. Tripoli, the only major Axis port in North Africa, was 1,300 miles from Alexandria in Egypt—1,300 miles—over twice the distance from the prewar Polish border to Moscow. So we're talking enormous, an enormous distance. Tripoli also had a limited capacity as a port. It couldn't have supported a major effort. Other ports to the east were also too small, and coastal shipping for both the Italians and Germans was in short supply. In addition, as one visualizes this combat across North Africa, there aren't huge flanking movements; this is a war of movement in a very narrow band. There was a single road that ran along the coast that moved from west to east. There was the Qattara Depression, which limited much of the movement to this territorial band close to the coast. So what you have is—it was very, very difficult to move supplies without those supplies coming under attack. Finally, British naval and air forces operating from Malta continued to harass any sort of supply efforts coming from Italy.

The problems of supply so hampered the armies, both Axis armies and Allied armies, in '40-'41 that they operated essentially almost as expeditionary forces. This problem of supply, of logistics, made it extremely difficult to sustain operations, so that much of the fighting in this theater tended to be back and forth, with the same territory between port cities being taken by the one side, then taken by another, back and forth, as they struggled with problems of water, oil, spare parts, and ammunition, so that it was very difficult to sustain the enormous operations that one saw elsewhere.

In 1941-42, then, there would be a major swing of fortune in the Middle East. It would be the British ability to resupply their forces in Egypt that ultimately would turn the tide in North Africa and the coast in the course of 1942. Rommel had initiated a new round of fighting in May of 1942, when he unleashed a new offensive. He followed the usual pattern until late in the month, when German troops took Tobruk, the important port city, inflicting terrible casualties on the British. In the process, they captured vast quantities of fuel, food, and drinking water. They also took 35,000 British prisoners. It was a tremendous victory for Rommel. He renewed the offensive again, and by late June, the Afrika Korps had thrust deeply into Egypt. By June 30, German troops had reached El Alamein, only 60 miles west of Alexandria.

Victory, at this point, seemed within Rommel's grasp, and Hitler rewarded him by promoting him to the position of field marshal.

The first battle of El Alamein, the gateway to Alexandria, in July, ended with the British holding firm but unable to push the Germans back, and so the old pattern returned, supplies being the key. The Germans simply couldn't sustain the offensive; they couldn't continue to push. The British at this point began to receive supplies. Supplies began to pour into Egypt, including American Sherman tanks, which began to arrive in large number for the British forces.

The RAF strengthened its forces, and Churchill decided to shake up the staff after the embarrassments of the previous month. In mid-August, he relieved his commander in North Africa and replaced him with General Harold Alexander, who would become a major figure for the British military during the rest of the course of the war. He was to command the entire theater.

And another equally important—in fact, probably more important—appointment that was made at this time was that General Bernard Montgomery was chosen to the lead the British Eighth Army. Montgomery was the son of an Anglican bishop. Militarily, he was a meticulous planner and a cautious campaigner. He would be the master of the so-called set piece, never wanting to move until he had all of his ducks in a row. He was tremendously popular with his troops. The Americans always thought that he drug his feet, was too slow, didn't seize the opportunities that were presented to him, but for British troops, "Monty" was seen as a great hero because he seemed to care about them. He didn't move until he had overwhelming superiority and was virtually assured of success. He was flamboyant; certainly the campaign in North Africa would see the emergence of two of the most flamboyant personalities and titanic egos of the Second World War, leaving Rommel aside. It would be the emergence of General Patton for the United States and, of course, Montgomery for the British.

Montgomery attacked with overwhelming force in October of 1942 in the Second Battle of El Alamein, on October 23, 1942. When he did, his forces outnumbered Rommel's 230,000 to 80,000. Armor: 1,500 British tanks, many of them American, to 500 German tanks; air superiority; and the role of Ultra, the intelligence intercepts, so that the British were able to determine when supplies were coming across from Italy, the German convoys were attacked in the Mediterranean, and Montgomery was able to anticipate Rommel's moves.

In the Second Battle of El Alamein, in October of 1942, a battle that would mark a important turning point, the British suffered terrible casualties, losing four times the number of tanks as the Germans, but Rommel couldn't take even these losses. Hitler, meanwhile, refused significant reinforcements. Rommel was constantly pressing—"We need help, we need help, we need help"—and there was very little help coming from Germany at this time, in part because of German involvement in the Soviet Union.

By November, Rommel was in retreat. That retreat proved to be a masterpiece and, combined with Montgomery's caution, allowed the Germans to escape back into Libya. So the question now was, was this going to be the beginning—was this really a turning point? Were the British now going to take the initiative and really drive the Germans out of North Africa? The Americans were now in the war; what was our role to be? And how would the Germans respond?

The American and British military—we'll talk about this more when we talk about D-Day—the British and the American military had begun common staff talks, planning. Roosevelt and Churchill were in agreement from the very outset, even before the American entry into the war. Should we come into the war, we both agreed that it would be a Europe-first strategy; Germany was the greater threat. But, having said this, there were significant differences between the American and the British assessment of the immediate strategic priorities. American leaders, particularly General Marshall and Secretary of War Stimson, shared the Russian view, which was that a second front was needed in northern Europe, and needed immediately. There was terrific fear in the Allied camp that the Russians were going to collapse, with a new German offensive again in the spring of 1942. Marshall, Stimson, most of the American commanders involved in common staff talks with the British, advocated a cross-channel invasion as soon as possible—at best in 1942, at worst in the following year.

The British, on the other hand, took a far more cautious approach. At the Arcadia Conference in December of 1941, the first wartime meeting between Churchill and Roosevelt, Churchill had broached the possibility of an Allied landing in French North Africa. He was putting forward, putting on the table with the Americans, a Mediterranean strategy. It would send Allied troops into Morocco, Algeria, and Tunisia. They would then press eastward toward Libya, catching the Germans in a vise—Montgomery and his troops moving from the east, the American and British force moving from the west.

Following the Arcadia Conference, the American military grew restive about Churchill's proposals. Marshall, Stimson, and General Dwight Eisenhower, chief of the War Department's operation division, all agreed that a North African operation would divert strength away from a buildup in England that was necessary for the cross-channel invasion. The Americans developed an alternative plan in March of 1942, Operation Roundup. The Allies, the Americans argued, should begin an immediate buildup of forces in Great Britain for a cross-channel invasion no later than the spring of 1943. In the meantime, they contended, a smaller landing in France could be made during the course of 1942, relieving some of the pressure on the Soviet Union. This would make Stalin happy. And this operation, this more modest cross-channel invasion to come in '42, was to be code-named Operation Sledgehammer.

Marshall was dispatched to London to convince the British that this was the proper course of action, and there he encountered terrific resistance. The British army chief of staff, Alan Brooke, who had been at Dunkirk, a veteran of the First War, began a policy—one sees this now in these inter-Allied relations—the British would always agree, "Yes, absolutely, we must have the cross-channel invasion. Of course, that's what we're pointing toward, the cross-channel invasion. This is the big show." So they would agree in principle, but then said, "Well, let's evaluate the situation. What's available to us as we look at the situation now?"

Brooke would say, "Well, there's a shortage of troops." This was undoubtedly the case at this point; the American army was not mobilized for a big cross-channel invasion at this point. There was a shortage of equipment, particularly landing craft. This hurt the Germans, now, Brooke argued, we have to be ready to do this as well.

He never actually made it crystal—well, he never made it explicit, but it was crystal clear that there was also a great deal of skepticism among the British high command about the battle-worthiness of the American troops—that the Americans were green. There was a lot of enthusiasm coming from Marshall and the American leadership about closing with the Germans, but the British had had a lot of experience dealing with the Germans, and none of their encounters had been very pleasant.

All the way through—also, I think, this is another point that we will certainly talk to as we talk about the background to Operation Overlord and D-Day—having suffered such colossal casualties in the First War, the British commanders, all of whom were—the most important ones had been— veterans of the First War, did not want to see another bloodbath on that scale. Also, the idea of launching an invasion prematurely, which might lead to failure—the British could not afford another failure at this point; Churchill felt that very, very keenly—the Americans might be full of vim and vigor about this, just chomping at the bit to get into the fray, but for Britain another defeat could not be tolerated.

In August of 1942, the Allies would launch the Dieppe raid on the coast—a cross-channel, a small raid—largely with Canadian troops, with 6,000 casualties. It was a disaster. And so, the British once again could say, "Well, we don't have this down yet. We're not ready." Brooke had no trouble convincing Churchill, who then urged Roosevelt to adopt the original plan for invasion of French North Africa. Roosevelt was swayed. Marshall was furious by this. The British strategy seemed to smack of British colonialism— defending the empire—this was something that didn't play very well in the United States. But Roosevelt abandoned Operation Sledgehammer and insisted on action nonetheless in 1942, and the only reasonable place for that action was in French North Africa.

The result was Operation Torch. It would be the first Allied joint venture. The man chosen to lead Operation Torch was Dwight Eisenhower. He was a staff officer par excellence. He had served twice as assistant to MacArthur. His real skills were in planning and organization and logistics. That recommended him, certainly, to the war plans division, where he had served since 1941. But it was as much, as important as those skills were, I think it was as much his personal and political skills that particularly recommended him to Roosevelt and others for this Allied command. He was a team player, a man capable of subordinating his own ego to the situation. He was adept at cooperation, and he possessed, by virtually everybody's description, great personal magnetism. Montgomery, who had more than his share of run-ins with Eisenhower over the course of the next few years, would describe him in this way: he said that Ike had, "the power of drawing the hearts of men toward him as a magnet attracts bits of metal. He merely has to smile at you and you trust him at once."

The plan was for Allied landings at Casablanca in Morocco, Oran and Algiers in Algeria, then to sweep eastward toward Tunisia. By landing so far to the west, the Allies were out of German airspace, the British argued, but it would mean a very long campaign. The key to this was how the French would respond. There were 200,000 French troops in Morocco and Algeria, presumably loyal to the Vichy regime. The French army and navy were loyal to Vichy. They harbored strong anti-British feelings as a result of the action we've described, and so it was decided that it would be best if the United States, rather than the British, led this operation.

There was also a problem with General De Gaulle. How would one deal with him? There was a good deal of anti-De Gaulle sentiment in the French military. They saw him as someone who had abandoned ship. He was hardly popular with the French military. The Allies didn't completely trust him, either. They considered him to have little support in metropolitan France or in French North Africa, and we feared leaks from De Gaulle's headquarters. Therefore, the Allies passed over De Gaulle and turned to General Henri Giraud, whom they smuggled out of southern France to be the new, handpicked leader of Free France.

The Allies may have recognized Giraud, but this infuriated De Gaulle. A compromise was finally worked out between the two of them. The Machiavellian details of this defy description. Needless to say that within a matter of months De Gaulle had outmaneuvered his opponent at every turn and would emerge in full control of the committee that would ultimately dominate French policy in North Africa.

The German response to Torch was to pour troops into Tunisia. I might say, the French did resist the invasion; there were 7,000 French causalities in the Allied invasion of French North Africa.

The Allies, having made a successful landing in November, found themselves bogged down in Tunisia. There was inter-Allied friction. Eisenhower was certainly under a great deal of pressure. The American troops did not perform with great distinction. In fact, in the first encounter with the Germans at the Kasserine Pass, the Americans had virtually collapsed—a fiasco. There began to be talk about replacing Eisenhower with General Alexander, who was now, in fact, placed in charge of field operations. But Eisenhower remained in position, named a new commander for the United States Army's Second Corps, General George Patton, and restored morale and discipline within the American forces.

By March of 1943, Great Britain and the United States had amassed great strength and began the final push toward victory. Rommel was unable to get resupplied; Hitler refused to the very end to see the potential of the Afrika Korps and too late—too late—began to try to reinforce it. Only after the Allies had already established a dominant position did Hitler attempt to reverse the situation.

The Germans had failed to hold North Africa. Operation Torch had succeeded. But from the American point of view—and we'll close with this—from the American point of view, it wasn't the worst-case scenario that they feared, it was the best-case scenario—because the very success of Operation Torch meant that there would be not only no cross-channel invasion in 1942, but also, they feared, none in 1943 either.

War in the Mediterranean—
The Invasions of Sicily and Italy
Lecture 16

We'll be examining the Allied invasions of Sicily and Italy, the campaign in Italy, the strategic debates between the Allies over the proper course of action in dealing with the Germans in Italy, the extent to which Italy was responsible for a delay in the cross-channel invasion, and just exactly what the implications of this enormous operation would be.

This lecture deals primarily with Operation Husky—the Allied campaign in Sicily and the subsequent invasion of Italy in September 1943. The Sicilian invasion—vehemently advocated by the British— was a logical extension of the Allied victory in North Africa. As U.S. commanders had feared, it locked them into a Mediterranean strategy for which they had little enthusiasm, and it forced postponement of the cross-channel invasion.

Eisenhower was again named commander-in-chief, but British General Alexander remained actual field commander. The Italians put up weak resistance to the Allied invaders, although German forces under Kesselring resisted impressively. Mass surrenders of Italian troops were common.

Generals Patton and Montgomery raced toward Palermo. Patton won the race after German resistance slowed Montgomery. Both generals subsequently raced toward Messina. Although Patton became a hero in the United States, he was subsequently removed from command for slapping two soldiers whom he had accused of cowardice.

The Allied victory in Sicily had important consequences. It drew the United States deeper into Churchill's Mediterranean strategy. Churchill renewed his emphasis on the "soft underbelly" of Europe—Italy, the Balkans, and Turkey. The Americans remained skeptical about this Mediterranean focus but had no alternative plans. The collapse of Sicily and the prospect of an Allied invasion of Italy led to Mussolini's fall from power on July 24, 1943.

A new government headed by Marshal Badoglio took power in Rome, while the Germans installed Mussolini as head of a puppet state in northern Italy.

The Italian campaign began with the Allied invasion of mainland Italy on September 3, 1943. Bowing to U.S. demands, General Badoglio's government surrendered. Hitler rushed troops to northern Italy and the area around Rome under General Kesselring.

The Allies launched the following three-pronged assault.

- British forces under Montgomery crossed the Straits of Messina and landed in the "toe" of Italy.

- Another British force stormed ashore at Taranto.

- U.S. and British troops under General Mark Clark landed south of Naples at Salerno. The near-failure of the U.S. landing reinforced doubts about the ability of American troops to make amphibious landings—and about the upcoming cross-channel invasion.

It's certainly true that American troops lacked combat experience in 1943. It is also true that German defenses were a great deal stronger in northern Europe in 1944 than they had been in 1943.

Italy proved to be anything but a "soft underbelly." The British seized the Italian air base at Foggia. The harsh Italian terrain worked to the advantage of the German defenders. The fighting in Italy was among the most arduous experienced in the war. In late 1943 the slow Allied advance halted at the "Gustav Line" some 100 miles south of Rome. The front stabilized in January 1944, making it possible theoretically for the Allies to shift troops from Italy to Britain for the cross-channel invasion.

In an effort to break the deadlock in Italy, Allied troops made an amphibious landing at Anzio (30 miles south of Rome) on January 22, 1944. The

American invasion force failed to drive inland rapidly and seal off the Germans in southern Italy; the Americans were again bogged down.

In February, Allied planes bombed the monastery of Monte Cassino. After several months of fierce German resistance, Polish troops finally captured Monte Cassino in May 1944. At about the same time, American forces broke out of Anzio. Instead of driving east to cut off the German retreat from the Gustav Line, Allied troops moved north to liberate Rome on June 4, 1944. Kesselring did not contest the city but instead withdrew north to the "Gothic Line."

The First Canadian Division.

The Italian campaign had many important effects, outcomes, and implications. For one, the campaign held down 20 German divisions. For another, throughout the effort, Allied progress was slow, costly, and destructive. Additionally, the campaign did not satisfy Stalin's demand for a second front against the Axis.

Detractors were convinced that the Italian operations delayed the cross-channel invasion. Could a major cross-channel offensive have been launched in 1943? As the British argued, German submarines in the channel still posed a major threat in 1943; the Allies lacked available landing craft and troops; and U.S. troops lacked combat experience. But sufficient landing craft and ships were available in the Pacific, and German defenses in northern Europe were stronger in 1944 than in 1943. German submarine strength and lack of Allied air superiority probably precluded a cross-channel invasion during 1943. ■

W. G. F. Jackson, *The Battle for Italy.*

John Keegan, *The Second World War*, Chapter 19.

Questions to Consider

1. What were the strategic implications and political consequences of the Allied invasions of Sicily and the Italian peninsula?

2. Was the Italian campaign responsible for the Allies' failure to launch a cross-channel invasion in 1943, as American war planners had feared?

War in the Mediterranean—
The Invasions of Sicily and Italy

Lecture 16—Transcript

In the spring of 1943, the Allies had emerged victorious from major campaigns in the South Pacific and in North Africa. They now confronted strategic options, and in the European Theater this was largely an option between pressing for a cross-channel invasion at some point in 1943 or some sort of alternative. The American position was for a cross-channel invasion as soon as possible, a position vigorously reinforced by Stalin, who continued to demand the second front, the second front, the second front—North Africa, in Stalin's view, did not constitute the second front.

The other option was an invasion of Sicily and Italy. That position was vehemently put forward by the British, and it is that option that we are going to be taking up in this, our sixteenth lecture. We'll be examining the Allied invasions of Sicily and Italy, the campaign in Italy, the strategic debates between the Allies over the proper course of action in dealing with the Germans in Italy, the extent to which Italy was responsible for a delay in the cross-channel invasion, and just exactly what the implications of this enormous operation would be.

In many respects, an invasion across the coast to Sicily from North Africa was a logical extension of the victory over German and Italian troops in North Africa. Indeed, the American commanders, as we've seen, had been deeply concerned from the very outset, not about the defeat, a defeat in North Africa, but just the opposite. What would be the implications of Allied success in North Africa? What if Operation Torch were launched and were successful? Then, Marshall, Eisenhower, and other American commanders feared, the United States would be drawn irrevocably into a Mediterranean strategy for which they had very little political enthusiasm, as it might be seen as supporting British colonialism; or military enthusiasm, since, the view was, an invasion of North Africa, if it's successful, will mean a postponement of the cross-channel invasion. And indeed, with the defeat of Rommel and the Afrika Korps, the Germans in North Africa, this is precisely the quandary in which the Allies found themselves. By the success in North

Africa, which came only in January-February 1943 and into the spring, a cross-channel invasion was impossible in that year.

Now, then, the option was to cross into Sicily. Operation Husky then is decided upon, set for July of 1943. Dwight Eisenhower was named commander in chief, but, as in North Africa, the British General Alexander was to be the actual field commander.

In Sicily, the Allies found Italian resistance to be weak. Mass surrender was commonplace. The Italians clearly had lost their stomach for the war. One of the arguments that Churchill had put forward about the importance of an invasion of Sicily and of Italy would be that it might topple Mussolini, pull the Italians out of the war—who knows, maybe the Italians would switch sides—that this would begin the unraveling of the Third Reich's position on the continent.

There was great pressure, from the very beginning of the operation in Sicily, on Mussolini. Italian troops clearly were not going to fight to the finish for the Duce or for this misguided policy of his—of his expansion in North Africa, which had drawn him into this conflict.

But, formidable resistance was provided by the Germans. General Kesselring had been dispatched to lead mobile Panzer units in Sicily, and Kesselring would bedevil the Allies both in Sicily and, even more so, in Italy. General Montgomery, according to the plan, was to race up the eastern coast of Sicily and seize Messina. But Kesselring interposed his troops, slowed Montgomery; and the American General Patton, meeting weak resistance, pushed straight across the island. He took Palermo on July 22, and then, what was often depicted as a race between Patton and Montgomery, developed, both trying to reach Messina.

Patton would become, as a result of his leadership—beginning in North Africa, but certainly in Sicily—would become a hero in the United States, given the nickname "Old Blood and Guts," especially when he reached Messina shortly before the British. Patton's moment of glory was to be short-lived, however. It would be shortly after this that the infamous slapping incident where Patton—incidents, I should say, two instances—

where Patton, in touring a military hospital, slapped a solider—an American soldier—whom he felt was malingering, suffering from shell shock; repeated this again shortly thereafter. This was covered by the press, and Patton would be removed from command—an irony which the Germans simply never quite understood.

The consequences of the Allied victory in Sicily were considerable. First of all, it drew the United States and Great Britain deeper and deeper into Churchill's Mediterranean strategy. Indeed, Churchill now renewed his emphasis on the so-called "soft underbelly" of Europe, arguing now that, having taken Sicily, that the next obvious step, the logic, the momentum of military operations, would be to jump across the "toe" of the boot and for an invasion of Italy proper. This would then be supplemented by support for the partisans in Yugoslavia, who were causing the Germans trouble across the Adriatic. It might even be possible to cajole the Turks into joining the anti-Hitler alliance.

In fact, what the Americans saw with great dismay was the emergence once again of a full-blown Mediterranean strategy, to which they were supposed to lend their support. The Americans were skeptical about this emphasis, as they had been from the beginning, but they had no real alternative plans. It was also quite clear by this point that there was no—what was the alternative? The alternative would now move troops back to Britain to begin the buildup for the cross-channel invasion, or pursue the military logic of the situation. We chose the latter.

The collapse of resistance in Sicily and the prospect of an imminent Allied invasion did indeed lead to Benito Mussolini's fall from power on July 24. King Victor Emmanuel III removed him as premier and replaced him with Marshal Badoglio, an Italian military commander who was certainly unenthusiastic about continuing the war.

Mussolini was rescued by German commandos and spirited away and ultimately set up by the Germans to run a puppet state—Fascist state—in the north, to continue resistance against the Allies. But this was a resistance that had German support and very little Italian support.

Negotiations with Badoglio were under way. Badoglio wanted, in fact pledged, that Italy would switch sides—not only withdraw from the alliance with Germany but actually switch sides—support the Allied war effort. However, the Allies continued to cling to the notion of unconditional surrender. This was a policy that was very dear to President Roosevelt. He had announced it at the Casablanca conference at the beginning of the year, and this caused some problems. Would unconditional surrender mean that the monarchy would go? Exactly what did it mean? What were its implications for Italy?

Hitler, meanwhile, sent troops into northern Italy in the area around Rome, and by September 3, when the agreement was reached, when Italy was called upon to surrender its navy, merchant marine, and air force to the Allies and join the coalition against Hitler, the Germans were firmly entrenched in northern Italy and all the way south of Rome.

The invasion of Italy began on September 3. It was a three-pronged assault. The British, led by Montgomery, crossed the Straits of Messina onto the toe of the boot, meeting very little resistance. A second British force stormed ashore at Taranto, the Italian naval base, meeting no resistance. And, at the same time, the Anglo-American Fifth Army, under General Mark Clark, the American, landed south of Naples, at Salerno. Clark wanted to land north of Naples, but was convinced by the British that this would be problematic, since that was too far north—couldn't be supported by Allied aircraft. So troops landed in Salerno. The goal, certainly Mark Clark's hope, was to take Naples within three days.

But Kesselring had rushed troops south, and one Panzer division was already in place in the mountains overlooking the Salerno beachhead. And the result was a near disaster. The Germans poured down artillery on the small beachhead for some time. The success of the landing was in grave doubt. Ultimately, the situation was saved by airpower and naval guns, finally allowing the solders on the beach to break out and push inland a bit, breaking the German siege.

This landing, I might add, at Salerno didn't do anything to win greater support for the United States and its determination for a cross-channel invasion among its British allies. The sense was this was a problematic invasion. They had almost been driven back into the sea. For a while, it looked as if the whole invasion at Salerno hung by a thread. So at this point, the two amphibious landings that the Allies had attempted against the Germans, one at Dieppe in '43 and now the Salerno landings, didn't give great confidence for the success of a cross-channel invasion.

Naples was not taken until October 1. Meanwhile, the British were able to seize Foggia, on the eastern side of the peninsula, a major air base, which was now converted to Allied use. That—taking Foggia was quite an important achievement. What this did was allow the United States and Britain to move air groups from North Africa onto the European continent, into Italy. It would bring the Balkans and southern Germany into range for American B-17s and B-24s. It would begin now, at this time, a double pressure on the Germans—attacks from the RAF and the American Eighth Air Force from Britain, now to be augmented by attacks from the south. The Germans, finding their position in Sardinia and Corsica in trouble, evacuated those territories in September and early October.

Things looked like they might turn out very well for the invasion, but Italy proved anything but a soft underbelly. The Italian terrain was ideal for defensive operations, and Kesselring, the German commander, proved to be an absolute master. The Apennine Mountains extending down the center of the peninsula created a formidable barrier. The numerous rivers were also difficult. The valleys oozed mud, and in the hills and the mountains the men had to deal with raw cold and snow and a lack of cover; indeed, were forced to depend on mules for supplies. And combat in Italy was frequently hand to hand. Anyone who'd been looking at brochures of sunny, pleasant Italy, were in for a real shock.

The combat in Italy was among the most difficult anywhere in the Second World War. The terrain was difficult, the conditions difficult, and a terrain which certainly did give the great advantage to the German defenders. During the fall and early winter, the Allies slogged slowly northward, but their progress was halted about a hundred miles south of Rome, where the Germans had created what they referred to as the "Gustav Line." By January 1944, the front had stabilized. The Germans had managed to blunt the offensive, and, at the end of 1943, Allied command and strategy had been altered.

At this point in the evolution of the campaign in Italy, the Allies really did have an option. They could have stopped. There was nothing now at this point—one could talk about the logic, the military logic or the momentum from North Africa to take them across to Sicily or then to extend the assault into Italy itself—but now Mussolini had been toppled. The British had seized the air base at Foggia. The Allies were in a position to make air attacks on southern Germany and important positions in the east. At this point, it would have been possible—this argument was certainly made—to simply halt. Why batter away at these German positions, these well-entrenched German positions, against this master of the defense in General Kesselring? Why not now begin to move more troops and prepare for the cross-channel invasion?

And in some sense, this is exactly what happens. There's certainly not a standstill in the Italian campaign, but at the end of 1943, Eisenhower was dispatched to London to become supreme commander of the forces preparing for the invasion of northwestern Europe. General Montgomery would follow as his field commander, and General Alexander, the British general, assumed command in Italy.

The Allies certainly had now moved to push for the cross-channel invasion, in part because at this time Stalin had reached the absolute limit of his toleration for this. At the Teheran conference with Roosevelt and Churchill, Stalin absolutely insisted on a firm commitment from Churchill that Britain was committed to a cross-channel invasion. And Roosevelt swung—in this delicate relationship, triangular relationship that these three powerful leaders had—Roosevelt swung his support clearly to Stalin, pushing Churchill, in effect, to declare, yes, we are committed and we are committed to doing this cross-channel invasion at the earliest possible time, and that would be in the spring and early summer of 1944.

Nonetheless, the campaign in Italy would continue as well, under General Alexander. In a dramatic attempt to break the deadlock, the Allies launched an amphibious landing at the resort town of Anzio, just 30 miles south of Rome, on January 22, 1944. General Clark was expected to move quickly inland, but his forces did not. Fearing a quick German response, just as at Salerno, Clark and his commanders had been cautious. Despite intelligence derived from Ultra that made clear that Kesselring couldn't send troops for about a week, Clark's commander on the scene failed to drive inland. And Kesselring shifted forces to prevent further expansion of the beachhead, so that instead of threatening to break communications between Rome and the Gustav Line—to cut the Germans off by driving across the peninsula, sealing off the Germans to the south, and then pushing on Rome—the Americans were bogged down again.

Once again, an amphibious landing had turned out differently than anticipated. Clark replaced his commanding officer with General Lucian Truscott, but he too was able to effect a breakout from the Anzio position. One of the problems, at this point now, was that with the main bulk of the American forces south of the Gustav Line, Anzio above it, one possibility now was to drive from the south to link up these forces.

Those forces pushing from the south found that the going was particularly difficult, and one place in particular, one logjam, was Monte Cassino. Allied solders believed that the Germans were using the old abbey, the ancient abbey at Monte Cassino, as an observation post, calling down artillery fire on their positions. Mark Clark was initially opposed to bombing the ancient structure, but General Alexander insisted, and on February 15, 1944, 200 bombers smashed the abbey. The Germans, as it turned out, had not been using the abbey as an observation post, but they now quickly used the ruins created by the bombing of the abbey to rush troops there. Now they had the observation post and good defensive positions. The bombing had had the opposite effect as intended. A second air raid, almost 500 bombers against the town, still failed to break German resistance.

The bitter fighting around Monte Cassino revealed the full diversity of Allied troops. At this point, we've talked about world war in the sense of the geographical spread of combat from the South Pacific to the Soviet Union to North Africa to Europe, but in the siege, the attack, on Monte Cassino, one really does see now the variety of Allied troops involved. There were Indian troops, troops from New Zealand, French troops, and it would be finally Polish troops who would storm the town. And indeed, it was in mid-May of 1944 that Polish troops actually reached the summit in Monte Cassino. In May, French units also broke through the Gustav Line and threatened the whole German position.

British troops would ultimately take Cassino; the Poles, the ruins of the old monastery; and five days later, the Americans broke out of Anzio and, at this point, still could have cut off the German retreat from the Gustav Line. It was still possible.

But Truscott received an order from General Clark. Instead of driving east to cut off the retreating Germans, he was to turn north, to take Rome. Rome was for the taking at this juncture, and if it wasn't the strategic prize, it was a political prize of considerable import. Truscott reluctantly complied—he didn't want to do this—and Kesselring was now able to extricate his troops, pulling them back once again in an effective fighting retreat. As he pulled back, Kesselring did make an important declaration. Rome was declared an open city to prevent its destruction by the Allied air forces.

This bombing of Monte Cassino was a very controversial matter, I think for everybody except those Allied troops who were down below Monte Cassino needing to get by it. I don't think they had very many qualms about what happened to the old abbey, but for everyone else it did become an issue. And so then behind this, of course, lurked the even greater question, what does one do about these great cultural monuments of Western civilization? Do you bomb Rome? The center of Paris had certainly been spared. The industrial ring around Paris had been bombed by this point, but now this question of what happens to Rome had loomed before the Allies. Kesselring made it clear that the Germans would not contest the city, and as a consequence Rome would be spared.

American forces entered Rome on June 4, 1944, two days before the Normandy landing. The Germans withdrew to yet another prepared position 150 miles to the north, the "Gothic Line," replacing the Gustav Line, stretching across the peninsula beyond Livorno and Florence, the soft underbelly. One has the impression we'd still be fighting in Italy had the war gone on, that the slow slogging up through this mountainous terrain—and I think for those of you who remember the war or were involved in it directly, the Willie and Joe cartoons of Bill Mauldin are largely from the Italian campaign. They're marvelous, marvelous cartoons, and certainly among the most popular from *Stars and Stripes*.

What then were the implications of the Italian campaign? Again, it had been a successful campaign, just as North Africa had been. The Germans were in full-fledged retreat. The Allies had been successful; Rome liberated by the summer of 1944. Its detractors would maintain, however, that the Italian operation delayed the cross-channel invasion on which the world waited. Did the Italian campaign delay the cross-channel invasion? I think there are a number of ways that one can approach this question. One is to look, as the British certainly did, at what was required for a successful cross-channel invasion into the teeth of what the Germans were calling Fortress Europe, the heavily fortified defensive positions along the coast of northern Europe. Could a major offensive have been launched in 1943?

One of the arguments that the British had used, and I think it's certainly a very powerful argument, was that the submarine offensive—the German submarine offensive—was still a major threat in 1943. That the safe convoying of enormous amounts of material and so on into England would have been a difficult task in 1943, whereas by 1944 the submarine threat had largely been removed.

In 1943, it is also clear that the Allies did have shortages of shipping. They had shortages in landing craft, equipment, and troops. It wasn't that the landing craft didn't exist in 1943; they were all the way across the world in the South Pacific being used, and we still needed more. So shortages of equipment, landing craft, shipping, troops—the American army was not yet at full strength and, as the British argued, the Americans, who were going to be pivotal players in this alliance obviously, had lacked combat experience in 1943, and had gotten that experience in the bitter fighting in Sicily and Italy. On the other hand, one could make a counterargument that the Allies, as I just indicated, did have the ships and landing craft, that they were simply in the Pacific, not in the Mediterranean and in Western Europe.

It's certainly true that American troops lacked combat experience in 1943. It is also true that German defenses were a great deal stronger in northern

Europe in 1944 than they had been in 1943. There were 49 German divisions in France in 1943, mostly second-line quality troops. They were short of armor. It was a quiet front for the Germans in 1943. In June of 1944, there would be 58 divisions, much more armor, and the coastal defenses had been greatly reinforced, largely under Rommel's instigation.

There was a claim made over and over again by Allied air commanders that one of the other key ingredients for a successful cross-channel invasion, air superiority—indeed, air supremacy—had not been achieved in 1943. Well, that's certainly true. It was a long way from being achieved in 1943. The argument the air commanders made was it could have been established in 1943 by the Eighth Air Force in England if the best of those units and support personnel had not been siphoned off to North Africa and then ultimately to Italy as well.

I think, of these arguments, the greatest threat in 1943 was undoubtedly the submarine, and it's doubtful that the Allies could have established air superiority in the course of 1943. If you recall, it was in the summer of 1943 that the Americans launched the two big daylight raids, the Regensburg-Schweinfurt raid in August of 1943, and then repeated it again in the fall with disastrous consequences. The planes got through, bombed the targets, but they had suffered grievous casualties in those two raids. The German air force was still very, very strong in the course of 1943.

It would only be at the Teheran conference, which we've indicated, when Roosevelt, Churchill, and Stalin all met for the first time, that Churchill finally gave in to pressure and committed himself to the cross-channel invasion as being the top priority for 1944. The plan was Operation Overlord, and at Teheran Roosevelt announced his decision to name Dwight Eisenhower supreme commander.

This was a surprise. It was not a popular decision. Both Churchill and Stalin preferred Marshall and were surprised at the choice of Eisenhower. Eisenhower had demonstrated certainly those characteristics, those political qualities, those qualities of personality that we've described in North Africa, and in his participation in the Operation Husky, but had not yet really demonstrated the ability to take charge of an enormous operation that was going to be the centerpiece of all of Allied strategy. Marshall seemed to be the most obvious choice, but Roosevelt said he simply couldn't part—he couldn't imagine a life in Washington without Marshall—he needed Marshall close at hand for advice. And so Eisenhower was named.

At the conclusion of the Allied campaign in Italy, the Germans were certainly pushed back. The frontiers of Fortress Europe were shrinking, but the German position in Western Europe was still enormously strong. And even in 1944, the odds for a successful cross-channel invasion were by no means great or obvious in favor of the Allies. It would still be an enormous risk, the implications of which—the stakes of which, cannot be exaggerated—and, after turning our attention in the next lecture to events on the Eastern Front, we will return to talk about the planning for that cross-channel invasion.

Stalingrad—The Turning Point on the Eastern Front
Lecture 17

**With this lecture … we will turn our attention to the great turning point
of the war on the eastern front, and that is the Battle of Stalingrad.**

The titanic struggle for Stalingrad between August 1942 and March 1943 marked the turning point of the war on the eastern front. In the spring of 1942 the Germans launched a new offensive against Stalingrad. Having abandoned earlier efforts to take Leningrad and Moscow, Hitler adopted new objectives. German forces would drive to the south of Kiev, seize the Caucasus oil fields, and take Stalingrad.

The Soviets appeared highly vulnerable. They had fewer tanks in 1942 than they had possessed in 1941. The Red Army was absolutely exhausted, and its best units remained positioned in front of Moscow. At first, the German offensive was highly successful. The Germans defeated the Soviets at Kharkov in May. The main German offensive began on June 28, 1942. Stalin remained convinced that Moscow was the Germans' main target. The Germans reached Sebastopol in July.

Soldier in Stalingrad.

Although Stalingrad was not yet secure, Hitler ordered a drive into the Caucasus. The drive by Germany's first panzer division proceeded with great speed into September. The Germans penetrated deep into Russia; the invasion force split, with part heading toward the Grozny oil field and the other toward the Black Sea. However, the euphoric Germans underestimated the Soviets.

The German drive slowed in late September and October as resistance by Russian defenders and local forces (e.g., the Chechnians) stiffened. The Germans faced mounting problems. Their front was now more than 500 miles long, and their supply lines were 1,300 miles long. Resistance activities behind the German lines were mounting. Concerned about the slow pace of the offensive, Hitler fired General Halder as chief of staff in November 1942.

> **The Germans, terribly still unprepared for this kind of warfare, now found themselves with a major defeat on their hands, and a defeat that could lead to real catastrophe.**

The Germans and Soviets fought a ferocious battle for Stalingrad. The Germans had to take Stalingrad in order to block Soviet troop movements to the South. The task was left to General von Paulus's 6th Army. German troops entered the northern suburbs and reached the Volga on August 22. The next day the Germans launched a terror air raid on Stalingrad with incendiary bombs. The Russians appeared to be trapped.

Russian resistance was fierce as the battle acquired enormous symbolic significance. The Germans were determined to take the city and the Russians to hold it at all costs. The two sides waged a ferocious battle of attrition. The fighting proceeded street by street, block by block, and house by house. The city was reduced to rubble, and movement was measured in meters. By early November, the Germans held 90 percent of the city.

General Zhukov, the savior of Moscow, took command in the south and planned a counterattack. Zhukov deliberately kept reinforcements of the city to a minimum as he massed Russian troops to the north and south of Stalingrad. All preparations for the counterattack were kept under tight security.

Zhukov unleashed the counterattack on November 19. The attack came on the northern and southern flanks, catching the Germans off guard. On November 23, the two Russian spearheads linked up 45 miles away from

Stalingrad, encircling the entire German 6th Army and one corps of the 4th Panzer army.

Hitler refused Paulus's request for permission to break out of Stalingrad. He ordered General Manstein to fight through to Stalingrad, but the effort failed. Doomed, Paulus's 6th Army was ordered to fight to the last man. Paulus held out until February 2, 1943, and then surrendered.

The battle for Stalingrad had important implications. It was a catastrophic defeat for the Germans. Two hundred thousand troops were lost, and 90,000 were captured. The summer offensive of 1942, concluding at Stalingrad, marked the end of German initiative on the eastern front. After Stalingrad, Germany remained on the defensive. Zhukov emerged as the leading Soviet commander. ∎

Suggested Reading

John Erikson, *The Road to Stalingrad.*

John Keegan, *The Second World War*, Chapter 11.

Richard Overy, *Why The Allies Won*, Chapter 3.

Questions to Consider

1. Which German miscalculations contributed to the defeat of Hitler's Stalingrad offensive?

2. What were the consequences and significance of the Battle of Stalingrad?

Stalingrad—The Turning Point on the Eastern Front
Lecture 17—Transcript

In our last few lectures we've been examining a series of turning points—major shifts in strategic impetus—in the drift of the war in the South Pacific, in North Africa. And, with this lecture, our seventeenth, we will turn our attention to the great turning point of the war on the Eastern Front, and that is the Battle of Stalingrad.

We stopped our discussion of the German advance into the Soviet Union with the Russian counteroffensive before Moscow in December of 1941. That winter offensive had ground to a halt in February, and in March of 1942 the Eastern Front saw no significant initiatives. The Russians were exhausted from their winter offensive; the Germans, still marshaling their forces for a new offensive in the summer.

As winter turned to spring, Hitler had developed a new set of objectives for his summer offensive. He decided to abandon the attempt to take Moscow and to break the siege at Leningrad and to concentrate instead on the south, on the Ukraine and beyond. The primary objective was to be the Caucasus oil fields—to deny Russia's resupply and to seize this valuable asset for Germany.

The plan was an ambitious one. It called for a three-phase campaign: the encirclement of Soviet troops west of the Don River, and then a dash southward along the Volga to Stalingrad. There General Paulus's sixth army and a Panzer army, the fourth, would establish a blocking position near the city to protect the southern force, which would drive into the Caucasus. Phase three, then, would be the drive of German troops deep into the Soviet Union to the south, claiming the Caucasus oil fields.

It was not as ambitious as Barbarossa, but its scale was still extraordinary. It was over 500 miles from Kiev to the heart of the Caucasus, and the German army in the Soviet Union was not as strong as it had been the year before. In fact, it had 350,000 fewer troops at its disposal for this summer offensive than Hitler had marshaled in the summer of 1941. The total tank strength of the German army was less than in 1941, though now it would be concentrated in the south rather than trying to reach three different objectives. Hitler was forced to rely in this offensive on Romanian, Hungarian, and even Italian units—imagine the poor, unfortunate Italian units that had been shipped off to the Eastern Front—and these were not as well equipped, nor as committed to the cause, as their German counterparts.

But if the German position was shaky, the Red Army's position was also problematic. The winter offensive during the worst winter in Russia in 140 years had left the Red Army absolutely exhausted. At this phase, in this period of the war, the Russians were still far more adept at defensive operations than offensive ones. They'd suffered tremendous losses—astonishing losses—in 1941, of both men and armor. Stalin remained convinced that when the Germans attacked—and everyone expected a new German offensive come spring—that this would be a renewal of their drive on Moscow. Therefore, the Red Army's best units remained in a blocking position in front of Moscow.

The Germans had planned to preface their offensive in June by eliminating a Soviet salient in the line south of the city of Kharkov, but before they could do so the Russians actually launched an attack themselves. Kharkov was the hub of the German communications network in the south of Russia and a prime target. Stalin and the Russian commander General Timoshenko decided to launch an offensive from the salient in May, over the objections of General Chuikov, who believed that this would be really folly when the Soviets needed to be concentrating their forces for offensives elsewhere. Timoshenko began his offensive on May 12, with great early successes, but he had in fact played directly into Germany's hands. Five days later the Germans cut off the Soviet spearhead, capturing 240,000 Russian prisoners and destroying over 600 tanks of the 840 that had been sent into combat in this offensive.

I think for most armies this would have been an absolutely crushing, devastating defeat, but the Soviets were resilient. Timoshenko, I might add, had begged Stalin for permission to retreat to more defensible positions, but Stalin had refused, and so the Soviets were trapped and forced to fight on to the end.

Thus, the German offensive in the summer of 1942 began almost a replay of 1941 of Operation Barbarossa, not in its scale but with still smashing German victory. Hitler was absolutely exultant. In the south, General Manstein, who had conquered the Crimea in the fall of 1941, began the siege of Sevastopol in early June, and, although the Russians held out for a month, Sevastopol fell on July 3, and over 100,000 more Russians were taken prisoner; 200 Russian tanks captured.

This was the offensive that was going to win the war, the Germans believed. The main German operation, the main German offensive, began on June 28. It made rapid progress against the weakened forces of the Red Army. The Soviet position was actually made worse by their own misguided Kharkov offensive and Stalin's continued conviction that the major thrust of the German attack would still be directed at Moscow. He simply couldn't—he wasn't going—to shift troops while there was any threat to Moscow.

The fourth German Panzer army drove 100 miles in eight days, reaching the Don in the south. There was a sense this was a replay, literally a replay, of the great German victories of the previous summer. But the Russians fought tenaciously there, allowing a withdrawal finally toward Stalingrad, though it still looked like a rout. "The Russian is finished," Hitler maintained, and his General Halder, chief of staff, agreed.

Hitler decided that it was now possible to move directly to phase three of the attack; that is, the sending of massive numbers of German troops to the south toward the Caucasus, without first securing his flank at Stalingrad. Stalingrad was important strategically. It was a blocking position to keep Soviet forces from the north from being shifted south to meet the German spearheads there. To strengthen the forces moving south, he diverted a Panzer army away from Stalingrad and left the task of securing that city to General Paulus's sixth army. This was an overwhelmingly infantry army with very little armor, and this decision would prove costly indeed. The fourth Panzer would probably have reached Stalingrad before the Soviet defenses were firmly established, and its presence was not necessary to help the forces moving south across the Don River.

nzer army then streaked southward against weak Soviet defenses.) it had pressed 200 miles southeast of Rostov and had reached oil fields in the foothills of the Caucasus. This was the deepest netration of the war.

Here another key decision was made. The Germans split their forces. One element moved east toward the Grozny oil fields; the other pushed towards the coast of the Black Sea. What one sees here, is, once again I think, too many objectives for the German army. Hitler makes decisions; things are going so well that he jumps the gun, decides to skip stages that were absolutely necessary. But within the German military, just as there had been the previous summer, a real sense of euphoria seemed to surge from the lowest ranks up to the top.

"The commanding officer says the Russian troops are completely broken and cannot hold out any longer," one German wrote home to his wife. "To reach the Volga and take Stalingrad is not so difficult for us. The Führer knows where the Russians' weak point is. Victory is not far away." That letter was written on July 29, 1942. On August 7, he wrote again: "Our company is tearing ahead. Today, I wrote Elsa, we shall soon see each other. All of us feel that the end, victory, is near."

In September, however, the offensive slowed—the offensive down into the Caucasus. In October and November, Russian resistance in the mountainous terrain stiffened, and the Germans were now fighting not simply the Red Army, they were fighting locals—Chechnian local resistance forces who were unhappy about the Soviets, but they certainly didn't want the Germans there either. So the Germans wind up engaged in combat with them.

The advanced elements of the German army did reach Mount El'brus, Europe's highest mountain, and a team of climbers actually were dispatched to place the German flag near the summit. This was to be literally the high watermark of the German advance.

But while this symbolic action was taking place, the problems for the German offensive were multiplying. The Germans were now stretched to the absolute limit of their capacity. Resupply was difficult, and they encountered shortages of fuel, difficult mountainous terrain, and tough resistance. As they moved farther and farther south, as well, resistance activities behind the front mushroomed. The German army was certainly deep in the Soviet Union, but the front was far more fluid than it appeared if one drew simply a map. Army Group South had begun the offensive covering a 500-mile front. Now, it was stretched over almost 1,300 miles, dangerously thin by any definition.

In September, Hitler was furious. He fired a number of his top commanders because the offensive which had been going so well since it had been launched in the early summer now was slowing down. The momentum seemed to be lost. Hitler was growing impatient. What was the matter? He obviously believed, and argued, there was nothing the matter with the plan; the plan was brilliant. It was his own, after all. The Russians were reeling. The Red Army was on the run, and still the offensive seemed to have lost momentum. What was wrong? Well, there was nothing the matter with the plan; there wasn't anything the matter with the German troops; it obviously had to be the generals. And so there was a wholesale firing of commanders on the Eastern Front, just as there had been, by the way, after the failure of the offensive before Moscow a year before. General Halder, who had been chief of staff of the German army since 1938 and one of the leading, if not the leading, strategists within the German high command, was removed. He was replaced by a younger and far more pliable staff officer.

With the German army now stretched deep into the Caucasus, this front of 1,300 miles, really the importance of Stalingrad as the hinge of this attack was extremely important. The task of taking the city, as I indicated, had been left to General Paulus's sixth army. It was mostly infantry, and still it had made steady progress throughout August. On August 22, in fact, the Germans had broken through, and a Panzer corps had fought its way into the northern suburbs of the city.

The Luftwaffe was called on to seal the fate of the Russians in Stalingrad. On August 23, 1942, the largest German air raid since June 22, 1941 was launched against the city. Air units from all over were brought to bear on Stalingrad. Over half the bombs dropped were incendiaries in order to set the maximum number of fires within the city. Nearly every wooden structure in Stalingrad, including acres of workers' housing, were burned in the raid.

The results were absolutely spectacular. Stalingrad before the battle had begun—already resembled—a devastated city. The fires were so intense, so vast, that one could read a newspaper 40 miles away by their flames. It was a terror raid, pure and simple—to kill civilians, to overload services, and to create panic in the population; to make it absolutely impossible for the Red Army to operate within this urban area, and to force a surrender. "The whole city is on fire," a German soldier wrote home. "On the Führer's orders our Luftwaffe has sent it up in flames. That's what the Russians need to stop them resisting."

But the city did not surrender. On August 25, the regional party committee of the Soviet Union proclaimed a state of siege. "Comrades and citizens of Stalingrad," their declaration stated, "we shall never surrender the city of our birth to the depredations of the German invader. Every single one of us must apply himself to the task of defending our beloved town, our homes, and our families. Let us barricade every street, transform every district, every block, every house into an impregnable fortress."

The Russians were determined to hold, and the Germans were determined to take the city. The battle for Stalingrad was assuming, gradually, monumental proportions. It was a ferocious battle of attrition, and it had enormous symbolic value. The fact that it was named for Stalin obviously plays a role here. And it was fought block by block, house by house, floor by floor, and room by room. The city itself was very quickly reduced to a state of rubble, and movement which had been measured in miles or kilometers by the hundreds, over the course of the battle of Stalingrad would be measured in meters.

There had been nothing like it since the colossal carnage of the First World War. It was, as one historian has called it, "Verdun on the Volga." The Germans were certainly aware of what this meant. General Doerr, one of the German commanders, described it in the following terms: "For every house, workshop, water tower, railway embankment, wall, cellar, in every pile of ruins, a bitter battle was waged without equal even in the First World War and its vast expenditure of munitions. The distance between the enemy's army and ours was as small as it could possibly be." Despite the concentrated activity of aircraft and artillery, it was impossible to break out of the area of close fighting. The Russians surpassed the Germans in their use of the terrain and in camouflage and were more experienced in barricade warfare for individual buildings.

Vasily Chuikov was in command of the city, and in late August Stalin ordered a change of command. Georgi Zhukov, the savior of Moscow, now replaced the commander in the south, Timoshenko, and Zhukov began to work his magic. While the battle raged in Stalingrad itself, Zhukov followed the strategy that he had employed the year before in Moscow. What he did was to deliberately withhold reinforcements, to keep those reinforcements to the garrison at an absolute minimum; that is, there were reinforcements he was building up, but they weren't being funneled into Stalingrad. The troops in Stalingrad were going to have to hold. This was clear to the defenders there. Instead, he began to mass troops north and south of the city. This is exactly what he had done around Moscow in December of 1941, so that the Germans concentrating on the front just before them would not be able to detect this buildup. Moreover, as Zhukov knew, both the northern and southern flanks of the German sixth army were held by Romanian troops, understrengthed and underequipped. The Russian preparations for a counterattack were kept under a very tight security.

Still, by early November the Germans held nine-tenths of Stalingrad. Hitler, in a very famous speech—the Beer Hall Putsch in Munich had taken place in early November 1923, and every year this was a big event on the German Nazi calendar. Hitler would always go back to Munich, address what they called the Alte Kaempfer, the old fighters from the party, and on this date, in early November 1943, he gave one of his patented speeches, in which he said something to the effect of, "Well, one can talk about different objectives in the Soviet Union, but I knew what I wanted. I've come to the Volga to a particular point, to a particular place. Don't think it's because it's named for Stalin. No, it could've been named for anybody else." Then he proceeded to reel off all of the statistics, which he always seemed to have at his disposal: There we will cut off so many tons of manganese. There we will seize so many tons of scrap iron. There we will cut off such and such—so many things of oil. So it is an extremely important economic point for us. It's a crucial battle. "And you know," he said, "we have it, actually. It's within our grasp. There are just a few small places left that are beyond our reach. But we are very clever. We will take them little by little by little, and ultimately prove triumphant."

But the German position in Stalingrad was a difficult one. It formed a salient with long, vulnerable flanks, and this is exactly the situation on which Zhukov was planning. On November 19, Zhukov unleashed his offensive against the Romanians, northwest and southeast of Stalingrad. The German high command was caught completely unprepared. The Romanians buckled, and on November 23, 1942, the two spearheads linked up 45 miles west of Stalingrad, encircling the entire sixth army and one corps of the fourth Panzer army. Paulus, seeing the desperation of his own situation, appealed to Hitler to allow him to break out of the encirclement and establish communication with German lines beyond the Russian positions. Hitler ordered Manstein to break through to Stalingrad, but he certainly refused Paulus's plea to allow the sixth army to try to break out. Instead, he promoted Paulus to the position of field marshal, pointing out to everyone in sight that no German field marshal had ever surrendered, and calling on Paulus to hold on at all costs, that help was coming from Manstein.

The whole issue of relief, however, was rendered moot by a second Russian offensive on December 16, pressing from the Don towards Rostov with the intention of cutting off all German forces to the south. A real catastrophe was now looming for the Germans.

Inside the city itself, though, the battle would continue to rage, and rage in ferocious fashion. To give you some sense of the changing mood in this cauldron that became Stalingrad, I'd like to read you a series of just brief descriptions from a German writing home about the Russians he's encountering. On September 1 he wrote home, "Are the Russians really going to fight on the very bank of the Volga? It's madness." The Russians literally were pushed up against the river. Any sort of reasonable military leader would've tried to get them back across the river. They were trapped. On September 8 he wrote, "This is insane stubbornness." September 11: "Fanatics." September 13: "Wild beasts." September 16: "Barbarism. They're not men but devils." September 26: "Barbarians. They use gangster methods." And then finally on October 27, "The Russians are not men, but some kind of cast iron creatures. They never get tired and they are not afraid of fire."

At first, the Germans in the city, with the offensive around them, the Germans in the city of Stalingrad still thought they had triumphed. Earlier on, a Russian described the Germans as being almost drunk with victory in the city. They had found vodka, were jumping down from their lorries, playing their harmonicas, dancing "like madmen," one Russian said, on the pavements. But that mood was soon to break. One of the frustrations—I'm going to read a number of these descriptions of the combat within Stalingrad, because I think both they're gripping and they also give you that sense of the enormity, and the brutality, and the hopelessness, in a way, of this struggle. Of two armies caught in a very small place with no place to go except the ruins of this destroyed city, and still fighting in this sort of "craters of the moon" sort of environment. You get the sense of frustration from one of the Germans as he wrote home, "We would spend the whole day clearing a street from one end to the other, establish blocks and fire points at the western end, and prepare for another slice of the salami the next day. But at dawn the Russians would start up firing from their old position at the far end. It took us some time to discover their trick. They had knocked communicating holes through between the garrets and attics and during the night they would run back like rats in the rafters and set their machine guns up behind some topmost window or broken chimney." The Russians seemed in this situation to be everywhere.

The Russians, on the other hand, with a sense of desperation—I think, if you were one of these Russian troopers in Stalingrad—a sense of there being no place to go, no escape. There was no help coming. It was clear that reinforcements—though there was a sense there might be reinforcements across the river—they weren't coming, and getting across the river was going to be impossible. So they fought and fought and fought, literally, as we've seen, house by house, street by street, room by room.

This is a Russian account: "We beat off the next attack with some stones, firing occasionally and throwing our last grenades. Suddenly from behind a blank wall from the rear came the grind of a tank's caterpillar tracks. We had no antitank grenades. All we had was one antitank rifle with three rounds. I handed this rifle to the antitank man, Berichev, and sent him out through the back to fire at the tank point blank. But before he could get into position he was captured by German tommy gunners. What Berichev told the Germans

I don't know, but I can guess that he led them up the garden path, because an hour later they started to attack at precisely the point where I'd put my machine gun with its emergency belt of cartridges. This time, reckoning that we had run out of ammunition, they came impudently out of their shelter, standing up and shouting. They came down the street in a column. I put the last belt in the heavy machine gun at the semibasement window and sent the whole of the 250 bullets into the yelling, dirty, gray Nazi mob. I was wounded in the hand but did not let go of the machine gun. Heaps of bodies littered the ground. The Germans still alive ran for cover in panic. An hour later, they led our antitank rifleman onto a heap of ruins and shot him in front of our eyes for having shown them the way to my machine gun. There were no more attacks. An avalanche of shells fell on the building. The Germans stormed us with every possible kind of weapon. We couldn't raise our heads. Again we heard the ominous sound of tanks. From behind a neighboring block, stocky German tanks began to crawl out. This clearly was the end. The guardsmen said goodbye to one another. With a dagger, my orderly scratched on a brick wall, 'Radimstev's guardsmen fought and died here for their country.'"

The battling in Stalingrad would continue in this vein through November into December and into the new year. The sixth army was given an order, finally, to fight to the last man. Utterly surrounded, with no way of resupply, General Paulus surrendered the sixth army on February 2, 1943. It was a catastrophe for the Germans.

The suffering in Stalingrad—much of the sense of what we have of the Eastern Front in the Second World War is from this incredible battle in Stalingrad. The temperatures had begun to drop again in November and December. Men froze to death. Frostbite was suffered by troops on both sides.

The Germans, terribly still unprepared for this kind of warfare, now found themselves with a major defeat on their hands, and a defeat that could lead to real catastrophe. There were 200,000 German losses at Stalingrad, 90,000 prisoners of war, and, with the defeat at Stalingrad, the entire front in southern Russia was now exposed. There was a very real danger, when Stalingrad fell in February of 1943, that the Soviet army would continue to move west, cutting off those German units that were down in the Caucasus, and that the entire Eastern Front could collapse for the Germans in one great counteroffensive by the Russians.

This defeat at Stalingrad, with so much symbolic and strategic importance, was the turning point of the Second World War on the Eastern Front. It was the great Russian victory that turned the tide, and, taken in conjunction with the victories of the Allies in North Africa, the invasion of Italy, the defeat of the Japanese at Guadalacanal, 1943 would come into being with great optimism for the Allies. The beginning of 1942, only a year earlier, had been the low point, the nadir, of the Allied position, and now as 1943 began—before the spring would come in 1943—now the question was where would the Allies strike, not where the Japanese or the Germans would attack.

Eisenhower and Operation Overlord
Lecture 18

[In this lecture] we're going to be examining the preparations for what was the largest amphibious assault in history—the D-Day invasions, the long-awaited cross-channel invasion of Normandy and Fortress Europe.

W e will analyze the Allied planning for the D-Day invasion of northwestern Europe—Operation Overlord—and the German preparations for the anticipated attack. In early 1944 everyone expected an Allied invasion of northwestern Europe. The only questions concerned where and when it would come.

Allied planners faced many difficult choices as they prepared the cross-channel invasion. President Roosevelt chose Gen. Dwight Eisenhower to be supreme commander. The British and Soviets had preferred Gen. George C. Marshall, and Marshall himself had wanted the assignment. But FDR decided that he could not spare Marshall's presence in Washington. So Gen. Bernard Montgomery was chosen to be ground commander and in charge of the actual operational planning of the invasion.

The Allies decided that the invasion force would land in Normandy. The Germans knew that the invasion was afoot, but they did not know where and when it would take place. Although Pas-de-Calais offered the shortest route to the Ruhr, which was the Allies' ultimate target, the Normandy ports would better accommodate the invasion force. An American force under Gen. Omar Bradley would land on the eastern end of the Normandy coast and advance on Cherbourg, while a British force would seize Caen. Paratroopers from the 82nd and 101st airborne divisions would land the night before, and seaborne troops would land at daybreak.

There were serious disagreements within the German high command over how to prepare for the invasion. Hitler knew that the Ruhr was the Allies' ultimate target, and so he decided to strengthen his western defenses. His calculations were largely political. If the invasion failed, another attempt would not be made for at least a year, and in the meantime the Soviets might make a separate peace with Germany.

Although Hitler expected the landing to occur in Normandy, both Rommel and Rundstedt expected the invasion force to land in the Pas-de-Calais. The latter was the worst-case scenario, and thus it was adopted as the basis for German defensive planning. Rommel argued for stopping the invasion force on the beaches, while Rundstedt favored a mobile defense that would launch a vigorous counterattack after the Allied forces had landed and the main invasion force had been identified.

The Allies tried to convince the Germans that the main landing would come at the Pas-de-Calais. A "dummy" camp under the command of Gen. George Patton was constructed near Dover, directly across the channel from Calais. Deceptive Allied radio traffic suggested that the landing would occur in Norway. The Allies learned through Ultra that the Germans had believed the deception.

Then at 21:30 on the evening of the fourth, at Southwick House, a weather briefing suggested that there might be a 36-hour respite after all, a brief break in the weather on the night and morning of June 5–June 6.

Weather conditions dictated that the invasion would have to occur in late spring or early summer. Eisenhower chose June 4, 1944, as D-Day. The Allied Expeditionary Force assault waves were loaded up on the evening of June 3. However, a storm developed on June 4, and the weather on June 5 was terrible.

Eisenhower faced a tremendously difficult decision about whether to proceed. If he decided to postpone the invasion, the tide and light conditions would not be right again until June 19. In addition, air support was questionable if the weather was bad. Eisenhower also had to consider the morale of his troops, who had already boarded the ships. Postponement might also risk the surprise element.

At 21:30 on June 4, Eisenhower's weather officer predicted a 36-hour break in the storm on June 5–6. Eisenhower decided to proceed. He issued an inspirational message to the invasion force: "You are about to embark on a great crusade. ..." He also drafted a second statement in which he accepted full responsibility in the event of failure. ∎

Suggested Reading

Stephen E. Ambrose, *D-Day, June 6, 1944: The Climactic Battle of World War II*, Chapters 1–9.

Dwight D. Eisenhower, *Crusade in Europe*, Chapters 13–14.

John Keegan, *The Second World War*, Chapter 20.

Richard Overy, *Why The Allies Won*, Chapter 5.

Questions to Consider

1. Why did the Allies choose Normandy as the landing point for the cross-channel invasion?

2. Describe the disagreements within the German high command over how to prepare for the invasion.

Eisenhower and Operation Overlord
Lecture 18—Transcript

Hello. Welcome to our eighteenth in this series of lectures on the Second World War. We're going to be examining the preparations for what was the largest amphibious assault in history—the D-Day invasions, the long-awaited cross-channel invasion of Normandy and Fortress Europe.

In the course of 1943, as we've seen, the Germans had suffered an enormous setback on the Eastern Front in Stalingrad, and slowly the Western Allies had slogged their way up the Italian peninsula. But it was still the great cross-channel invasion, the second front for which Stalin had been clamoring for years, that was to hold the real key to the success—to victory—for the Allies. This commitment to a cross-channel invasion had been—was quite controversial. The British had favored a Mediterranean strategy, as we've seen, had encouraged an invasion of North Africa, then Sicily, then Italy; while the Americans had impatiently sought the cross-channel invasion. And of course Stalin had been relentlessly demanding a second front which would relieve pressure on the beleaguered Russian troops in the east. It would not be until the Teheran conference in November of 1943, when Franklin Roosevelt, Churchill, and Stalin all met for the first time, that Churchill finally gave way to pressure from Stalin, now reinforced very vigorously by Roosevelt, and committed himself to make the cross-channel invasion of northern Europe the top priority for 1944. Churchill was not happy with this decision at Teheran. He would be ambivalent about it all the way down to May, really almost to the eve of the invasion itself. But he certainly, at Teheran, at last committed Britain to this great undertaking.

The plan was to be code-named Operation Overlord, and at Teheran Roosevelt announced his decision to name Dwight Eisenhower as commander in chief. There was a good deal of controversy about this. Both Churchill and Stalin had expected, and in fact wanted, General Marshall. He was by far the most respected man in the American military establishment. Marshall himself had hoped for the appointment. But Roosevelt insisted on Eisenhower. On the one hand he argued that he really couldn't imagine his life in Washington without Marshall. Marshall was his military confidante. He was the man that the president leaned on for advice. His calm, his steady—his rock solid and steady personality were essential—his judgment essential in Washington, Roosevelt felt. And, from a military point of view, Dwight Eisenhower had presided over, as commander in chief, three amphibious assaults already—Torch, Sicily, and Italy as well. So there was a good deal of rationale for the appointment of Eisenhower. British Air Marshal Sir Arthur Tedder was to serve as Eisenhower's deputy, and Montgomery was given command of Allied ground forces and really given the responsibility for the actual planning of the ground operations, the invasion itself.

Everyone in Europe understood, in the winter and early spring of 1943, that the invasion was coming. Fortress Europe was going to be assaulted by the Western Allies. The question was, where and when? The Allies had decided in their planning that the attack would come in Normandy. Why Normandy? Well, the reasoning was that it contained two important ports, Cherbourg and Le Havre, for resupply. These were considered absolutely essential to any sort of sustained military operation on the continent. The projected landing areas lay to the east of the Cotentin Peninsula, which juts out into the English Channel and thus protects the beaches from the prevailing westerly winds.

The Germans also, of course, expected the invasion to come in the Pas-de-Calais 200 miles to the northeast. The distance across the Channel was only 20 miles at that point. It offered the shortest route both into France, and then, of course, a quick drive through France and into the heart of Germany. The Germans very clearly understood the goal of the Allied invasion was to get through France as quickly as possible, through the Low Countries and into Germany Proper and particularly into the industrial heartland of Germany, which was the Ruhr. An attack across the Pas-de-Calais would offer the most obvious, shortest route to that objective.

But for the Allies, the ports across the Channel from Normandy were larger and could handle the massive ship and troop concentrations that were going to be necessary, and so for these reasons, the Normandy area suggested itself as the best place for this great undertaking.

The plan that would evolve in the last part of 1943 and into '44 called for an invasion of six divisions—three American, two British, one Canadian. This was to be the seaborne assault force. The Americans would be commanded by General Omar Bradley and were to land near the eastern base of the Cotentin Peninsula and drive towards Cherbourg, the nucleus of the first army. The British and Canadians were the advance guard of the British second army and were to land farther east near the mouth of the Orne River. Their objective was to seize the city of Caen, which Montgomery believed he could do within the first 24 of the invasion. Caen was a major road and rail junction and a key objective for the D-Day landings. The seaborne troops were to land at daybreak. But during the preceding night two American airborne divisions were to be dropped west of the American beachheads to destroy communications and to block avenues to the beach. This would be the 82nd and 101st Airborne Divisions. One British airborne division was to carry out a similar operation east of the British and Canadian landing sites.

While the ground troops fought inland, prefabricated concrete harbors called "mulberries" were to be towed across the Channel in sections and put in place off the Normandy coast. This was one way of resupply. It was an extraordinary engineering feat developed precisely for the Allied landing.

The planning that went on through the winter of 1943 and into the early spring of 1944 was intense and secret, and was extraordinary in its attention to detail. The scale of the planning was absolutely awesome. This would be the largest amphibious assault in history, as we've indicated, and on its success—Roosevelt, Churchill, the Allied command felt—hung the success of the Second World War.

Operation Overlord would be the best-kept secret—remarkably enough, given the number of personnel involved, the long run-up, the planning, and so on. It was an extraordinary feat of security. It was incredibly tight, but in the spring of 1944 everyone in Europe and the United States knew that the invasion was coming. The only questions, as we've said, were where and when.

Hitler was certainly very aware of the stakes of this approaching contest. He believed that the outcome of the battle would be the critical turning point of the war, and in November of 1943 he issued Führer directive number 51. "For the last two and a half years," the directive states, "the bitter and costly struggle against Bolshevism has made the utmost demands upon the bulk of our military resources and energies. The situation has since changed.

The threat from the east remains, but an even greater danger looms in the west: the Anglo-American landing. In the east the vastness of space will, as the last resort, permit a loss of territory, even on a major scale, without suffering a mortal blow to Germany's chance for survival. Not so in the west. If the enemy here succeeds in penetrating our defense on a wide front, consequences of staggering proportions will follow in a short time."

It was clear for Hitler what the objective would be, and it would be the Ruhr. There was no territory to give in the west. "For that reason I can no longer justify the further weakening of the west in favor of other theaters of war. I have therefore decided to strengthen the defenses in the west," he wrote.

Hitler's calculation was largely political. If the invasion failed, the Western Allies would not try again, he believed, for at least a year, and the Russians might actually seek a separate peace. At this point, after the catastrophe at Stalingrad, it was clear that the Germans were going to be on the defensive in the east, but they were still very deep inside the Soviet Union. So here one sees—one's no longer talking about a grandiose New Order in Europe and a Grössdeutsches Reich. One's talking about survival of the Third Reich, and here—the way to do this clearly was now a separate peace with the Soviets, or with the Western Allies. The Russians, though now certainly on the offensive, were still an awfully long way from Germany. If they reached the start line of 1941 they would still be 2,000 kilometers from Berlin.

So as 1943 turned to '44, the Germans concentrate now on the anticipated invasion of northern Europe. Field Marshal Gerd von Rundstedt was named to command all German forces in the west, but Erwin Rommel, the hero of the Afrika Korps, by far the most popular military figure in Germany, was placed in command of all ground units in the key areas of northern France, Belgium, and the Netherlands. This was an odd arrangement, and it would have important implications because the unity of command would be in question from the very beginning, with Rundstedt commander in chief in the west but Rommel in charge of the defenses of the key areas where the invasion would likely come.

Both Rundstedt and Rommel believed that the invasion would come in the Pas-de-Calais, looking at the situation from a military point of view, and of course Rundstedt, thinking back to German plans from the summer of 1940, believed that this was the obvious place. One had to make the preparations for it, even if the Allies should go—take a different route. The Pas-de-Calais was so crucial because it was only 20 miles across the Straits of Dover, the narrowest part of the Channel. Therefore, they had to concentrate there.

Hitler, on the other hand, originally believed, looking at the map, that the invasion, when it came, would come not at the Pas-de-Calais but in Normandy. In part I think this was consistent with Hitler's own sense of daring—to do the unexpected, to strike at the least obvious place, and Normandy certainly didn't suggest itself as an obvious target for the invasion. But over the course of time Hitler himself was increasingly convinced by Rommel, by Rundstedt, by his military, that the major defensive energies of the Germans should be devoted to the Pas-de-Calais area.

And, of course, the worst-case scenario carried the day. Even if the Allies were to land at the Pas-de-Calais, they would simply have a straight shot across Belgium and the Ruhr, and that had to be prevented at all costs. There might be time if they landed in Normandy, but the worst-case scenario was an invasion in the Pas-de-Calais. Despite the so-called "Atlantic wall," the German defenses, the defensive network that had been established along the coast, Rundstedt and Rommel were keenly aware of Frederick the Great's dictum that he who defends everything defends nothing. And as they looked at this western coast of Fortress Europe, running from Norway all through the Low Countries to France, into Brittany, this was an extraordinary defensive problem that they had to confront. They had to make guesses; they had to make calculations.

Adding to these inherent strategic difficulties, German defensive thinking was also hampered by serious differences about how to defend against the invasion. Rommel was convinced that the Allies had to be stopped on the beaches—hit them as they come off their landing craft, halt them at the beaches—that if they get ashore successfully then the battle's lost. We have to stop them within the first 24 hours. It was for this reason, Rommel argued, that first 24 hours of the invasion would be what he called "the longest day," the day on which the fate of Germany would hinge. Rundstedt, on the other hand, believed that trying to halt the Allies on the beaches was a virtually impossible task. After all, you would have to build up these defenses all across the likely landing areas, over several hundred miles, and so the best defensive strategy would be to certainly hold the beaches as much as possible, but to have a mobile strike force, a mobile defense, with a vigorous counterattack after the invasion, after the main thrust of the invasion had been identified. Both Rommel and Rundstedt, as well as Hitler, all believed, of course, that there would be a diversion. There might be some sort of diversionary attack one place, and then the main thrust of the attack would come elsewhere. So between Rommel and Rundstedt, both charged in different ways with the defense of Western Europe, there are these significant differences.

Complicating these arrangements was another problem, and that was the two important Panzer divisions that were going to be key elements of any German defensive strategy. Whether it was Rommel's "halt them on the beaches," or, more obviously, Rundstedt's mobile defense position, these two Panzer divisions had to be sent to throw back the main Allied invasion. Neither Rommel nor Rundstedt had the authority to dispatch those Panzer divisions, which were in the north, closer to the Pas-de-Calais and Paris. Only Adolf Hitler could release those Panzer divisions for dispatch to the front. So unity of command was not achieved by the Germans as they prepared for this decisive battle.

The Allies certainly planned to invade Normandy, but in early 1944 and right down to D-Day itself, the Allies did everything they could to convince the Germans that the invasion would indeed come in the Pas-de-Calais. The Allies created a dummy headquarters under Patton's command, with elaborate radio traffic, supply depots, railway sidings, inflatable tanks, cardboard trucks—an extraordinary effort to confuse the Germans, who believed that no invasion would come without Patton, the hero of the American army as far as the Germans were concerned, being a key player.

The British also created a dummy army in the north, also with radio traffic, with a whole series of ploys to make the Germans believe that an invasion of Norway was in the works—that the British were going to launch an attack in Norway. And although Hitler did not reinforce the German troops in Norway, the 13 German divisions that were stationed in Norway remained in place even as the spring approached and invasion season was upon the Germans.

Ultra, the Allied intercepts of German code traffic, reported that the Germans had indeed bought the deception. So the question of where was successfully disguised by the Allies. Everyone knew that the invasion would come sometime in the late spring or early summer and the timing would be largely dictated by weather conditions. The Allies would need calm seas, they would need clear skies, if they were to take advantage of one of the great advantages they possessed, and that was air superiority.

So, the question of when. The Germans understood this as well as the Allies. Late spring, early summer. This was the time that one could expect it. Eisenhower, in planning, had set June 5 for D-Day, and the cumbersome loading process had begun on May 31. I always find it remarkable to think that this massive movement of troops—of vehicles of every sort, trucks, tanks, jeeps, all sort of artillery pieces—all of southern England, beginning on May 31, was simply in motion, as these troops moved by train, some by foot, some in convoys, began moving to the ports from which they would load the ships and begin to move. All along the route, British civilians were out waving at the troops. It was clear to anyone around that this was the big event; this was the long-awaited invasion. It was finally coming. And yet the Germans were in the dark about this.

By the evening of June 3, the assault waves of the Allied expeditionary force were loaded up, all prepared for the invasion on June 5. The ships assembled were extraordinary. Two thousand seven hundred and twenty-seven ships: battleships, destroyers, minesweepers, huge LSTs—landing ships to carry tanks, heavy supplies, troops, and so on. Nine hundred and thirty-one of these ships were headed for Omaha and Utah beaches, the two American beaches to be hit—the western naval task force. The eastern naval task force contained 1,796 ships bound for Gold, Juno, and Sword beaches, the code names for the British beaches. In addition, 2,600 landing craft, Higgins boats and other smaller vessels that were simply too small to make the cross-channel trip on their own, had been loaded up onto these giant LSTs so that, all together, an armada of 5,333 vessels had been assembled in the south of England to prepare for this enormous undertaking.

By June 3, all of the supplies, all of the men, had been loaded. And then, on June 4, a major weather front hit—howling winds, plunging temperatures, and rain falling in horizontal sheets. Still, the thousands of ships in the vast armada had begun to move out of their harbors and to form up into convoys.

Eisenhower got more bad news at his weather briefing at 04:00. The situation, he was told by his chief meteorologist, who was a 28-year-old Scotsman by the name of J. M. Stagg—one thinks about the responsibility that this man shouldered in these days—Stagg told Eisenhower at 04:00 the situation was deteriorating rapidly, that the weather was going to get worse and, even more, it was unpredictable. It was not at all clear if the weather would break, when it would break—that predicting the weather for more than 24 hours under these circumstances was almost impossible.

At 06:00 Eisenhower gave the order to put everything on hold. The troops in the ships were miserable. Caught in the storm out in the Channel, seasickness—awful conditions for the troops.

Eisenhower now was confronted with a choice. To postpone the invasion would mean putting things off until June 19. There were only three days in each two-week period in June when the two conditions he needed could be predicted; that is, when low tide and first light came together. Essentially, he had to have these conditions because of German defenses. They were concentrated in the tidal flats, so you wanted to be able to see them. The naval people bringing the boats in wanted to be able to see the underwater obstructions that would be obscured at high tide; and, also, the airborne operations required at least a half moon, and that reduced the availability of days to an even shorter period. If he postponed to June 19 and the weather were bad then, then one's talking about a postponement of an entire month— you'd lose a month of campaigning; the security might be breached. It was a nightmarish situation for Eisenhower.

Then at 21:30 on the evening of the fourth, at Southwick House, a weather briefing suggested that there might be a 36-hour respite after all, a brief break in the weather on the night and morning of June 5-June 6. A cheer went up from the gentlemen who were present at Southwick House at that meeting. They were gathered at the mess room there. As one person who was present said, he'd never seen so many middle-aged men cheer as vigorously at one time as when Stagg brought the news about this possible weather break. In fact, Stagg was quite certain about it. The pressure on Eisenhower at this moment was intense. Leigh-Mallory, in charge of air operations, urged postponement. Air Marshal Tedder, Eisenhower's deputy commander, agreed. It was simply too dicey to undertake air operations if the weather was going to be this chancy. Eisenhower turned to Montgomery and asked him. And Montgomery, ever ready for this sort of thing, said, "I would say, go." Eisenhower paced the room and then decided—Overlord, the largest, most complex, and diciest amphibious assault in human history—an assault on which the outcome of the war would ride—would be launched on June 6 in weather conditions that boded only ill. It was a gamble of astronomical proportions.

When Eisenhower awoke at 03:30 on June 5, the wind was literally shaking his trailer. Rain fell in sheets, and the storm continued to rage. At a weather briefing, Stagg arrived with good news. He insisted, despite all of the conditions that Eisenhower and everyone present could see—the howling wind, the rain coming in sheets—Stagg absolutely insisted that the weather was going to break, and added a new note: It would only be a break, and then conditions would deteriorate again. The operation would have, at most—at most—48 hours of reasonably good weather.

Already the ship convoys had been forming up since midnight, and the men were forced to ride out the storm bobbing in the heavy surf. At this point Eisenhower could still have ordered a postponement, and, at a last briefing with his staff while the rain continued to pelt against the window, Eisenhower, supported once again by Montgomery, made the final decision. "OK," he said simply. "Let's go."

Eisenhower would draft a message to the troops of the Allied expeditionary force which, I think, is one of the most powerful and moving documents of the Second World War, and I would like to read it. This was to be given to all troops involved in the Normandy landings. "Soldiers, sailors, and airmen of the Allied expeditionary force, you are about to embark upon the great crusade toward which we have striven these many months. The eyes of the world are upon you. The hopes and prayers of liberty-loving people everywhere march with you. In company with our brave allies and brothers in arms on other fronts, you will bring about the destruction of the German war machine, the elimination of Nazi tyranny over the oppressed peoples of Europe, and security for ourselves in a free world. Your task will not be an easy one. Your enemy is well trained, well equipped, and battle-hardened. He will fight savagely. But this is the year 1944. Much has happened since the Nazi triumphs of 1940-41. The United Nations have inflicted upon the Germans great defeats in open battle, man to man. Our air offensive has seriously reduced their strength in the air and their capacity to wage war on the ground. Our home fronts have given us an overwhelming superiority in weapons and munitions of war and placed at our disposal great reserves of trained fighting men. The tide has turned. The free men of the world are marching together to victory. I have full confidence in your courage, devotion to duty, and skill in battle. We will accept nothing less than full victory. Good luck, and let us all beseech the blessings of Almighty God upon this great and noble undertaking. Dwight Eisenhower."

Eisenhower, in these terribly tense moments on the eve of D-Day, also drafted a second message. He put it in his pocket. He wrote, "Our landings in the Cherbourg–Le Havre area have failed to gain the satisfactory foothold, and I have withdrawn the troops. My decision to attack was based on the best information available. The troops, the air and navy, did all that bravery and devotion to duty could do. If any blame or fault attaches to the attempt, it is mine alone." That was a message that he desperately hoped he would never have to print.

At 19:00 hours on the fifth of June, Eisenhower would visit the 101st Airborne units. They were to be among the first to land in Normandy. The die was now cast, the invasion was about to begin, the machinery was all in place, the ships underway. The great moment had at last arrived.

D-Day to Paris
Lecture 19

In this lecture, we're going to examine the course of events on that June 5–June 6, and then the Allied movement from Normandy toward Paris and the liberation of that city and of France.

Erwin Rommel, the German commander in charge of defending northwestern Europe, argued that the key to German victory was to defeat the Allies at the beaches, and that the first 24 hours of the invasion would be decisive. It would be, as he put it, "the longest day." This lecture traces the last agonizing stage of planning and then the launching of the D-Day invasion, the course of the battle in Normandy, and the liberation of Paris.

The seaborne invasion force was preceded by Allied paratroopers who dropped into France the previous night. On June 5, Eisenhower visited troops of the 101st Airborne, of whom some 80 percent were expected to become casualties. These troops carried a daunting amount of equipment. Most pilots of the C-47s were going into combat for the first time; their planes were neither armored nor armed. The planes formed a 300-mile "V" formation. At first they maintained an extremely tight formation while crossing the Channel, despite no radio communications. They dispersed, however, after they hit a cloud bank.

Very few paratroopers of the 82nd and 101st units were actually dropped where they should have been. Some were mistakenly dropped at sea; some were dropped at a too-low altitude; some were dropped into flooded fields and drowned.

Due to this dispersal, the Germans received reports of invading paratroopers from all across Normandy. Meanwhile, the French resistance began to cut German communications. Both factors caused the German response to be slow.

The seaborne invasion force landed in Normandy early on D-Day. Strategic surprise was achieved at Normandy, especially due to the poor weather.

Rundstedt and the high command were still convinced that the Normandy landing was a diversion and that the main invasion would come in the Pas-de-Calais. Hitler was not awakened with the news, and the key Panzer units were delayed for several hours. The German response was slowed by poor intelligence, the role of the French resistance, and the inability to move troops rapidly to the front.

The Allied landings at Juno, Sword, and Utah beaches were successful. U.S. troops were pinned down for

Soldier checking for snipers in a French town.

hours on Omaha beach. They broke out and moved inland only late in the day. Keep in mind that the success of the D-Day landings had not been a foregone conclusion.

The Normandy landings were merely the prelude to a long and murderous campaign in Normandy and later for France. The breakout of Allied troops from Normandy went very slowly. By July 1, almost one million Allied troops had landed. The impenetrable hedgerows made fighting particularly difficult. Montgomery was slowed by tenacious German defenses at Caen, which did not fall until July 18. The breakout of Patton's Third Army in July opened the war of movement.

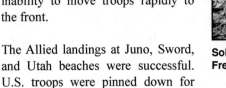

Indeed, the summer of 1944, both on the Eastern and Western Fronts, did represent the beginning of the war's final phase.

Allied forces trapped an entire German army group in the Falaise Pocket, where the fighting and destruction were particularly intense. The landing of a second invasion force in mid-August 1944 presaged a debate among Allied commanders over the liberation of Paris. Eisenhower wanted to bypass the city, which had little strategic importance and would only slow the Allied advance. De Gaulle wanted his Free French forces to liberate Paris before the Communist Parisian resistance did. Eisenhower relented on August 22 and ordered Gen. Leclerc to advance on Paris. The Parisian resistance rose anyway, and Hitler ordered the city's destruction.

The liberation of Paris was the final chapter in the battle for France. By September, Allied armies were advancing on Germany, and the outcome of the war in Europe was no longer in doubt. ■

Suggested Reading

Stephen E. Ambrose, *Citizen Soldiers: The U.S. Army From the Normandy Beaches to the Bulge to the Surrender of Germany*, Chapters 1–5.

———, *D-Day*, Chapters 10–32.

Dwight D. Eisenhower, *Crusade in Europe*, Chapter 15.

John Keegan, *Six Armies in Normandy*.

Questions to Consider

1. What explains the failure of the German forces in France to contain and defeat the Allied invasion force?

2. Evaluate the debate among Allied leaders over whether to liberate or bypass Paris.

D-Day to Paris
Lecture 19—Transcript

In our last lecture, we examined the planning for Operation Overlord, the cross-channel invasion of Hitler's Fortress Europe. That was to come on June 6, 1944. The outcome of that battle would be decisive for the outcome of the war. Everyone involved was clearly aware of that, and, on the eve of the invasion, as the troops had gathered in the Channel, the seaborne assault forces already in the Channel, Dwight Eisenhower, the supreme commander of the Allied expeditionary force, went to visit members of the American airborne units that would be dropped into German-occupied Europe, into Normandy, in the night of June 5-June 6. In this lecture, we're going to examine the course of events on that June 5-June 6, and then the Allied movement from Normandy toward Paris and the liberation of that city and of France.

We begin with Eisenhower himself. We talked in the last lecture about the loneliness of the decision that he made when many of his commanders, especially his air commanders—Leigh-Mallory, Tedder, Tedder in particular, whose views Eisenhower respected greatly—were worried; in fact, favored postponing the invasion. Leigh-Mallory estimated that, under the best of conditions, that the airborne units that were going into Normandy would suffer 80 percent casualties. This weighed very heavily on Eisenhower, as the decision had been made and he waited for the invasion to begin. And at 19:00 on June 5 Eisenhower visited the troops of the 101st Airborne. I think many of you have seen the film clip of Eisenhower walking among these airborne troops. The troops are in their charcoaled faces, ready for their loading up to go. Eisenhower walks around, talks to them, he seems confident, he seems not quite jovial but just exudes that sense of confidence—the confidence that he certainly did not necessarily have at that moment. I think he went because these were the troops that he was sending into combat and into harm's way first, and I think that sense of the 80 percent casualties—that figure that Leigh-Mallory continued to press upon him—weighed very heavily on Eisenhower as he talked to those troops.

There would be about 13,400 American, 7,000 British, paratroopers who would be dropped into Normandy—the first Allied troops to land in Nazi-occupied Europe. Those parachute units were about to undergo an amazing operation. Standing there waiting to climb into the C-47s, their equipment alone was daunting. I'd like to read you the description of what one typical airborne trooper had with him as he got ready to climb into the C-47 for this flight: "one suit of olive drab worn under my jumpsuit"—and this was an order for everyone—"helmet, boots, gloves, main parachute, reserve parachute, Mae West"—the yellow inflatable life jacket—"rifle, 45 automatic pistol, trench knife, jump knife, hunting knife, machete, one cartridge belt, two bandoliers, two cans of machine gun ammo totaling 676 rounds of 30 caliber ammo, 66 rounds of 45 caliber ammo, one Hawkins mine capable of blowing off the track of a tank, four blocks of TNT, one entrenching tool with two blasting caps taped on the outside of the steel part, three first aid kits, two morphine needles, one gas mask, a canteen of water, three days' supply of K rations, two days' supply of D rations, six fragmentation grenades, one gammon grenade, one orange and one red smoke grenade, one orange panel, one blanket, one raincoat, one change of socks and underwear, and two cartons of cigarettes." So loaded with equipment were these airborne troopers, if they sat down or fell over backwards they literally had to be helped up by their buddies to climb into the troop transports that would carry them to their date with destiny in Normandy.

One always thinks of the extraordinary armada that had set sail from England headed for the continent when one thinks of D-Day, but this armada of C-47s, these transport planes that would take off on the night of June 5 into June 6, was also a sight to behold, and I'd like to read you one description of what that looked like to those who were taking part. First of all, most of the pilots who would be flying these troop transports were going into combat for the first time. They had not been trained for nighttime flying, remarkably enough, or to deal with flak or bad weather. The C-47 was primarily designed to carry cargo or passengers, not for this sort of operation. The C-47 was neither armed nor was it armored. Their gas tanks were neither protected nor self-sealing, so they were extraordinarily vulnerable aircraft. There were so many planes in the air that the chance of a midair collision was on everybody's mind. It took 432 C-47s to carry the 101st Airborne to Normandy; about the same number for the 82nd Airborne. They were flying in what was called a "V" formation. Stretched out across the sky, it was 300 miles long, nine planes wide, all without radio communication. Only the lead pilot in each serial of 45 planes had a Eureka set, with a show of lights from the Plexiglas astrodome for guidance for the following planes. The planes were 100 feet from wingtip to wingtip in their groups of nine, 1,000 feet from one group to another, with no lights except the little blue dots on the tail of the plane ahead. It was an extremely tight formation even by daylight standards, but to do this at night was very chancy indeed. They crossed the Channel at about 500 feet or less to escape German radar detection, and then were to climb to 1,500 feet to escape the antiaircraft fire along the Channel Islands. Six hundred feet was the jump altitude.

When they crossed the coastline heading out across the Channel, everything was fine. The formation had been able to come together, to form up. But then, as they moved across the Channel, they encountered an enormous cloud bank, and when they did, the formation simply came apart. Some dropped below the cloud bank, some climbed above it, some peeled off to the right, some to the left. It was absolute chaos. And then when they finally crossed into France, they were widely separated, and as they came out of the cloud bank over the continent, as one of the pilots said—in fact many of them said—"all hell seemed to break loose"—searchlights, tracers, antiaircraft fire, everything. And the troop carriers began to move toward the jump zones.

The problems with the C-47s meant that very few of the 82nd or 101st Airborne units actually were dropped where they were supposed to. Many of the—a number of the units were actually dropped across the—out into the sea. The planes had gone all the way across the Cotentin Peninsula and dropped them on the other side. Others had come in very low—dropped them at too high a speed so that the paratroopers were scattered. Rather than coming down in—they were supposed to come down in sticks, but instead they were scattered everywhere. It looked like a catastrophe in the making. One American paratrooper who had landed safely managed to—was looking up and saw another C-47 coming across at extraordinarily low altitude. He saw them disgorge a stick of paratroopers, and he wrote later, "Their chutes were pulling out of the tray packs and just starting to unfurl when they hit the ground. Seventeen men hit the ground before their chutes had time to open. They made a sound like ripe pumpkins being thrown down to burst against the ground." In addition to those who were dropped actually out at sea, were those who were dropped too low or were dropped with the planes going too fast.

Other paratroopers that night drowned in water that was two feet deep. The Germans had flooded fields around the Normandy area. The flooding could not be picked up by aerial photographs or Allied intelligence because of reeds, hay, and so on. And so, when paratroopers came down on what looked like a field, in the dark of course, hit the ground, and rolled as they were supposed to, they wound up with all of this equipment rolling up in their parachutes in water two feet, three feet deep, and were unable to disengage themselves, and simply drowned.

One other group of paratroopers came down in spectacular fashion in the absolute center of the village of Sainte-Mère-Église, a critical point in airborne operations they were supposed to take—they were not supposed to land in the town. As coincidence would have it, a fire had broken out in one of the buildings in the town. Lights were on, the huge fire was going, the villagers were out putting out the fire—and of course the German troops were out as well in the village—as down suddenly out of the sky, after hearing the droning of planes coming over, thinking, of course, this would simply be another Allied air raid—instead the sky was filled with parachutes coming down, and the troopers landed right in the middle of the village and were cut to pieces.

One man, a radio operator, who landed on that night, would recall he landed with his radio set in a leg bag attached to his leg—so additional equipment— fell into the water with 140 pounds of radio equipment securely fastened to his body and a back injured by the opening shock—that's when the parachute snapped open. He lost his knife as he struggled to cut his way out to the surface, and was reprieved of his last gasp when his parachute collapsed and ceased to drag him along the bottom. "The terror of that first night," he recalled in 1967, "remains so vivid even today that sometimes I wake up in a cold sweat and nearly jump out of bed."

What might not have been a propitious beginning to this most ambitious operation turned out to be a godsend. The Germans began to receive communications from all over Normandy, from all over the area, that paratroopers had landed, paratroopers had landed. And so even though the French Resistance had begun to cut communications, making it difficult for the Germans to get accurate reporting from the landing sites, at German high command they began to say, "Well, there are paratroopers here, here, here, and here." It didn't seem to make any sense. What was the actual—was this simply a diversion? Was this simply a small action? What was going on? It was not at all clear.

As the paratroopers were climbing into their planes, the BBC had broadcast in its broadcast to France, which were done every evening, the second part of Paul Verlaine's poem "The Song of Autumn," which was the code word for the French Resistance to know, to say, "This is it." The second half meant, the invasion is coming. And so as the paratroopers were flying across the Channel and preparing to land, French Resistance groups were out beginning to cut lines of communication and so on. The Germans decoded this—understood what this meant—but were unable to act on it. The Abwehr, the German counterintelligence people, were enormously frustrated by this, believing that they understood that this was the signal, but were unable to act on it in a forthright fashion. The Germans then were slow to respond because of the chaos caused by the cutting of communication, and also these contradictory, or at least what seemed to be, bizarre reports from the front, of paratroopers.

At dawn on the sixth of June, 1944, the vast armada that had been composed in Britain approached the shores of Fortress Europe. The Germans there were caught off guard despite the breaking of the code. Rommel, so confident that the weather was so abysmal, so terrible, that no Allied landing would come now, had actually left Normandy, left France, on his way back to Germany—it was his wife's birthday—to visit her. Other key commanders of the German high command in France were away from their posts going to war games, because also they were convinced that the weather would prevent any sort of Allied landing at this particular point.

Gerd von Rundstedt, the German commander for the Western Front, was slow to react. Certain, when finally enough coherence could be achieved from the reports, that a landing had taken place in Normandy, Rundstedt was still slow to react because he believed this was the diversion. It was too far away, it was not the Pas-de-Calais, and he was wary of taking premature action. Finally, he demanded that Hitler release the two Panzer divisions, but Hitler would not be awakened and thus 12 precious hours were lost, and several more before the Panzers could actually get underway. A great deal is actually made of this, of Hitler sleeping through the night—Nero fiddling while Rome burned. But in some ways, one suspects that even had Hitler been awake and had been apprised of the developing situation in Normandy, that he would have also been wary of dispatching his Panzers that far south, and would still hold on to them for some time because of the fear that the real invasion would come at the Pas-de-Calais.

The plan that had been devised for D-Day was that the operation was to unfold in three stages: what was called the break-in—D-Day itself—get the lodgment to safely land. Then the buildup, and then finally the breakout. All went well at the Allied invasion beaches except at Omaha Beach, where the navy launched troops too far out in the choppy sea; there was ferocious resistance on the part of the Germans; the Americans were pinned down for hours. Until late in the afternoon it appeared that the situation at Omaha might really get out of hand and that the entire invasion front might collapse if the Germans could split the Allied invasion front. But, late in the day, the Americans finally were able to move off the beach and to begin to press inland.

The British landing at Gold, Juno, and Sword beaches moved ahead. Their landings went much more smoothly. They moved inland much quicker. They too failed to take their original objective on D-Day. Montgomery had been—though he would later maintain this was not the case—confident that he was going to be able to take Caen the first day, in the first 24 hours. This was their objective. But although the Germans had been caught off guard and had been slow to respond, they put up terrific resistance, especially as the British began to move inland toward Caen.

By the seventh of June, 100,000 Allied troops had landed on the coast of Normandy. Within 10 days, a half a million Allied troops had come ashore. By July 1, almost a million Allied troops had managed to land.

It's interesting as one thinks about what might have happened had Eisenhower decided to postpone the invasion, because on June 19 one of the largest storms in the English Channel in the twentieth century hit. A huge, ferocious storm, it destroyed the mulberry off the American landing beaches—this artificial port that had been established. It would have been an absolute disaster if they'd tried to launch it then, or it might have been postponed yet again.

The D-Day invasion had succeeded. I think there is a tendency to think, in retrospect, that victory there was a foregone conclusion, but it was anything but that—anything but that. And the extraordinary feats of heroism on that day, I think, 50 years after the fact, still boggle the mind. I'm struck as I think about the fiftieth anniversary of the D-Day landings, when a number of American Rangers who had taken part in one of the most remarkable achievements of that day—a specially trained group of Rangers were supposed to climb Pont du Hoc, this sheer bluff, to get these German guns at the top. They had managed to do it, climbed this against terrific resistance, and as I looked at the veterans standing there on this fiftieth anniversary, standing at the bottom of the beach looking up at these sheer bluffs, one man turned to one of his buddies and said, "Would somebody here please tell me how we did this?" It was such an amazing individual feat. The day was filled with those.

There's a second tendency, I think, a second, and understandable, temptation also, to think of that dramatic day, "the longest day" as Rommel referred to it, as in itself decisive for the outcome of the war. But that epic battle, in which 4,000 Allied soldiers would become casualties, was in fact just the beginning of a long, murderous campaign in Normandy, whose outcome was still in doubt weeks after June 6. Indeed, the Allies were still bogged down in Normandy a month later, the Americans slogging through the hedgerow country, the so-called bocage country. Saint-Lô would fall only on July 18, and the British were still pinned down before Caen. That unfortunate city had been the British objective for D-Day, but would fall to British and Canadian troops only after a massive RAF raid virtually leveled the city on July 18.

What's remarkable, in a way, about the Battle of Normandy is that one almost gets the impression that the Allies were so focused on the planning on D-Day itself—getting the troops ashore, landing them, being able to supply them—that less thought had actually been given to the terrain, the conditions of combat in Normandy itself. The Americans in particular, finding themselves in Normandy—in this bocage country, the hedgerow country—Allied intelligence was unprepared for this, remarkably enough. These hedgerows were anything but sort of small decorative shrubs. These in many cases were centuries old—huge hedgerows, mounds that were almost like bunkers with a deep system of roots, so that a tank couldn't even penetrate them. And each row and each field was boundaried by these hedgerows. As a consequence, a German force—even an undermanned German force—could fight, hold up an advance for much of a day, move back to the next hedgerow, the next hedgerow, and so on. It was absolutely murderous for the troops bogged down in this area.

It would not be until August that the American breakthrough occurred, when General Patton was at last dispatched to the continent to lead the American Third Army, and it came roaring out of the Cotentin Peninsula and raced to the east-northeast towards Falaise. At this point General Montgomery—and at this point and certainly in retrospect after the war—always would maintain that the original plan, his original plan, had called for him not necessarily to take Caen, but to use that as the hinge, and then the Americans would be the door that would swing for the great breakout. This is some creative retrospective thinking, I think, on the part of General Montgomery, but certainly it would be Patton whose Third Army would begin the war of movement, breaking out and tearing into the Germans. At Falaise, an entire German army group would be trapped by the Americans coming from the south, the British and Canadians moving down a bit from the north. The killing and destruction in the so-called "Falaise Pocket" was so intense, the slaughter so overwhelming, that Allied pilots flying over the battlefield at 1,500 feet could smell the stench of death rising from the battlefield.

In mid-August the second Allied invasion occurred on the Mediterranean coast of France, led by a joint American and French force that rapidly began to push northward. At this juncture, the only issue remaining for the campaign in France was the fate of Paris. Would the Allies attempt to seize the city? Would the Germans defend it—leading, almost everyone agreed, to the city's destruction? Eisenhower's intention originally was simply to bypass

Paris. It was, as far as Eisenhower was concerned, of very little strategic importance. The political significance of it, the symbolic significance of it, was obviously important, especially to the French, but in terms of military operations, Eisenhower believed that it would simply slow down the Allied advance. The Allies would be forced to supply the city of Paris, the civilians of Paris, and that this would be a diversion of much-needed resources.

Initially, the decision to bypass Paris had been supported by General De Gaulle, who had been promised by Eisenhower when the two were in Africa that Paris would be liberated by French forces. The question now was, which French forces. As the Allied troops broke out of Normandy, Resistance forces in Paris, indeed all over the country, had risen up. The French Resistance, which had struggled against the Germans and German occupation since 1940, now came out in full force. De Gaulle had created a general staff or what he called FFI, the French Forces of the Interior, and had convinced Eisenhower to recognize him as a co-equal of the other national commanders under supreme headquarters of the Allied expeditionary force. De Gaulle was, in the best of times, a difficult person to deal with. His sense of pride had been wounded over and over and over again by the Allies, who were not completely—who did not consider him completely trustworthy. Nonetheless, De Gaulle was particularly worried that the Parisian Resistance, with its heavy communist influence, would seize the city. If the city were going to be liberated, De Gaulle argued, it had to be liberated by the FFI, by his forces—liberated from without, not by the Communists within the city. He ordered the Parisian Resistance, under no circumstances, to unleash what he called a premature rising against the German garrison. There were two concerns for De Gaulle. One was that if the Resistance in Paris, largely dominated, he was afraid, by the Communists, did in fact rise against the Germans, that it would lead to the destruction of the city; that the Germans would use this as an—that the fighting in the city would destroy Paris, the jewel of Western civilization as far as De Gaulle was concerned. And second, he didn't want there to be what he called a second commune—there was the commune of 1871, when the Germans had surrounded Paris and a left-wing uprising had sent the city and French political culture into a crisis.

On August 22, 1944, with the threat that De Gaulle would, on his own initiative, send French troops to Paris, Eisenhower relented and General

Leclerc was ordered to advance with his French armored division on the city. In a mad dash for Paris 120 miles away, Leclerc, supported by American forces, entered the city, whose Resistance had risen anyway—De Gaulle was unable to actually control events in Paris—and accepted the surrender of the German garrison. The Germans had indeed planted, begun the process— German demolition teams had begun the process of mining the Eiffel Tower, the Louvre, all the bridges on the Isle de la Cite, the Isle Saint Louis, the major cultural monuments of Paris—but the German general there was finally convinced that he did not want to be the man who would be remembered for the destruction of Paris.

The fall of Paris, then, was the final installment in the battle for France which had commenced on D-Day, June 6. By early September, the Allied armies had reached Belgium and Holland and were approaching the German frontier. The war in Europe in the late summer of 1944 seemed to be drawing to a speedy close. And indeed, the summer of 1944, both on the Eastern and Western Fronts, did represent the beginning of the war's final phase. The Allied success in France was matched by a devastating defeat meted out to the Germans by the Red Army in July, when the entire center of the German front in Russia collapsed and the Russians began the long, arduous push toward the eastern frontiers of the Third Reich.

But the war was not over. The dying continued for almost a year after D-Day. In fact, the largest pitched battle in American history remained to be fought, the Battle of the Bulge, in December and January of 1944–1945. But after the events of the summer of 1944, after the success of D-Day, the outcome of the war in Europe was no longer in doubt. The tide had been irrevocably turned, and the liberation of Europe from Nazi tyranny was at hand.

Operation Market Garden and the Battle of the Bulge
Lecture 20

[In this lecture] we're going to examine Allied operations from the fall of Paris, in late August of 1944, through the winter, looking at particularly Operation Market Garden, the Allied plan to get across the Rhine in 1944, and then the German counterattack, the Ardennes offensive, in the winter of 1944 and into January, 1945.

After the fall of Paris in August 1944, the Germans seemed defeated, and the Allies were poised for a final assault on Germany. The success of the battle for France raised new strategic choices for Allied commanders. The Allies debated the best way to break into Germany and bring the war to a conclusion in 1944. Montgomery urged a single-thrust strategy aimed at taking the Ruhr. But Eisenhower advocated a broad front strategy.

Various problems beset the Allied armies. First, they faced a troop shortage. The British were at the limit of their manpower reserves,

The 60th Infantry Regiment advances into a Belgian town under protection of a heavy tank.

and the United States was stretched by the demands of a two-theater war. Also, in late 1944, the Allies suffered from overconfidence and faulty intelligence. They were convinced that Germany was on the brink of defeat; Allied intelligence underestimated German potential in the west.

The Allied armies also faced enormous logistical problems. Advancing troops were outrunning their supplies. A port closer to the front—Antwerp—was desperately needed. Although Antwerp fell in September, Hitler remained in control of the Scheldt estuary, which made the port useless.

Operation Market Garden was planned for September 1944. Montgomery advanced a daring plan to jump the Rhine in Holland, thereby outflanking the Ziegfried line to the north. The goals of the operation were to cross the last river barrier that guarded Germany, outflank the northernmost fortifications of the West Wall, and threaten Germany's V-2 launching sites in Holland.

The Allies faced formidable problems. They had to cross numerous rivers and canals and seize many bridges. They suffered again from overconfidence, expecting to brush aside two defending German armored divisions. And the Allied forces moved very slowly. Thus, Operation Market Garden ended as an abysmal failure. The defeat of the Allies meant no Rhine crossing in 1944.

Meanwhile, Patton and the Americans bogged down in Lorraine. The First Army took Aachen on October 21. Nevertheless, Allied progress was slow in late 1944 and victory remained elusive.

Hitler struck back with the Ardennes offensive in December 1944. He hoped that one last dramatic stroke in the west would split the Allies between Montgomery in the north and the Americans further south. The German high command, meanwhile, sought to find defensible positions behind the Rhine. They worried that Hitler's plan would weaken Germany's position in the east and consume its last troop reserves.

The failure of Hitler's offensive in the Ardennes would mark the last gasp of Nazi Germany in the west.

The plan called for smashing the Allies in the Ardennes Forest, then making a massive armored drive for Antwerp, then driving a wedge between the Allied armies and destroying them piecemeal. The Allies assumed that the Ardennes was impenetrable, especially in winter. German radio silence meant that Ultra was of little use to the Allies. Despite telltale German troop movements, the Allies were still caught off guard. They continued to exhibit fatal overconfidence.

Hitler's Operation "Autumn Fog" commenced on December 16, 1944. It caught the overmatched Americans completely by surprise and unprepared. Allied air power was neutralized by bad weather for more than a week. The German drive created a huge bulge in the American lines. American prisoners were massacred at Malmedy. Despite being surrounded by Germans, isolated U.S. units held out at the key road junctions of Saint Vith and Bastogne. Patton's army finally broke the siege of Bastogne on December 26. When the weather cleared, the Americans rallied their air power and halted the German offensive by the end of January.

The Battle of the Bulge further weakened the German army. Hitler had sacrificed his last reserves and best armor on an essentially doomed enterprise. German troops were caught west of the Rhine. The battle gravely weakened the German position in the east on the eve of a massive Russian offensive in Poland in January 1945. The failure of the Ardennes offensive represented the last gasp of the Third Reich. ∎

Suggested Reading

Gerald Astor, *A Blood-Dimmed Tide: The Battle of the Bulge By The Men Who Fought It.*

Carlo D'Este, *Patton: A Genius For War*, Chapter 43.

Dwight D. Eisenhower, *Crusade in Europe*, Chapter 18.

John Keegan, *The Second World War*, Chapter 23.

Questions to Consider

1. Evaluate the disagreement between Montgomery and Eisenhower over how best to end the war following the fall of Paris.

2. What were the goals of Operation Market Garden? Why did it fail?

Operation Market Garden and the Battle of the Bulge
Lecture 20—Transcript

By the late summer of 1944, the Western Allies stood in control of most of France; Belgium, Holland lay before them; the frontier of Germany beckoned. In this, our twentieth lecture in the series on the Second World War, we're going to examine Allied operations from the fall of Paris, in late August of 1944, through the winter, looking at particularly Operation Market Garden, the Allied plan to get across the Rhine in 1944, and then the German counterattack, the Ardennes offensive, in the winter of 1944 and into January, 1945.

At this point in the war, with the fall of Paris, the breakout out of Normandy, it really did seem as if the war might come to an end in Europe in 1944. The Germans seemed to be reeling; were defeated. At this point, a debate broke out within the Allied high command, between General Montgomery, the British commander, who would advocate what he called a single thrust strategy, aimed at driving directly toward the Ruhr and possibly even on to Berlin if necessary, and General Eisenhower, who would prefer a broad front approach to the strategic advance toward Germany.

The Allies would encounter several problems in this period. One was a shortage of troops. We would discover in 1944 that, despite the enormous mobilization of manpower in the United States, that the American army was actually too small for the task that it had been assigned—to fight in two theaters of war—in the Pacific and now in Europe. There would also be a problem of overconfidence—extraordinary overconfidence on the part of the Allies—in the summer and fall of 1944, for which the Allies would pay a terrible cost in the Ardennes in the winter, with the German offensive that would come to be known as the Battle of the Bulge.

The Allied debate over offensive strategy really burst forth with the fall of Paris on August 25. The "City of Light" was spared by the Germans and by the Allies. It was declared an open city. Leclerc and Bradley's troops entered the city. Some of the American troops were somewhat bitter, because they got to march down the Champs Élysées, march through the city, out the other side, only then to get put back on trucks, or march, and move on toward the front, after the Germans.

But shortly thereafter, the British Second and Canadian First, the American First Armies, slammed into Belgium, and by September 15, almost all of Belgium and Luxembourg were in Allied hands. Meanwhile, Patton's Third Army had swung into the northeast portions of France and was making rapid headway. Indeed, the German frontier was now only a few miles away. The offensive needed to halt, not so much because of German resistance, which seemed to be cracking at every possible place, but simply because the armies were outrunning their supplies.

Supply would become one of the major problems, as well. Fuel shortages began to develop. The only real operative ports, beaches, were still in Normandy, and as—the farther the American troops, the Allied troops, pushed, the farther away from those resupply centers they came.

The debate, then, centered around General Montgomery's position. Montgomery argued with Eisenhower, urging what he called a single thrust strategy, with the British Second and American First Armies, under his command naturally, driving toward the Rhine and the Ruhr; while the Canadians and the Americans under Patton would halt in order to conserve fuel and supplies, and those scarce supplies and fuel would be funneled to Montgomery's forces in the north. Eisenhower, on the other hand, advocated a broad front strategy, with all armies moving ahead simultaneously, putting pressure on the Germans, stretching German resources across a broad front.

Montgomery was certainly unhappy, and later argued that Eisenhower's decision permitted not only the early encirclement of the Ruhr, but a dash all the way to Berlin. Montgomery, after the war, would maintain that Eisenhower had made a terrible decision here, that victory really was within the Allies' grasp in the summer of 1944, and that if only he, Montgomery, had been given the necessary fuel, supplies—had been given precedence over Patton and the others—then it would have been possible to concentrate Allied forces, smash the Germans, cross the Rhine in the north, and drive directly to the Ruhr, knocking the Germans out of the war early—or, then, even continuing on, this great juggernaut headed toward Berlin.

Montgomery is probably correct about the advance to the Rhine. There's no question that had he been given the resources, Allied forces under his command—the British Second Army, American First—could have driven toward the Rhine with great force in the summer of 1944. But crossing the Rhine was still going to be a very difficult proposition, and Montgomery was wildly optimistic about the possibility of a drive to Berlin, or even actually into the Ruhr itself. The Allies lacked the supplies for such an ambitious policy, and there was no solution in sight to that supply problem. This was something that Eisenhower understood.

That problem, the problem of getting supplies to the advancing Allied armies, was eased somewhat by the capture of Marseille, but the Allies still badly needed a major port in northwestern Europe, nearer the action. Moving supplies from Marseille in the south, or from Normandy, still was taking too long. The obvious choice was the Belgian port of Antwerp, one of Europe's largest and most important ports. And Antwerp actually fell to the British on September 4, with the port intact, an important achievement for the British.

But the problem was not solved by the seizure of Antwerp, because Antwerp lay on the Scheldt River, 60 miles from the North Sea, and the Germans continued to control the Belgian and Dutch territory that bordered the river's estuary—so that while it had the port, one still had to send the supplies up and down that river to get to the port, and the Germans were able to harass any sort of ship movement and make any major resupply impossible by that route. Hitler planned to hold on to this estuary for as long as possible—the Allies certainly knew this—to deny the use of the port. And indeed the Germans continued to hold out in the Scheldt estuary until November 9, and until that time Antwerp was absolutely useless to the Allies.

A second debate would break out in the Allied camp in roughly this period. Montgomery, thwarted in his single thrust strategy, now put forward a new plan: a plan to cross the Rhine in the north, in the Netherlands. If it worked, he argued, the Allies would jump the only major river barrier that guarded Germany and would outflank the northernmost fortifications of what was called the West Wall, sometimes called the Siegfried Line, along the Dutch-German border. It would also threaten the V-2 launch sites in Holland.

One of the aspects of the D-Day attack that we did not mention, in talking about the operations on the continent, was Hitler's launch in the aftermath of D-Day of the so-called V weapons—Vergeltungswaffe. In German, it means revenge or vengeance weapons—the buzz bombs that would chug, chug, chug, chug and could be heard coming across the Channel, the first missiles, certainly, of modern warfare. You could see them. They could be actually shot down, traced on radar and shot down by the RAF or the Americans, with some difficulty. These were terrifying enough, but the Germans would also begin, shortly thereafter, launching the V-2s, rockets that, fired above the stratosphere, would come down with devastating impact on London and could not be seen, could not be anticipated—basically would arrive with devastating impact.

So, getting to these launch sites in the Low Countries was a major concern for the Allies, in Holland in particular, in 1944. However, a drive to the Rhine in Holland would require crossing four rivers and three canals before reaching the lower Rhine at Arnhem. It would require airborne troops to seize bridges all along the route, with British ground troops pushing north to relieve them. The plan that Montgomery came up with, to drop large numbers of airborne troops all along the way, as far north as Arnhem, about 65 miles away—they would seize the crossover; seize the bridges, allowing the Allies pushing from the south a long route north to actually cross the rivers and get across the Rhine. This last bridge at Arnhem was 64 miles away.

Eisenhower was dubious about this plan, but he agreed, approved Montgomery's plan, and what came to be known as Operation Market Garden was launched. The American 101st and 82nd Airborne divisions, the British First Airborne division—the so-called Red Devils—were to be dropped, with the bridge at Arnhem to be taken, the key bridge at Arnhem to be taken, by the Red Devils.

Market Garden began on September 17, 1944, with a huge parachute drop. It was a daring enterprise, an enormous enterprise. There is a film called "A Bridge Too Far," from the Cornelius Ryan book by the same name, which has a visual depiction of this. It's remarkable even in the later filming, an enormous parachute drop. That went successfully, but problems quickly emerged. For one thing, there were two German Panzer divisions within the vicinity of Arnhem. What is remarkable about this, and symptomatic of the period, I think, is that Ultra had already informed the Americans—or we'd been informed by Ultra—of the presence of these armored divisions in the area, and yet the parachute drop went ahead on schedule.

I think what one sees in this is the beginning—that it reflects, I think, this excessive optimism, the sense that the Germans were beaten. We were now going to be able to push the Germans out, and even though these two armored divisions were present, they could be brushed aside. It is this overconfidence, in this period, that would prove to be nearly fatal.

The British drop was also too far away from the objective, and their advance was quite slow. The American 82nd Airborne had difficulty capturing the bridge over the Waal River, and so there was a great deal of delay in the operation; things didn't go as smoothly as anticipated after the initial drop. Also, the advance of the main force, the ground force moving from the south, was glacially slow. It moved along one major road, and the Germans quickly brought this under artillery fire, so that the progress to relieve the airborne troops in the north—the progress was unbelievably slow.

Finally, relief arrived to all of the paratrooper units except the British airborne at Arnhem. This was indeed, as Cornelius Ryan has argued, "a bridge too far." It was too far away, and after nine days of intense fighting, the Red Devils managed to break out of—break through German lines and to link up with the relief force. When they did so, of the 9,000 British paratroopers that had gone into Arnhem, 2,400 emerged to link up with the relief column.

The failure of Operation Market Garden—and it was an abysmal failure—ended all hopes of crossing the Rhine in 1944, and for all intents and purposes really ended the possibility of the war coming to an end in the west in 1944. There would be no easy crossing of the Rhine in the north.

U.S. forces under Hodges, his First Army, and Patton were probing into Germany, but the going was very, very slow. German resistance was tenacious; the terrain was bad. Patton was bogged down in Lorraine, slogging away in the most unproductive campaigning of Patton's career in Europe. The First Army would take Aachen, the first German city to fall, on October 21, after a month of slow and heavy fighting, particularly in an area called the Huertgen Forest, where the fighting was brutal, resistance terrible, the terrain difficult. The fighting in the Huertgen Forest was especially bloody, and resistance terrific. Patch's Seventh Army and de Lattre's French troops were advancing from the south, but they encountered the Voge Mountains, the long, low range along the border of Alsace, and also their advance slowed.

So, what had seemed to be this initial burst out of France, and coming after the liberation of Paris, now, on all and every direction, north, east, and from the south, all were slowed. Even the existence of the Red Ball Express, this extraordinary resupply system of roads being taken over and run in a one-way street literally to the front and then the trucks revolving on a 24-hour basis, couldn't keep up the necessary supplies to the troops at the front. Summer had turned to fall, and victory in Western Europe was still elusive.

In this situation, Hitler decided to take one last gamble in the west. He wanted one last offensive, a desperate effort to split the Allies in the west, an offensive to drive between Montgomery's armies in the north and the Americans farther to the south, with Antwerp in the middle. When Hitler presented his ideas for this to his commanders, Rundstedt and the others were absolutely mortified. Of all times, this was the time to marshal one's resources. This was the time to begin to pull back to defensible lines, to hold. The Russians were still hammering away in the east, advancing on a broad front toward Germany. Now the key was to find defensible positions, to pull back beyond the Rhine, to hold the Americans and the British, to force them into a long, slow, arduous advance.

Hitler would have none of it. Instead, there was going to be a coup de grâce, a dramatic stroke, that would smash the Allies in the west and possibly lead to some sort of negotiated peace. Hitler's plan was to smash into the Allied forces through the Ardennes, in the Ardennes, then send armored spearheads dashing for Antwerp. This would isolate Montgomery's forces in the north. It would deny the Allies the use of the port. He assembled 24 divisions, including 10 Panzer divisions equipped with the newest German tanks, the Tigers and the Panthers. It was a larger force than the Germans had used in the invasion of Western Europe in 1940. And many of these troops, especially the armored divisions, were battle-hardened veterans, not of the Western Front but the Eastern Front, who had been brought back—SS units, as well, Waffen-SS units, brought back, elite troops for this assault in the west.

The Allies had only weak forces at this point along many areas of the front—weak in the sense of underequipped, understaffed, and certainly inexperienced. It was at this point in the war that already the needs of manpower were being felt and the Allies were already contemplating the idea—the Americans already contemplating the idea—of actually pulling ground troops out of the Army Air Corps units stationed in England and Italy and giving them rifles and sending them into infantry units—the area that was weakest—there were only four divisions of Hodges's First Army along the Ardennes.

The Germans—and there was an amazing intelligence lapse here—on the one hand, one wonders, the Allies looking at this situation in the winter of 1944 now, they have fairly strong forces in the north, Patton's position is still down in Lorraine in the south, and the Ardennes, right in the center, this key area in the center of the line, is considered by the Western Allies to be impenetrable to the Germans: The Germans can't launch an offensive operation there, particularly in the winter, and particularly with armor, despite the fact that the Germans had invaded through the Ardennes in 1870 and in 1940 with great effect. In addition, intelligence reports were filtering back to Allied high command that there was a considerable amount of troop movement, tank movement, from east to west. Radio silence meant that Ultra was of little help. But in fact, the very lack of radio traffic should have alerted the Allies that something was afoot. Part of this was explained away: The Germans were closer to their own turf; they didn't need to use radio transmissions as much; there were other ways of communicating. All of this was true, but, one senses here this, again, almost fatal overconfidence of the Allies.

The Allies did detect the transfer of Panzer divisions from the east and actually intercepted messages concerning German air reconnaissance over the Ardennes. And yet, no particular steps were taken to face the possibility of a German offensive, simply seen as being impossible. It was one of the great intelligence failures of the Second World War.

On December 16, 1944, the Germans launched what Hitler called Operation "Autumn Fog." He caught the overmatched Americans unprepared. German troops, some of which were dressed in American uniforms, were able to infiltrate Allied lines. They picked English-speaking and American-sounding Germans dressed in American MP uniforms behind the lines to change signs and to generally cause havoc and confusion. The German forces overwhelmed the outnumbered Americans over a 70-mile front, and Panzers headed for the Meuse River. Low overcast kept the Allies—kept Allied airpower—neutralized for a week, so that what was the great Allied advantage, complete air superiority, indeed air supremacy, was of no value. This was actually one of the great strokes of luck for the Germans, that the weather was so bad during this time. The fighting was intense and conditions terrible—heavy, wet snowfall. It turned out to be the coldest winter in Europe in the twentieth century to that point.

The first SS Panzer division was particularly aggressive. It would be during this German offensive in the Ardennes that troops largely from the Eastern Front—used to fighting in conditions at the Eastern Front, where prisoners were not taken, where the rules of war were not observed, where the Geneva Convention meant nothing—these SS troops were now employed in the west, leading to the murder of a number of American prisoners of war; the most notorious incident, of course, near Malmedy, where 86 American prisoners were machine-gunned and shot by SS troops.

Isolated U.S. units continued to hold out, especially at two key road junctures in eastern Belgium, at Saint Vith and at Bastogne. These were crucial, crucial road junctures that the Germans had to seize. Speed was of the essence for the Germans. They understood this. They were lucky; the weather was still holding out—bad for the Allies—and so, they needed to break through. They couldn't be held up. The longer they were held up, the dicier the operation became. Saint Vith fell on December 22, but Bastogne held. Reinforced by the elements of the 101st Airborne, Bastogne would be surrounded and the Germans would offer—the German general offered the American commander there, Anthony McAuliffe, the opportunity to surrender.

This of course has gone in the lore of the Second World War. It's not quite, "Give me liberty or give me death," but when the German commander sent formal word, using all of the courtesies and so on, the formal courtesies of German military lore, to offer surrender to the American forces at Bastogne, McAuliffe, supposedly stumbling around, said "Aw, nuts!" and one of his associates said, "Well, just say that. Send that message back." And so to the German offer of surrender—in this sort of flowery, formal, German proposal—the response went back, "Nuts." It would go down as one of the great comments of the Second World War. I think McAuliffe regretted it almost ever after, since he was constantly asked about this after the war, but it seemed to be the essence of defiance.

The 101st, as well as McAuliffe's troops, held out, and on December 23 the skies cleared and the Allied planes were at last able to take off. The Allies were able to employ their airpower, and they decimated the German armored spearheads, who were deprived of fuel. Here one sees the impact of something we're going to talk about in a future lecture, which is the impact of Allied airpower, hammering away at German oil supplies, so that one of the goals was not simply to reach Antwerp—to deprive the Allies of the port, split the Allies—but also to get the oil supplies of the Allies built up in the west.

On December 26 Patton's troops, who had turned from Lorraine and raced northward, broke the siege of Bastogne. Montgomery, who had been charged with lifting the siege, and who would create enormous ill will over this episode, arrived at Hodges's headquarters, and according to—even one of Montgomery's own men said he arrived at Hodges's headquarters with the air of Christ come to cleanse the temple. He had ridden to the rescue of the Americans, who had mucked everything up. Patton would lift the siege of Bastogne December 26. Montgomery did not launch his assault to come to the relief of the Americans until January 3.

At this point, the German offensive had ground to a halt without crossing the Meuse River. Autumn Fog had been a wildly ambitious German operation. It created a bulge in Allied lines 45 miles wide and 65 miles deep, hence the name the Battle of the Bulge. But it really had no chance of reaching Antwerp.

Rundstedt wanted to withdraw, to pull his troops back, but Hitler refused. And by the end of January, the bulge in Allied lines had been eliminated. Hitler had sacrificed his last reserves and his best armor in this undertaking. He had delayed the Allied offensive in the west, but he had exhausted his strength on the enterprise—on an enterprise which had virtually no chance of success. Everything would've had to break right for the Germans for this operation to have achieved the strategic objectives that Hitler had foreseen. And, of course, it desperately weakened German strength in the east— armored strength particularly—at a critical juncture. The Russians were preparing a massive offensive in Poland for mid-January, and German troops there would find themselves drastically overmatched.

And Hitler also refused to withdraw troops to the east bank of the Rhine, as Rundstedt and the others had begged him to do. Instead, he demanded that German troops would fight for every inch of German soil. It was absolutely suicidal. His commanders understood it—that German troops would find themselves caught between the Allies in the west and the Rhine, and were in for a desperate winter.

The failure of Hitler's offensive in the Ardennes would mark the last gasp of Nazi Germany in the west. There was, at this point—by the end of December, beginning of January, 1945—the Germans could not win the war in Europe. The last gasp—the last hope for some sort of miraculous victory—had now vanished. And yet the war would go on until May of 1945. But Germany now would be in retreat and on the defensive.

Advance Across the Pacific
Lecture 21

In this lecture, we're going to shift our focus geographically, across the world to the Pacific, examining the American strategy in the Pacific, the debates within the American high command about roots for the advance towards the Japanese home islands, and to examine the beginning of the campaigns that would lead American forces slowly, inexorably, and with terrific losses, toward the final assault on Japan.

U.S. debate over command structure and strategy in the Pacific theater led to a compromise solution. The Pacific war was to be largely an American responsibility. Meanwhile, Britain would retain operational control over Burma and Southeast Asia. There was little inter-Allied squabbling, as there had been in Europe, but serious inter-service rivalry occurred within the American command structure.

FDR favored appointing a single commander-in-chief for the Pacific Theater. Admiral King and FDR wanted Admiral Nimitz. MacArthur's escape from the Philippines made him a hero in the United States and complicated the decision. FDR resolved the disagreement by dividing the command structure in the Pacific. MacArthur was named commander of Allied forces in the southwest Pacific. Nimitz was named commander of the north, central, and south Pacific theaters. The southwest Pacific was an Army theater, and MacArthur reported to Marshall. Nimitz reported to Admiral King. The British retained operational control in Burma and the rest of Southeast Asia.

The strategic debate followed service lines. The Navy favored a central Pacific strategy based on an advance through the Marshalls, Carolines, and Marianas. This would allow concentration of resources and afford the most direct route to Japan. The Army preferred a drive through northern New Guinea and thence on to the Philippines and the southwest Pacific.

The result was a compromise solution. The Joint Chiefs chose a two-pronged strategy, merging Army and Navy proposals. The Navy strategy took highest priority. The advance on Japan would proceed on two axes—the southwest and central Pacific. Both offensives would employ the "island-hopping" tactic.

U.S. forces launched a series of operations against the Japanese in the southwest Pacific during 1943 and 1944. MacArthur and Halsey commanded Operation Cartwheel in the southwest Pacific, which was launched in June 1943. The key targets were New Guinea and the Solomon Islands (especially Rabaul and Truk). Fighting was particularly intense, and the flamethrower was a major combat weapon. MacArthur's progress along the coast was monumentally

The progress across the Pacific was filled with these intense short conflicts and a growing horror ... that a new kind of war had been entered into with an enemy that was almost beyond comprehension.

slow, but by late 1943 his forces were closing in on Rabaul, where the Japanese had constructed strong defenses. Ultimately MacArthur decided to bypass Rabaul entirely. By February 1944, MacArthur had achieved his objectives.

Meanwhile, U.S. forces advanced in the Central Pacific. Nimitz launched assaults on the Gilberts (especially Makin and Tarawa), Marshalls, and Marianas. The battle of "Bloody Tarawa" began on November 20, 1943. The invading forces used "amtrack" vehicles to cross the reefs. The tides were low, as the planners had feared. Most of the Marines had to wade hundreds of yards to reach the beach. Tarawa provided a rude shock to U.S. military planners

Digital Stock World War II CD.

U.S. Marine Raiders on Cape Totkina on Bougainville, the largest of the Solomon Islands.

and the U.S. public; U.S. casualties were high, and the Japanese defenders fought to the last man.

Nimitz then leapfrogged the Carolines and attacked the Marianas. These islands, unlike Tarawa, were substantial and lay within striking distance of the Japanese home islands. Saipan was Nimitz's key target. U.S. forces invaded in June 1944. The ensuing combat was extremely bloody, with Japanese defenders engaging in suicide charges and 8,000 Japanese civilians on the island committing suicide. Saipan offered a stark picture of what U.S. forces invading the Japanese home islands could expect.

The battle of the Philippine Sea took place in June 1944. U.S. forces had huge air superiority; U.S. carrier-based aircraft intercepted Japanese planes in "the Great Marianas Turkey Shoot." Japanese sea power suffered a crippling defeat. Tinian was invaded on June 24, and Guam was invaded on July 21.

The loss of the Marianas was devastating for Japan. The Tojo government fell nine days after the fall of Saipan. The capture of Tinian brought Japan into range for attack by B-29 bombers. ■

Suggested Reading

Eric Bergerud, *Touched With Fire: The Land War in the South Pacific*.

John Keegan, *The Second World War*, Chapter 16.

Ronald H. Spector, *Eagle Against The Sun*, Chapters 11–14.

Questions to Consider

1. How did Roosevelt and the U.S. Joint Chiefs resolve the inter-service rivalry over U.S. strategy in the Pacific theater?

2. What were the military, political, and psychological consequences for Japan of its loss in the Battle of the Philippine Sea?

Advance Across the Pacific
Lecture 21—Transcript

In the last set of lectures we've been examining events in Europe, and the European Theater of operations, examining strategic dilemmas, strategic problems, confronted by both the Allies and the Axis powers. In this, our twenty-first lecture, we're going to shift our focus geographically, across the world to the Pacific, examining the American strategy in the Pacific, the debates within the American high command about roots for the advance towards the Japanese home islands, and to examine the beginning of the campaigns that would lead American forces slowly, inexorably, and with terrific losses, toward the final assault on Japan.

The war in the Pacific was to be largely an American responsibility. In the division of labor, the British were to take care of Southeast Asia, coming out of Burma, India, and so on, while the United States would shoulder the responsibility for the larger Pacific. So that whereas we've been talking about conflicts between British and Americans over strategy, the Mediterranean strategy versus the cross-channel invasion, there would be no replays of this inter-Allied conflict in the Pacific Theater; rather, here the strategic debates would be between the various armed forces of the United States—the Navy versus the Army, MacArthur versus Admiral King and his Navy counterparts.

Initially, in 1942 and 1943, progress was slow. The initiative had been wrested away from the Japanese at Midway and at Guadalcanal, and gradually the gap between the industrial capacities of the two powers began to widen. The great fear of Yamamoto at the outset of the war—that if the war went beyond several months, if the Americans were not brought to the bargaining table within a matter of months, that over the long haul Japan simply could not compete with American industrial strength, American industrial production, and American manpower. As time passed this became increasingly clear. The gap would grow at a spectacular pace that would profoundly affect the outcome of the war.

Initially, Franklin Roosevelt had favored one commander in chief for the Pacific Theater, in many ways the counterpart to Dwight Eisenhower in his position in Europe. But Admiral King and FDR both had hoped that Admiral Nimitz would be that man; on the other hand, General MacArthur. The defender of the Philippines and his dramatic escape from Bataan had made MacArthur a hero in the United States. The solution: King, Nimitz, Roosevelt, were all fairly convinced that one commander in chief was necessary and believed that it should in fact be Nimitz, but there was the problem of MacArthur—what to do, what to do with the Philippines. The solution, and one that was not an entirely happy one, was a divided command structure in the Pacific. General MacArthur would be commander of Allied forces in the Southwest Pacific, responsible for Australia, the Solomons, New Guinea, the Bismarck Archipelago, the Philippines, the Dutch Indies, except for Sumatra; while Admiral Nimitz would retain his position as commander of the Pacific fleet and become commander in chief of north, central, and southern Pacific Theaters of operation. The Southwest Pacific, then, was an army operation, and MacArthur reported directly to General Marshall, while the navy ran the other operations and Nimitz remained under the control of Admiral King. Britain, meanwhile, retained operational control over Burma and the rest of Southeast Asia.

With this divided command structure there was obviously a strategic debate. The navy favored what came to be known as a Central Pacific strategy, an advance through a series of island chains, the Marshalls, the Carolines, and the Marianas, island chains and individual islands which were certainly obscure, hardly known by anyone in the United States before 1942-43, but would become etched in the experience and memories of hundreds of thousands, indeed millions, of Americans over the next few years. This Central Pacific strategy, this advance through the Marshalls, the Carolines, the Marianas, offered, Nimitz argued, the most advantageous and direct route to Japan. It would allow a concentration of resources, and these three far-flung island chains contained over a thousand small islands, and the Japanese simply couldn't defend all of them. The United States, according to this strategy, would be able to pick and choose its targets; it would be able to maneuver. The Japanese would be stretched to the utmost, and finally the conquest of the Marianas would bring the Japanese home islands into range of American heavy bombers. The Solomons, New Guinea, and even Rabaul, the major Japanese base and garrison, could be bypassed and the Japanese troops there simply allowed to, as the navy put it, "wither on the vine." The key to this strategy was the capture of the Japanese naval base at Truk in the Carolines.

The army, on the other hand, and MacArthur most certainly, preferred a drive along the northern coast of New Guinea, then an attack on the Philippines. Not surprisingly, this strategy would concentrate the American effort in the Southwest Pacific under—no surprise at all—General MacArthur's command. The result: just as there had been a compromise on command structure, there would now be a compromise on strategy.

In April of 1943, the Joint Chiefs of Staff opted for a two-pronged strategy, merging both army and navy proposals. They believed that the navy's Central Pacific strategy should in fact be the highest priority, but recognized that too much blood had already been spilled in the Solomons and New Guinea simply to abandon operations there. So the American advance on Japan would proceed on two axes—the Southwest, an army area of operations, and the Central Pacific, a navy area of concentration. The offensives were based on what came to be known as the "island-hopping" technique, seizing key islands or parts of island chains, then jumping forward several hundred miles, followed by another leap, leaving possibly pockets of Japanese defenders isolated. Japan would be kept guessing, would stretch their resources to the breaking point, and the Allies, the Americans, would move inexorably on toward the Japanese home islands.

The offensive in the Southwest Pacific would come in 1943 and into '44. The Joint Chiefs had laid down the guidelines for strategy that MacArthur and Halsey, Admiral Halsey, under MacArthur's general direction, would follow in 1943. This operation was called Operation Cartwheel. The two key targets of this operation were in the Solomons, New Guinea, northwest of Guadalcanal, and Bougainville. Successful landings there would permit Halsey's forces to bypass most of the Solomons, and provide air bases for assault on Rabaul. The importance of land-based aircraft and land-based airpower was driven home in March of 1943 in what came to be known as the Battle of the Bismarck Sea, when General George M. Kenney, in his Fifth Air Force under MacArthur, began experimenting with B-25 Mitchell bombers, lightweight, two-engine bombers, attacking at low level. During the winter of 1943, pilots had been specially trained for these low-level operations, and then in March, Ultra indicated a Japanese convoy containing seven troop carriers and eight destroyers had left Rabaul for New Guinea. B-17's, the big four-engine bombers, tried to attack, and in fact sank two of the troop ships. Then the B-25's and lower dive bombers sank all of the troop carriers as well as four destroyers. For the first time, land-based aircraft had destroyed a Japanese fleet without the aid of naval forces.

It strengthened the American resolve to gain advanced air bases and the determination to build airfields, to use air power in conjunction with the navy, and ground forces to pressure the Japanese. Admiral Yamamoto, I think sensing that awful sense of the tide turning against him, inexorably turning against him, tried to reverse this virtual tidal wave of rising U.S. air power by sending 300 Japanese planes to attack American bases in the Solomons and New Guinea in a series of major air raids, but in each suffered very serious losses without reversing the balance of air power. Believing that he had in fact achieved a victory—he'd been getting incomplete reports of great damages to American aircraft—Yamamoto decided to visit Bougainville to congratulate his pilots; there was an intercept, Ultra intercepted this and his plan to visit. Eighteen American P-38 Lightnings jumped his plane—shot it down as it approached Bougainville—and Japan lost one of its great military figures before Operation Cartwheel was even underway. Yamamoto, who had warned of the dangers of an all-out conflict with the United States, would not be alive to see his worst fears realized.

Cartwheel was launched in June of 1943, against New Guinea and the Solomons. New Georgia and Bougainville would allow Halsey's forces to bypass most of the Solomon Islands and provide air bases for raids on Rabaul. The sense that Rabaul was the key—it and Truk—these two key Japanese positions had to be taken. And so, air bases for raids on Rabaul. Assaults began in late June, fighting was intense and horrific, in a rugged, jungle-choked terrain, intricate Japanese defenses; for the first time in combat in the war, the flame-thrower would be used as a major weapon in combat on the ground. A series of naval engagements resulted in Japanese defeats, at sea as well as on land, and Bougainville was especially important, since a foothold there would allow the Americans to build airfields closer to New Britain and fighter planes could then escort bombers on raids against Rabaul.

By November, Japanese resistance in Bougainville had come to an end, had been broken.

Meanwhile, MacArthur continued his operations along the northern New Guinea coast, using American and Australian troops. Progress along the coast was agonizingly slow. The Japanese fought tenaciously, and in December launched an attack on New Britain in torrential rains, fighting in the monsoon season, something that virtually everyone thought was impossible and was absolutely miserable. Nonetheless, by the end of 1943, the Allies were closing in on the fortress Rabaul from the western end of New Britain, and Bougainville, and New Georgia. By March 1944, the Allies had seized Los Negros and the Admiralty Islands and now closed the fence around Rabaul. At this point the temptation was to launch a major assault. In fact, MacArthur had thought from the outset that there would have to be a major battle over Rabaul, where the Japanese had a great many troops; but, it was already decided that it would be possible, seeing the way the course of the conflict was going, to actually bypass it, simply to seal it off, not have a frontal assault on this highly fortified Japanese position, and this is exactly what happened.

So, there's progress being made in a slow, agonizing way, fighting engagements across the islands in the Southwest; meanwhile, in the Central Pacific, Admiral Nimitz had built up far larger naval forces than were available for Operation Cartwheel. The Fifth Fleet under Admiral Spruance commanded eight carriers, seven battleships, seven heavy and three light cruisers, 34 destroyers, and, in addition, a new advance in technology was now available to the Americans, and that was the arrival of the Hellcat fighter plane. It would become the best carrier-based aircraft in the Pacific and the day of the Japanese Zero was quickly going to pass.

The first objective for Nimitz in the Central Pacific was the Gilberts—the objectives two small atolls, hardly visible on the map. One was Makin at the northwest extremity, but the other, a tiny island, near the center, was going to be the real key, this was Tarawa. Tarawa was well defended by a garrison of some 5,000 Japanese troops. It was actually not one island but a number of islands and coral reefs along a fifteen-mile lagoon. The key point was Betio, a stretch of island two-and-a-half miles long but at its widest portion across only 800 yards deep, a tiny island. The taking of Tarawa was considered essential. Intelligence had warned Admiral Spruance that the November tides were highly unpredictable, and raised fear that the invasion force would become stuck on the reefs that were just underneath the surface of the sea just around the coral reef that surrounded the islands. The Admiral, however, decided not to postpone the attack—he didn't want to wait until December—and so on November 20, 1943, marines stormed ashore at Tarawa.

The first three waves were able to take advantage of a new item in the inventory of naval and amphibious warfare. This was the "Amtrack," the vehicle which was able to move across the reefs. The tide was low, just as intelligence had feared, but instead of being caught on the reefs, these Amtracks were able to go over the reefs and deliver the first three waves of marines onto the beach, where they encountered fierce resistance. For all of the remaining waves of incoming marines, the deeper, clumsier landing craft ran aground on the reef, on the coral reef. The marines were dislodged hundreds of yards from shore, and had to wade in chest-deep water, through withering Japanese fire, until they reached the beach. It was a brutal encounter. By nightfall, the beachhead was only 300 yards deep, and 1,500 of the 5,000 marines on shore were either dead or wounded. Resistance on Tarawa would end on November 23, but Tarawa, "Bloody Tarawa" as it came to be known, was a rude shock, a shock to the marines and to the American military planners, and also a shock to the American public. Here was this tiny atoll, hardly could be found with a magnifying glass on the map, and 1,000 Americans were dead and 2,000 were wounded. For the Japanese, the toll was even grimmer. Of the 5,000 Japanese troops on Tarawa, 17 survived. Was this, American planners and the public worried, was this a prelude, is this what all of these islands would be like, this island-hopping strategy, this advance across the Pacific toward Japan—was each one of these islands going to be contested in this sort of way, with this level of casualties? It was a terrifying prospect.

From the Gilberts, Nimitz would make a leap to the Marshall Islands. There things went far more smoothly. By bypassing the outer islands and leaping 400 miles into the center of the chain, the neutralization of the Japanese base at Truk, in the Carolines, in the western rim of the Marshalls, was important; it was a very important naval and air base that could threaten all American operations. This was carried out in mid-February, when carrier-based American planes destroyed over 200 Japanese aircraft, sank eight warships, damaged one carrier, and ended Truk's value as an airbase and a base of naval operations.

The assault then was pressed on, into the Marianas, to Guam, and Saipan, and Tinian, all hallowed names in marine corps and naval history. The decision was made to leapfrog all the other Caroline Islands and to move 1,000 miles northwest to this series of islands—Saipan and Guam and Tenian. These, unlike the islands already encountered, certainly unlike Tarawa, were substantial islands, and they lay only 1,200 miles from the home islands of Japan. Taking them would open a variety of strategic options—an assault on the Philippines in the west, something that MacArthur was certainly still very keen on; a northwards thrust toward the Bonin Islands within 700 miles of Japan, establishing important air bases for long-range American bombers. The B-29 with its great range was already becoming available to American forces here, so the taking of the Marianas would move American airpower, land-based airpower, within striking distance of Japan itself. So, the Marianas loomed extremely large in American strategic thinking in the summer of 1944.

Nimitz's key objective in the Marianas was to be Saipan, and on June 15, 1944, as the Allies had been on shore for a little over a week in Normandy, American forces stormed ashore at Saipan. There, the fighting was, at it had been at Tarawa and elsewhere, incredibly bloody. On July 6, 1944, Admiral Nagumo and General Saito committed suicide to inspire their troops, and on the night of July 6 and 7, the Japanese launched a massive frontal assault, a suicide charge that decimated the remaining Japanese troops. It was a suicide charge. The marines had seen this before, but nothing like this, of this scale, this magnitude. The suicide of the Japanese commanders struck the Americans as being not brave, but as simply bizarre, fanatical, beyond comprehension. And, one gruesome chapter would remain, as 8,000 Japanese civilians committed suicide on Saipan, throwing themselves off the cliffs on the northern side of the island, blowing themselves up with hand grenades, drowning themselves in the ocean—in many cases with American troops within earshot of the Japanese, pleading with the civilians not to take this sort of action. What provoked this—was it fear of the Americans? Certainly the indoctrination of the Japanese that if they fell into American hands the women would be raped, the men would be mutilated and murdered, was part of it. The cult of suicide that was very powerful within Japanese society also would play a role, and then, just the desperation and the fear of surrender. For the Americans witnessing this, there was a horrifying sense that this really was a prelude—a preview—of what would happen if American forces—when American forces—reached the Japanese home islands. If Japanese civilians would commit mass suicide on Saipan, the Japanese commanders would commit suicide; if there would be a bonsai charge, a suicide charge of large numbers of Japanese troops when it wasn't about victory, wasn't to reverse the tide, the outcome of the battle—this was already sealed—this was about dying. This was something else, and there was the horrifying sense that each step closer to Japan was simply going to bring greater and greater scenes of this sort of horror.

While the fighting was going on on Saipan, American forces continued to press—naval forces continued to press on—the battle of the Philippine Sea in June of 1944 would see more horrific losses for the Japanese. The Americans in this conflict, this struggle, would use carrier-based aircraft to intercept a number of Japanese, a huge number of Japanese planes. The huge American air superiority, about 1,000 versus about 200 Japanese, led to staggering losses for the Japanese, who lost 275 of 373 planes shot down, to only 29 losses for the Americans. Two American subs sank two Japanese carriers. It came to be known as "the Great Marianas Turkey Shoot," so crippling a defeat was this for Japanese forces. It was a defeat not only of airpower, but of Japanese naval power as well, and it was a defeat from which the Japanese would never recover.

On July 24, Tinian was invaded, to once again repeated scenes of fanatical suicide charges, blind heroism on the part of the Japanese, or crazed fanaticism, depending upon one's point of view. It was over within eight days. Guam was invaded on July 21, where the beachhead was resisted and once again more suicide charges, but the outcome was never in doubt. On August 1, organized resistance on Guam ceased.

The loss of the Marianas was a shattering blow to the Japanese. Tojo's government fell nine days after the fall of Saipan, and the United States was now in a position to strike the Philippines as MacArthur wanted to do, and to threaten Japanese oil supply from the East Indies. The Americans also began preparing new airbases for the B-29 Superfortresses that were arriving steadily, preparing for the strikes at the Japanese home islands.

The progress across the Pacific was filled with these intense short conflicts and a growing horror that the war in the Pacific, while going extremely well for the Allied cause, for the Americans and this island-hopping technique, that a new kind of war had been entered into with an enemy that was almost beyond comprehension. One American pilot who was fighting the Japanese at this point, a naval aviator, said in his memoirs about this particular period of the war and then what would follow, the emergence of the Kamikazes, that one always wanted to think that the soldier, the airman, the sailor on the other side was somebody just like you, somebody who wanted to do his job, believed in his cause, and then wanted to go home. But at a certain point in this campaign of island hopping across the Pacific, Americans came to believe that, as he said, "For us, the war always seemed to be about winning; for the Japanese, it seemed to be about dying."

Turning Point in the Southwest Pacific—
Leyte Gulf and the Philippines
Lecture 22

We want to examine two major engagements that would really seal the fate of imperial Japan. One is the Battle of Leyte Gulf, which would inflict a terrific defeat on the imperial Japanese Navy and render it, really for the remainder of the conflict, of secondary importance; and then, the liberation of the Philippines.

The Battle of Leyte Gulf, fought in October 1944, was the most decisive naval battle fought in the Pacific war since the Battle of Midway in 1942. It broke the back of Japanese naval strength and secured the American landing in the Philippines. This lecture will trace the course of that great naval encounter, in which the Japanese employed for the first time the *kamikazes*. We will then analyze the American invasion of the Philippines, which began in December 1944 and raged well into the new year, with massive Japanese, Filipino, and American casualties.

The invasion of the Philippines was prefaced by the struggle for Peleliu and the Battle of Leyte Gulf. The fighting that came to be known as the "tragedy of Peleliu" took place from September to November 1944..Fighting conditions on Peleliu were unbelievably bad—tremendous heat and ferocious Japanese resistance. The capture of Peleliu was ultimately unnecessary to the success of the Leyte landings.

The Battle of Leyte Gulf took place on October 23–25, 1944. Admiral Toyoda's goal was to force a decisive naval battle involving the whole combined Japanese fleet. If his daring plan had succeeded, it could have reversed the U.S.-Japanese balance of forces in the Pacific. The Japanese operation was conducted without carrier-based air support. Victory came within Admiral Kurita's grasp when Halsey decided to pursue Admiral Ozawa's decoy carrier force. However, Kurita made the fatal decision to turn back after Halsey had taken the bait.

In this battle, the Japanese introduced a new weapon—the "*kamikaze*" suicide air assaults. These had a hugely negative impact on U.S. morale. The outcome of this confrontation—the largest naval battle in history—was the destruction of Japanese naval power in the Pacific.

The battle for the Philippines took place between December 1944 and March 1945. The brutal fighting in Manila (February-March 1945) was reminiscent of Stalingrad. The Bataan Peninsula and Corregidor

Although [the kamikaze] was not capable of reversing the tide of battle, [it] would certainly have a dramatic impact on American morale and would inflict terrific casualties.

fell in late February 1945. MacArthur sent troops to each of the islands, ignoring the high command's decision to bypass them. He was determined to keep his promise to the Filipino Resistance. The Japanese withdrew into the interior of Luzon and continued to fight until the war's end. The battle for the Philippines was Japan's most costly defeat in the entire war. ■

Suggested Reading

John Keegan, *The Second World War*, Chapter 30.

Samuel Eliot Morison, *The Two-Ocean War: A Short History of the U.S. Navy in the Second World War*, Chapter 14.

E.B. Sledge, *With The Old Breed: At Peleliu and Okinawa*, Part I.

Ronald H. Spector, *Eagle Against The Sun*, Chapters 19, 22.

Questions to Consider

1. What were the key turning points in the Battle of Leyte Gulf? Why did the Japanese lose the battle?

2. How did the outcome of the Battle of Leyte Gulf shape the later course of the Pacific war?

Turning Point in the Southwest Pacific—
Leyte Gulf and the Philippines

Lecture 22—Transcript

Hello, and welcome to our twenty-second lecture in this series on the Second World War. In our last lecture we followed the progress of the American drive across the Central Pacific, examining Admiral Nimitz's strategy, the island-hopping technique of moving across the various island chains of the Central Pacific, aiming toward the home islands of Japan. In this lecture we want to shift our focus to that second axis of American advance across the Pacific—this, the Southwest Theater, dominated, of course, by General Douglas MacArthur, an Army theater for the most part. And yet it would be here that one of the major campaigns of the Second World War would occur, indeed the largest naval engagement of the Second World War would take place, and that is the Battle of Leyte Gulf in October of 1944.

So we want to examine two major engagements that would really seal the fate of Imperial Japan. One is the Battle of Leyte Gulf, which would inflict a terrific defeat on the Imperial Japanese Navy and render it, really for the remainder of the conflict, of secondary importance; and then, the liberation of the Philippines. Douglas MacArthur had promised when he had left the Philippines in early 1942 that he would return. He would fulfill that promise in this, what would become the largest engagement battle in the Pacific during the Second World War—the Battle for the Philippines.

The prelude to both of these, the Battle of Leyte Gulf and the Battle of the Philippines, has to be seen in MacArthur's original intention to begin the conquest of the Philippines by invading Mindanao. But Admiral Halsey suggested bypassing and landing instead at Leyte on the eastern edge of the Philippines. MacArthur and Nimitz would ultimately agree about this. But Nimitz insisted on the invasion of a series of islands about 500 miles to the southeast of Mindanao, the Palau Islands, as an advance base for the invasion. On October 20, the original date for the invasion was set as October 20, 1944, the invasion of Leyte. But first, it was going to be necessary, MacArthur believed, to seize Peleliu. And the First Marine Division was sent to take this small island as a blocking position for the invasion.

The tragedy of Peleliu would begin on September 15, 1944. The fighting on this island was in a series of engagements, where one is always tempted to say this was the most savage, this was the most brutal—conditions on Peleliu were unbelievably bad. The fighting took place in 115-degree heat, against heavy Japanese fortifications, in conditions that were really indescribable. I think, in fact, the most powerful book of personal recollections about the entire Second World War is written by a veteran of the Peleliu campaign. That's E.B. Sledge, Gene Sledge's *With the Old Breed*, an absolutely devastating account of the day-to-day conflict on Peleliu in this unbelievable heat against great Japanese resistance. The marines and army units involved in the Peleliu campaign would suffer 6,000 casualties. And resistance on Peleliu, which was expected to be squashed within a matter of a week, maybe two, would only be brought to an end on November 26. And, ironically enough, Peleliu would ultimately be irrelevant to the success of the Leyte landings—unnecessary, as it turned out.

On October 20, U.S. Army forces landed on Leyte, and within three days had seized the capital and two important airfields. MacArthur landed on the first day, making the statement as he walked ashore, "People of the Philippines, I have returned!" The Japanese at this point were in a desperate situation. Could the tide of events in the Pacific be reversed? Objectively speaking, I think if Yamamoto had been around, he might have argued, "Well, at this point there is no way to reverse the tide of events." Possibly, with one dramatic stroke, somewhere around the Philippines, maybe it would be possible to inflict a major defeat on the Americans—and somehow, if not reverse the tide, the overall tide of events in the Pacific, at least to blunt the American offensive.

The Japanese developed a plan for a major naval engagement. The objective was to force a decisive naval battle with the American Pacific Fleet, which might still provide victory for Japan—victory on a much more circumscribed scale than had been their original intention. Admiral Toyoda devised a master plan that called for the entire combined fleet to converge on the Philippines. A northern force under Ozawa was to move south from Japan as a decoy to lure Admiral Halsey's Third Fleet away from Leyte. This northern force of Ozawa's included Japan's four remaining aircraft carriers. This was clearly a decoy for the Japanese. The four carriers contained only 110 aircraft. And while this force was to be seen as a decoy, to lure Halsey's Third Fleet away from the Philippines, at the same time two Japanese task forces were to steam northward from the Singapore area, wind their way through the congested waters of the Philippines, and merge on Leyte Gulf from two directions. Their mission was to destroy the American transports carrying the troops for the invasion of the Philippines and the supporting warships. A twofold objective—destroy important elements of the U.S. fleet, and nip the American invasion of the Philippines in the bud. This, then, was the Japanese objective.

One of those task forces, under Admiral Kurita, contained five battleships, including the super ships *Yamato* and *Musashi*, the two largest battleships in the world, as well as 12 cruisers and 15 destroyers—an enormous naval task force. It would move through the San Bernadino Strait, and close on Leyte from the north. Meanwhile, Admiral Nishimura's force of two battleships, a heavy cruiser, four destroyers would steam through the Surignao Strait to the south, and would be joined by yet another task force dispatched from Japan. Toyoda's plan was daring; it was typically ambitious. The maneuvering of these three task forces with timing to converge in the Philippines with the decoy force and so on, was typical, I think, of Japanese naval planning. And, if it succeeded, it would deal a severe blow to the United States, and possibly even reverse the balance of forces in the Pacific. But, it relied heavily on precise timing, it relied heavily on maneuvering through very congested waters, and the entire operation was to be undertaken without carrier-based air support. Only land-based planes from the Philippines would attempt to offset the great American air superiority provided by the American carriers.

The battle would take place between October 23 and October 25. On October 23, American submarines sighted Kurita's huge force, and alerted Admiral Halsey. They also sank two heavy cruisers and disabled a third. But Kurita continued on toward the San Bernadino Straight. On October 24, American aircraft attacked and sank the giant battleship *Musashi* and damaged three others. When Kurita turned west, Halsey believed he was withdrawing, and therefore shifted his Third Fleet northward to intercept the Japanese carrier force, Ozawa's decoys to the north. He did not even leave a covering force at the San Bernadino Strait, and he did not inform Admiral Kincaid, whose Seventh Fleet remained on station with only five small escort carriers, three destroyers, and a number of smaller vessels. He had taken the bait. He had seen, he had word of the carriers, and he was off to get them. Kurita then swung back, pushed through the San Bernadino Strait, where his vast armada broke on the startled Americans. He thought that he was confronting the big American carriers and he pressed in for the kill. This was the exactly the decisive engagement that the plan had called for. But—and this was very rare for the Japanese, who were extremely good at nighttime maneuvers; Japanese naval practice was very skillful in nighttime maneuvers—his force became dispersed, confusion followed, wild sort of fighting. Several destroyers were sunk; one of the small American carriers. Indeed, the Japanese seemed on the verge of inflicting an annihilating defeat on American forces. Nothing remained between Kurita and the Leyte invasion force except a number of small carriers.

Victory was, indeed, at this point, within his grasp. But because his attack had moved beyond his control, his vessels were dispersed in a way that he was uncomfortable with; and also because he still thought the big American carriers were present, instead of pressing his attack, he broke off, believing that the large American carrier force he thought present would annihilate his strung-out forces. Instead, that large carrier force was hundreds of miles away with Halsey, searching down the Japanese carriers of this northern decoy force. Kurita withdrew back through the San Bernadino Strait, and an opportunity for the decisive engagement that the Japanese sought had been missed.

Halsey, meanwhile, did press his attack against Ozawa's forces in the north. He sank all four of Japan's remaining carriers. Five hundred aircraft, landed and ship-based, were lost. The United States sank three battleships, four cruisers, 11 destroyers; in fact, destroyed Japanese naval power in what proved to be the largest naval battle in history. It was, indeed, the decisive engagement that the Japanese had hoped for, but the outcome went in the other direction—in fact, a more predictable direction.

It was at the Battle of Leyte Gulf, as this engagement came to be known, that the Japanese had produced a new weapon, and one that, although it was not capable of reversing the tide of battle, would certainly have a dramatic impact on American morale, and would inflict terrific casualties. This, of course, was the "Kamikaze," or the "Divine Wind," the special suicide planes, suicide units employed by the Japanese, now in desperation, to break the momentum of American forces. The term Kamikaze, or Divine Wind, referred to the typhoon that had destroyed the Mongol fleet of Kublai Kahn in the late 13th century, saving Japan from invasion. A suicide unit now composed of pilots who deliberately crashed their TNT-laden planes into American ships would now be launched at the Americans.

The Kamikaze special attack corps was to inflict both material and morale damage on U.S. forces. The first attack came on October 21, a foretaste of what was to come. But the main assault would come on October 25, 1944. Two hundred Japanese suicide planes would slam into the American fleet. The response of American sailors seeing this, of pilots—naval aviators—desperately trying to shoot down these planes, the stunning shock of seeing planes come in for what looked like a standard dive bombing attack, only to keep going and keep going and keep going, was unbelievable. If one sees film footage of these engagements with the Kamikazes roaring down in the Battle of Leyte Gulf, I think it's some of the most dramatic footage of the entire Second World War, shot in many cases in color in a way that the scenes from the European Theater so rarely were, but of flak of all sorts of anti-aircraft fire, a hail of anti-aircraft fire, and these Japanese planes bearing down on the American planes, and then slamming into the sides or the decks of the carriers or the other ships. The Kamikazes in the Battle of Leyte Gulf would sink 24 American vessels, seriously damage 27 others. They would inflict 2,100 casualties, 738 of whom were killed.

The Kamikazes, along with the Bonsai charges, the refusal to surrender, these sorts of practices that one had seen with the Japanese, the mass suicides elsewhere, simply drove home yet again—completed, in fact—a Western view of the Japanese as a fanatical enemy ready to die rather than face defeat, rather than surrender. And, once again, it's the sense of, "Is this a preview of what we're to anticipate as we draw closer to the Japanese home islands? Mass suicides on Saipan, these Kamikaze attacks, the Bonsai charges. Was there no limit to this?" And this sense, I think, that the Pacific Theater would offer, in terms of combat, such a different frame of mind for American servicemen confronting this enemy—even, I think, a more stark and strange experience than those Americans who were confronted with the real evils of the SS.

The Battle of Leyte Gulf, then, would seal the fate of the Japanese navy in the Second World War. The invasion of the Philippines which followed would go a long way toward breaking the back of Japanese military power in the Southwest Pacific. Leyte was invaded on December 10, Mindoro on December 15. The invasion of Luzon at Lingayen Bay on January 9, 1945, against General Yamashita, would mark the beginning of the American assault on the Philippines. Clark Field, which had fallen to the Japanese at the very beginning of the war, would fall back into American hands on January 30, 1945. The fighting for Manila from February 3 to March 3 was a struggle unmatched in the Pacific Theater. It was more reminiscent of Stalingrad, of the major battles in Europe, of urban fighting, than any other conflict in the Pacific Theater—block by block, war on a European scale. It's estimated that 100,000 Filipino civilians died in the fighting or fell victim to Japanese atrocities, as the Japanese were pushed out of Manila—almost a replay of the rape of Nanking—scenes of horrendous torture, execution of Philippine civilians suspected of being resistance fighters, or simply civilians who happened to be at the wrong place at the wrong time.

The Bataan Peninsula fell by late February, 1945, as did Corregidor—the fall of these positions so important symbolically for the United States after their loss so early on in the war in 1942. That marked a major, I think, morale booster for the American population, certainly thinking about possibly the end of the war against Japan. The Japanese would withdraw into the mountainous interior of Luzon, and bloody fighting would continue until the very end of the war—all the way through the summer of 1945, Japanese resistance would continue in the Philippines. MacArthur sent American troops to each of the islands, ignoring a Joint Chiefs of Staff decision to bypass them. As far as MacArthur was concerned, he had pledged to return. He had pledged to liberate the Philippines. He had a made a pledge to the Filipino population. And while in some ways it didn't seem to make a great deal of military sense, it was a pledge to a Philippine population which had the largest resistance groups in all of Japanese-occupied Southeast Asia and the Pacific. Indeed, the Philippines would be really alone, outside of China, as fostering a major resistance group to the resistance organization against the Japanese.

The Battle for the Philippines was the largest military engagement fought by the United States in the Pacific. The United States would suffer 48,000 wounded and 14,000 deaths in the liberation of the Philippines. The Japanese would suffer 350,000 losses. It was the most costly defeat for the Japanese in the entire Pacific war. At this point, with the fall of the Philippines, with the defeat of the Japanese navy at Leyte, with the Americans moving along the Central Pacific axis, and now also through the Southwest, the war in the Pacific could have—one could argue *should* have—come to a close at this point.

The first American bombing raid on the Japanese home islands had come in June of 1944. It would be the spring of 1945 when the massive raids would begin, the major B-29 raids launched by General Curtis LeMay, something that we'll talk about in a future lecture. The war might have come to an end at this juncture. American submarines were slowly but surely choking Japan. Submarine warfare, American submarine warfare against the Japanese, had been enormously successful. Slowly, the Japanese were cut off from their trade, cut off from their raw materials, cut off from food supplies. The stranglehold of the American navy on the Japanese home islands, and especially through the use of the submarine, the noose was growing tighter and tighter. Air power was about to be visited upon Japan in a major way. Up until the spring of 1944, the United States, and what few efforts it had made to actually bomb the Japanese home islands, had largely concentrated on high altitude, daylight, precision bombing. In the spring of 1945, that policy would change, as we will see, and the United States would go over to a different sort of bombing policy. The war might have ended here, but it did not.

The advance would have to continue. There would be no Japanese surrender. The Americans advancing now again across the Central Pacific continued to move. Nimitz planned to continue his drive through the island chains toward Japan. And while the Battle of Manila was still raging, Nimitz would launch an attack on the Bonin Islands, which stretched from near Saipan close to the Japanese home islands. These islands, the Bonin Islands, would eliminate attacks by Japanese fighters, operating from the islands. American fighter planes would now be able to use bases there to escort B-29's, and this might also serve as an advance base for the Superfortresses themselves. If nothing

303

else, this last island chain would provide emergency landing facilities for B-29s returning from Japan to their airbases in the Marianas, to Tinian in particular.

The islands were not the sort of jungle islands, the jungle-choked terrain of Guadalcanal and so on, but rather were volcanic. And the island targeted for the first invasion was perhaps the most inviting, was Iwo Jima, which means "sulfur island." It was a barren, desolate, pork-chop-shaped island, and it was to be the key in the new American advance, closer to the home islands of Japan. The Battle of Iwo Jima would be launched in February of 1945 and would last through March. Iwo Jima abounded with bubbling sulfur pits, casting a dense acrid smell over the island. The beaches held no sand, but instead consisted of black volcanic ash, so soft that just walking across it was difficult. A man sunk up to his ankles in this black volcanic ash. Although the island's volcano, the 550-foot high Mt. Surabachi, was dormant, the marines found that if they tried to dig into the ash-covered beaches, the earth was hot to the touch several inches down. This battle—the Battle of Iwo Jima, and the battle which would follow it, the Battle of Okinawa—would mark the last two stepping stones in the American march across the Pacific.

At this point in the spring of 1945—February-March—the war in both Europe and Asia seemed to be coming to a close. The Battle of the Bulge had been successfully brought to a close in Europe; the Germans' last gap offensive blunted. And in the Pacific, the inexorable march of American forces across the Pacific now seemed to be homing in on the Japanese home islands. It was at this point, that already one began to see, and we'll talk about this in future lectures, that questions about the post-World War—thinking about a post-war environment—began to occupy Franklin Roosevelt, would occupy Winston Churchill, certainly occupy Stalin. But there was still the business at hand. The business at hand was the final defeat of Nazi Germany and the defeat of Imperial Japan. And that was going to extend across certainly the spring in Europe, and through the summer in the Far East.

The Final Drive for Japan—
Iwo Jima, Okinawa, and the Fire-Bombing of Tokyo
Lecture 23

The battle for the Philippines was still very much underway as marine and army forces gathered for the assault on Iwo Jima. The goal in taking this island was that it would eliminate attacks by Japanese fighters on American aircraft making their way towards the Japanese home islands.

This lecture examines the two climactic battles in the final drive for Japan in 1945: Iwo Jima and Okinawa. We will trace the strategic considerations that prompted these battles and follow the course of the bloody fighting.

The battle of Iwo Jima took place in February and March 1945. The objective of the battle was to secure airfields for the final air assault on Japanese home islands. The assault was postponed until February due to slowness in subduing Leyte.

On February 23, a Marine patrol reached the summit of Mount Surabachi on Iwo Jima and raised the U.S. flag. A.P. photographer Joe Rosenthal captured the moment in a famous photograph.

Digital Stock World War II CD.

Soldiers raising an American flag at Iwo Jima in an iconic snapshot of World War II.

The fighting on Iwo Jima was indescribably brutal. The terrain was difficult, and Japanese defenses were formidable. U.S. Marines suffered terrible casualties on the exposed beaches. More than 6,000 American soldiers were killed at Iwo Jima, and 17,000 were wounded. Virtually the entire Japanese garrison perished, including General Kuribayashi.

A debate ensued over whether the conquest of Iwo Jima was worth the high price in lives lost. Was the battle necessary? Might Iwo Jima have been bypassed?

The battle for Okinawa—the last fought in the Pacific war—took place in April 1945. Okinawa was a very substantial island, 76 miles long and at some spots 18 miles wide. It was located just 350 miles from the southernmost Japanese island, and it possessed excellent airfields and two good anchorages. It was garrisoned by the largest Japanese military force (120,000 troops) that U.S. forces engaged during the Pacific war. It also held a large civilian population. Okinawa would provide a major jumping-off point for an invasion of Japan.

The United States assembled the largest ground force and naval armada deployed during the Pacific war. U.S. naval forces numbered 1,300 vessels, including 40 aircraft carriers. One hundred eighty thousand Marines and soldiers went ashore. Their numbers ultimately rose to 250,000. The Japanese responded with 10 mass kamikaze assaults that sank 34 ships, damaged 350 others, and killed 4,900 U.S. sailors.

There seemed to be a growing conviction on the part of American policymakers and military men that the Japanese high command was perfectly prepared to go down literally in flames, taking every last man, woman, and child in Japan along with them.

The losses were staggering for both sides. Of all U.S. Marines killed in World War II, 14 percent died at Okinawa. Of all naval casualties suffered during the war, 20 percent were sustained off Okinawa. Despite these huge losses, the Japanese military showed no inclination to surrender following their defeat at Okinawa. Six weeks of desperate combat convinced the Americans that the Japanese would fanatically resist any invasion of their country's home islands.

The United States also waged an air war against Japan. The original strategy involved daylight strategic bombing. Raids were carried out by

B-29 Superfortresses flying from bases in China and, in spring of 1945, the Marianas. The first raid on the home islands came in June 1944. The early bombing was ineffective, and Air Corps leaders sought a different strategy.

Gen. Curtis LeMay's new strategy departed from Air Corps doctrine. He shifted from daytime strategic bombing to nighttime area raids. This shift allowed the planes to fly at lower altitudes and thereby avoid disruption by the jet stream. The new raids would include the use of incendiaries.

The first night raid on Tokyo was conducted on March 9–10, 1945. The city was massively fire-bombed. Some 80,000–100,000 Japanese died in the resulting firestorm. The Tokyo attack inaugurated a campaign of fire-bombing raids against Japan's major cities that continued into the summer. Military rather than racial considerations dictated this change in bombing strategy. The U.S. invasion of Japan was tentatively scheduled for November 1945. General Marshall expected one million U.S. casualties. ∎

Suggested Reading

John Keegan, *The Second World War*, Chapter 31.

Bill D. Ross, *Iwo Jima: Legacy of Valor*.

E.B. Sledge, *With The Old Breed*, Part II.

Ronald H. Spector, *Eagle Against The Sun*, Chapter 21.

Questions to Consider

1. How did combat conditions for U.S. forces on Okinawa differ from those on Iwo Jima?

2. Was the capture of Iwo Jima worth the price that was paid to achieve it?

The Final Drive for Japan—
Iwo Jima, Okinawa, and the Fire-Bombing of Tokyo
Lecture 23—Transcript

Hello, welcome to our twenty-third lecture on the Second World War. We had stopped in our previous lecture with the American forces just off the shore of a volcanic slab of rock in the Bonin Islands—the island of Iwo Jima, a name that very few people would've been able to identify before February of 1945, but has been certainly with us ever since. The battle for the Philippines was still very much underway as marine and army forces gathered for the assault on Iwo Jima. The goal in taking this island was that it would eliminate attacks by Japanese fighters on American aircraft making their way towards the Japanese home islands. It would also possibly be a forward base for American aircraft, eliminate the Japanese radar and early warning for American assaults on the Japanese islands, and, finally, would be an emergency landing strip for the gigantic B-29's that were now beginning to take part in these raids.

The assault on Iwo Jima was originally planned for January 2 but had been postponed until February 19 because of the very slow going on Leyte. The Japanese position on Iwo Jima was very strong indeed. The garrison there was reinforced during January, during the delay, reaching 21,000 troops, and the Japanese defenses were made even more effective by the terrain. Mount Surabachi dominated the southern end of the island; the wider northern end was dominated by a plateau that rose 350 feet and rippled with a set of rough volcanic ridges. Both Surabachi and the northern ridges contained numerous caves, reinforced by a network of pillboxes and bunkers. These positions housed mortars, huge artillery pieces, and machine guns, linked together by an elaborate system of tunnels, underground barracks, and ammo dumps.

General Tadamichi Kuribayashi did not intend to contest the American landing on the beaches. This he had seen in previous campaigns and believed it had been a mistake for Japanese forces. Instead, he would have fire directed on those landing zones, but would not have Japanese forces present close by. He could bring murderous fire on the beaches, and because of the volcanic ash and a series of steep volcanic terraces that rose abruptly from the beaches, movement off the landing zones would be slow. This he realized.

When the marines came ashore on February 19, 1945, they were pinned down on the exposed beaches and suffered terrible casualties. The four days of pounding by American naval guns and aircraft, instead of the ten days of firing that the marine commanders had requested, had done little, ultimately, to reduce the Japanese gun positions and artillery, and mortar fire would rain down on the marines. Six thousand, two hundred men were pinned down on a 3,000-yard strip of sand, two marines for every yard along this beach. It was a slaughterhouse. As one historian described it, sand hummocks, appearing as giant dead anthills moments before, spewed machine gun fire from apertures hardly visible above ground level. Mortars fell in cascades from hundreds of concealed pits. Heavy artillery and rapid-firing anti-aircraft guns, barrels lowered to rape the beaches, slammed shells into the oncoming landing craft and support vessels. Land mines sown like wheat in the field exploded in sickening blasts on the terrace as marines stumbled across them. Fifteen-inch coastal defense guns and large mortars rained down from Surabachi's base, slopes, and crater. There was no way to dig a foxhole. As fast as loose volcanic ash was scooped out, the hole filled up again as in a bin of wheat. Men burrowed into the sand, or pressed against porous rocks, or hugged the sides of shell craters, anything for a shield from the withering enemy fire. When vehicles and artillery made it ashore, they were immediately mired to the hubs in the sand. Damaged Higgins boats and larger landing craft quickly filled with water and made them unmovable. It was a scene of twisted boats, burning jeeps and trucks, and bogged down cannon. Still, somehow, miraculously, by nightfall, the marines had made it off the beach, had fought their way across the island, and had actually cut off Mount Surabachi.

In the days of intense fighting that followed, the marines would inch their way up the heavily defended shores, slopes of the volcano. On February 23, a patrol reached the summit and planted a small tattered flag. Later, elements of a platoon, some 40 men, made it to the top carrying with them a much larger flag, an eight-by-four-foot flag that could be seen well from below. As the handful of marines struggled to raise the flag, A.P. photographer Joe Rosenthal snapped what would become the most famous picture of the Second World War. Of the 40 men of that platoon that had fought their way up the slopes of Surabachi that day to raise the flag, only four would survive until the end of the battle.

The raising of the flag was a moment of great symbolic value, but the battle for Iwo Jima had just begun. Now the marines faced the task of moving on to the northern plateau with its rugged terrain and intricate fortifications. The troops pushed forward, yard by yard against ferocious resistance. The fighting was intense as the marines sought to clear the cages and flame throwers, dynamite. They fought hand to hand facing fanatical resistance, including an array of devilish booby traps, often on bodies, sometimes on prisoners who committed suicide by surrendering, having their bodies booby-trapped—would then explode with a handful of marines around them. The battle raged on through weeks of indescribable brutality in which every cave, every ditch, every slope was contested, and the casualties mounted. Finally, with all hope of victory gone, the Japanese would resort to bonsai charges one after another until, in the end, virtually the entire Japanese garrison had perished, including the commander, Kuribayashi, who committed suicide.

The costs of the battle of Iwo Jima were absolutely staggering. When the fighting stopped on March 23, over 6,000—6,821 to be precise—Americans were dead; 17,000 were wounded. American losses at Iwo Jima, for the first time in the war in the Pacific, actually outnumbered Japanese casualties. The Japanese of course lost virtually their entire force, but the losses were staggering on both sides. Three marine divisions were ground up in the fighting for Iwo Jima. One-third of all the marines who were killed in the Pacific Theater died on Iwo Jima. It was an island four-and-a-half miles long, two-and-a-half miles wide. As the coverage of the battle sunk in—and at this point during the war it's very interesting, I think—part of the reason that we have this remarkable photograph and the coverage of the battle was that navy censorship of the combat had relaxed so that there was much greater coverage. And Iwo Jima, while it certainly provoked an enormous outpouring of patriotism at home, it seemed to be the very symbol of devotion to duty, of sacrifice, of fighting under terrible conditions. It also created the beginning of a mounting firestorm of concern about an ultimate invasion of Japan. As American forces moved closer and closer to the Japanese home islands, the costs of victory were rising, and rising astronomically.

An issue was raised before the fighting at Iwo Jima was even completely over—that, in fact, the entire campaign might have been a mistake, that Iwo might have been bypassed. Given the casualties, had Iwo Jima been worth the cost? One of the major arguments subsequently made was that B-29's on their way to Japan made emergency landings at Iwo Jima and were able to land there, that about, oh, 240 B-29's made it down in the area in the remaining period of the war, 11 crew members per plane. If one calculates the casualties, it would seem that the losses might not have been worth it. Certainly this was raised at the time, provoking great controversy, as I said.

And yet no matter how one evaluated the military value of the island, none could dispute the valor of those that fought and died there. The battle yielded the most powerful visual image of the American war effort, in Joe Rosenthal's stern photograph, and 27 Congressional Medals of Honor, 17 of them posthumous, were awarded for actions on Iwo Jima. Still, there was this lingering doubt. The battle had been a success. An airstrip was created there that was able to handle the B-29's. It did, in fact, give a clear beacon toward the Japanese home islands, but had it been worth it, had it been worth it? If, a marine historian would later argue, an invasion of Japan had indeed been necessary, those three marine divisions that were chewed up so mercilessly on Iwo Jima would have been sorely missed indeed.

With Iwo Jima in American hands, there would be one final assault before the ultimate invasion of Japan, and this was Okinawa, only 350 miles from the southernmost of the major Japanese home islands. This was not a small volcanic atoll or a tiny jungle-choked speck on the map, but was a very substantial piece of real estate, 76 miles long and at some spots 18 miles wide. It held excellent airfields and two equally useful anchorages. It was, in short, an ideal base for the anticipated final assault on Japan itself.

The Japanese defenses on Okinawa were predictably strong—120,000 Japanese troops were stationed on the island, the largest force to confront the Americans in the Pacific. The southern portion of the island where the Japanese determined to make their stand was dominated by limestone cliffs, which were honeycombed with caves, pillboxes, and tunnels. The Japanese could also bring land-based aircraft to bear, and the greatest concentration of heavy artillery in the Pacific was also prepared for the invaders. The Japanese plan was to allow the Americans to land and to hold this heavily fortified southern portion of the island.

For their part, the Americans assembled the largest invasion force in naval armada in the Pacific war. Thirteen hundred vessels assembled off the shores of Okinawa, including 18 battleships, 200 destroyers, and 40 aircraft carriers. If one thinks about this, if one thinks about the distance traveled by the United States since that attack on Pearl Harbor in December of 1941, when less than a half a dozen carriers were available, now 40 aircraft carriers have been marshaled for the invasion of Okinawa. In addition, 180,000 marines and army troops would be thrown into the fray. At one point during the battle, 250,000 American troops would ultimately participate in the assault force on Okinawa.

The invasion itself began on Easter Sunday, April 1, 1945. All went relatively smoothly for over a week, with little substantial contact. I think there was a sense that it was almost eerie, that one knew that there was an enormous Japanese force on Okinawa. The question was, where was it located, when would there be contact made, when would the Japanese come, would there be some massive bonsai assault, would there be more of the Kamikazes—just exactly how would this play? But instead of there being the climactic battle that had been anticipated, or the withering fire on the beaches as there had been at Iwo Jima, instead the Americans came ashore, and began to move in search of the Japanese enemy. Then the force of 180,000 American troops encountered the main Japanese defenses. Six weeks of desperate combat would follow.

At one point in the final week of May, 12 inches of rain fell, turning the battlefield into an enormous quagmire of mud. Finally, on May 31, the Japanese would abandon Shuri, one of Okinawa's two towns in the south, and withdrew to a final line of ridges and cave-infested hills. Another month of gruesome fighting was required before the last Japanese resistance was finally broken. The Kamikaze assault around the island was particularly terrifying, sinking 34 ships and damaging 350 others in one last desperate spasm of violence. The Japanese mounted ten masked Kamikaze attacks, of 50 to 300 aircraft. In these attacks, almost 5,000 American sailors would die. The battle did not end until June 21, 1945. The anticipation was that the assault on Okinawa would take four, maybe five weeks; it came closer to eight, and the total by anybody's reckoning was hideous. Seven thousand Americans had been killed on land; almost 5,000 at sea; 32,000 thousand Americans wounded in combat on Okinawa itself; another 4,800 at sea.

Twenty percent of all casualties suffered by the American Navy in all of the Second World War, in all theaters, were sustained in the waters off Okinawa. Fourteen percent of all marines killed in the Second World War died there.

The Japanese also suffered grievously as well. One thousand, four hundred, and sixty-five Kamikazes; of the 120,000 troops, all but 11,000 were killed. Eleven thousand Japanese actually would surrender on Okinawa. It was the largest surrender of Japanese forces ever encountered by the United States. Most of those surrenders came in the last days of the battle. For the most part, the Japanese troops fought as they had elsewhere, to the absolute bitter end, with General Ushigima and his entire staff committing suicide. It's also I think indicative of the intensity of the combat, and the desperate nature of the battle, that the American commander on Okinawa was also killed—that was the Army General Simon Bolivar Buckner, who was killed in action on Okinawa.

There was something else that was different as well about the fighting on Okinawa, similar more to the situation in the Philippines than to Iwo Jima or the other major battles in the Pacific, and that was there was a large civilian population on Okinawa. A hundred and fifty thousand Okinawan civilians would die in the fighting that raged across their island—an enormous number, many caught simply between the Japanese forces and the Americans, not knowing which way to turn. Many had retreated to caves, seeking to get away, only to discover that when the American troops would approach them and ask them to come out, they were terrified, wouldn't do it. The Americans didn't know what to do—thought in many cases that these were Japanese troops—tossed hand grenades in, or flame throwers. One saw this over and over again on both sides as the Okinawan civilians now were caught in the middle of this catastrophic battle. Both sides would suffer 35 percent casualties in what seemed at times like a return of World War One's artillery barrages and frontal assaults.

General MacArthur and others were highly critical of the conduct of the land operation on Okinawa. General Buckner had sent his troops into frontal assaults, into the teeth of highly fortified Japanese positions, with the resultant terrible casualties. There was a growing sense of concern, I would say almost frustration, at this point in the war—when in June of 1945, the war in Europe is over; American forces are moving closer and closer to the

Japanese home islands; and in each one of these assaults, it seems as if there is a new horrifying clue or a presentiment of what is likely to come if this invasion of Japan actually is necessary. Plans were already underway, the planning underway, the operational plans being laid for this final assault on Japan, which was to begin at the latest in November of 1945. Okinawa had fallen, the costs had been horrific, and so as the Americans advanced closer and closer to the home islands, the price of victory had grown and grown, and contemplating an assault on the Japanese home island was neither a popular thing at home nor certainly within the military itself; and yet the Japanese leadership showed absolutely no signs of buckling, no signs of surrender. It is true, and we'll talk about this in a subsequent lecture when we talk about President Truman's struggles about whether or not to use the atomic bomb. There was certainly at this point indications that some within the Japanese diplomatic community, within what one might loosely call the civilian element of the Japanese government, was interested in some sort of peace-feelers to the United States, going through, in fact, the Soviet Union. But the military still called the shots in Japan and there was absolutely no hint whatsoever at this juncture that the Japanese military was prepared to accept the outcome on the battlefield, and surrender.

What makes this even more incomprehensible in some ways, and terrifying in another, is that as these battles, these two great climactic battles in the Pacific—Iwo Jima and Okinawa—were unfolding in such grisly horror, the great air assault by the United States on the Japanese home islands had begun and had begun with great fury. Much as we've seen of the island hopping, of the attempts to seize new bases closer to the home islands, had been based on the idea of creating forward jumping-off points for the American air assault on Japan. The instrument for a massive campaign of high altitude strategic bombing as it had been practiced in Europe was to be the new, high-tech B-29 bombers, with terrific range, with the capability of carrying a much higher bomb load; and those B-29's would become available in early 1944, would be operational from bases in China initially, but because of mechanical problems in the early models and the meager supplies reaching the 20th Air Force in China, the B-29's were unable to mount a sustained attack against Japan.

The first raid against the home islands had come on June 14, 1944, when 60 B-29's attacked the iron and steel complex at Yawata, with little damage.

The attacking planes, flying at altitudes of 30,000 feet, had encountered very strong winds. We discovered something over Japan that we really hadn't had much of a sense of at this point, and that was something called the jet stream. At 30,000 feet, the B-29's attempting to move over the target, using the Norden bombsight, using high-tech aiming devices with all of their calculations, discovered that if they flew at 30,000 feet, they zipped across the target area—it threw all of their calculations off, and so the bombing had been highly ineffective. In addition, cloud cover was common over Japan, particularly during the daytime, and Japanese industry tended to be dispersed. The early raids from the Marianas in the fall of 1944 were more intense and certainly more effective, but still plagued by these same problems and didn't produce the results that were to be expected.

Then, in the early spring of 1945, as the engagements at Iwo Jima and subsequently Okinawa would be underway, the commanding general Haywood Hansell was replaced as Commander of the 21st Bomber Command by Curtis LeMay, a man who had been a pioneer in the tactics of daylight strategic bombing in Europe. LeMay, at 39 years of age, was the youngest general in the United States Army air forces, and he began by initiating a dramatic shift in American bombing strategy. Since the target areas in Japan were almost always covered by clouds in daytime, and had to be bombed by radar, and since the tremendous strength of the jet stream and winds over Japan made accuracy almost impossible, LeMay decided to scrap the policy of daylight strategic bombing and move over to nighttime attacks. There, he discovered, if one went at night, the cloud cover was thinner; anti-aircraft fire was less accurate. The Japanese possessed very few night fighters, so that the planes could fly at lower altitudes, escaping the problems of the jet stream, sometimes as low as 5,000 feet, unheard of in any sort of air operation in Europe. A shift from daylight strategic bombing to area raids, using incendiaries. Japanese cities with their wood and paper structures were highly vulnerable to this type of attack, and these structures tended to be densely clustered around the decentralized industrial facilities. Finally, a new type of incendiary had been developed and used in Europe against the Germans—napalm—which would spread rivers of fire through the attacked areas.

LeMay ordered his bombers to drop their machine guns in order to carry the heavier loads; assured them that they would be safe. No one was very convinced about this, bomber crews thinking if one flies low, anything lower than 20,000 feet is asking for trouble—anyone who'd had experience in Europe understood this. When LeMay started talking about 5-to-10,000 feet, this seemed absolutely suicidal, but LeMay insisted. Dropping their machine guns in order to carry heavier loads also seemed to be asking for trouble, but, despite a good deal of skepticism at this breach in army air force doctrine, and a move from daylight strategic bombing to nighttime bombing, in spite of this resistance, LeMay insisted, and on the night of March 10, 9-10, 1945, 334 B-29's appeared in the black skies over Tokyo.

For over three hours, the giant bombers rumbled over the city, attacking a mixed area of private dwellings and factories, turning them into a raging inferno—a firestorm on a scale similar to that of the RAF's raids on Hamburg and later Dresden. Temperatures in Tokyo reached over 1800 degrees Fahrenheit—literally, a firestorm that sucked the oxygen out of the center of the city—howling winds that were so powerful that it literally sucked some of the planes out of the sky. When it was at last over, 16 square miles of Tokyo's built-up area was utterly destroyed, and between 80- and 100,000 people had been incinerated. It was probably the largest number of casualties from any raid during the Second World War. Within days, the 21st Bomber Command launched firebombing raids on Nagoya, Osaka, Kobe, and Yokohama, and others would follow. The raids would continue into the summer of 1945, so that the battles that we've been talking about, of Iwo Jima and of Okinawa, were being fought against a backdrop of these mounting raids against the Japanese home islands.

The departure from air force doctrine was based on military considerations. There's been a good deal of talk since the war about the role that race played in American thinking about the conduct of combat against the Japanese. Curtis LeMay, who would make the decision to move over to nighttime raids, to area raids, away from the American doctrine of daylight strategic bombing—the notion of pinpoint bombing that had been pioneered and of which LeMay was an enormous enthusiast—the decision to move away from this was based not on questions of morality, not on questions of race, but rather on what was militarily the most effective. The raids at high altitude over Japan had been a failure; this was Haywood Hansell's problem, LeMay argued—so that if daylight precision bombing didn't work over Japan, then one went to the alternative.

Before the war, American strategists had already made studies of the feasibility of bombing Japan, and it was very clear to everyone from the very beginning of the conflict that Japanese cities were ideal targets for this sort of incendiary bombs that we had used also against the Germans in Europe. So, I think what added to the enormous sense of frustration and puzzlement, bewilderment, on the part of American policy makers, as well as American military men, as we confronted the prospect of a final assault on Japan, was here was a nation which had now suffered one string of catastrophic military defeats after another, all the way through the Central Pacific, all the way through the Southwest Pacific as the Americans moved closer and closer and closer to Japan, and now as a backdrop, a series of absolutely horrific raids launched against the Japanese home islands, the war in the spring of 1945 was brought home to Japan. The bombing of Germany had been going on since 1940. A half a million German civilians would be killed by Allied bombing. The Japanese would come close to that figure in just through the spring and the summer of 1945. And yet, as the pressure mounted, there still seemed to be no indication that Japan was about to buckle—no sense that the military had come to its senses. Indeed, there seemed to be a growing conviction on the part of American policy makers and military men that the Japanese high command was perfectly prepared to go down literally in flames, taking every last man, woman, and child in Japan along with them.

The planning for the invasion of Japan had begun already before the fighting on Okinawa had been brought to a conclusion. The tentative jump-off date was set for November; Okinawa as well as the Philippines were to be forward staging areas for the assault on the southernmost Japanese island. General Marshall, a man not given to exaggeration or hyperbole, estimated at this point that an invasion of Japan would cost the United States a million casualties. This was the prospect that confronted American policy makers as summer began to wane in 1945.

War in the Air
Lecture 24

What I'd like to do in this lecture is to examine the Allied bombing policy during the war, looking at largely the European case, to talk about the experience of the air war in Europe, and what it meant both to be on the receiving end, and also in the planes flying at 20,000 feet during the course of the Second World War.

Air power and strategic bombing were the key to Allied victory, and they transformed the nature of warfare between 1939 and 1945. The United States and Britain had a distinctive conception of air power. Unlike the Germans or Japanese, the Americans and British emphasized strategic rather than tactical bombing. For the British, a strategic bombing capability substituted for the country's lack of a large land army. The British emphasized nighttime area bombing.

The U.S. Army Air Corps endorsed high-altitude "daylight precision bombing," which offered the political advantage of limiting casualties. Strategic bombing doctrine was embodied in Air War Plans Department One, which called for a sustained air offensive against the Axis powers to destroy their will and capacity to wage war. It was hoped that air ascendancy would make an invasion of the continent unnecessary.

The RAF was the first to test the concept of strategic bombing. It tried but soon abandoned daylight operations in Germany: casualty rates were high. Casualty rates remained high following the shift to nighttime bombing, and inadequate technology made it hard for RAF pilots to defend themselves and locate targets.

In February 1942, the British shifted their bombing policy; they acquired new radar equipment and new four-engine bombers—the Lancasters. Also in 1942, the RAF shifted to area bombing of Germany's large industrial cities. It began to measure its success in terms of urban acres destroyed and industrial man-hours lost. In February 1944, the RAF began to measure success in terms of the number of German workers killed per raid.

The new commanding officer of Bomber Command, Arthur Harris, championed area bombing. During the spring and summer of 1942, Harris launched three devastating RAF raids on German cities, in part to score propaganda points. However, radar proved to be ineffective as an aiming device for bombing. The Germans developed the means to jam British radar, and German night fighter defenses increased the RAF's aircraft losses.

The United States entered the air war in Europe in 1942. U.S. bombing commanders remained committed to daytime bombing assaults against industrial targets. The Eighth Air Force slowly built up its forces in Europe. The equipment needs of Operation Torch slowed its buildup.

"The bombing was much more effective than the Allies believed. The important consequence of the bombing was not that it failed to stem the increase in arms production, but that it prevented the increase from being very considerably greater than it was."—British historian Richard Overy

The Allied air policy adopted at the Casablanca Conference in January 1943 was "round-the-clock" bombing. American forces would bomb Germany during the day, and the RAF would bomb at night. U.S. and British bombing offensives were combined but not coordinated. Bomber Harris ignored pressure to attack priority industrial targets and continued to attack urban centers. He failed to follow up U.S. raids against industrial targets.

The RAF launched a huge but disastrous air offensive against Berlin between November 1943 and March 1944. Harris followed up this failure with another disastrous raid on Nuremberg. These failures undermined Harris' contention that Germany could be defeated through air power alone, and without an invasion. In mid-1943, the United States accepted sustained bombing of Germany. Its first raid—against Schweinfurt and Regensburg— ended in disaster.

The experience of aerial combat really did amount to the experience of life and death at 20,000 feet. It was very hard for large groups of bombers to maintain formation as they flew through flak over German targets. The B-17 and B-24 heavy bombers were on the cutting edge of technology. However, they were not pressurized; waist windows were open and the turrets were not sealed, so that temperatures inside the planes often fell to 20–40 degrees below zero. Heavy losses suffered by U.S. bombers showed that they needed fighter support. The deployment of P-51 Mustangs in early 1944 allowed huge bomber formations to challenge the Luftwaffe over Germany.

What did U.S. and British strategic bombing achieve? German war production increased in tandem with the tonnage of Allied bombs dropped on Germany. The shortcomings of Allied strategic bombing campaigns were attributable to poor coordination, the impossibility until late in the war of relentless attack on key priority targets, and technological and operational shortcomings that continued to make precision bombing difficult. However, the bombing was more effective than the Allies realized. It prevented German war production from increasing faster than it actually did. ∎

Suggested Reading

John Keegan, *The Second World War*, Chapter 22.

Richard Overy, *The Air War, 1939–1945*.

———, *Why The Allies Won*, Chapter 4.

Geoffrey Perret, *Winged Victory: The Army Air Force in World War II*.

Questions to Consider

1. Why did the U.S. and British forces adopt strategic bombing? What purposes did it serve?

2. Evaluate the contribution of strategic bombing to the success of the Allied war effort.

War in the Air
Lecture 24—Transcript

In our last lecture we had begun to address the issue of strategic bombing, particularly a shift in the American strategic thinking with regard to air power in the assault on Japan in the spring and summer of 1945—the movement away from what the Americans had called daylight precision bombing to a campaign of nighttime area raids. What I'd like to do in this lecture is to examine the Allied bombing policy during the war, looking at largely the European case, to talk about the experience of the air war in Europe, and what it meant both to be on the receiving end, and also in the planes flying at 20,000 feet during the course of the Second World War.

It was air power, but particularly strategic bombing, that transformed the nature of war between 1939 and 1945 and rendered the Second World War so terrifyingly different from its predecessors. In the First World War, the vast and grisly carnage had been confined largely to the front, to the soldiers, fortresses, and trenches strung along no man's land, and to the sailors and their ships at sea. The use of air power to smash an enemy's capacity to wage war, to demolish its industrial base, its energy sources, its communications network, its system of transportation, and ultimately the will of its people to resist was a radically new departure for military planners on the eve of the Second World War. And it fundamentally altered the nature of warfare, not simply in this war, but for all modern war.

Although Hitler, as we've seen, had used the threat of colossal air offensives against civilian targets for diplomatic advantages in the 1930's, the Luftwaffe was neither equipped nor trained for such a mission. For Germany, air strategy remained tied to land operations and was dominated by the army. It was a strategy that served the Wehrmacht well in its blitzkrieg stage of war in 1939 through 1941, but its narrow focus would come back to haunt German air planners as the conflict progressed, and Germany confronted powers whose air doctrine was quite different. Among the major powers, only Great Britain and the United States adopted a broad view of air power, which placed strategic bombing rather than tactical bombing at its center. Political as well as military factors weighed heavily in the decision of both countries.

In Britain, a commitment to a general conception of air doctrine was an alternative to a large land army, which the British did not have in the 1930's and didn't feel they could afford. And unlike Chamberlain, Neville Chamberlain, who in 1937, 1938, had lobbied for international agreements to actually banish bombing, Winston Churchill had early on shown himself to be an enthusiastic supporter of Britain's strategic bombing program. Churchill couldn't find language bloodthirsty enough to satisfy him when it came to talking about bombing, especially in these early stages of the war when this was the only, only option—offensive option—open to the British.

In the United States the concept of strategic bombing had been worked out in the Army Air Corps Tactical School during the 1930s, and would guide its operations during the entire Second World War. Their Army Air Corps strategist developed the doctrine that came to be known as high altitude daylight strategic bombing. It was a concept based on the premise that a massive fleet of heavy bombers, big, four-engine planes with high tech aiming devices, this would be the Norden bombsight, and flying at altitudes above effective enemy anti-aircraft fire—that is, above 20,000 feet—could identify and then destroy carefully selected strategic military and industrial targets. This was the idea.

The concept offered Franklin Roosevelt a politically attractive prospect of American involvement in the war without heavy casualties. This is always the lure of air power, and it was embodied in what came to be known as AWPD-1 (Air War Plans Department One), a statement of American air power at the very outset of the war. The plan called for a general air strategy that would not only, and I quote, "Provide for the close and direct air support of the surface forces and the invasion of the continent (meaning Europe) and for major land campaigns thereafter, and a strategic defense against Japan Pacific, but also to conduct a sustained and unremitting air offensive against Germany and Italy to destroy their will and their capacity to continue the war." Air planners in the United States actually hoped that this air offensive, "might make an invasion of the continent unnecessary." This was always the argument that would be put forward by Hap Arnold, the head of the Army air forces, by major American air planners, as well as Bomber Harris of the RAF. Give us enough materiel. Give us the priorities and we will make a land operation, an actual invasion of Europe, not to mention Japan, unnecessary.

This Air Wars Plan Division One was replaced after Pearl Harbor with a new document, but still with renewed emphasis on establishing complete air ascendancy over the enemy as a prelude to close support operations. But the United States, like Great Britain, entered the Second World War with a commitment to the concept of strategic bombing.

The RAF would be the first to test the theory. During 1940, RAF Bomber Command attempted daylight bombing of the Ruhr and other industrial and military targets in Germany on a very limited scale. But daylight operations were quickly abandoned because it was apparent that the bombers simply could not defend themselves against either German fighters or against anti-aircraft fire. In addition, the equipment and technology proved inadequate to the task. Bombing was carried out in 1940 and 1941 with smaller two-engine planes, the Stirlings, with very limited bomb loads, and navigational problems were really paramount. It quickly became apparent to virtually everyone in the command structure that the theory of strategic bombing clearly outran the RAF's ability to execute it.

This disturbing fact was driven home in August of 1941 when a committee headed by a man named D.M. Butt issued a report on the performance of Bomber Command against targets in France and Germany during the preceding two months. It did not make happy reading for Churchill or the head of the British air arm. The findings of his committee came as a shock. Commissioned by Lord Cherwell, Churchill's science advisor, this independent report found that on any given night, one-third of all attacking aircraft failed to bomb the primary target. One-third. Of the remaining two-thirds, only one in three had come within five miles of the aiming point. On moonlit nights, two of five aircrafts bombed within five miles of the aiming point, but on the far more frequent moonless nights, especially in Northern Europe with cloud cover, the ratio fell to 1 in 15. The problem wasn't so much one of aiming. The problem was of navigation. The crew simply couldn't find the targets. In addition, the shift to nighttime bombing, which had been in part to get away from the heavy casualties taken by the RAF in the daytime, didn't solve that problem either. Losses remained extremely high. There was one aircraft lost for every 10 tons of bombs dropped. The entire front line of Bomber Command had been wiped out, statistically speaking, in the last four months of the war before the report.

Clearly, something had to be done, and that something was a shift in bombing policy for the British that came in February of 1942, before the United States had really had a chance to enter the war in Europe. A new radar navigational aid had been developed to help the bombers find their way to the target. It was crude, but it was an improvement. It was called GEE. But also important technologically was the emergence of the new giant four-engine bombers, especially the Lancasters. They were capable of delivering a bomb load of 14,000 pounds. With the advent of this new radar equipment, it became possible to send the entire bomber force along the same route, concentrated in both time and space. It was a great improvement for bombing over the earlier freelance approach in which the planes would've found their way to the target, the individual navigators doing the work, and hopefully arriving more or less on schedule. Now a bomber stream could be sent, a bomber stream which was much better for delivering bombs to the target, but it was also quite obviously hardly a way to provide a tighter close formation such as the Americans would later employ. Thus, rather than abandoning strategic bombing, the RAF merely refined its approach.

1942 also brought a very important shift in targeting as well. The new directive indicated the targets for future operations for the RAF were to be Germany's large industrial cities. So no group commanders would miss the point, Air Minister Sir Charles Portal explained it to them in a memo that read, "Reference the new bombing directive. I suppose it is clear that the aiming points are to be the built-up areas, not for instance the dock yards or aircraft factories. This must be made clear if it is not already understood." The RAF, in other words, had decided to embark upon a strategy of area bombing. It was no longer going to be a matter of trying to pinpoint a military or industrial objective, but area bombing.

Just a month later, in March of 1942, a new report elaborated that strategic decision and provided a means of measuring Bomber Command success. The RAF in 1942 would swing over to a new way of evaluating what was a successful rate and what wasn't. They came up with a formula; a formula that for every x square miles of urban landscape laid waste, y number of Germans would be left homeless. The point, as Bomber Command put it, was to "de-house" the German working class. This is the term that was used, to de-house them, to destroy urban landscape. By concentrating on cities of over 100,000 in population, large targets that would be easier to find and to hit, over a third of the German population could be left homeless. From 1942 until early 1944, Bomber Command would measure its success by acres of built-up area destroyed; a correlation between acres of concentrated urban devastation and industrial manhours lost.

In February of 1944, however, the RAF went over to a new formula, a different one. It was no longer to be acres that were to be measured, but rather a new labor target would replace the area target. Success would henceforth be measured by a formula which estimated the number of German workers killed per raid. To the point, we're not talking now about factories, we're really, by February '44, Bomber Command is talking about estimating the number of German workers killed. The man who would execute this policy was the new C.O. of Bomber Command, Arthur Harris, who would become the leading champion of area bombing.

During the spring and summer of 1942, Harris gave a terrible hint of what was in store for the Germans when he launched three monster raids on German cities, using every available aircraft and all combat crews, trainees, instructors, as well as veterans—anything that would fly—in order to be able to announce that 1,000 planes had raided the German city. On May 30, 1942, 1,000 planes bombed Cologne, 900 were sent to Essen, 1,000 to Bremen in early June. Harris couldn't sustain these sort of numbers. In some ways—I'm not saying they're a publicity stunt—but it was clearly, there was a propaganda element in this as well as a serious military objective. He couldn't sustain these sort of numbers and subsequent RAF raids would be lighter; but he certainly had made his point, not only to the Germans but to the English public, and to the other services, who were very unhappy at this time about the high percentage of the war budget that Bomber Command claimed. It was about a third of the entire British war budget was now being claimed by Bomber Command, but there were still terrific problems. The radar was a reasonably good navigational aid, but it certainly wasn't much of an aiming device for bombing. The Germans, meanwhile, had developed jamming devices to frustrate English radar, and advances in German night fighter defense also raised Bomber Command's losses throughout the summer to above the 4% rate, which Harris considered acceptable.

While the RAF was struggling in the summer of 1942 with these problems, the United States entered the air war in Europe. The Americans came with their own theories of strategic bombing, and the Eighth Air Force became operational in the European Theater of operations. This was the unit charged with executing American strategic bombing policy, and the commander was General Carl Spots—Eighth—who commanded the Eighth Air Force. Eighth Bomber Command was led by General Ira Eaker. During the course of 1943, Eaker would assume command of the Eighth and Spots would then move on to be the head of all U.S. Army air forces in Europe. Both men were avidly committed to the concept of strategic bombing, but with a major difference in their approach from their British counterparts. Both of these men were eager to put American ideas of daylight precision bombing into practice to identify key industrial and military bottlenecks, and using the sophisticated Norden bombsight, destroy those targets. In other words, they were not at all convinced by Harris's commitment to nighttime area raids, which killed civilians without, they believed, delivering a decisive blow to German industrial targets.

The buildup of American strategic presence was slow and there were a lot of conflicting priorities. Just as the Eighth Air Force began to get its—to build up crews, to get aircraft arriving, to have the facilities in England—Operation Torch came along, the intervention of the Mediterranean campaign. And so the most experienced crews, aircraft technicians, and so on were moved off to North Africa to be involved in the raids there. The first mission flown by the Eighth Air Force had been on August 17, 1942, but by early 1943, thanks to Operation Torch, the Eighth Air Force still had fewer than 100 operational heavy bombers—this at a time when the British were already launching these big, thousand-plane raids.

At Casablanca, in early 1943, Churchill, the Allied hike man, agreed on what was called a combined bomber offensive. There was a lot of pressure on the Americans at the end of 1942. Raids hadn't gone very well. We didn't have many planes up. The weather was bad. It's one thing to talk about daylight precision bombing if what you're doing is bombing Alamogordo, New Mexico, or out in Arizona; a whole other matter if what you're trying to do is define targets in Northern Europe, which tends to be cloudy. The weather is—even in a good spell—is not really conducive to this kind of thing. The

Americans were under great pressure to shift their priorities, to swing over as part of the RAF's nighttime bombing campaign. The Americans resisted. Eaker made a plea, particularly to Churchill, and wrote up at Casablanca, in which he argued, "Well, what we need to do is let the RAF continue to bomb at night; we'll bomb during the daytime; and what we'll do is bomb around the clock." And I think Winston Churchill, who never met a phrase that he didn't like if it was a well-turned phrase, was really taken with this idea of "around the clock" bombing. This sounded good. The Germans would get no breathing space. The RAF would bomb them at night; the Americans in the daytime. He didn't believe daylight precision bombing would work at all. He thought the Americans were misguided about this, but this gave Eaker the opportunity to continue with the American air offensive.

What followed the Casablanca conference into 1943 was something called the combined bomber offensive. This was to be—this implied cooperation between the RAF and the Americans, this round the clock bombing—but the combined bomber offensive was anything but a combined bomber offensive. It was not coordinated. Despite the apparent coordination of air operations between the Americans and the British, there was no genuine coordination, but instead two distinct efforts. Bomber Harris routinely and maddeningly ignored all pressure to send his planes against priority targets, as ostensibly agreed upon, and instead continued to press against the large urban centers that he was so fond of attacking—that he believed would win the war. He continued to talk about—in private conversations with the Americans— Harris would call these things panacea targets. The Americans believed you had to find—you identify some sort of production bottleneck, ball bearings, for example—and then what you do is, you hammer away at ball bearings productions; destroy that, you bring the whole war machine down. Harris thought this was absolute nonsense. Panacea bombing wouldn't work, and as a consequence, never really followed raids up. The American idea was, we would go over, bomb Schweinfurt, let's say, in August of 1943, the first big American raid in Germany against ball bearing plants. The plan was for the RAF to come over at night. They didn't. They bombed Hamburg instead. Harris just resisted, and Churchill and no one else actually called him on the carpet for this. He flagrantly ignored demands that he follow the combined bomber offensive target priorities, and in November of '43 he claimed that 19 German cities had been totally destroyed by Bomber Command. Then he asserted, with typical Harris rhetoric, "We can wreck Berlin from one end, from end to end if the Americans will come in on it. It'll cost us between four and 500 aircraft, 10 men to a crew. It'll cost the Germans the war."

But Harris's four-month long battle for Berlin—it was called the Battle of Berlin, this big air offensive launched by the RAF, with some American participation, not much, between November of '43 and March of '44—it was a failure by his own standards. The city was relentlessly bombed, but the factories continued to produce, and Bomber Command lost 1,000 aircraft in this period alone. It was a disaster. By the spring of 1944, Harris had largely failed in his repeated promises to break Germany through saturation bombing, and his losses at the Battle of Berlin, and an absolutely disastrous raid on Nuremberg in March of 1944 when Bomber Command lost 100 planes in a single night—big, we're not talking small planes, we're talking about these larger bombers—had cost a great deal of his credibility with both Churchill and with the Allied military planners who were now getting ready to think about D-Day, Operation Overlord—not convinced by Harris. Harris and the American air commanders continued, literally up to, I think, the day of D-Day, to keep saying, "This is unnecessary. We can do this. We can beat the Germans without an invasion if you'll just give us the priorities." But it was fairly clear to most objective observers, and Eisenhower was one of them, that they had oversold their case.

For their part, the Americans were in no position to embark upon sustained bombing of Germany until mid-1943. The first major raid deep inside of Nazi Germany was the so-called Regensburg-Schweinfurt raid in August of 1943, and it proved to be a disaster. The planes made it through. They were not turned back. They bombed the target; hit Schweinfurt, one set of, several groups hitting Schweinfurt, some going on to hit Regensburg and the Messerschmitt factories there. But 60 B-17s were lost in that raid. And in October of 1943, the Eighth lost 148 bombers during a single week in a series of raids against targets in Germany, culminating in a second attack on Schweinfurt on October 14, in which another 60 planes went down in one single day. It was the absolute low point of American operations in Europe.

The losses during the first year of the American air war were indeed staggering. A tour of duty in the Eighth Air Force was set at 25 missions, but between August of 1942 when the Eighth began flying its missions and August 1943, only 30 percent of Eighth Air Force bomber personnel actually survived 25 missions to the continent. Thirty-seven percent were lost before they had completed five missions. Even in early 1944, the life expectancy of an Eighth Air Force bomber crew was 15 missions. In fact, the rate of loss for bomber crews was higher than for any other branch of the American military in the Second World War, comparable only to losses in the RAF Bomber Command, and to German U-Boats.

All combat is obviously terrifying, but I think there was something about the air war and bomber operations that was particularly unnerving. On the bomb run, the American idea of strategic bombing was that massive formations would fly in a very tight formation, not quite wing tip to wing tip, but close. Huge formations of these bombers moving, trying to bomb, hit precision targets, meant that if when one began the bomb run from what was called the IP, the Initial Point, to the target, the planes had to fly at a set speed, at a set altitude. They could not take evasive action. They had to fly directly over the target in exactly this formation. What this meant was to fly directly into German flak, which began to be radar guided so that the Germans, as the approaching planes, as the approaching formations, were seen, could lock on. There were different kinds of barrages flying through literally seas of flak, flak so thick, as bomber crews used to say, "You can get out and walk on it."

The planes themselves were, for the time, absolutely the cutting edge of technology—the B-17 Flying Fortress, the B-24 Liberator were enormously successful aircraft. But—and they looked enormous as one stood outside them—but inside those aircraft, these were not aircraft built for creature comfort. They were not pressurized, so that as soon as the planes went over 10,000 feet, the crews had to go on oxygen. Raids into central Germany would be nine hours or so, on oxygen, so you were tethered to your oxygen mask. The windows of the B-17, the waist on the Liberators, the windows on the waist were open. The turrets were obviously not sealed, and the bomb bay doors would swing open, so that in the aircraft itself, when the planes reached operational altitude at 20,000 feet, the temperature inside the planes in Northern Europe would be 20 to 30, to sometimes 40, degrees below zero.

To touch anything, any metal object, without gloves at operational altitude, meant you lost a finger, sometimes a hand.

The Eighth Air Force would lose as many people to frostbite in the first year of operations as they did to enemy action, and anoxia, simply passing out, people going off of oxygen, oxygen valves freezing up. Bundling up in clothing of several layers thick, with an electric flying suit underneath it, maybe—this was fine as long as the electrical system in the plane worked. If it didn't, and that went out, you were simply stuck. All crewmembers had to be tested for claustrophobia. The losses for the Eighth Air Force would remain extraordinarily high, and also for the 15th flying out of Italy, where targets in southern Europe, from which targets in southern Europe were hit.

The losses suffered by the Americans in these daylight raids prompted a fundamental rethinking of the American approach. In the end, American planners decided that it wasn't so much the strategy that was wrong, but the technological ability to carry it out—that the bombers simply could not fly into Germany without fighter support. They couldn't defend themselves. This had been the argument they'd made with all of the machine guns available on a B-17 and a -24. Now they were going to have to have fighter support, and in early 1944, the P-51 Mustang, which had already been developed, was now deployed in large numbers in Europe, capable of flying all the way with the bombers to the targets as far away as Berlin. And this marked a major turning point in American air operations. It allowed the great bomber formations to fly on into Germany to defeat the German Luftwaffe, which was done in the beginning of what was called Big Week in February of 1944, and then on down to the D-Day invasion. The Mustangs were given their permission to leave the bomber formation. They didn't have to fly along with the bombers, but to go seek out Luftwaffe planes wherever they were found. As a result, the Luftwaffe, between February of '44 and the summer of 1944, had been defeated. And the American onslaught against German targets continued shifting in early 1944, from oil, and aircraft production, submarine bases, to transportation, to bomb the access to the D-Day invasion beaches.

What, at the end of the day, did the American air assault and the English air assault against Germany achieve? What was the effect of strategic bombing, daylight strategic bombing, or the nighttime raids of the British? Did it work? What was its contribution to the war? Here, I think we're confronted by a very odd paradox. As Allied tonnage of bombs dropped on Germany increased by leaps and bounds during 1943, and into 1944, so, too, did German war production. Take your pick: tanks, planes, weapons, you name it; in fact, in virtually every category identified as a priority target by the combined bomber offensive, production increased dramatically between 1942 and the fall of 1944. The American strategic bombing survey, which was done right at the very conclusion of the war in Europe, indicates this: that ironically, the apex of German war production came in the summer of 1944 in July, at that point at which the Allies had established air superiority. Thereafter, from July to April 1945, the index for German industrial output plunged.

What were the factors that limited Allied success? First, one would have to note the lack of real coordination. This round the clock bombing sounded good, but it wasn't the coordinated effort. Second, the theory of strategic bombing as envisioned by the Americans—to conduct a sustained and unremitting air offensive against Germany and Italy to destroy their will and capacity to continue the war—it simply didn't work. The theory implied a relentless attack on key priority targets, returning to hit them over and over again—but this the Allies were unable to do until the final six months of the war. Indeed, only in the campaign against oil, which really began after D-Day, was this sort of coordinated sustained targeting carried out, and then it worked. Finally, the Allies discovered that theory simply outran operational capabilities. Even if the Allied air forces could've agreed upon one set of priorities in cooperating in attacking them, such a sustained assault was simply impossible until the spring of 1944. Shortages of aircraft and crews remained until '44, and tactically the doctrine of daylight precision bombing had proven impossible without long-range fighter support available— unavailable until early 1944. And finally, the technology of the period, the state of plane-based radar to locate targets and the operational problems, such as the effectiveness of anti-aircraft defenses, continued to make precision bombing a goal rather than a reality.

On the other hand, part of the explanation for—part of the paradox is somewhat misleading. You'll recall from an earlier lecture, when we talked about the blitzkrieg strategy, that we indicated that German war production had been based on a blitzkrieg strategy—production in breadth, not in depth. The Germans had, remarkably, not mobilized their economy, not even begun to mobilize it for total war, until late—until finally 1943 and into 1944. There was so much slack in the German economy that the Germans finally, under Albert Speer, were able to get it out only in the course of 1944. Thereafter, then, the air offensive really did make a difference. We saw this in the Battle of the Bulge, when the Germans really didn't have the oil necessary.

In evaluating the impact of Allied strategy, strategic bombing, I'm inclined to agree with the British historian Richard Overy, the economic historian, who has argued that, if anything, "The bombing was much more effective than the Allies believed. The important consequence of the bombing was not that it failed to stem the increase in arms production, but that it prevented the increase from being very considerably greater than it was." Bombing placed a ceiling on German war production, which was well below what Germany was skillful, and more urgent management of its resources was capable, of producing after 1943. Substantial though increases in German output appeared, they might have been greater still but for bombing. The absence of bombing would've freed resources held down. In anti-aircraft—over a million people were involved in this in 1944 in repair work—would have eliminated wastage caused by bombing and would have allowed the industrial planners the same freedom as that enjoyed in the United States to plan, build, and operate the war economy without interruption and as near to the economic optimum as possible.

Hitler's New Order in Europe
Lecture 25

In this lecture I'd like to turn our attention then to Hitler's New Order in Europe, the fruits of which were yielded up in these last months of the war—the racial war conducted by the Nazis in Europe against the Jews of Europe.

H itler's wars against the Allied powers and against the Jews must be viewed together This is because in many ways the Holocaust, the systematic destruction of the European Jewish community, is inconceivable without the war itself. Nazi racial policy evolved during the 1930s. In 1933 and 1934 the Nazi regime issued anti-Jewish legislation. A Nazi boycott of Jewish businesses was called off almost immediately when it proved to be unpopular. Jews were eliminated from the civil service and certain professions. The anti-Jewish policy seemed to lose momentum in 1934 and 1935.

Hitler accepting the ovation of the Reichstag.

The Nuremberg Laws of 1935 revoked the citizenship of Jews. Marriage and sexual relations between Jews and "Aryans" were prohibited. In November 1938, Goebbels' propaganda ministry orchestrated the *Reichskristallnacht* (night of broken glass) pogrom throughout Germany. This was the first instance of violence against the Jews clearly directed by the leadership of the regime. The policy of forced emigration was instituted in 1938.

The Nazi regime gradually moved toward the "final solution." In January 1939 Hitler threatened the destruction of the Jewish race in Europe, and he linked Bolshevism with "world finance Jewry." In November 1939,

333

Himmler became responsible for Nazi racial policy. He delegated this work to Heydrich, who designated Poland as the concentration point for Jews in preparation for their deportation to the east.

The *Einsatzgruppen* (3,000 special SS commando units) were responsible for rounding up the Jews. Various solutions to the "Jewish question" were discussed within the SS leadership during 1940 and 1941. These included the settlement of all Jews in Madagascar. The "Commissar Order" informed the German Army on the eastern front about the SS "special tasks," which included the massacre of Russian and Ukrainian Jews behind German lines. In late summer 1941, Hitler issued a verbal order to Himmler regarding the final solution.

Heydrich developed a plan for systematic mass murder of Jews, which he presented at the Wannsee Conference on January 20, 1942. The system of death camps was established during 1942. Ten percent of the inmates would be put to work, and the rest would be killed. European Jews were deported to the east.

The Allies faced difficult choices in considering how to respond to the Holocaust. They were aware of SS activities but did not have extensive knowledge about the death camps. There was considerable skepticism and even disbelief within the Allied camp about these reports. Many of the information sources were regarded as suspect.

Various factors worked to discourage a vigorous Allied response. The Allies discussed bombing either the camps or the rail lines leading to them. It was feared that such bombings might inadvertently kill numerous inmates, and that they might detract from the broader military effort. Latent anti-Semitism in official circles contributed to a reluctance to publicize accounts of Nazi atrocities against the Jews. In sum, Allied policy held that the best way to save the Jews was to rapidly win the war against Nazi Germany. ∎

To prevent further death, to save more lives, the Allied governments argued, the war had to be brought to a speedy conclusion, that anything that detracted from that would only protract the war and cost more lives.

Suggested Reading

Yehuda Bauer, *A History of the Holocaust.*

Christopher Browning, *Ordinary Men: Police Battalion 101 and the Final Solution in Poland.*

Henry Friedlander, *The Origins of Nazi Genocide From Euthanasia to the Final Solution.*

Raul Hilberg, *The Destruction of the European Jews.*

Questions to Consider

1. Trace the evolution of the Nazi regime's "final solution to the Jewish problem." What role did the "final solution" play in Hitler's larger ideological program?

2. What considerations discouraged the Allies from responding aggressively to the Holocaust? Was their restraint justified?

Hitler's New Order in Europe
Lecture 25—Transcript

Hello. Welcome to our twenty-fifth lecture on the Second World War. We've been examining in our past few lectures the closing in of Allied forces, the American forces, on Japan, and looking also at Allied air policy, both in the Pacific Theater and also in Europe. In the spring of 1944-45, the vise was closing, not only on Japan, but also on Germany—the air war bringing the war home to both the Japanese domestic population and the Germans. And also, in the European Theater, as the Allied armies began to close in on Hitler's Third Reich. The Russians moving relentlessly from the east, the Anglo-American forces from the west; the Third Reich began to yield its grisly harvest, as the Allies broke into Germany proper to uncover the horrors of Dachau and Buchenwald; the Russians to uncover the truly astonishing and horrific bestialities of Auschwitz and the German concentration camp system in Poland. In this lecture I'd like to turn our attention then to Hitler's New Order in Europe, the fruits of which were yielded up in these last months of the war—the racial war conducted by the Nazis in Europe against the Jews of Europe.

We talked about, in an earlier lecture, Hitler's foreign policy—his ideological conception of an assault against the Soviet Union as being not simply an exercise in geo-politics, but also an ideological crusade, a crusade against what he considered to be the center of Judeo-Bolshevism. But the war against the Soviet Union was a war to eliminate Communism—Bolshevism. But in Hitler's thinking, there was no distinction to be made between Jews and Bolsheviks. The war against the Soviet Union would be a war of annihilation, not only against the Red Army and the Russians, but also against the Jewish community of Europe. I'd like to look at the evolution of Nazi policy, to look at Nazi racial policy during the pre-war era, and then to look at the impact of the war itself on Nazi policy. In many ways, in fact in a crucial way, it seems to me that what we now call the Holocaust, the systematic destruction of the European Jewish community, is virtually inconceivable without the war itself—that the war and the Holocaust must be seen together.

In 1933, when Adolf Hitler was named the Chancellor of Germany, he came to power with roughly a third of the vote in Germany. He was hardly swept into power on a tidal wave of mass public support. The National Socialists had received at the height of their popularity in the summer of 1932 just about 37 percent of the vote. Part of the Nazi campaign had always been the appeal, the ideological core of the National Socialist party—the Nazi party—had been anti-Semitism: to eliminate the influence of Jews from German society. In the shorthand version, as Hitler would talk about this, and his paladins would talk about it during the rise to power, it wouldn't simply be to eliminate the influence of Jews, but to use a variety of ways of saying, "We want to eliminate the Jews from German life, to expunge the presence of Jews from German life." We know from studies of Germany in the period just before the rise to power that the anti-Semitism of the regime was not what drew the vast majority of Germans to it, but rather its radical nationalism, its determination to undo the economic woes of the Weimar Republic, and so on. But after 1933, with the regime in power, it is precisely this aspect of National Socialist ideology that would be translated into reality.

The Nazis, as it turned out, had been deadly serious about the anti-Semitic planks of the Nazi platform. In 1933, shortly after Hitler's appointment as chancellor, there had been a boycott call of Jewish businesses in Germany. The boycott was intended to last for months on end. It was called off after 24 hours. It had been an abysmal failure—unpopular at home, certainly unpopular abroad. It was bad publicity for the new National Socialist Regime. In these first months of the regime in '33, the Nazis also introduced a series of laws to eliminate Jews from jobs in the civil service, to restrict the practice of law, medicine, and so on by Jews.

But between 1933 and 1935, a period during which Hitler consolidated his grip on the German society and the German state, the regime seemed to lose momentum in its Jewish policy. There were no new initiatives. There was a great deal of harassment and persecution of Jews on the local level. If one were Jewish in Germany, it depended on where you lived. You might be relatively free from harassment, if you lived in Cologne, but if you had the misfortune of living somewhere in Franconia, Nuremberg, because the local Nazis there were far more radical in this sense, your life might be a living hell. But there was no new initiative from the national regime. It tended to be local, regional.

But then, in 1935, the regime would introduce what came to be known as the Nuremberg Laws. These were laws which, in effect, would eliminate Jews as citizens of the Third Reich. Jews were no longer citizens in Germany with full civil rights, but rather subjects of the Third Reich. Those laws also introduced a series of strictures against Jewish intermarriage with so-called "Aryans"—sexual relations, and so on. The regime after the Nuremberg Laws in 1935 once again seemed to lose momentum in its racial policy. There were no real new initiatives in racial policy between 1935 and 1938. It was not at all clear that the regime was pursuing a consistent policy. In this period, the SS, Hitler's elite *Schutzstaffel*, the black-suited SS elite organization with Heinrich Himmler at the head, and his trusted lieutenant Reinhard Heydrich, certainly pursued Jewish policy. But Nazi policy with regard to the Jews of Germany in the period before the war was largely to encourage Jews to leave. There's a particularly ugly German term called "Entjudung." It's no less ugly in English. It means de-Jewification. The German government encouraged Jews to leave; did everything they could to make life unpleasant at home so that Jews would leave. It was not a situation like the Soviet Union after the Second World War where it was difficult for Jews to leave. The regime certainly didn't stand in the way, but Jews could leave, basically penniless if they were to go.

In 1938, there was a new ratcheting up of Nazi policy with regard to the Jews. In November of 1938, a pogrom occurred all over Germany. It was called "The Night of Broken Glass," *Kristallnacht*, or the *Reichkristallnacht*, in German. It was a pogrom conducted all over Germany, largely by Joseph Goebbels, head of the Reich Propaganda Ministry, in response to the assassination of a German diplomat by a young Polish Jew in Paris. It was presented as a spontaneous reaction of outraged German citizens. In fact, it was a very carefully orchestrated pogrom carried out by Goebbels' propaganda minions all over the country. It's important because it really represents the first clearly orchestrated act of violence against the Jews that was directed from the top. This was not local. This was not a regional phenomenon. This wasn't the work of local radicals. This was national policy, and it could not be presented as anything but.

So, the regime before the outbreak of war in September of 1939 certainly had pursued an anti-Semitic policy. One can look at it as a steady ratcheting up or escalation of steps taken against the Jews. First, boycott; then made non-citizens in 1935; then this first act of violence in 1938. In addition, a series of economic limitations on Jewish life in Germany, also in 1938. And then the war.

The war would be the major turning point in National Socialist racial policy. And I think it's important as one thinks about motivation, one thinks about the evolution of Nazi policy, that on January 30, 1939, the anniversary of Hitler's appointment as chancellor—he'd been appointed chancellor on January 30, '33—Hitler spoke to the German Reichstag—the German legislature, the national parliament—and he made the following declaration: "One more thing I would like now to state on this day, memorable perhaps not only for us Germans. I have often been a prophet in my life and was generally laughed at. During my struggle for power, the Jews primarily received with laughter my prophecies that I would someday assume the leadership of the state, and thereby the entire "*volk*," and then, among many other things, achieve a solution of the Jewish problem. I suppose that meanwhile the then resounding laughter of Jewry in Germany is now choking in their throats. Today I will be a prophet again. If international finance Jewry within Europe and abroad should succeed once more in plunging the peoples into a world war, then the consequence will not be the Bolshevization of the world, and therewith the victory of Jewry, but on the contrary—the destruction of the Jewish race in Europe."

This is months before the outbreak of the war. And what we have in this statement is that typical combination in Hitler's mind, "world finance Jewry" on the one hand and Bolshevization on the other. But the invasion of Poland in September of 1939, and even more so the invasion of the Soviet Union in the summer of 1941, would catapult the Nazis into a position to, as Hitler had put it, "solve the Jewish problem in Europe." Indeed, the invasion of Poland and then the Soviet Union put Germany in control of Europe's largest Jewish communities. The Jewish population in Germany before the war had been one-half of one percent of the overall population. And now the Germans, with the invasion of Eastern Europe, found themselves in control of these large Jewish communities.

In October of 1939, a month into the war, Heinrich Himmler, head of the SS, was named Reich Commissar for the strengthening of German "volkdom," a new title that gave him responsibility for Nazi racial policy in all of the occupied territories. Himmler delegated that authority to his trusted lieutenant Reinhard Heydrich, in a so-called Reich Security Central Office, where SS specialists were already at work in finding a solution to either the "Jewish problem" or the "Jewish question." The Nazis used variations on this term over and over again—immigration, forced immigration, "Entjudung"—the policy of pre-war Germany would now really become expulsion. Expulsion of the Jews from Germany. Expulsion of the Jews from those areas of Eastern Europe that the Nazis were going to incorporate into this new Grössdeutsches Reich. In a memorandum drafted on September 19, 1939, entitled "The Jewish Question in the Occupied Territories," Heydrich laid out the foundations of Nazi policy. In those territories annexed to Germany, all non-Germans were to be expelled. Those territories were to be cleansed of non-Aryans, both Slavs as well as Jews, in preparation for future settlement by Germans. This meant the evacuation of Poles, Czechs, and so on to the so-called Government General of Poland—the new Polish states—the rump Polish state created by the Nazis on October 12, 1939. This Government General of Poland would serve as the dumping ground for Jews rounded up all over Europe, and it would ultimately become the killing grounds for the Jews of Europe.

Moreover, all Jews were to be rounded up and concentrated in a few selected urban areas. Heydrich's memorandum in September of '39 suggests that "ghettoization" was not the final aim, that creating big ghettos in the east was not the final aim, but represented an intermediate step. These ghettos, or concentration centers, in the east were to be located near major rail lines, he indicated, hinting that further transport was being considered. It was at this time that another idea was circulated very secretly among the top Nazi leadership—the idea of creating some sort of, what they called a Jewish reservation, almost like an Indian reservation in the United States— somewhere out vaguely in the east, somewhere off in Eastern Europe. The responsibility for executing this policy, the rounding up, the ghettoization, was placed in the hands of special SS forces, the so-called *Einsatzgruppen* and special SS commando units developed for the move into Austria. These were men, for the most part, with special training and indoctrination in Nazi

340

racial policy. Others were simply police officers. They numbered about 3,000 men.

It's estimated that approximately 1 million people were rounded up and forced into ghettos in the Government General of Poland in the course of 1939-1940. In fact, by October of 1939, the SS had begun the deportation of Jews from Austria and Czechoslovakia to the Government General. But problems with this scheme emerged relatively quickly. The army high command was appalled at the sheer brutality of the *Einsatzgruppen*, who moved in right behind the Wehrmacht troops, prompting complaints to various Nazi officials, including Himmler, and to Hitler himself, that the *Einsatzgruppen* and the SS were causing difficulty with military operations.

As the war continued and spread to the west in 1940, the German in charge of the government, General Hans Frank, complained that his area, the Government General of Poland, was simply being reduced to little more than a dumping ground, and he was not going to be able to manage this situation if the trends continued. By October of 1940, Jews were being deported from Western Europe to the Government General. Himmler, at this point, ordered the construction of a camp at Auschwitz in Poland near Krakow, and in early 1941, the commandant was ordered to expect as many as possibly 30,000 inmates. Still, no ultimate solution to the "Jewish question" had been found.

The SS considered several options at this time. In February of 1940 the idea of a Jewish reservation somewhere in Eastern Europe seems to have been approved by Goering, by Himmler, by Hans Frank, and then was dropped. We're not quite sure why. The paper trail is not at all evident. But nobody could agree about where the location of this should be. At roughly the same time, another plan was put forward within the SS, that had been discussed off and on really since the outbreak of the war. And this was an idea—sounds fantastic in a way—of settling of all of Europe's Jews somewhere in Africa; in fact, in the French colony of Madagascar off the southeastern coast of Africa. In May of 1940, Himmler wrote a memorandum to Hitler entitled, "Treatment of Foreign Nationals in the East," in which he stated, and I quote, "I hope to see the concept of Jews completely obliterated with the possibility of a large migration of all Jews to Africa or else to a colony." In other words, the SS was taking this idea of the "Madagascar Plan," as it came to be known, quite seriously. They drafted numerous memoranda on issues of international law. They considered questions of transport, and so on, in pursuance of this option.

But as 1940 turned into 1941, the National Socialist Regime still didn't seem to have a very clear idea as to what a solution to the "Jewish question" was going to be. The Royal Navy made the idea of Madagascar fairly unworkable, since transport was not going to be possible. And, of course, by August of 1941, German troops were now deep inside the Soviet Union, and as the war against the Soviet Union would progress, it would profoundly affect Nazi racial policy.

We talked, when we talked about Operation Barbarossa, about this infamous "Commissar Order" delivered to German troops going into the Soviet Union, in which they were told that they would face four implacable enemies: commissars of the Bolshevik party, partisans, saboteurs, and Jews—that these groups were to be eliminated wherever they were found, whether they were engaging in active or passive resistance. The mistakes of the Polish campaign, where there were conflicts between SS, *Einsatzgruppen*, and the German army, were now to be eliminated. The German army was given to understand very clearly that the SS going into the Soviet Union had "special tasks" to deal with and the army was to give them leeway.

Throughout the summer and fall of 1941, as the German troops dove deeper and deeper into the Soviet Union, with the *Einsatzgruppen* moving along with them, the *Einsatzgruppen* conducted what was a massive bloodbath all over the Soviet Union behind German lines, the major victims of which were Russian Jews, Ukrainian Jews. They engaged in mass shootings—the Jews, partisans, Slavic "Untermensch," "sub-humans," as the Nazis referred to their Slavic enemies. They also began experimenting in 1941—the shooting of Jews, where whole villages of Jews would be marched out, forced to dig a trench, and then shot—shot by the *Einsatzgruppen* personnel—in some cases shot by regular German army troops who would be drawn into this in one way or the other. Whether or not the army troops were drawn directly into these sorts of actions or not, they saw it. German troops took photographs of this; sent the photographs home; wrote home about what they had seen on the Eastern Front with these mass shootings. And, at this point, the SS began to experiment with another means. This sort of action was too public. It was too sloppy. It was too inefficient. In the summer of 1941, the SS began experimenting with mobile gas vans, special mobile units that would be drawn up behind the Front and poison gas used. In September of 1941, Auschwitz was used for the first gassing of victims. The first victims of gassing at Auschwitz were 600 Russian prisoners of war.

It is sometime in the summer of 1941, in this summer when the Germans believe they've won the war, when all is going well for them in their deep drive into the Soviet Union, when victory over the Bolsheviks seems at hand, that Hitler issued a verbal order to Heinrich Himmler to seek what was called a "final solution" to the "Jewish question" in Europe. The date is uncertain. We're never going to know. There is no paper trail. But it is quite clear that late in the summer of 1941, that Himmler, as well as Reinhard Heydrich, his deputy, began to speak of a Führer order. This is the way Hitler did business anyway: verbal orders; don't write it down; begin speaking of a Führer order to find a "Gesamptloesung," a "total solution," an "Endloesung," a "final solution," to the "Jewish question." And that responsibility was delegated from Himmler to Reinhard Heydrich. He would become the real architect of what came to be known as the "final solution."

He drew together several existing policies and institutions. The concentration camp system. The camps in Germany—I think this is important that one understand—the camps inside Germany were not big death camps. They were horrible institutions. People died there—tortured, beaten to death, starved to death, and so on. But they were largely for political prisoners. The camps now that were going to be created for the extermination of the Jews were to be built in Eastern Europe, in Poland, for the most part. These were to be "Vernichtungslager"—"death camps," different from those inside of Germany. The Jews of Europe would be "resettled." The Nazis were keen on euphemisms. Rather than talking about mass murder, they talked about "resettlement," or "special treatment." And, at these concentration camps, these special "Vernichtungslager," special gas installations, gas bunkers were to be created so that one wouldn't have mass shootings, but rather the use of poison gas.

What Heydrich had embarked upon—had come to the conclusion that he would do by the late summer, early fall of 1941—was nothing less than a systematic plan for mass murder. I say Heydrich because it's clear that Hitler saw himself as a "big picture" man. He gave the direction to policy. It was Heydrich, or Himmler, or others, who would work out the details of how this would work. And it seems clear that at some point Heydrich presented this plan to Hitler, who obviously okayed it. It is clear from testimony in October that Himmler already understood what was afoot. He told one foreign office official, and I quote, "The destruction of the Jews is being planned. Now the destruction of the Jews is imminent."

An invitation was issued to a small group of Nazi officials, party officials, state officials, to the Berlin suburb of Wannsee, to meet in December of 1941, in which this would be presided over by Heydrich, where he would present this final solution to those who were gathered. The meeting had to be postponed. It was postponed to January 20, 1942, in part because of the Soviet counter offensive before Moscow, the American entry into the war, and so on, and so it was pushed back until January of 1942. At this Wannsee Conference—Hitler didn't attend it, none of the other major Nazi officials, not Goering, not Goebbels, and so on, not Himmler—but Heydrich presided over the meeting. And he announced to the SS representatives, state officials, and so on gathered there—a meeting that took, oh, a little over an hour—what the plan would be.

A series of death camps would be created in Poland. Those that existed, like Auschwitz, would now be expanded to handle thousands, hundreds of thousands, indeed possibly millions, of victims who would be transported there. Many, he figured, would die in transit. Others would simply be worked to death once they arrived. Still others would be liquidated on the spot. Mothers, small children, the old, the infirm—were on principle deemed unfit to work—would simply be liquidated as soon as they arrived at these camps. Poison gas would be used. The need for secrecy was emphasized. The German public, the Nazis felt, was not prepared for this sort of thing, not this kind of radical action. They certainly didn't want foreign propaganda to get hold of this information. And the third thing was that the ignorance of the victim had to be maintained. People couldn't know, the Jews of Europe weren't supposed to know, what fate awaited them at the end of the long train journey.

A series of these camps were created beginning in the spring of 1942. The process would largely be the same from camp to camp. There were some variations, but for the most part, the procedures were the same. Approximately 10 percent of any arriving shipment of Jews would be selected for work. The others would be instructed to undress. Women and girls frequently had their hair cut—the Germans used the hair for industrial purposes. They were marched between files of auxiliary police to what they were told were shower stalls—the big underground bunker with shower heads sticking out of the ceiling. They were told, in many cases, "You've had a long journey. You're going to now have a bath." In some cases, they went so far as to issue soap. The victims were led down from the train platform into these "shower" installations, and at this point, all pretense was lost. People were rammed into these underground bunkers. The Germans calculated at one person per square foot, and then gas would be released from above. The gassing process itself could last anywhere from 10 to 30 minutes before the last person had finally died. Between 1942 and January of 1945, when the camps were closed down by the advancing Allies in the east, the Russians, over 6 million Jews would die in the camps, and millions more—Russians, Poles, gypsies, and others—would simply vanish into the gas chambers, victims of Nazi racial policy.

In recent years there has been an increasing discussion about exactly what was known about this. I'm not going to talk about what the Germans knew. There were rumors. Certainly this was not reported in the German press. The Nazis didn't talk about it, but there were rumors. People heard things about what was going on in the east. And of course, a great many people were actually involved in the process itself. The Allies also had heard reports about a variety of sources—about what we now think of as the Holocaust— as early as the summer of 1941. And it's this I want to talk a little bit about. Allied intelligence services had begun to receive numerous reports in 1941 and '42 from Poland and the Soviet Union. There's a series of articles about this in the press over the last year and a half about disclosures, about what was known. In fact, what was known—and this was known at the time, and talked about at the time—was the activities of the *Einsatzgruppen*, this kind

345

of mass pogrom across the Soviet Union. About a million people—probably a million and a half people—died as a result of these *Einsatzgruppen*. This was certainly known. But, Allied governments had a difficult time figuring out what all the pieces of the intelligence added up to. The Soviet Union provided very little hard information, stressing Nazi brutality and barbarism, but rarely singling out the Jews specifically. The three so-called Molotov Notes of January, April, and October of 1942 about the conditions and German atrocities in the East, mentioned certainly atrocities, but against all Soviet peoples, not necessarily against the Jews. Then in December of 1942—now the camps had been up and running since March '42, for the most part—the Soviet Foreign Ministry's Information Bureau issued a brief, unsigned statement dealing with Nazi plans "to exterminate the Jewish population in the occupied territories of Europe," and went on to mention that millions of Jews from all over Europe were being concentrated "for the purpose of killing them." The international press picked up such items, but did not emphasize them. These bits and pieces of news from suspect sources—Polish underground, Hungarian soldiers returning from the Eastern Front, and so on—were certainly there.

There's a book by Walter Laqueur called *The Terrible Secret*, in which he talks about what exactly was already published in the newspapers during the course of the war. But this tended to be swamped by more pressing, and clearly documented, news from the fronts. Nonetheless, in June of 1942, the BBC broadcast a report that 700,000 Jews had been killed so far. But only in the summer of '42 did the Allied governments slowly begin to realize that these actions were not simply pogroms of a kind of a traditional sort, but something far more sinister was afoot. A *Daily Telegraph* story in England, also in June, reported that a million were dead. There were mass meetings in Madison Square Garden in the United States in July and August, and in other cities. The World Jewish Congress began to make appeals to the Foreign Office in Britain, and to the State Department in the United States, encountering tremendous skepticism.

The official response, both in Britain and the United States, to Jewish groups and to others that raised the issue of what was going on insofar as one was able to piece this together, was that any sort of effort to, for example, bring the camps under attack, would sidetrack the Allies from military objectives.

And, to give you some indication of the lack of sympathy that was frequently heard by Jewish groups, a Foreign Office official in England said, and I quote, that such efforts to rescue the Jews would "waste disproportionate amount of time in dealing with wailing Jews." There was considerable reluctance to publicize atrocity stories. The Ministry of Information believed in England that the public thought that people singled out as victims were probably a bad lot. There was also a fear that there'd been a lot of Allied propaganda during the first war about German atrocities in Belgium, most of which turned out to be untrue. And so there was a reluctance to take this up. And finally, there was latent anti-Semitism in official circles, both in Britain and in the United States—skepticism about what was being told.

Here, I think, one has to come to the conclusion that the Allies were getting by 1944 a considerable amount of information. It was only in '44 that we discovered what Auschwitz actually was. What policies might have been undertaken? Bombing certainly, the camps, bombing the railroad tracks leading to the camps. These things were discussed. But the Allies felt that while it was theoretically possible, if you'll recall that raids deep into Germany were extremely costly to Allied planes, personnel, and so on, as late as early 1944—mid-1944. And the other thing, the idea of bombing the railroads—one of the things the Allies had discovered about bombing transportation in France: you don't bomb them once. You bomb railroad tracks, you bomb a marshaling yard—you don't just do it once. You've got to keep coming back and doing it over and over and over again. The best way to save Jewish lives, the official position was, was to win the war as quickly as possible, and this would save lives.

I think the other thing, too, is that if one puts oneself in the position of someone to make a decision, do you want to be the person who is willing to make a decision to say, "Yes, we're going to bomb the camp at Auschwitz," to be responsible for the death of tens of thousands of Jews. One could say, "Well, possibly in the long run this might have saved lives." But I think it would have been extremely difficult for any elected official in the West to take on that responsibility. The BBC would broadcast in the summer of 1944 a warning to anyone in Europe who was participating in the deportation of Jews that they would be held accountable at the end of the war. Finally, I think, one of the problems for the Allies was that if they could not prevent the murder of the Jews, then to talk about it—to raise it as a public issue—they felt, would simply reveal their own weakness.

All of these things taken together meant that there was a great reluctance on the part of the Allied governments, even with mounting information. The simple fact was that this was not part of the war objectives of the Allied cause. To prevent further death, to save more lives, the Allied governments argued, the war had to be brought to a speedy conclusion, that anything that detracted from that would only protract the war and cost more lives. It was a controversial decision; one that, I think, looking back, we might dispute. But at the time, I think there was a growing sense that the horrors, most of which were already in the past by the summer of 1944, could only be halted by the destruction of Hitler's Third Reich.

"This Man's Army"
Lecture 26

American production would be one of the real miracles of the Second World War, creating a military machine and industrial machine of unparalleled proportions; and the American army, too, considering that on September 1, 1939, that it was the 19th largest army in the world, that the Poles had a larger military establishment than the United States at that point.

The U.S. Army had to be virtually created during the late 1930s and early 1940s because it had been neglected during the inter-war years. Five years after the end of World War I, U.S. Army strength stood at 132,000 troops. President Hoover cut pay for officers by 15 percent and for enlisted men by 30 percent. Early in his presidency, FDR threatened to slash the military budget by 51 percent, relenting only when Douglas MacArthur threatened to resign as chief of staff. The military budget began to rise again in 1935. When war broke out in Europe in 1939, army strength stood at 190,000 troops.

The turning point came with the fall of France in June 1940. The Army received a huge budget allocation of $9 billion. The first U.S. army draft in peacetime was introduced in September 1940. Gen. Marshall relied on Major Albert Wedemeyer to rebuild the Army. Wedemeyer had to find manpower to fill 800 divisions and construct a fleet within two years. The federal government bought or seized land to establish the huge military camps that would be needed to accommodate the millions of new army inductees.

Much of what Marshall insisted upon was a series of things to make life better for soldiers, sailors, everyone in the military.

Although FDR hoped that the United States would outproduce its enemies in equipment and munitions, the United States had no large munitions industries in 1941. Gen. Marshall and Secretary of War Henry Stimson reorganized the

War Department. The U.S. Army never reached the 8.8-million-man size projected by Wedemeyer. At its height, it was half the size of the Red Army and slightly smaller than the German army.

The world of the citizen-soldier was characterized by OD (olive drab) and khaki. The prospective soldier's first contact with the army came through the Selective Service System. At the reception center, the soldier entered a new world in which privacy was unknown.

The army served as a melting pot, revealing the nation's diversity to many soldiers who had previously not traveled far from their homes. It was a kaleidoscope of regional and religious diversity. The bomber crew was a microcosm of American society. African-American soldiers remained second-class and were over-represented in the service units. Gen. Marshall resisted any effort to use the armed forces to resolve the nation's racial tensions.

Gen. Marshall emphasized measures to boost morale among the troops. These included USO entertainment; the V-mail system (63 million pieces of V-mail were sent per month); regular food and drink; and good pay. ∎

Suggested Reading

Paul Fussell, *Wartime: Understanding and Behavior in World War II.*

Gerald Linderman, *The World Within War: America's Combat Experience in World War II.*

David Reynolds, *Rich Relations: The American Occupation of Britain, 1941–1945.*

Questions to Consider

1. What challenges confronted Major Wedemeyer as he attempted to rebuild U.S. military strength in the late 1930s? How successful were his efforts?

2. In what ways did the U.S. armed forces constitute a "melting pot"? What were some of the social consequences of the experience of military service?

"This Man's Army"
Lecture 26—Transcript

Hello. Welcome to our twenty-sixth lecture in this series on the Second World War. We're going to shift our focus in this lecture and the next, to examine two of the most extraordinary achievements of the Second World War, feats of the Second World War. One is the creation of the American military machine during the course of the war, something that had not existed when the war broke out in Europe in September of 1939—the construction of this enormous military machine, both in terms of the personnel as well as the equipment. And in our next lecture, we're going to look at the United States on the home front during the war—the arsenal of democracy, the mobilization of the home front, victory gardens, rationing, and so on.

American production would be one of the real miracles of the Second World War, creating a military machine and industrial machine of unparalleled proportions; and the American army, too, considering that on September 1, 1939, that it was the 19th largest army in the world, that the Poles had a larger military establishment than the United States at that point. The juggernaut that we've talked about pushing its way across the Pacific, driving across North Africa, up the Italian peninsula and onto the continent of Europe in 1944, was a product of a—it was a civilian army; the citizens in uniform and a creation that had really appeared from virtually nothing. It was one of the most astonishing accomplishments of the war. The army that would storm ashore at Normandy or even Guadalcanal simply did not exist in 1939. Its creation was the act of extraordinary imagination, organization, and will.

Within five years of the end of the First World War, the American army had fallen to a strength of 132,000 troops. The Germans, who had complained so bitterly about the Treaty of Versailles with its limitations of manpower to 100,000 troops, had an army virtually as large as that of the United States. The army of the depression years was the army at its nadir—pay was dismal, promotion was rare; the hard-drinking club of officers and NCOs of the interwar army as captured, I think best, in James Jones's classic, *From Here To Eternity*. Hoover, President Hoover, would cut officers' pay by 15 percent, enlisted men's pay by 30 percent, and Franklin Roosevelt, upon his coming into office, threatened to slash the military budget by 51 percent in the early days of the Roosevelt administration. His Chief of Staff, Douglas MacArthur, was so infuriated by this, that he threatened to resign—he rebelled, and FDR would back off.

Beginning in 1935, appropriations for the military began to rise after years, four straight years particularly, of decline. Still, as we've said, when the war broke out in Europe in September of 1939, the United States Army could muster only 190,000 troops; three infantry divisions in the United States, one in Hawaii, one in the Philippines, all drastically under strength. Even the outbreak of the war failed to bring significant increases in manpower. A ceiling was set in 1939 with 227,000 troops for an army that might be able to protect the frontiers of the United States, but not much else. When General Marshall begged for emergency funds in May of 1940, Franklin Roosevelt refused. There was still no pressing need.

The turning point, the turning point, as it was for so much else, was the fall of France. For the British and for the Americans, this sense that France would hold out, that there was time, that one could play for time, now was gone. Now there was a real crisis and the crisis was that the Germans dominated all of Europe and there was no room for maneuver. Roosevelt in this situation relented and the army was actually flooded with funds, $9 billion worth from 1940 to 1941. It was more than all of the money spent by the War Department since 1920. Marshall at this point envisioned an army of 1 million men by October of 1941. One thinks about this, going from 190,000 to 1 million by October of 1941, 2 million men by January of 1942. So, quantum leaps forward.

Where was all of this manpower to come from? Who would be the troops? Well, the country's first peacetime draft would be introduced, legislation to that effect coming in June of 1940. It was enormously controversial, tremendously unpopular, at this juncture as well. But on September 16, 1940, FDR would sign the Selective Service Act, instituting the draft. The law authorized the induction of 900,000 men for a year; called up the National Guard—that was 270,000 troops. It raised regular army strength to about 500,000 troops. A civilian-run system of draft boards began operating within 30 days and every male from the age of 21 to 36 was given a number from 1 to 7,386, which was the largest number that any one draft board had on its books. The President himself did the first drawing and the first number pulled was number 158. So important I think and so etched in memory are these experiences from this period that all the way through my childhood, the man in my small town just outside of Chattanooga who had that number and was the first one drafted was Frank Calloway, who ran Calloway's Service Station. And there on the back, all the way through as long as he lived, there was the photograph of him taking the number, saying, "Frank says he's ready to go." I think this was not an untypical attitude. It would become far more typical after the Japanese attack on Pearl Harbor.

But would this be enough? How did Marshall calculate the men and the machines necessary to fight a war? He relied, improbably enough—and this is one of the whole series of improbable things in this—he relied very heavily on Major Albert Wedemeyer. Wedemeyer had just recently studied at the Kriegs Academy in Berlin. He impressed Marshall—and I think this is also one of the typical things of Marshall, and this is one of the reasons that Roosevelt didn't want to let him out of Washington to go run Operation Overlord—is that Marshall was a very, very good judge of personnel. He impressed Marshall, and in July of 1940, Marshall charged him with coming up with a plan to figure out, to calculate, manpower needs and the equipment needed to create the army that Marshall had in mind. Army intelligence at this point estimated that Hitler and his allies could field 400 divisions by the end of 1943. Since the standard military wisdom of the time insisted that one needed a two to one ratio for offensive operations, Wedemeyer then was charged with coming up with manpower for 800 divisions. The British had maybe the potential for a hundred. The Russians had the potential certainly for hundreds and hundreds, but at this point, when Wedemeyer begins his calculations, it is not at all clear that the Soviet Union was going to be able to withstand a German attack; indeed, and as the plans continued, it seemed that the Russians were about to fold in the summer and the fall of 1941. To put a division of 15,000 troops into combat, another 25,000 would be required to handle supplies, training, communications, and so on. So, doing the math, 700 divisions at 40,000 men, worked itself out to about 28 million troops. The American population in 1941 was approximately 135 million. Since a modern economy, in a modern economy, only about 10 percent of the population could be spared for military duty without wrecking industrial productivity, the armed forces could safely take only 13.5 million, he calculated. After making the calculations for the navy and the air corps, Wedemeyer established that at its peak strength, the United States could field an army of perhaps 8.8 million men. This of course would then set off a chain reaction of needs. To move 5 million men to Europe and to supply them would require at least 1,000 ships of at least 7,000 tons each. To build such a fleet, again starting virtually from scratch, he figured would take two years. To raise and equip such an army would take also at least two years. And planning was necessary to establish production schedules for everything from G.I. soap to trucks to tanks. Bases had to be built. The army alone was going to require huge camps to house and train troops. The existing ones had to be expanded and new ones had to be built.

In 1940 and 1941, there was a land rush by the Federal Government, buying up land, seizing land, all over particularly what we now call the Sunbelt, to establish a series of military camps for training of army personnel. By May of 1941, so in very rapid-fire order, the army had 46 big new camps waiting for a flood of inductees. I think what's remarkable to me about this is that so many of these temporary barracks and buildings, annexes, and so on that were built in this land rush era at the very beginning of the Second World War and were built largely to last a matter of several years, were still in operation, wooden structures still in operation, still being used during the Vietnam era. So the army was now preparing for a flood of new inductees. The army air corps always wanted to do things slightly better—at least a hundred Miami Beach luxury hotels for basic training for its men.

What about equipment? What about munitions? FDR and others had worked on the assumption—as Roosevelt thought about this in the approach of war—had worked on the assumption that the United States would simply out-produce its enemies. The American economy still had an enormous amount of slack in it as a result of the depression. We hadn't tapped nearly anything close to the potential of the American economy. But, how was it going to do this? How was one going to mobilize the economy? It was quickly pointed out to the President that nothing was inevitable about success in this. The United States in 1941 did not have a big munitions or arms industry. One had to be created.

During the First World War, American soldiers had largely used equipment provided by Great Britain and France. As one general wrote in a memo to the War Department, and I quote, "It would be unwise to assume we can defeat Germany simply by out-producing her. Wars are won by sound strategy implemented by well-trained forces which are adequately and effectively equipped." Marshall and Stimson reorganized the military and the War Departments, respectively; Stimson believing that the War Department needed a great deal of change and a great deal of reform. "It's just like the alimentary canal," he said. "You feed it at one end and nothing comes out at the other but crap." Something had to be done to make this an efficient organization capable of handling the monumental tasks foreseen for it.

One didn't have to start absolutely at scratch, and one of the most foresighted aspects of American military thinking in the interwar years, the army had established the so-called Army Industrial College in 1924, conducted annual surveys of industry, yearly updates, and detail annexes. Thinking about potential needs, what one was seeing already here is the beginning of what would later be called the military industrial complex, thinking about needs and the relationship of industry to the military. Still, the American army was never to reach Wedemeyer's projections. The total number of divisions was 92. At its peak, 5.9 million soldiers, 2.3 in the army air corps, it was slightly smaller than the German army and only slightly larger than Japan's. It was only half as big as the Red Army. And even in 1941, when the Selective Service Act had to be renewed in October, it passed by one vote. There was hardly a great commitment to this enterprise at this juncture.

For those who found themselves now caught in the Selective Service System, or for those who after—on the Monday following December 7, 1941—would rush off to join the army, they would be introduced into a world of khaki and OD It was a time when OD referred to olive drab and not overdose. And a new phenomenon was born in American life, the GI, the Government Issue. The introduction came via a series of steps: the reception center— the citizen soldier entered another world. After being inducted locally and given two weeks to settle his affairs, the soldier travels by train to one of the vast reception centers that were set up around the country. Here began the introduction to the army. Civilian clothes were shipped home, hair cut, GI clothing issued; the usual complaint, "Does anything here ever fit?" An utter lack, getting used to the utter lack of privacy, the utter lack of individuality, life in the barracks, the latrine, and so on, learning all of the things that would become the standard sort of approaches to this, that there was the right way, the wrong way, and the army way to do everything. They would be subjected to a series of tests, the general classification test, the mechanical aptitude test, given an Army Serial Number, and then on to another camp for basic training. Seventeen weeks of inculcating army discipline, then on to unit training—the total process expected to take 52 weeks. What was created was a remarkable organization.

One saw, in the army of the Second World War, the United States really as melting pot. In an era when people didn't travel very much and there wasn't a lot of what social scientists call spatial mobility, it's something that had also been inhibited by, of course, the privations of the Great Depression. Suddenly the human variety of America came as a revelation to most young men, especially from rural or small town backgrounds. One of the things that's very interesting, David Reynolds—a wonderful English historian—several years ago wrote a book called *Rich Relations: The American Occupation of England, 1942-45*, and one of the things he points out is that something like 40 percent of the American soldiers who found themselves in Great Britain prior to the D-Day landings, 40 percent of them had come from homes that did not have indoor plumbing. For many people who entered the army in 1941, '42, this was a step up in some ways—regular food, regular work after the depression, and certainly this ethnic and regional kaleidoscope in a period, as I said, when people didn't travel very much. If one reads through the letters or gathers experiences of veterans from this period, many of them have to do with encountering the inevitable person from Brooklyn or the Texan or hearing the first southern accent and so on. One has the sort of—the World War II image of the standard bomber crew where there had to be—there had to be usually the—somebody from Brooklyn had to be on the crew. I think central casting dictated that every bomber crew in the United States Army air corps, and probably naval aviation, had to have at least one person from Brooklyn, some slow-talking southerner, or the big Texan—this sort of Van Johnson, peaches and cream complexion, blonde-headed, Midwestern guy. All were there. And in fact, much of the, I think, the wartime experience, actually does reflect that Hollywood stereotype—that people were thrown together for the first time. And if one reads letters from servicemen from this time, it's commented on, the sort of north/south battles that were fought and so on.

The exception of course to this, within all of the ethnic diversity and intermingling of crews and companies, was with black soldiers, with African-Americans, who would remain during the Second World War as one said, "second class citizens, whether in the army or not." A 1940 directive set racial policy for the war. It promised that the percentage of blacks in the military would correspond to the percentage of blacks in the overall population, about 10 percent. African-Americans would serve in every branch of service, combatant and non-combatant, but were still terribly over-represented in the so-called service units. Twenty-five percent of the quartermaster corps, 15 percent in engineering, five percent in the infantry, only two percent in the army air corps. No blacks were to be members of bomber crews. There was, of course, the first black fighter squadron in the 99th, established in 1941, that would become quite famous during the war. Separate but equal was the policy. No blacks were to command white units. Most black units were commanded not only by whites, but in a perverse twist that I think defies understanding, by white southerners; no intermingling of black and white enlisted personnel in the same regimental organizations was permitted. As General Marshall put it, pragmatist to the end, a policy of integration, and I quote, "would be tantamount to solving a social problem which has perplexed the American people throughout the history of this nation. The army cannot accomplish such a solution and should not be charged with the undertaking." When this would, the situation was driven home in the war in a number of different ways.

There was a very famous incident written up in *Yank* magazine, where a corporal Rupert Trimmingham, who was stationed in Arizona, was traveling with a number of other black soldiers and had had to stop over in Louisiana and had gone into—the only place they could get something to eat was at the railroad station—had gone into the railroad station, were not permitted to enter. The white personnel there refused to allow them to enter. They had to go around to the back, which was standard operating procedure in the south at this time, where they would be fed by the kitchen people out back. While he and his soldier friends were out back eating, a number of German prisoners of war were brought into the main dining room of the train station. They sat down, were served, laughed, joked, treated very well. And Trimmingham wrote a biting letter to *Yank* and I'd like to read it. "Here is a question that each Negro soldier is asking. What is the Negro soldier fighting for? On whose team are we playing? Myself and eight other soldiers were on our way from Camp Claiborne, Louisiana, to the hospital in Arizona. We had to lay over until the next day for our train. On the next day we could not purchase a cup of coffee at any of the lunch rooms around here. As you know, old man Jim Crow rules. The only place where we could be served was at the lunch room at the railroad station." And then he proceeds to tell the story I've just related. "I could not help but ask myself these questions. Are these men," talking about the Germans, "sworn enemies of this country? Are they not taught to hate and destroy all democratic governments? Are we not American soldiers sworn to fight for and die if need be for our country? Then why are they treated better than we are? Why are we pushed around like cattle? If we're fighting for the same thing, if we're going to die for our country, then why does the Government allow such things to go on? Some of the boys are saying that you will not print this letter. I'm saying that you will." He certainly did print it and it provoked a huge outpouring of letters to *Yank*, the weekly army magazine, all registering the same sort of outrage that something like this would take place.

The army also was determined during the war—well, one of the complaints about the army during the Second World War subsequently was, well, there just wasn't enough political indoctrination. The troops just didn't know what they were fighting for. This was borne over and over and over again in various surveys that were done about troop morale. What were we fighting for? The four freedoms—nobody seemed to know quite what those were. Less than 13 percent of the men in one survey could identify even two of the four. The average GI clearly did not have a clear set of ideals for which he was fighting, except to get the thing over with and go home as quickly as possible.

There was a very famous story written by John Hersey during the war. He had been a—he would subsequently write a number of things, as you know, *Hiroshima, A Bell for Adano* in 1945, but he was a war correspondent early and the war was Guadalcanal. He'd been with a group of marines tramping through the jungle and had been in fire fights and so on and they'd stopped at a clearing to rest. As they were all sitting around, he said, "You know, what do you think this war's all about? What are you fighting for?" All of the marines, I'm sure 18 to 19, maybe 20 years old, all looked down at their boots, embarrassed by this question. And nobody said anything. He kept looking around; nobody said anything. And then finally somebody said, "Jesus, I'd love to have a piece of blueberry pie." Then somebody else said, "Well, I prefer mince." Then somebody else went on, "Well, I like apple crumb southern-style," or whatever it was. And they went on talking about this for a few minutes. And Hersey said, "You know, what this was really about, this was what they were fighting for. And it wasn't mom and apple pie, it wasn't that. But this was the way they articulated their war; that this is what it meant to them." He wrote this up and sent it back as an article and it became an enormously popular piece during the Second World War.

Marshall understood this and he believed that rather than attempting to indoctrinate troops, although the troops were supposed to see all of the Frank Capra *Why We Fight* films, which were—even for Frank Capra, who made such wonderful films as *It Happened One Night* and oh, the Jimmy Stewart film for Christmas time, *It's A Wonderful Life*. The *Why We Fight* series—was pretty heavy-handed, heavy-handed; it's tough going. Marshall understood that what troops wanted was morale; it wasn't ideals and this sort of propagandistic sense. And so much of what Marshall insisted upon was a series of things to make life better for soldiers, sailors, everyone in the military. One of those things was mail. One of the most innovative aspects of the Second World War was something called the V-mail system. Not e-mail, but V-mail, which was to take a form, an actual letter-sized form, write on it, and then this would be taken and microfilmed to a much smaller version which could then be sent. Sixty-three million V-mail letters a month would originally have weighed 400 tons. As V-mail, they weighed 400 pounds, so that it was possible to send massive amounts of mail back and forth from the most obscure places in the Pacific, not always in great delivery, or from Europe. So mail, the USO system with entertainment, movies—though certainly people would complain that they saw the same *Hopalong Cassidy* movie for a year and a half on ships in the South Pacific. Beer was supposed to be three bottles a week per man. I'm sure that some had more than their quota, some less. Food was, for many people—although soldiers love to complain about everything and food is one of them—the food was, regular pay, compared to any other armed forces in the world, was extremely good. Still, the citizen soldier could always complain. He was, as one author has written, suspended between two ways of life. Physically, he had left civilian life, yet mentally he never joined the army. He was in the service, but not of it.

I think one gets a wonderful sense of this in the letters that were written into both *Stars and Stripes* and to *Yank* magazine. I'd like to read you a couple. This is from 1945. "Dear *Yank*, on the troop carrier I was on, the PX rationed chocolate. One day I purchased a Hershey bar with almonds as did the soldier in front of me. It developed upon eating our chocolate bars, that his Hershey contained nine almonds, while mine only seven. Is this fair?" This provoked a response a couple of weeks later in another letter. "Dear *Yank*, in a recent issue of *Yank*, T-5 Nebbling stated that the man preceding him in the chocolate bar ration line received nine almonds in his Hershey bar, whereas he himself only received seven. We feel that we can clearly clarify the situation by pointing out that through some gross and unpardonable error, the other soldier undoubtedly received an officer's Hershey bar."

Lest one think that only letters were the form with which GIs could express themselves, there was also poetry. It was a standard feature of *Yank*. Some of it I'm afraid I can't actually provide you with here, but this is one that I particularly like dealing with, a real source of trouble for all GIs and that was supply. "Back in Texas where I took my training, I had no galoshes when it was raining. Straight to supply and down on my knees, 'No soap,' said the sergeant. It's all overseas. Then to England we sailed. 'No supply troubles now,' I wailed. Went to the sergeant with my song and dance. 'T.S. my boy, it's all in France.' Some day soon I'll cross the Rhine. Everything then should really be fine. The supply angle would be terrific. When I get there, it'll all be in the Pacific."

These aspects of day-to-day life for this new creature, the GI; it would be this institution, the GI, the serviceman, would become the central figure of the United States during the Second World War, a new citizen in uniform. But lest one think that all of the letters and all of the poetry was funny, there's also a very moving poem that I would like to close with, written by Sergeant Harold Applebaum at an army camp in North Carolina, also in 1945. It's called *The Death of Private Jones*. "Let's say that Private Jones died quietly.

Let's say that when the first wave stormed the shore, a single shot went through his heart and he slipped lifeless to the sand. Not one man saw him die, so busy they with lying head and crawling on, yet all men felt the breath of leaden wings come close. And when they did, it made his passing seem a public death. So much for Jones. He died as one of scores and on a distant beach. But when they bring the news to those who count the costs of wars, a private's death becomes a private thing. How strange that war's arithmetic discounts the spread of sorrow as the sorrow mounts."

Daily Life, Culture, and Society in Wartime
Lecture 27

[In addition to creating a military machine,] an extraordinary achievement of the war years ... is the transformation of the American economy from largely a depressed economy on the eve of the war to the most productive, astonishingly productive, industrial economy in the world.

By 1944, the United States had become the "Arsenal of Democracy." The U.S. economy accomplished prodigious feats of wartime production. At the outbreak of war, U.S. industrial facilities operated nowhere close to their potential, due to lingering effects of the Depression. War contracts began to flow in 1939 and especially in 1940. Henry Ford's bomber site at Willow Run produced huge numbers of aircraft.

Henry J. Kaiser became the world's largest ship builder. Kaiser built one-third of the U.S. Navy's "Liberty ships." Naval tonnage grew by 42 percent. During 1942, U.S. production equaled that of all the Axis powers. By 1944, U.S. production was twice that of Germany and Japan combined. By 1945, the United States produced 40 percent of the world's armaments.

To facilitate economic planning, Roosevelt established the War Resources Board, the War Production Board, the Office of Economic Stabilization, and the Office of War Mobilization.

Rosie the Riveter.

The war generated social strains and social change. Despite a 1943 strike by the United Mine Workers, there was remarkably little labor strife during the war. Women's roles changed importantly during the war. The share of women in the work force rose from 25 percent during the 1930s to 36 percent during the war. For the first time, married women outnumbered single women in the work force. Germany, by contrast, avoided introducing German women into the work force and relied instead on slave labor. "Rosie the Riveter" symbolized the entry of women into jobs traditionally reserved for men. Although women did not have wage parity with men, their wages rose faster than men's wages did.

Civilians, simply assuming that [victory gardens] had been done during the First War [and that] it was going to be done again, began a project to create these victory gardens.

The position of African-Americans also changed. Blacks left the South in large numbers to take industrial jobs in the Midwest and California. The army had no plans to induct black troops into the Army. In the summer of 1941, A. Philip Randolph threatened a march by blacks on Washington to protest discrimination. FDR established a Fair Employment Practices Committee, but tensions remained rampant. Detroit, Philadelphia, and other cities experienced race riots and strikes during 1943 and 1944. The U.S. Armed Forces remained segregated.

Japanese-Americans suffered discrimination. There was considerable fear of a possible Japanese invasion of the U.S. West Coast. FDR bowed to pressure in February 1942 and approved the "relocation" of Japanese-Americans. Ten major relocation camps were established in barren regions in seven Western states. Most of the forced evacuations were completed by August 1942. The Nisei 442nd Regimental Combat Team was established in 1943.

The war also altered daily life. Rationing and blackouts were common. Automobile production was halted; gas was rationed; and tires were invaluable. Various consumer goods were rationed.

Cities on both coasts were blacked out in 1942. A spirit of volunteerism prevailed. Civilians planted 18 million "victory gardens" on their own initiative. "Eat what you can and can what you can't," was their mantra. And Hollywood stars were mobilized to assist in eight major bond drives.

Cultural life was also affected. Night life flourished. And the government tried to mobilize the music industry to produce patriotic songs. War-weariness, however, gradually set in, contributing to Republican gains in the 1942 election and restricting FDR's victory margin in 1944. ∎

Suggested Reading

John M. Blum, *V Was For Victory*, Chapters 4–6.

John Keegan, *The Second World War*, Chapter 10.

William O'Neil, *A Democracy At War*.

Richard Overy, *Why The Allies Won*, Chapter 6.

Questions to Consider

1. How did the war affect the social and economic roles of women in the United States? How lasting were these changes?

2. What admirable traits or qualities did the wartime experience elicit in the U.S. civilian population? Did wartime conditions also reveal certain negative traits?

Daily Life, Culture, and Society in Wartime
Lecture 27—Transcript

Hello. Welcome to this lecture on the American home front during the Second World War. In our last lecture we had focused on what was really one of the remarkable achievements of the war years, and that was the creation of an American army, a gigantic American military establishment from virtually nothing. In this lecture we're going to focus on what is an equally remarkable feat—an extraordinary achievement of the war years—and it is the transformation of the American economy from largely a depressed economy on the eve of the war to the most productive, astonishingly productive, industrial economy in the world. We're going to look at the social changes that the war would bring in its wake, and examine some of both the social tension and social achievements of the war, and also what I would call the transformation of everyday life, to look a little bit at popular entertainment and so on during the war years.

At the outset of the war the United States was still lingering under the effects of the Great Depression, and yet within a very short period of time, really from 1939 to America's entry into the war in 1941, in late 1941, one sees already an enormous spurt forward in production, prodigious feats of wartime mobilization—the numbers are absolutely staggering. Aircraft production rose from less than 6,000 in 1939 to over 96,000 in 1944; naval tonnage grew by 42 percent in the same period. Already during 1942 the United States' production equaled that of all the Axis powers; in 1943 it was one-and-a-half times as great; by 1944 the United States was producing twice as much as Germany and Japan combined. In that same year, the United States would produce 40 percent of the world's armaments.

The United States had become by 1944 quite genuinely the "Arsenal of Democracy," as it was frequently called at this time. This drastic acceleration or expansion of the economy was possible in part because, at the outbreak of the war, American industrial facilities were nowhere close to their potential because of the depression. Although the United States produced more steel than any other country already in September of 1939, we were using only one-third of our capacity at that point, so there was a great deal of slack in the economy. There were still 10 million men unemployed in 1939. The New

Deal had not solved the problem of unemployment; wartime production certainly would. The economy began to accelerate with the war. Contracts in 1939 and early 1940 acted to jumpstart the economy. These contracts were not simply American but also French and British, placing orders with American factories to produce all sorts of armaments for the war in Europe. It began the crossover for American industry even before the United States has entered the conflict in order to meet these orders from Europe. With the Japanese attack on Pearl Harbor, American industry was primed for expansion.

The real turning point when, just as it was when we talked in our last lecture about the mobilization of American manpower, it was really the fall of France that acted as the shock, the shock that sent virtually a shockwave of warning to the United States that there was no time, there was not going to be a long run-up to war; that France, which had been expected to hold out for some time, had fallen rapidly, and now we were moving very quickly toward the front lines. Automobile plants, particularly after the Japanese attack on Pearl Harbor, began producing tanks, trucks, aircraft.

One of the most, I think probably the most, famous of all of the various industrial sites of the Second World War in the United States was Henry Ford's extraordinary bomber site 27 miles west of Detroit, Willow Run it was called. It was by its very proportions staggering. The main building consumed 67 acres; the final assembly line to build B-24 Liberators was one mile long. Willow Run would produce 8,564 B-24's over the course of the war. At top speed, this was absolutely astonishing; at top speed one B-24 came off the assembly line every 63 seconds. When one thinks about Hermann Goering's, head of the German Luftwaffe, observation in 1940-41 about American production, he says, "Well, they make good razor blades;" didn't think that there would be a way for the United States to mobilize its economy for any sort of major effort in Europe. These sorts of numbers would've been absolutely mind-boggling. One sees similar sorts of achievements in other fields of industrial production. In shipbuilding, for example, where Henry J. Kaiser, who had become easily the most famous industrialist of the war, before the United States entry into the war, Kaiser had not produced a ship, not laid a hull, not been involved in this sort of thing at all, but he came to represent this sort of "can-do" attitude of the war, a captain of industry who was capable of taking any sort of mission and performing remarkable feats. He would become the world's largest shipbuilder during the course of the war, employing 250,000 workers, 12 shipyards. When he came on board in 1941, it took a year to produce the basic sort of ship involved in transport, the so-called "Liberty ships." Very quickly, Kaiser would accomplish this in a matter of days; in fact, at one point produced a Liberty ship in fewer than five days. He would build a third of the Liberty ships produced during the Second World War, giving him the nickname "Sir Launch-a-lot."

These sorts of entrepreneurial initiatives, achievements, also took place within a context of economic planning provided by the government. Franklin Roosevelt would begin with a series of production boards, agencies, created to evaluate martial resources. In 1939 he had created the War Resources Board; there would be a War Production Board established in 1941; an Office of Economic Stabilization; and then finally the Office of War Mobilization, headed by James Burns, the senior senator from South Carolina and a Supreme Court justice, to head it. It would be this Office of War Mobilization that would really coordinate these various endeavors. Needless to say, this arsenal of democracy, this transformation of the American industrial scene, produced considerable social change and considerable social tension. It's remarkable in some ways that the war years would pass with as little labor trouble as there was—in part at the beginning of the war there was hardly a problem with labor; there was a labor shortage—but, there would be strikes, John L. Lewis's mine workers, United Mine Workers, strike of 1943 being the most obvious one. But, for the most part, the war years would pass with remarkably little labor strife, with labor and management pulling together for the war effort. The labor shortage at the beginning of the war was so acute that there were signs placed around in various places, even in restaurants, one which I particularly like, this is "Please Be Nice To Our Waitresses, They're Harder To Get Than Customers."

That comment, talking about waitresses, actually also points to one of the most obvious changes in the labor force during the Second World War in the United States, and one of the most obvious changes, social changes, that the war would bring on the home front, and that would be a massive influx of women into the American labor market. Women would move into the labor market in enormous numbers; the number jumped from 25 percent of the workforce before the war to 36 percent of the workforce during the course of the war. Between 1940 and 1944, the number of employed women rose by half, reaching a high of 19 million, and for the first time, married women in the workforce would outnumber single women. Women over 35, in fact, accounted for 60 percent of the increase in women coming into the labor force. By 1944, at the peak of women's wartime employment, the percentage of the female workforce in clerical, sales, or service jobs had declined to 34 percent, while the percentage increase in the number of women employed in what were called war industries, in metals, chemicals, rubber, and so on, had grown by 460 percent. So women were moving out of the traditional sort of women's clerical sorts of jobs into jobs that had traditionally been held by men. Although most saw this influx as temporary, to be reversed when the boys came home, the changes wrought in the gender composition of the workforce by the war were indeed historic—from a relatively small labor force composed largely of young, unmarried women, to an enormous force comprised for the most part of older, married women over the course of the war.

This is in stark contrast—I think this is a point that one ought to make—it's in stark contrast to, for example, Germany, which during the war did not want to employ women. Despite the tremendous strains on German manpower during the course of the Second World War, the National Socialist Regime was very, very reluctant to introduce women in significant numbers into the workplace. I think we alluded to this in a previous lecture, that while American factories, British factories, certainly Soviet factories were really operating 24 hours a day running shifts, German factories never would do this during the course of the war. They didn't employ women to the same degree as certainly we did in the United States or in the other Allied countries, and instead tended to rely on slave labor, which was notoriously and obviously unproductive, worked in abysmal conditions, and so on.

So this introduction of women, the successful introduction of women into the labor force, was a considerable and important change during the course of the war. Certainly the most potent symbol of this entry of women into the labor force would be "Rosie the Riveter," sort of becomes a folk hero, folk emblem for women who have taken on now men's jobs, and it bore some relationship to reality. Women held 20 percent of the jobs in the aircraft plants in Detroit; in Seattle, the home of Boeing, it was 47 percent of the workforce was female. There was no wage parity, of course, in the period, but raises for women during the course of the war far outstripped those of men in the labor market; for example, in the aircraft industry over the course of the war women saw their wages go up by 100 percent, whereas men's rose by only about a ninth. So there were very real gains and the picture of women we have here in the studio—for those of you who are listening simply on audio, we have here in the studio a picture of one of the most famous posters from the Second World War, the War Production Coordinating Committee, "We Can Do It," with this woman with her hair up in a kerchief showing her bicep—this, I think, was certainly one of the most powerful images of the war, going along with the "Rosie the Riveter" idea.

Another change in the labor force also needs to be mentioned as one looks at the war years, and this is the introduction of black Americans, African-Americans, into the labor force, and the spatial change, the geographic shifts that would take place. Black Americans would leave the South in record numbers during the course of the Second World War; or one of the things about the war, of course, was that the entire society seemed to be in transit, producing enormous strains on the transportation system, the trains for the most part. And one of the greatest migrations was the migration of African-Americans out of the South, leaving for industrial jobs primarily in the Midwest but also in California, along the West Coast.

The army had no plans to utilize black labor—even the black men who were taken into the army would be underutilized in the military. There were about 5 million employed blacks, over one-half male, in 1940, virtually none in well-paying war industries. So before the war began, even before the war began, there was already the beginnings of some sense of protest about this state of affairs, when A. Phillip Randolph, the President of the Brotherhood of Sleeping Car Porters, which was really the only really influential black labor union, the only one with any real clout, called for a march on Washington in December of 1941. He did this in part, having seen the figures on the low employment of blacks in war industries, and also having seen a report that indicated that something like 40 percent of all management personnel in war industries said that they didn't have any interest in employing blacks. So A. Phillip Randolph called for a march on Washington in the summer of 1941.

It was estimated that about 50,000 black citizens would come to join in this march to protest racial discrimination in both industry and in the Federal Government. This was a source of great embarrassment to FDR and to the government. Randolph's plans were supported by the NAACP, and only four days before the march, President Roosevelt invited Randolph and Walter White, who at this point was the head of the NAACP, to Washington. The upshot of this visit was an executive order. The President issued an executive order to establish the Fair Employment Practices Commission. It would prompt employers to break with past practice and to see that certainly the major war industries would be integrated.

This was considerably, this initiative on the part of FDR, was certainly aided by the labor shortage that would be felt in 1940-41 and into early 1942. By 1944, blacks held 7.5 percent of all jobs in war industries. This still meant the blacks were under-represented, but it represented a vast improvement over their status at the beginning of the war.

Still, racial tensions in the United States were never very far from the surface and they regularly erupted. There was a great deal of tension on military bases or in areas where there were military bases with black population around—fights between black and whites; riots between soldiers in El Paso, Texas, in 1943; a gunfight between black soldiers and MP's at Camp Stuart, Georgia left one dead and five wounded in 1943. Also labor trouble, having to do with the integration of the labor force, when 12 blacks were promoted at a shipyard in Mobile, Alabama, white workers went on a rampage, injuring 20 blacks. And easily the low point of race relations during the war would come in the summer of 1943 in June, when a riot broke out in Detroit that would leave 25 African-Americans dead; nine whites were killed; the National Guard had to be called out to restore order; over 700 people were wounded and 1,300 people put under arrest, here in what was really a massive race riot in Detroit. These kinds of tensions would surface at different points. Detroit was the worst instance during the war, but, in the summer of 1944 in August, white transit workers in Philadelphia struck the Philadelphia Transit Company to protest the promotion of eight black porters to the status of drivers in the Philadelphia transit system. So bitter was this resistance to this sort of change that once again the regular army had to be called out by

President Roosevelt to run the transit system in the city of Philadelphia, this in the summer of 1944.

So while there was enormous unity in the country at one level about the war effort, the social changes brought by the transformation of the labor market would be felt in all sorts of ways. The NAACP would see its membership rise tenfold during the course of the war, reaching a half a million by 1945, and although gains by blacks both within the labor market and within the military were certainly held within bounds—we talked about the policy of racial segregation really within the military in our last lecture—the Second World War would act as an accelerating factor in the momentum that would build after the Second World War for racial integration in the United States.

The low point of wartime domestic affairs, however, did not come even with the race riots in Detroit or the labor trouble in Mobile, or in Philadelphia, but rather had come earlier, in February of 1942, when the President bowed to pressure and approved an initiative to remove 112,000 Americans of Japanese ancestry and resident Japanese aliens from their homes along the West Coast, and place them in what were euphemistically referred to as "relocation centers." This was Executive Order number 9066, issued on February 19, 1942. It was, for this great bastion of democracy, a country at war with oppressive regimes in Asia and in Europe, a shameful violation of civil rights. It was the result of a widespread hysteria, along particularly the West Coast, at the very low ebb of American military fortunes, at the end of 1941, beginning of 1942; there was considerable fear of fivers, fifth columners, Japanese gardeners, barbers, and so on. If one's ever seen the Frank Capra *Why We Fight* series, there's a film called *Know Your Enemy—Japan* and there is a passage there where the camera focuses in on the Japanese barber who doesn't talk as he's cutting Americans' hair, or the Japanese gardener who while tending the roses along the sea coast is actually flashing signals to Japanese submarines off the coast. This is a film made much later in the war. On February 23, a Japanese submarine had actually shelled an oil refinery near Santa Barbara, and the next night a weather balloon had gotten loose and strayed over the skies of Los Angeles. It was mistaken for a Japanese air raid and in the hyper-tense feelings of the period, panic and virtual hysteria swept the West Coast. Still, it was not until March 29, 1942, that the forced evacuation of Japanese-Americans began.

Most evacuations were completed by August of 1942. Anyone with one Japanese great-grandparent was to be interned. The FBI, the Office of Naval Intelligence, and the Army's G2 had actually done investigations of Japanese civilians before the outbreak of the war, identifying those Japanese residents, Japanese-Americans, who they thought were genuinely subversive, or who might be guilty of some sort of anti-American acts. So there already had been research done, investigations done to actually arrest or at least take into custody, protective custody, those individuals, so that this kind of massive sweep of the Japanese population of the West Coast was by and large unnecessary. Earl Warren, Attorney General of California, was very much in favor of this action, indeed argued, to I suppose his everlasting regret, that while it might be possible to determine whether Italian-Americans or German-Americans were loyal, that these inscrutable Orientals were simply impossible to understand and, therefore, these measures were going to be necessary.

There were 10 major camps, most of them in barren settings, severe climates, two in California, two in Arizona, one in Arkansas, one in Wyoming, one in Utah, and for reasons that have always defied my understanding, two in Arkansas, where Japanese-Americans from the west coast were put to work in the Mississippi Delta over the course of the war.

Beginning in 1943, with the fortunes of the war having changed considerably, Japanese-Americans were allowed to begin to leave the camps, but the relocation centers remained in operation until January of 1945. In early 1943 the army began accepting recruits for an all-Japanese military unit; it came to be known as the 442nd Regimental Combat team, the Nisei. In all, 33,000 Japanese-Americans would serve in the Second World War in the European Theater. The 442nd became an elite unit with the strength of 3,000 men. By war's end, it counted 9,486 dead and wounded. It was the most decorated combat unit in the American army—one Congressional Medal of Honor, and a series of Silver Stars, Distinguished Service Crosses, and so on. The treatment of Japanese-Americans, the racial tensions within the United States, represent many of the problems that one encountered during the course of the Second World War.

There were other aspects of American day-to-day life that were more obvious to the vast majority of Americans. The spirit of volunteerism—one always obviously can talk about rationing and the blackouts; car production stopped; gas began to be rationed on December 1, 1942; tires became invaluable; a thirty-five-mile-per-hour speed limit was passed for the country; pleasure driving altogether was outlawed on the East Coast of the United States in January of 1943; it was impossible to go anywhere without the slogan, "Is This Trip Necessary?" being seared into one's consciousness. "Don't you know there is a war on?" is a comment for anyone complaining about the lack of any particular item. Blackouts were slow to come but did on both coasts.

The government—it's interesting that during the First World War the government had sponsored and been very much behind the idea of "victory gardens;" that is, private people growing small plots of vegetables around. The government during the Second World War didn't initiate the program; civilians, simply assuming that this had been done during the First War, it was going to be done again, began a project to create these victory gardens. There would be 18 million of them, small vegetable plots all over the country, 18 million victory gardens as they were called. In 1943, 8 million tons of produce was grown on 20 million individual plots, from tiny little backyard gardens to, in cities, miniscule little plots. What couldn't be eaten was to be saved or canned. One of the slogans from the war, "Eat what you can and can what you can't," was current about the victory gardens.

It was impossible to get through any particular period of the war on the home front without seeing children, in particular, involved in scrap collections of one sort or another, collecting string, rubber bands, aluminum of all sorts. At one point, the government claimed that there was a shortage of aluminum for aircraft production, and so women voluntarily came forth with all sorts of pots and pans and we discovered the sort of aluminum necessary for aircraft production was not that kind of aluminum—this stuff was melted back down and sold back to women later on. But it was indicative, I think, of the spirit of volunteerism, that people came without being asked, volunteered to bring in the pots and pans and so on. The scrap iron collections, tin cans, tin foil, as I said, rubber bands—these were collected in balls—bottle caps, chewing gum wrappers, flashlight batteries, collections particularly by children would become part of the everyday scene.

Bond drives—the government was determined to finance some of this enormous expenditure during the war by selling bonds. There would be eight major bond drives during the course of the war, smaller ones as well. Hollywood was mobilized for this, the stars going on big motorcades and train trips around the country for bond drives, "Buy Bonds." Carol Lombard was actually killed flying back from one of these bond drives. Dorothy Lamour, the costar of Bob Hope and Bing Crosby in the various road pictures, was credited with raising $350 million worth of bonds during the course of the war, showing up all over the country.

It was a time, when, if one thinks about the austerity of the war, it was also a time, though, of great night life in the United States—night life flourished, nightspots, bars, all over the country. One saw this particularly reflected, I think, in November of 1942, with this awful fire at the Coconut Grove in Boston, in which 500 people were killed, trapped in this nightclub that evening. The government certainly tried to mobilize Hollywood, mobilize the music industry in particular, to establish a sort of wartime anthem. There were a number of very patriotic songs that various government agencies fastened onto as being things that would fire up the home folks. "Remember Pearl Harbor" was one—this didn't do very well; "Praise The Lord And Pass The Ammunition" was somewhat better; "We Did It Before And We'll Do It Again," all of these to inspire patriotism on the home front but these songs, there were some that were a lot less elevated, "You're A Sap, Mr. Jap" was one. The most popular wartime song, by a long shot, was actually never played on the radio, either in the United States or in Britain, because it was seen as scatological, and it was Spike Jones' "De Führer's Face" in which the chorus was "Heil 'pfltz,' heil 'pfltz,' right in the Fuhrer's face."—this was just seen as too much. It was a wildly popular song in the United States and in Britain and yet never, ever was actually allowed to be on the airwaves. The most popular song of all time also came during the Second World War. It emerged in a film that came out in, of all times, August of 1942, called "Holiday Inn," and Bing Crosby sang it—it was Irving Berlin's "White Christmas." It would become the all-time leading song. Hollywood, though it turned out a number of propaganda films, war films, by far the most popular were simple entertainment films—people didn't want to be propagandized during the course of the war.

By 1944, one could see, despite the enormous mobilization and support for the war, overwhelming support for the war, by 1944 a war weariness had begun to set in on the home front. Already in 1942 the Republicans had scored big gains in Congressional elections, and, in 1944, FDR had won reelection, but by his smallest margin ever. After D-Day in the summer of 1944, too, the assumption seemed to be that the war with its privations was basically over, that the Germans were on the verge of collapse, that the end was finally in sight. The German offensive in the Ardennes, the Battle of the Bulge would change all of that, but the public, as a whole series of indicators suggested, was growing increasingly restive with the demands of total war. This would be particularly acute after the fall of Germany and V-E Day in May of 1945, just as the American policy makers began to confront the daunting task of planning for the invasion of Japan, and possibly a war that would carry on into 1946 or even beyond. It was against this background that Harry Truman, who would become president in April of 1945, would have to make his decisions about the future course of the war.

The Race for Berlin
Lecture 28

In this lecture we're going to examine the thrust of the Russians on the Eastern Front, from the aftermath of Stalingrad down to the final climactic battle in Berlin.

Following the failure of Hitler's Ardennes offensive, both the Western Allies and the Russians resumed their inexorable march toward the Reich. The Red Army advanced on Germany from the East during 1943 and 1944.

The Red Army assumed the offensive against the Germans with the battle of Kursk in July 1943—the largest armored battle in history. This battle ended Germany's ability to launch Panzer offensives. In November 1943 the Soviets recaptured Kiev, and in January 1944 they reached the prewar frontier of Poland. The Red Army's summer offensive of June 1944 was directed against German Army Group Center and resulted in a bigger defeat for Germany than Stalingrad.

Serious tensions emerged in mid-1944 between Hitler and the German high command. Hitler narrowly escaped assassination in July 1944. In a foretaste of the coming Cold War, in August 1944 the advancing Red Army halted outside of Warsaw as the Germans crushed the Polish underground insurgency. As the Red Army pushed into Finland in September 1944, Germany's satellite states began to desert the Axis. Hitler refused pleas from his military commanders to withdraw German troops from the Baltic states and form a new defensive line against the Soviets. In January 1945 the Soviets moved through Poland. German forces were heavily outmatched. By February the Red Army was just 65 miles from Berlin.

Meanwhile, British and American forces drove toward Germany from the West. The invasion of Germany began when Anglo-American forces crossed the Rhine. The Allied plan called for three-pronged advance to clear the Rhineland. The British and Canadians proceeded slowly against bitter German resistance. They did not reach the Rhine until February 21, 1945.

Montgomery understood that his troops would have priority to cross the Rhine first. Cologne fell to the U.S. First Army on March 5. Two days later, the U.S. Third Army crossed the Rhine at Remagen.

On March 23, Montgomery launched what was to have been the main offensive across the Rhine. By March 25, all organized resistance west of the Rhine had ceased. By March 27, all seven Allied armies had crossed the Rhine.

The Anglo-American forces then raced toward Berlin. The Allied forces' next objective was the Ruhr, which was encircled in April. German forces resisted fiercely, even though they had already effectively lost the war.

On April 11, Simpson's Ninth Army reached the Elbe, where Eisenhower ordered him to halt. Simpson was overextended and short of supplies. The Germans were planning a last-ditch offensive action. By April 16, the Russians were poised at the Oder River. The Big Three had agreed at Yalta that Berlin would be part of the Soviet zone of occupation. The Allies were unsure of Hitler's whereabouts. They were fooled by German plans to construct an "Alpine redoubt." Eisenhower directed the main thrust of the Allied assault at Bavaria.

The final Soviet drive for Berlin began on April 16, 1945. The Soviets unleashed a huge artillery barrage against the city. Russian units linked up west of Berlin on April 25 and then invaded the city. Hitler committed suicide in his bunker on April 30.

The great evil of National Socialism had been defeated, but at absolutely staggering costs.

The Soviets lost more casualties in the Battle for Berlin than American troops had suffered throughout the war in Europe. If U.S. forces had seized Berlin and incurred similar casualties, it would have been very difficult for them to have subsequently turned the city over to the Soviets per the Yalta agreement. In his "last testament," Hitler blamed the Jews for provoking the outbreak of war in 1939. V-E Day was declared in the West on May 8, 1945. ■

Suggested Reading

John Erickson, *The Road to Berlin.*

John Keegan, *The Second World War*, Chapters 25–28.

Questions to Consider

1. Describe the collapse of the German military position in the East during 1944 and early 1945.

2. In view of later events, was Eisenhower right to order Gen. Simpson's Ninth Army to halt at the Elbe while the Soviets captured Berlin?

The Race for Berlin
Lecture 28—Transcript

In the spring of 1945, the war in Europe was reaching its final climax. In this lecture we're going to examine the thrust of the Russians on the Eastern Front, from the aftermath of Stalingrad down to the final climactic battle in Berlin. We'll examine western strategy, the controversy over Eisenhower's decision not to press on to Berlin, the role of Yalta, the political decisions involved in this, and then take stock of the final fall of Hitler's Third Reich.

We had stopped our discussion of the war on the Eastern Front with the German defeat at Stalingrad. It had been an enormous, catastrophic loss for the Wehrmacht, and it did represent the final offensive thrust of German power in Eastern Europe. After the fall of Stalingrad in the early spring of 1943, there would be no new major German offensive on the Eastern Front. There would be a number of what might be called tactical offenses, but nothing in the way of a major offensive along the lines of Operation Barbarossa, obviously, in the summer of 1941, or the renewed German offensive toward the Caucases in the summer of 1942. Instead, for the first time in the war, it would be the Red Army that would now begin to be able to mount a sustained series of offenses aimed at breaking German power in Russia itself, driving the Germans from the soil of the Soviet Union, and then pursuing the Germans back inside the frontiers of the Third Reich.

The beginning of that Soviet rollback of the German position would begin in the summer of 1943 in what was the Battle of Kursk in July of that year. The Red Army had at last marshaled its forces, preparing not so much to counter-punch a German offensive, but was now planning a major armored assault aimed at the German positions. The Germans, too, at this point were also planning a minor tactical assault on a Russian salient. What one had with the Battle of Kursk is two forces, both planning an offensive, that rushed literally into one another. It would become the largest armored battle in history. At the high point of the battle, 3,000 tanks were employed on the field. There had been nothing like it. There has been nothing like it since. Both sides suffered grievous losses, but at this point in the war, the Soviet Union, whose factories were producing on a scale that was not quite that of the United States, but still remarkable production figures—the Soviets could afford to accept those losses. The Germans could not. The Battle of Kursk in July of 1943 marked the end, really, of the German ability to launch Panzer offensives. After this, the Panzer forces of the Wehrmacht really never recovered, and would be largely used for defensive purposes.

In November, Kiev in the Ukraine was retaken by Russian forces, and by the end of that month, the Soviets had reached the pre-war border of eastern Poland. So, the Russian offensive from the summer continues to move across this great line in the East.

It would be the summer of 1944; just as the Allies were beginning to launch the great offensive Operation Overlord in Normandy, the Soviets were also preparing a major offensive in the East. The two things were to correspond, to put enormous pressure on the Germans, to stretch them as much as possible. The summer offensive, which would be aimed at the German Army Group Center, began in June. It was an even greater defeat for the Germans than the Battle of Stalingrad had been. The Russian offensive in June destroyed 25 divisions of the Wehrmacht with a total of 350,000 German casualties and prisoners of war. It was an absolutely devastating blow. In some respects, it's hard to imagine how the Germans—that Army Group Center almost like a beacon aiming directly into the heart of Germany—with the collapse of Army Group Center, it's almost hard to see why it wasn't that the Soviets couldn't simply continue to move in this juggernaut sort of fashion into Germany itself. But the Russians began to encounter some of the problems that the Germans had a year before and two years before, and that is, as they began to move west, they began to outdistance their own supply lines. They were now fighting over terrain that the Germans had used, had devastated, and now their supply lines were going to be stretched to the maximum. It would be difficult to maintain this sort of momentum. Nonetheless, the pressure was clearly on.

It is also at this point, in the summer of 1944, that real tensions within the German high command—between the high command and Hitler in particular—make themselves felt. In July of 1944, on July 20, Claus von Stauffenberg, a colonel in the German army, badly wounded in North Africa, in Rommel's Africa Corps, would place a bomb just a few feet from Hitler, at Hitler's briefing room in Rastenburg in East Prussia—the "Wolf's Lair," it was called. Hitler spent more and more of his time, less in Berlin, rarely back at his residence down in Berchtesgaden of pre-war years, more and more time at his field post in Rastenburg. It was called the Wolf's Lair.

Stauffenberg placed a bomb less than six feet from where Hitler was standing at an enormous oaken table. An elaborate plot had been hatched within elements of the German army, called Operation Walkyrie. Stauffenberg was to place the bomb, kill Hitler, make it back to Berlin, and then a code word would be issued to the German high command all over Europe; so that even those generals who were not involved in the plot, would, hearing this code word, think, "Ah, something's happened." This was a plan to deal with the question of—the probability or the prospect of some sort of sabotage or assassination of Hitler. Even those who were not involved in the actual plan would hear the code word, assume that something had happened, and then take action. The bomb went off. Stauffenberg had placed the bomb down, escaped from the room. Ordinarily, the briefing would have been held at Hitler's underground bunker—concrete, reinforced, and so on—but on this day it was held in a small wooden annex. Stauffenberg, who had excused himself after placing the bomb, walked out of the building, made his way toward a plane that was going to take him out, talked his way past the first guard, past the second. At that point, the wooden structure where Hitler was holding the briefing blew sky high. Stauffenberg assumed that Hitler and everyone in the room was killed. Miraculously, Hitler survived. We don't know for certain, but it seems, in trying to reconstruct it, apparent that one of the people sitting beside Stauffenberg had kicked the briefcase holding the bomb, (it was uncomfortable), and must've taken it and placed it on the outside of a huge oaken table leg. So that when the bomb went off, the main thrust of the blast went down one side of the table, killed two people there, severely wounded others. Hitler had his pants blown off, his eardrum perforated, but survived.

Nonetheless, after the 20th of July, Hitler never regained full trust in his military; was always wary that there would be another plot, that the army—he'd always felt that these old Prussian traditions, it was Claus von Stauffenberg, an aristocrat—that the army couldn't be trusted. And on the Eastern Front, this was particularly the case. There was a great deal of tension as the Russians began to press relentlessly from the east. And then, of course, with Operation Overlord, a real sense that Hitler was moving into a kind of "Never Never Land," where he was beginning to move divisions that didn't exist. Many of his closest military advisors would find themselves fired or removed from positions of authority. This was the situation, then, in August of 1944 as the Russian troops approached the city of Warsaw. There were logistical problems of a nature that we've just described. The Russians were at the end of their supply lines. But in August of 1944, the Polish underground—the so-called Polish Home Army—staged an uprising in Warsaw. The Polish Home Army was loyal to the so-called London Poles, the Polish government in exile that had very strong western attachments. The Soviets, on the other hand, had recognized their own representatives, the so-called Polish Committee of National Liberation, which they would set up themselves later in the city of Lublin. And the Red Army, just as the Warsaw uprising broke out by the Polish Home Army aimed at defeating the Germans, the Soviets stopped. They stopped east of Warsaw, did not give aid to the Polish Home Army, and the Warsaw uprising was brutally crushed by the Germans. It was a foretaste of what we would come to know as the Cold War, already a sense that the Russians were working on a political agenda that was not shared by the western Allies. The failure to support the Warsaw uprising, to help lift the siege around Warsaw of the Germans, was seen by the western Allies as a very suspicious act on the part of the Soviets.

The Red Army offensive would continue in the fall of 1944. In September, units of the Red Army would push into Finland; Romania, Bulgaria, Slovakia, and Hungary would all now begin to desert their alliance. They were satellite states of the Grössdeutsches Reich, and now would begin to desert the Axis as the Red Army approached. Hitler's Eastern European Empire was collapsing. In the Baltic states, Hitler issued an order saying that no German troops should retreat one inch. They should hold. They should hold. They should hold. So that even as Guderian and others were urging Hitler, "Withdraw the troops, pull the troops back, let's have defensible lines here," to keep the Russians out of Germany, there was a growing sense of doom foreboding, not only among German high command, but certainly among German civilians, that these years of brutal repression, brutal actions in the Soviet Union, were now going to be repaid, and repaid in spades by the Russians as they approached Germany. Guderian and others urged Hitler, "Pull the troops back, pull them out of the Baltics, so that there can be a defensive line to hold." Hitler refused to do it, and over a dozen divisions would be left dangling up in the Baltics, literally cut off from Germany, and played no role in this final act of the Third Reich.

The drive through Poland would begin in January of 1945. The Russians—to give one some sense of just exactly what sort of military force the Soviets now were able to marshal—as they began to launch the offensive in Poland in January of 1945, just as the Allies in the West were finally blunting the German offensive in the West, the Soviets marshaled a million-and-a-half troops for this offensive into Poland—thirty-three hundred tanks; 10,000 aircraft; 28,000 artillery pieces of varying sizes. Against this force, the Germans had available 600,000 men; 700 tanks; 1,300 planes. They were in a desperate position where there was simply no remedy. One of the things that the army had hoped to achieve with the assassination of Hitler in this coup d'etat in July of 1944 was to make a separate peace with the West, but hold in the East. Hold in the East, hoping that they could split the alliance and keep somehow the Bolsheviks—keep the Red Army—out of Germany. This was clearly not going to happen. Warsaw was finally seized, and by February 1945 Russian spearheads were 60 miles from Berlin. In front of this advancing tidal wave of the Red Army, a flood of German refugees now filled the roads. German civilians from the eastern provinces, from western Poland, Germans who had been resettled in the annexed parts of Poland, now all took to the roads in sheer panic. It was difficult for the Wehrmacht in some cases to maintain military positions because of this flood of civilians who were moving west. If one reads through the National Socialist newspapers from these last few months of the war, there is—of course, there's no bad news ever given in the Nazi press—but over and over again, around the periphery, one has this awful sense of German civilians in full panicked flight from the Russians. "The Russians are coming! The Russians are coming," really was the great fear of the German population at this point. Fanatical resistance was going to be necessary. And, of course, it was clear to the German intelligence people that the Red Army now was simply unstoppable, absolutely unstoppable.

Meanwhile, in the West, as the Russians began to close in on Berlin, the Western Allies had finally shaken themselves free of the aftermath of the Battle of the Bulge. The Ardennes offensive of the Germans had been blunted, and now Eisenhower was able to plan the advance into Germany itself. The plan was for a three-pronged advance to clear the Rhineland. The British and the Canadians would strike southward toward the Ruhr. Bradley would drive toward Cologne and Bonn, and then pivot south to link up with Patton's Third Army moving along the north bank of the Moselle. Further south, Patch's Seventh Army would make contact with Patton near the city of Koblentz. The plan went well, but the British and Canadians moved very slowly. They didn't reach the Rhine until February 21. There was bitter resistance on the part of the Germans that flooded fields, did everything they could to thwart the advance. It was Montgomery's understanding that his troops in the north were going to be given the top priority, although he had accepted Eisenhower's overall strategy of a broad-based push into Germany—there was an understanding that Montgomery had the priority to cross the Rhine, and that once the Rhine was breached, this was really going to be the breakthrough point.

Cologne fell to the American First Army on March 5, and as American troops entered this city, this great city on the Rhine, it was a picture of sheer devastation. As American and British troops got into Germany and saw firsthand on the ground the devastation brought by the Allied air forces, they were astonished. Instead of cities—cities that they had seen on the map, cities that some of them might have even seen photographs of from the pre-war years—shells of buildings. Cologne in particular. There's, as many of you must know, there's an enormous cathedral in Cologne, a huge cathedral. In 1945, as American troops entered the city, the cathedral was still standing. It had certainly been damaged, but it was still there, remarkable since right beside it was the main Cologne railroad station, which was completely devastated. The cathedral was virtually the only structure left standing and intact in the center of Cologne. The full devastation of Germany's cities would now be witnessed firsthand.

Fifteen miles south of Cologne, elements of the First Army, probing along the mountainous area there, came across an astonishing sight. There, at a small town called Remagen, they saw a bridge—a bridge across the Rhine. It was a sight that no Allied soldier had ever seen, because the Germans had blown all of the bridges across the Rhine. And here, where it was not supposed to be, was an intact structure going across the river. On March 7, 1945, the troops stormed the bridge and quickly established a bridgehead. Within 24 hours, 8,000 men were across the river. It was an astonishing achievement, also astonishing because they weren't supposed to cross the Rhine. This was not the plan. But there was the bridge. They crossed it. The bridge itself, to say that 8,000 troops got across it in 24 hours is important, because shortly after it, the bridge collapsed. The Germans had been sending frogmen down the river trying to bomb it, trying to shell it. They had mined the bridge; set off the charges; it didn't go. And so these 8,000 troops get across the river at this moment. Hitler was so furious that the bridge had not been destroyed, he fired Rundstedt—I think this was the third time that Rundstedt had been fired by Hitler for one thing or another. The Third Army would then secure a foothold on the east bank of the Rhine, southwest of Frankfurt, on March 22. And only then, on March 23, did Montgomery launch the attack that was to have been the main Allied offensive in the west across the Rhine. The Rhine—if one has never seen the Rhine, it is certainly a big river, and it is a fast-moving river, and especially in the spring. So when that bridge at Remagen went, a pontoon bridge was set up across the river. That by itself was an extraordinary engineering achievement. It was a major defensive position and now it had been breached.

By March 25, 1945, all organized resistance west of the Rhine had ceased. Now Hitler paid the price for his decision to fight west of the river. Rundstedt had told him, "Withdraw across the river, make the river the barrier," but those German troops that were west of the Rhine were now trapped, and the Allies were able to inflict huge casualties. In March and into early April, 290,000 prisoners of war would be taken by the Allies in this position. By March 27, all seven Western Allied armies were across the river and Germany's position in the West was now utterly hopeless.

Now the Allies faced another strategic decision. Could Allied forces reach Berlin? Now, what was shaping up in the spring of 1945—if not among the political leaders, among the military men looking at this situation—now it seemed as if the West was engaged in a race for Berlin. Who was going to get to Berlin? Could the Western Allies reach Berlin? Certainly looking at this Northern German plain, it seemed to beckon. It's ideal terrain for rapid tank movement. The Ruhr was the next obvious objective, the one that Eisenhower had singled out. The Ruhr would be encircled on April 1, and after two weeks of fighting the Ruhr pocket collapsed. Three hundred twenty-five thousand Germans surrendered. At this point there was absolutely no point for the war to go on. The war was lost, but the National Socialist Government refused to surrender.

Simpson's American Ninth Army reached the Elbe River on April 11, and on April 13 established a bridgehead on the eastern bank. He was 50 miles from Berlin. Simpson at this point anticipated orders giving him the go-ahead to make a dash for Berlin. Eisenhower issued orders for him to halt. Why was this? This would become one of the most controversial decisions of the war. In fact, I think it is probably less controversial than it should be. For one thing, Simpson—although it is true that he was only 50 miles from Berlin—his position was greatly overextended. He was short of supplies. He had 50,000 troops available to him to attack the city of Berlin, and the Germans were preparing a last-ditch major defensive effort for the capital city. Hitler had gone to Berlin on January 16 and would not leave the city. The Soviets on April 16 were poised at the Oder River, ready for a great jump across the river and the final assault on the capital city. And also in February of 1945, Roosevelt, Churchill, and Stalin at Yalta had agreed on zones of occupation for a defeated Germany. Berlin lay deep within the Soviet zone. Eisenhower, evaluating the situation, realized that while it might be possible, it might be, though it would be a dangerous attempt for this relatively small and undersupplied force to make a dash for Berlin, but having reached the city, the Germans lose; the Americans were simply going to have to turn this territory back over to the Russians for the Russian occupation zone. He decided to wait.

Eisenhower, also at this point—we didn't know where Hitler was—Eisenhower and the West in general had been really hoodwinked, taken in, by a German plan to construct what is called the "Alpine redoubt." Intelligence sources had been getting information that the Germans were funneling elite troops, supplies, and so on down to the area around Berchtesgaden, that this was where Hitler was, and that Hitler was going to conduct a last-ditch defense in the Alps that might go on for months, months, and months. Instead of sending troops on a dash for Berlin for territory that he was going to have to give back to the Russians, Eisenhower sent the main thrust of the

American offensive at this point into the south, into Bavaria, with Patton headed toward the Czech frontier, and then south into Bavaria itself.

Meanwhile, the Russians were prepared for the assault on Berlin. On the 16th of April, 1945, the Soviets launched their long awaited offensive. They were not over-extended. It was the largest military force the Russians had been able to marshal in the entire Second World War. When they began, the artillery barrage, the rocket barrage—the "Stalin organs," they called them, these rocket launchers that fired off rockets with this incredible "whooshing" sound—the barrage that the Russians set off on April 16 was so thunderous, so enormous, that in the eastern suburbs of Berlin, 60 miles away, one could see the eastern horizon lit up, and one could feel the tremors of the earth that far away, so intense was the barrage. The Russians pushed ahead toward Berlin, reaching the suburbs on April 22. And then in a great pincer movement, Russian troops linked up west of the city on April 25. They began fighting within the city, block by block, house by house. By April 28, they were less than a mile from Hitler's Reich Chancellery, where Hitler was in the bunker, from the Reichstag building close by, as well. On April 30, with the Russians literally a block away, Adolf Hitler committed suicide in the bunker in Berlin.

If one thinks about the cost of the seizure of Berlin for the Russians, between April 16 and May 8, 1945, in this last battle for Berlin, the Soviets lost 304,887 troops—killed, wounded or missing—more casualties than suffered by the United States in the European Theater in the war. This was something that Eisenhower understood. It was the biggest battle. The Battle for Berlin was won by the Russians at enormous costs. And this was against an understaffed, underarmed German defensive position with teenagers, elderly men left to fight. The losses suffered by the Red Army in the Battle for Berlin were the largest suffered by the Red Army in the entire Second World War. To have suffered those casualties coming from the west, and then to have turned that territory over to the Soviets, as according to the Yalta agreement, would have been a very difficult thing indeed for Eisenhower and for the West.

When Hitler committed suicide in the bunker on April 30, 1945, he wrote out, or dictated, a last political testament. Unregenerate to the last, he closed his political life with one final blast of hatred at those people against whom his entire political career had been directed. "It is not true," he wrote, "that I or anyone else in Germany wanted war in 1939. It was desired and provoked exclusively by those international statesman who were either of Jewish ancestry, or who worked for Jewish interests. Centuries may pass, but out of the ruins of our cities and cultural monuments, hatred will again arise against that people who are ultimately responsible for our misery—international Jewry and its accomplices." Within days after Hitler's suicide, an attempt to continue the Third Reich, to pass the leadership on, failed. The Third Reich unraveled without Hitler. And finally, on May 8, 1945, V-E Day was declared in the West; May 9, 1945, by the Russians. The war in Europe had finally come to a close.

The great evil of National Socialism had been defeated, but at absolutely staggering costs. For the Germans, 1,800,000 military dead; 1,200,000 missing; 500,000 civilians killed; 4 million evacuees in this great wave of people moving to the West, escaping the Russians—4 million of them simply vanished. No one knows what happened to them. The Russians, of course, had suffered unbelievably. Eleven million military casualties; 2,500,000 Russian prisoners of war would die in German captivity; 7 million Russian civilians, not counting those murdered in the Holocaust. Ten percent of the population of the Soviet Union had perished by the time the Germans surrendered in May of 1945. Hitler's death in the bunker; the linkup of American and Russian troops finally brought the war in Europe to a close. But the war in Europe did not bring the Second World War to a close. That final chapter would have to be written all the way across the globe in the South Pacific and in Asia.

Truman, the Bomb, and the End
of the War in the Pacific
Lecture 29

Franklin Roosevelt had passed away on April 12, 1945, in Georgia, and had been followed as president by Harry Truman; and it would be Harry Truman, a man not terribly well known to the American public, who would be responsible for making some of the most fateful decisions of the entire Second World War in the spring and summer of 1945.

In the summer of 1945, with Germany defeated and signs of war-weariness surfacing in the United States, the new American president, Harry Truman, confronted the dismal prospect of a bloody invasion of the Japanese home islands. In August Truman chose to use a revolutionary new weapon, the atomic bomb, against the Japanese, hoping to induce the imperial government to surrender.

Several factors influenced President Truman's decision to use the atomic bomb. For one, the Japanese military showed no sign of surrendering. In the wake of Iwo Jima and Okinawa, Truman worried about the high U.S. casualty rates that would result from an invasion of the Japanese home islands.

The Manhattan Project was a joint U.S.-British effort. It was motivated by the Allies' knowledge that Germany was developing a similar weapon. It was assumed initially that the bomb would be used against Germany. Both Roosevelt and Truman came to see the bomb as a

Digital Stock World War II CD.

Atomic bomb.

large conventional device with which they hoped to shock the Japanese into surrender.

Truman received word of the successful testing of the bomb on July 15, 1945, while he was attending the Potsdam Conference. Truman insisted at Potsdam on maintaining Roosevelt's demand for unconditional Japanese surrender. U.S. terms for accepting Japanese surrender were contained in the "Potsdam Declaration." The Japanese were threatened with "complete and utter destruction" if they failed to accept the Declaration. Truman interpreted the vague Japanese response as a rejection.

The first bomb was dropped by the *Enola Gay* onto Hiroshima, destroying 60 percent of the city and killing some 80,000 to 100,000 Japanese. Truman suggested to Japanese leaders that the United States possessed a stockpile of atomic bombs. The Soviet Union declared war on Japan on August 8, 1945, shortly after the Hiroshima bombing. The Navy argued that a blockade and air raids were sufficient to secure Japanese surrender, while the Army advocated the use of the atomic bomb.

Truman faced limited options in the summer of 1945. Neither an effective blockade nor terror bombing had succeeded in ending the war. The availability of just two bombs discouraged the use of one for demonstration purposes.

> **"It is my earnest hope and indeed the hope of all mankind, that from this solemn occasion a better world shall emerge out of the blood and carnage of the past."**
> **—Gen. Douglas MacArthur**

On August 9, 1945, a second bomb was dropped on Nagasaki, killing some 35,000 people. It is ahistorical to argue about Truman's "decision" to use the bomb, since no such decision was made. Use of the bomb was a foregone conclusion. The Japanese military continued to reject surrender even after Nagasaki. There were plans to kidnap the Emperor, who had spoken in council in favor of surrender.

On August 14, Hirohito addressed the nation for the first time, announcing that the war was over. August 14 was designated as V-J Day. ■

Suggested Reading

John Keegan, *The Second World War*, Chapter 32.

Ronald H. Spector, *Eagle Against The Sun*, Chapter 23.

Stanley Weintraub, *The Last Great Victory: The End of World War II, July/August 1945*.

Questions to Consider

1. What considerations led Truman to authorize the use of the atomic bomb against Japan?

2. Was his decision to do so morally justifiable?

Truman, the Bomb, and the End
of the War in the Pacific

Lecture 29—Transcript

The war in Europe had come to an end in May of 1945. It was a bitter disappointment in one sense that the American leader who had led the country through the war, had been the architect of much of the great alliance aimed at National Socialist Germany, was not alive to see the conclusion of the war there. Franklin Roosevelt had passed away on April 12, 1945, in Georgia, and had been followed as president by Harry Truman; and it would be Harry Truman, a man not terribly well known to the American public, who would be responsible for making some of the most fateful decisions of the entire Second World War in the spring and summer of 1945.

Looking at the international situation from Washington in the late spring, early summer of 1945, Truman was faced with some very difficult decisions. The war in Europe had been brought to a close but there were ongoing troubles with the Soviets. The relationship between the United States and the Soviet Union, which had always been tenuous, always been problematic, now threatened to become even more difficult. Franklin Roosevelt had always believed that his great charm, his personal appeal, would be enough to continue to draw Stalin into some sort of post-war international order, but Harry Truman would have less of Roosevelt's idealism, less faith in the powers of his own personality, and a great deal more skepticism about the Soviet Union in Europe.

But in the spring and summer of 1945, it was not so much the position of the Soviet Union in Europe that weighed heavily on Truman's mind, but rather the war that was not yet over in the Pacific. For months it seemed that the end of the war against Japan was in sight, and yet the Japanese had shown no signs of surrender. There had been peace feelers; there had been indications of a willingness on the part of some within the Japanese ruling class to make some sort of arrangement; no direct contacts with the United States or with Great Britain, but through the Soviet Union. But the real power in the Japanese government were not people in the foreign office, but rather the Japanese military, and there was absolutely no sense at all that some end of the war might appeal to them.

In the three months of Truman's presidency, the United States had suffered nearly half of all the casualties inflicted upon it by the Japanese in three years of combat. The specter of Okinawa loomed extremely large in Truman's thinking. Iwo Jima, Okinawa had seen, as we've talked about and discussed, tremendous American casualties; Truman wanted a careful review of American options. It was estimated in a discussion with the Joint Chiefs of Staff that an invasion of Japan would bring catastrophic casualties. Truman listened at one such meeting with the Joint Chiefs as Admiral Leahy estimated that an invasion of Kyushu, the southernmost main island of Japan, that 268,000 of the 770,000 Americans participating in the planned invasion would become casualties—more casualties, in other words, than in the entire Pacific war to date. It was estimated that the Japanese possessed 14 divisions on this island alone. They'd had two reinforced divisions at Okinawa—and that thousands of Kamikazes remained in place and available to the Japanese for a final defense of the home islands. And, of course, looming beyond Japan itself, the Japanese had the largest concentration of their military forces still in China, so an invasion now seemed for Truman an enormously high price to pay.

He had been made aware, upon taking office as president, of the progress now of something called the "Manhattan Project." The Manhattan Project had begun in 1940 as a joint British-American endeavor, to find out about the feasibility of an atomic weapon. Fear of German engineering and knowledge that the Germans had embarked upon a similar project, certainly acted as a spur to the Americans and to the British, and all through the early years of American participation in the war, the assumption was that if the bomb were available, if it were possible to actually develop such a weapon, that it would be used against Germany if necessary. The prospect I think that was particularly haunting to Roosevelt, certainly to the American scientists—it ultimately became an American project—working on this, was the prospect of the Germans developing an atomic device, an atomic bomb, and also the missiles to deliver it. Although the American government ultimately came to the conclusion that the Germans had dropped out of the nuclear race, that they had given up on their project to develop a nuclear bomb, the Manhattan Project, as the American undertaking came to be known, would continue on in preparation for ultimate use of an atomic weapon should it have been necessary.

Truman's choices at this juncture in the war were all difficult: war against Japan, an invasion of the Japanese islands were expected to take maybe a year and a half before the fall of Japan. Casualty estimates varied enormously. MacArthur estimated over a million; Marshall tended to agree with this. Some argued that the casualties would be nowhere nearly as high, a mere 63,000 American dead for an invasion of Japan, hardly a very happy prospect for Roosevelt or Truman, anyone else thinking about an invasion of Japan. The fighting in Iwo Jima and Okinawa led Truman to believe that Japan would resist an invasion with absolutely fanatical determination, fighting down to the last man, woman, and child. Moreover, the Japanese still had 2 million troops in the home islands, over 10,000 aircraft. They still had looming across onto the Asian mainland the Japanese army in China. So, the bomb might prevent the same kind of bloodbath that had been seen on Okinawa and prevent not only American casualties but also Japanese as well, certainly reduce them enormously.

Nonetheless, preparations were underway on Okinawa and in the Philippines for an invasion of Japan set to begin in November of 1945. It's clear looking through the papers of both Roosevelt and Truman that both men tended to think of the bomb as essentially a much larger explosive device, a kind of conventional weapon, only of a much greater scale, and maybe if the weapon were even as remotely destructive as they anticipated, its use might shock the Japanese into surrender. There was no real sense, looking through Roosevelt's papers or Truman's either, that at this stage of the war that Truman had any understanding of the nature of what one was talking about with an atomic weapon. The bomb was tested on July 15, 1945, and it revealed that it was even more terrible than the scientists or the political or military people believed. Truman received word about the successful test of the bomb while attending the Potsdam Conference in Germany, and for the first time informed Stalin that the United States possessed a weapon of enormous destructive power. Truman was reserved in the way he put this, but he was surprised a bit—the Americans were surprised that Stalin wasn't more inquisitive or didn't seem more surprised about this disclosure, some new weapon that had been developed. Well, Stalin already knew about the bomb—he'd found out through the Soviet espionage ring—and Stalin had some news for Truman. He informed the president that the Japanese had been making peace overtures to the Soviet Union for the possible surrender of Japan. Stalin was a little surprised that Truman was not more interested in this, but of course Truman already knew this because Truman had been receiving this information through the code breaks of the Japanese.

Truman insisted at Potsdam on maintaining the policy that Roosevelt had enunciated at the Casablanca Conference in early 1943 of unconditional surrender—this had been the formula in Europe and it was going to be the formula applied to Japan. At Potsdam, Truman would push for what came to be known as the "Potsdam Declaration," signed by the United States, Great Britain, and China. That Potsdam Declaration demanded of the Japanese that they put an end first to Japanese militarism; that there would be a punishment of Japanese war criminals; there would be a military occupation of Japan; the Japanese would have to evacuate all occupied territories; and would have to agree to complete disarmament—this was really unconditional surrender. The Allies, on the other hand, promised to establish a democratic government in Japan; to help rebuild Japanese industry destroyed in the massive American air raids on Japan; and to end the military occupation of Japan when it was clear that the Japanese had established a "peacefully inclined and responsible government." Should the Japanese fail to accept the Potsdam Declaration, they were warned that they would face "complete and utter destruction."

The Japanese response to the Potsdam Declaration was vague and evasive, and it convinced Truman and his advisors that it was tantamount to a rejection. The Japanese were clearly—the councils of state within Japan were clearly—discussing some form of surrender. One of the big problems about the formula of unconditional surrender was the position of the emperor. The emperor was not immortal, but a god in Japanese society, Japanese culture, and unconditional surrender could conceivably mean that the emperor would go, and this no one within the Japanese hierarchy, civilian or military, was really willing to contemplate. So military advocates in Japan for continuing the struggle prevailed, at least for now.

The British government at this point gave its approval for the use of the atomic weapon. On August 7, 1945, Colonel Paul Tibbets, Jr., at the controls of the *Enola Gay*, took off from Tinian in the Marianas carrying a 9,000-pound bomb with the destructive power of 20,000 tons of TNT. Just before 8:15 the giant object tumbled from the bomb bay. The plane had been seen approaching Hiroshima. It was by itself. The Japanese, on the ground, thought it must be an observer plane or a spy plane but certainly not a single aircraft off on an attack. But the giant object, the bomb, tumbled from the bomb bay just after 8:15. When it reached a point 660 yards from the ground, a blinding flash illuminated the sky, and a split second later a gigantic fireball burst over the unsuspecting city. Shockwaves of colossal force roiled like a typhoon of scalding air, leveling almost everything in its path. A cloud, a mushroom cloud, something that had never been seen by anyone before, rose to an altitude of 55,000 feet. In his logbook, Robert Lewis, the copilot of the *Enola Gay*, wrote simply, "My God." Beneath the cloud, 60 percent of what had been the city of Hiroshima disappeared. No one knows how many people died in Hiroshima on that day, but estimates range from 80,000 to 100,000 in that initial blast. The estimates virtually double when one talks about casualties a year later and so a year and a half later from radiation.

Later on that same day, Truman warned the Japanese leadership that unless surrender was forthcoming more cities in Japan would experience the same horror. He gave the impression to the Japanese leadership that more of these bombs, a stockpile of these bombs, was available and would be used. On August 8, the Soviet Union, one week earlier than anticipated, declared war on Japan. One of the major motivations of the Yalta Conference and much of the motivation of the Roosevelt administration and its dealings with the Soviets, as well as Churchill, was to coax, cajole, convince the Soviets to enter the war against Japan, which the Soviets had not done because of the obvious reasons of its life-and-death struggle with the Germans. Now, when it became possible for the Soviets to enter the war in Asia, the United States was far less interested in Soviet participation. Stimson, the Secretary of War at this point, urged Truman to make a concerted effort for peace, some new overture to the Japanese leadership, but Truman continued to insist on the Potsdam Declaration, and the Japanese at this point still did not seem willing to accept those stark terms. Truman was getting different advice. Certainly Stimson, as Secretary of War, Admiral Leahy, in fact most of the naval personnel, were very wary of the bomb, not at all convinced that it was necessary. The navy leadership in particular argued and argued quite correctly that the American Navy could blockade Japan; was in fact already doing it, and doing it very successfully. A ring of submarines around and surface vessels around the Japanese home islands had effectively strangled Japanese trade; Japan was slowly starving to death; a blockade, they argued, as well as continued air raids, fire bombings, could bring the Japanese to their knees and it would not be necessary to use the bomb. Marshall and MacArthur, on the other hand, had certainly argued in favor. No one was eager for an invasion; the army people were certainly not eager for an invasion of Japan. Among the army personnel, among the army leadership, Dwight Eisenhower would really be the only one who would speak up forcefully against the bomb, and that would be in retrospect, not prior to its use.

What were the options that Harry Truman, this man who had not anticipated being president, certainly had not anticipated being in this position at this juncture—what were the options that he actually had in the summer of 1945? Was the bomb really necessary? Why couldn't Truman wait? Why not accept the idea of a blockade? Why not accept a blockade in conjunction with additional air raids, conventional air raids, on Japan? Well, neither an effective blockade, which had already been in effect for some time, or terror bombing had worked. The Japanese military seemed unwilling to accept the realities of this situation. The Japanese military simply wasn't listening. They seemed to be willing to go down in a great flame of glory. It hadn't worked, conventional bombing and the blockade, Truman felt, simply hadn't worked. How long would this take? How long would it drag out? There was some discussion about the possibility of, "Well, why not a demonstration?"—that is, a use of the bomb on some sort of atoll or off the coast of Japan to demonstrate the great explosive power of this new weapon. The problem with this was that despite the implication of there being a stockpile of such atomic bombs, there in fact were two: one that was used on Hiroshima, and the one that would be used on August 9 against Nagasaki. If one of these two had been dropped on some sort of Pacific atoll or off the coast of Japan and you had only one other one, then how effective would this be? What happened if it didn't work? What happened if the Japanese didn't accept this? What happened if it didn't go off? There was always the possibility that it wouldn't work. So that didn't seem to be much of an option.

On August 9 then, a second bomb, a plutonium device this time, was dropped on Nagasaki, killing 35,000 people. The force of this bomb, although it was a more powerful bomb than the Hiroshima bomb, was reduced by the geographic position of Nagasaki, the force held in by the hills surrounding it.

One might argue that there was some question about if one could say the first bomb was necessary, that Truman really didn't necessarily have the options, hoping that the bomb would have a shock effect on the Japanese leadership. I think a more legitimate question could be raised about the use of the second one so quickly. Just 48 hours later—it was not at all clear reading through the papers of the Japanese government, it was not at all clear that they understood what in fact had happened to them at Hiroshima. At this point, however, no one in the White House, no one, certainly Harry Truman, was not willing to wait. The second bomb coming so quickly would have even more shock effect, hopefully to finally bring the Japanese military to their senses.

Also, I think there is in the debate and especially a debate which incidentally was not much of a debate in 1945, or even 1946, but as time passes has become more of a debate about whether or not the bomb, this awful weapon, should have been unleashed. In many ways I think it's a historical argument. In the context of 1945, to be the president of the United States, with a war-weary population, facing the prospect of an invasion of the home islands of Japan, which might take a year and a half, where the worst case scenario was a million American casualties, who knows how many millions of Japanese would've perished in such an invasion—what choice, one might argue, would Harry Truman have. One of the most unsavory aspects of the debate, I think, about the bomb that had erupted in the United States over the display of the *Enola Gay* on the anniversary, the 50th anniversary, was the argument made to say, "Well, only 63,000 Americans might have died in an invasion of Japan rather than a million." I think as president of the United States, sending telegrams to 63,000 more families would not have been a terribly attractive prospect in the summer of 1945. As one military man who was in the White House, served in the White House map room at the time, remembers, and I think this is absolutely true, he wrote, "Truman made no decision, because there was no decision to make. He could no more have stopped it than a train moving down a track. It's all well and good to come along later and say the bomb was a horrible thing; the whole goddamn war was a horrible thing."

On the day after the second bomb, the Nagasaki disaster, Hirohito, the emperor of Japan, took an extraordinary step. He broke a deadlock in the supreme war council, overcoming the military's continued opposition to surrender—even after the second bomb, the supreme war council had deadlocked with the military still resisting surrender. Hirohito, whose presence at these councils—he never spoke, ever, at these meetings—his presence was largely symbolic—he intervened and he broke the deadlock, speaking in favor of surrender. He directed the cabinet and the council to consent to the Potsdam Declaration. There was some hope there would be at least one proviso, that is, that the emperor himself would retain his position for domestic stability within Japan itself. On August 11, a compromise seemed to have been worked out whereby the emperor would be retained but under an Allied supreme commander. Still, at this point, the military within the circles of government in Japan resisted the idea of surrender. After the war was over and much of the debate about the use of the bomb, much of the criticism of Truman has been that, "Well, he didn't give negotiation a chance. He really wasn't willing to wait, talk, that the Japanese were going to be brought to their senses by either blockade or by the continuation of the American conventional air raids against Japan."

There's absolutely no evidence from the internal documents of Japan to support this view. The Japanese military who still exerted enormous powers within the policy making bodies of Japan absolutely refused to see reality; and even after the emperor had intervened, making the historic step of actually speaking in one of these councils, plans were hatched among junior officers (close to their equivalent in a sense of the Joint Chiefs of Staff), to actually kidnap the emperor, and to tell the Japanese public, "Well, that he had fallen under the influence of defeatist subversive elements." A number of conspiracies were hatched in these last frantic days of August, trying to prevent the actual surrender of Japanese forces by the emperor. Nonetheless, Hirohito would once again break a deadlock on August 14, once again reiterating his conviction that surrender simply had to come, that Japan could not continue to face this kind of destruction.

On August 15, 1945, Hirohito, emperor of Japan, addressed the Japanese nation for the first time. No one had heard his voice—he was a deity—and now was speaking to the Japanese nation, announcing that the war at last was over. He didn't instantly say that Japan had surrendered, but it was obvious. The Japanese had failed in their efforts in the war; the suffering was at last to come to an end. August 14 was then to be V-J Day, though the war officially did not end until September 2, when the Japanese formally signed the document of surrender aboard the U.S.S *Missouri* in Tokyo Bay. At that signing, historic signing, Douglas MacArthur made the following statement, "It is my earnest hope and indeed the hope of all mankind, that from this solemn occasion a better world shall emerge out of the blood and carnage of the past, a world founded upon faith and understanding, a world dedicated to the dignity of man and fulfillment of his most cherished wish for freedom, tolerance, and justice." The war in the Pacific had come to a close, and with that signing, the Second World War, a war that actually linked these conflicts that we've talked about over the past lectures, finally drew to its bloody conclusion.

The Costs of War
Lecture 30

In this concluding segment, we want to turn our attention to the historical consequences of the Second World War, to talk about its political implications; the long-term economic implications of the war, and also to talk about the human costs of this greatest of all conflicts in human history, to examine the epoch of the Second World War, which is really only now, 50 years after the guns fell silent, coming to a close.

The war fundamentally altered the balance of power in the world. It marked the emergence of the United States and the Soviet Union as superpowers. It led to the cold war. It led to the eclipse and (temporary) division of Europe. It intensified and accelerated anti-colonialist movements around the globe. It intensified demands for a greater state intervention in domestic affairs, as illustrated by the emergence of the welfare state. Returning veterans made new socio-economic demands on the state.

The human costs were very high. Fifty-five million people perished in the Second World War. No corner of the globe was left untouched. The human costs of the war are poignantly depicted in the story of the last U.S. bomber crew shot down over Germany during World War II. ∎

Remembering the war, the Second World War, which consumed 55 million lives, means remembering not only the extraordinary acts of unparalleled heroism, bravery, self-sacrifice, devotion to duty that would be the hallmark of that war, but the grief, anxiety, and heartbreak in which it was shrouded.

Suggested Reading

Thomas Childers, *Wings of Morning*.

John Keegan, *The Second World War*, Chapter 33.

Questions to Consider

1. How did World War II shape world politics during the postwar decades?

2. How does the study of World War II highlight both what is best and what is worst in human nature?

The Costs of War
Lecture 30—Transcript

Hello. Welcome to our final lecture in this series on the Second World War. In this concluding segment, we want to turn our attention to the historical consequences of the Second World War; to talk about its political implications; the long-term economic implications of the war; and also to talk about the human costs of this greatest of all conflicts in human history; to examine the epoch of the Second World War, which is really only now, 50 years after the guns fell silent, coming to a close.

We began our examination of the Second World War by pointing out that the war fundamentally altered life in the 20th century on this planet. The balance of power in international politics was dramatically changed by the course of the Second World War. It marked the emergence of the United States and the Soviet Union as superpowers. The United States before 1939 obviously had been a major power, certainly a major economic power, but had not yet, despite American intervention in the First World War, had not yet emerged as a major player on the international scene. That obviously would change with the powerful events of 1941 to 1945. The Soviet Union would emerge from the Second World War with its ghastly casualties, the terrific devastation of the war in the Soviet Union, as the other great superpower. The political conflicts between the United States and the Soviet Union, between the Soviet Union and the West that began to emerge in the final year of the conflict, would of course cast their shadow over the subsequent 50 years of history.

The Cold War was of course born out of the Second World War. The war, with its great devastation of Europe—Europe at the end of the war found its cities, major cities, destroyed, its populations displaced, economic turmoil—there was great concern that Europe itself might be convulsed by political revolution and more conflict. And, yet, the division of Europe, which would certainly follow in the Cold War, would finally be ended, and ended only actually in this decade of the 1990s.

The period of the Second World War, we tend to think of as beginning in 1939 with the German invasion of Poland. But in fact, this epoch of the Second World War, I think in larger historical terms is really going to be seen as beginning in 1914. I think that these two great conflicts of this century, the Great War, as the First World War was called, and the Second, are ultimately going to be seen, despite some differences in motivation and certainly differences in the nature of regimes involved, as one great war of the 20th century; total war in which the resources—human, economic, psychological—were mobilized for conflict.

It would intensify demands for a greater intervention of state in domestic affairs. The millions of returning veterans everywhere would demand of their government something more than simple benign neglect, having made great sacrifices. One sees in Europe certainly, to a lesser degree in the United States, but certainly in Europe, really the emergence of the modern welfare state in which the domestic populations of France, of Germany, of Italy, of Great Britain, all would demand of their states some sort of support and repayment in a way for the great sacrifices made during the course of the Second World War. The nature of the state itself after the Second World War would be ultimately different.

Also, if one thinks about the human costs of the Second World War, 55 million people would perish across the globe in this conflict. No corner of the globe would be left untouched. We talked in our last lecture about the casualties in Germany—1,800,000 military dead; a million plus missing; 500,000 civilian dead; 4 million who simply vanished in the trek from Eastern Europe to the West. In Great Britain, 390,000 fatalities; in France, 810,000; the United States, 259,000. Japan would lose 1,800,000; Poland, 4.5 million, over 4 million of whom were civilians. The Soviet Union, with the most dramatic of all of course as we've seen, 11 million military casualties, deaths; 2.5 million who died in German captivity, 7 million civilians, 22 million altogether; a tenth of the entire population of the Soviet Union—death on a scale never before imagined—and, of course, the 6 million who would perish in the Holocaust. These numbers are staggering, impossible, I think, to comprehend. And yet those human costs, I think, are things we must struggle to understand, must come to terms with, and the numbers themselves in many ways leave us blank. They're too big, too staggering. Individual stories, I think, bring the meaning of this war much closer to home. And so, as we conclude this series of lectures on the war, I'd like to tell a story, an individual story. A story that begins in the final days of the Second World

War and I think captures both the devastation, bravery, and heartbreak of the war.

In the final days of the war in Europe, American and Soviet troops were linking up on the Elbe; the Allies had overrun almost all of Germany; the Russians had reached the very suburbs of Berlin. The Third Reich was in its death throes. On April 21, 1945, at just after 10:30 in the morning, a formation of 137 American heavy bombers, giant B-24 Liberators, took off on its way to a target deep inside Nazi Germany. Only three days before, the Allied high command had declared the strategic air war in Europe to be over. There simply were no more strategic targets left for the heavy bombers. There would still be air attacks certainly, but those attacks would be carried out by dive bombers and by small lightweight attack aircraft. Still, one last mission had been ordered. General Eisenhower was convinced that Hitler was preparing one last-ditch stand in the Bavarian Alps and was funneling men and materiel into this alpine hideout.

So the target for the bombers on this day was a railroad bridge in the vicinity of Salzburg, considered to be a key transportation link that was to be destroyed. But the weather had been terrible all morning. Low clouds, fog, hung over the bases in England and over the continent. The situation deteriorated. Banks of leaden cloud, like mammoth slabs of concrete, stretched out in every direction. The weather ship, flying in advance of the formation—in all of these formations' big bombing raids, there would be a weather ship that would fly out in front of the main body of the formation to check weather conditions at the target. The primary was to be bombed, in this instance, visually. This weather ship, flying in advance of the formation, sent back a steady stream of directions, leading the formation on a meandering course through the cloud banks. Like explorers crawling through the murky crevices of a cave, the formation twisted and turned as the ships climbed and dropped, swung to the left and right, seeking a gap in the mountainous clouds. Buffeted by strong winds and pockets of turbulence, the formation formed and reformed, swinging at last to the southwest toward the I.P. Maintaining a tight formation was out of the question; holding to the briefed course was impossible.

Then, just past 10:30, the weather ship reached Salzburg to discover a towering weather front: solid cloud, thunderstorm, and rime ice from 15,000 to 20,000 feet. The weather ship advised abandoning the mission. The command pilot, riding in the lead aircraft, who was in charge of the mission—it was his decision to make ultimately: turn back, proceed on to the target, proceed to the secondary. The secondary target on this day was also a target in the Salzburg area, so the command pilot felt that he could not move to the secondary. Also, because American troops were moving through the area, moving into the southeast towards Salzburg, finding a target of opportunity, which would have ordinarily been another alternative, was also ruled out. The command pilot reluctantly agreed to abort the mission and return to base in England. He gave a signal for a turn to the right. But such a course, navigators and pilots throughout the formation realized, was a mistake. It would lead them directly over the city of Regensburg, one of the most frequently bombed and heavily defended cities in Germany. It was the home of a Messerschmitt factory that had been bombed in the first major American raid deep into Germany in August of 1943. The command pilot insisted, despite protests from various navigators throughout the formation, and high above Regensburg, the giant formation began a sweeping turn to the west.

On this day, April 21, 1945, luck was with the formation. It might have been a disaster. But on this day, only one flight battery was still operating in the city. And it cut loose with only two salvos. A bomb group used to seeing a sky filled with deadly black puffs of smoke saw only eight, nine of these sooty bursts in the sky around them. Anti-aircraft fire that morning was later described to be meager, but it was accurate. One plane, the lead ship of the Third Squadron, appropriately enough named the Black Cat, was not lucky that morning. At 10:32 a.m., an 88 millimeter shell ripped through the left wing of the plane between the number one and number two engine. Instantly, a plume of red-orange flame shot back, and then within seconds the wing folded and the plane flipped over onto its back and began a long, lopsided spiral into the clouds below. Throughout the formation, men strained to see parachutes, to see if anybody got out.

Just a few weeks later, on May 8, 1945, in a small town in Tennessee, Callie Goodner was waiting for her husband to return home from work when across the street the Western Union truck pulled up. It was a dreaded sight, one that anyone living at home through the war recognized with great terror. The Western Union boy crossed the trolley tracks and approached the front porch. He handed her a telegram. It was from the War Department. She opened the telegram on May 8 with cars blaring, their horns blaring, bells chiming throughout the town. It was V-E Day in Europe. The war was over. The radio broadcasts from London were already talking about celebrations in London, chanting crowds of happy civilians in the capital of Great Britain. And with her hands trembling, she opened the telegram. It read, "The Secretary of War desires me to express his deep regret that your son, Technical Sergeant Goodner, Howard G., has been missing in action in Germany since 21 April. If further details or information are received, you will be promptly notified." Within a matter of hours, Callie Goodner was in touch with families in St. Louis, in New York, in Peoria, Illinois; the crew—the families of the crew of the Black Cat who had remained somewhat in touch throughout the last part of 1944 and into 1945. "Have you heard anything? Have you received a telegram?" Rushing to her bedside table where she kept letters from her son, she tore open the last letter that she had received from him and looked at the date. The date was April 21, 1945. Howard had written a letter. In it he said that the war was winding down; the Russians were approaching Berlin, but he had to get to bed and get this war over with. But he sure wished he was at home in Tennessee in the spring time. It didn't look like he would make it this spring. But the letter was from April 21. How, she thought, could it be possible that he was missing on April 21 when she had a letter?

That evening, phone calls began coming in from New Jersey, from Chicago, from various places where families of the crew also reported that they, too, had received a missing in action telegram. In the following weeks, one by one, the eleven-member crew of the Black Cat's families would receive a second telegram, confirming that their son or husband were not missing in action, but in fact had been killed in action over Regensburg on April 21, 1945. It was a typical bomber crew. It could have been a typical outfit, a squad in the infantry, part of a ship's detachment from any branch of service. They were from all over the country; Jewish, Catholic, Southern Baptist. The youngest, a young Armenian from Brooklyn, was 18. One of the waist gunners was 17 actually when he enlisted; his—forged the papers, got into the army air corps, and was 18 when the plane went down. There were two married men on the crew. The old man of the crew, a waist gunner from Peoria, Illinois, was 29. They called him "Pops." He had two children.

One by one, the families received the second telegram, but not the Goodners. No telegram arrived. And days passed and days passed. Could it be? Then the second word began filtering in. Parachutes had been seen coming out of the plane. The whole crew might not have gone down. And then, a remarkable phone call from Brooklyn; the tail gunner was alive. He'd been liberated from an American—from a German prisoner of war camp just outside of Munich. He was alive and so was the bombardier—two of the crew members. Were others still alive? What about Howard? Was he alive? There'd been no second telegram.

Members of the 466th bomb group began returning to the United States in this period on their way to—for redeployment in the Pacific in preparation for the invasion of Japan. The families interviewed, called, wrote, or were contacted by other members of this bomb group, desperately trying to find out details, information about what had happened on this mission on April 21. Some people said there were two chutes, three chutes, four chutes had been seen coming out of the Black Cat as it spiraled into the clouds over Regensburg. Then on June 24, a second telegram was received at the Goodner household. Callie, her hands shaking, received the telegram and ripped it open. She read only as far as the first line. It began, "The Secretary of War desires me to express his deepest regret." It, too, confirmed that her son Howard Goodner, 21 years old, had been killed over Regensburg.

Resigned and despondent, her husband Ernest, in November of 1945, now the war over, the veterans returning triumphant, appealed to the Adjutant General in Washington for information, posing the same question that had tormented all of the families of the Black Cat since May. "We've had very little information from your office in regards to how my son met his death or where he is buried," the letter read. "We've talked to several members of the 466th bomb group who were on the mission, and they offered different—they have differed on the number of chutes that we have seen—they saw coming from the ship. According to records that you sent me, Howard was killed in action over Regensburg, Germany, on 21 April 1945. Could you tell me whether my son was found in the ship, or did he parachute out? I would also like to know what means were used to identify him." The family was tortured with the idea that somehow he had escaped, was wandering around somewhere in the chaotic state of occupied Europe at this point. In a final plea, he added, "I know you have thousands of letters like this and that your office is a very busy place, but please try and understand my position as a parent, and that I want to know every detail regarding my son. For the sacrifice that he made for our country, I feel sure his country will give me all the details that we have on my beloved son." The War Department was unable to provide those details, and the family, as all the members of this crew, and the families of servicemen all across the United States, would now suffer from the lack of information. There would be no more news from the War Department; only in 1948, the return of his body from Europe.

If any war can be described as just or successful, the Second World War would be a prime candidate. It was the Good War, with hard-won victories over the barbarism of Nazi Germany and the aggressive militarism of Imperial Japan. But to Callie Goodner, whose son Howard perished over Regensburg on what proved to be the last Allied bombing raid in Europe—it was the last American bomber lost over Europe, and one of the war's bitterest ironies for her and for the family—triumph over Hitler was a cold consolation for the loss she had suffered. For almost half a century after her son's death, she could not believe that he was never coming home.

For Vincent O'Brien, the war ended and his struggle with its meaning began on the day after Christmas, 1944, when his son's personal effects arrived home in a small box. Opening the parcel, he found a neatly folded dress uniform, a few dog-eared photographs, and a small paper bag containing a jeweler's ring, the silver wings of a navigator, a wristwatch, a pair of sunglasses, and three coins. "I sat staring at the box in which these things had come," he wrote. "It was such a small box to hold all the laughter, tears, all the hope and apprehension which had been packed into it. So much gaiety and tenderness; so much virile beauty. It was hard to believe that it had all vanished, leaving only a little heap of clothes in a torn paper bag. It was incredible that of high adventure in a far land, nothing was left but a three-pence and a watch that had stopped ticking." That scene of quiet anguish was repeated in hundreds of thousands, indeed millions of homes, throughout the United States, England, Germany, the Soviet Union, Japan—all across a world convulsed by war.

After all these years, its memory lingers like a wound that will never heal. Remembering the war, the Second World War, which consumed 55 million lives, means remembering not only the extraordinary acts of unparalleled heroism, bravery, self-sacrifice, devotion to duty that would be the hallmark of that war, but the grief, anxiety, and heartbreak in which it was shrouded. We must, in short, preserve and remember not only the remarkable triumph and valor of those traumatic years, but also the colossal human tragedy that lurks in the cold and unforgiving heart of every war, no matter how just.

On the 50th anniversary of the Black Cat's demise, on April 21, 1995, the families of the crew of the Black Cat convened in a village just outside of Regensburg where the plane had come down. Remarkably, the villagers there had constructed a cross and a small plaque for the crew of the Black Cat. And as the families of that crew gathered with about 150 German villagers, many of whom had been children or young adults and watched that awful scene of the plane cartwheeling out of the sky on April 21, 1945, we gathered to mark the end of the war and the epoch that it dominated. And as we did, the memory of that crew, as for all the losses of war, spoke out to us across the decades, reminding us that in war there are no winners and that even in victory there is heartbreak. Thank you.

Timeline

The War in Europe

Jan. 30, 1933 .... Hitler appointed Chancellor of Germany.

March 16, 1935 .... Germany renounces disarmament clauses of
Versailles Treaty, introduces conscription, and
begins construction of an air force.

March 7, 1936 .... German remilitarization of the Rhineland.

July 18, 1936 .... Beginning of Spanish Civil War.

March 1938 .... The Austrian crisis and the *Anschluss*.

September 1938 .... The Sudetenland crisis.

Sept. 29, 1938 .... The Munich Conference.

March 1939 .... German occupation of Czechoslovakia.

August 23, 1939 .... The Molotov-Ribbentrop Pact.

Sept. 1, 1939 .... Germany invades Poland.

Sept. 29, 1939 .... Russia and Germany divide Poland.

Nov. 30, 1939–
March 12, 1940 .... Russo-Finish War.

April 9, 1940 .... Germany invades Norway.

May 10, 1940 .... Germany invades Holland, Belgium, and France.

May 29–
June 4, 1940 .... British and French troops evacuated
from Dunkirk.

June 10, 1940 .... Italy declares war on Britain and France.

June 22, 1940 .... France signs armistice.

July 8–Nov. 1940 .... Battle of Britain.

October 28, 1940 .... Italy invades Greece.

April 6, 1941 .... Germany invades Yugoslavia and Greece.

June 22, 1941 .... Germans launch Operation Barbarossa.

Sept. 4, 1941 .... German siege of Leningrad begins.

December 6, 1941 .... Russian counterattack before Moscow.

December 11, 1941 .... Hitler declares war on the United States.

January 20, 1942 .... Wannsee Conference in Berlin.

July 2, 1942 .... New German offensive in Soviet Union.

August 22, 1942 .... Battle of Stalingrad begins.

September 21, 1942 .... Soviet forces counterattack, begin the
encirclement of Stalingrad.

November 8, 1942 .... Allied invasion of French North Africa begins.

January 17–27, 1943 .... Casablanca Conference.

February 2, 1943 .... German 6th Army surrenders at Stalingrad.

February 8, 1943 .... Battle of Kursk.

May 8–12, 1943 .... End of German resistance in North Africa.

July 10, 1943 .... Allied forces invade Sicily.

July 25, 1943 .... Mussolini forced to resign.

August 17, 1943 .... American air raids on Schweinfurt
and Regensburg.

September 2 1943 .... Allied invasion of Italy.

September 9, 1943 .... American forces land at Salerno.

November 6, 1943 .... Russians retake Kiev.

January 22, 1944 .... Allied forces land at Anzio.

March 15–
May 18, 1944 .... Allied attacks on Monte Casino.

June 4, 1944 .... Anglo-American troops enter Rome.

June–August 1944 .... Soviet offensive against German Army
Group Center.

June 6, 1944 .... D-Day: the invasion of France.

July 1944 .... The Warsaw uprising.

August 25, 1944 .... The liberation of Paris.

September 17–26, 1944 ...... Operation Market Garden fails.

December 16–25, 1944 ...... The Battle of the Bulge.

January 12, 1945 .... Russians take Warsaw.

February 7, 1945 .... Yalta Conference.

March 7, 1945 .... American forces cross the Rhine at Remagen.

May 1, 1945 .... Battle of Berlin begins.

May 7, 1945 .... German surrender to Western Allies at Reims.

May 8, 1945 .... V-E Day in the West.

The War in the Pacific

September 1931 .... The Mukden Incident and Japanese attacks
in Manchuria.

February 18, 1932 .... Japanese declare the independence
of Manchukuo.

July 7, 1937 .... Japanese hostilities with China commence.

December–
January 1938 .... The "rape of Nanking."

December 7, 1941 .... Japanese attack on Pearl Harbor.

December 25, 1941 .... British forces at Hong Kong surrender.

January–March 1942 .... Japan seizes Dutch East Indies,
Singapore, Burma.

January–April 9, 1942 .... Battle of the Philippines.

April 18, 1942 .... The Doolittle raid on Tokyo.

May 7, 1942 .... The Battle of the Coral Sea.

June 4–7, 1942 .... The Battle of Midway.

Aug. 1942–Feb. 1943 .... The Struggle for Guadalcanal.

June 1943 .... MacArthur launches Operation Cartwheel.

November 1943 .... The fighting on Tarawa.

February 2, 1944 .... Invasion of the Marshall Islands.

June 16, 1944 .... Invasion of the Marianas.

August 11, 1944 .... Conquest of Guam.

October 19, 1944 .... MacArthur opens offensive in the Philippines.

February–March 1945 .... Battle of Iwo Jima.

March 9–10 1945 .... First fire-bombing of Tokyo.

April 1–June 21, 1945 .... Battle of Okinawa.

August 6, 1945 .... Atomic bomb dropped on Hiroshima.

August 8, 1945 .... Soviet Union enters war against Japan.

August 9, 1945 .... Second atomic bomb dropped on Nagasaki.

August 14, 1945 .... Allies accept Japanese surrender.

September 2, 1945 .... Formal surrender signed on board U.S.S. Missouri in Tokyo Bay, marking end of Second World War.

Glossary

anschluss: the "connection" of Austria with Germany in March 1938.

Blitz: "lightning" in German; refers to the German aerial assault on British cities between 1940 and 1942.

Blitzkrieg: "lightning war"; term referring to Germany's form of warfare in the first phase of the war, 1939–1941.

Einsatzgruppen: Special SS commando units that conducted a bloodbath on the eastern front against the Jews.

kamakaze: "Divine Wind"—special suicide planes used by the Japanese for the first time in the Battle of Leyte Gulf.

lebensraum: "living space"—term employed by Hitler to describe Germany's need for expansion to the east in order to claim land for the Reich's swelling population.

SHAEF: Supreme Headquarters Allied Expeditionary Forces in the European Theater of Operations, commanded by Gen. Dwight Eisenhower from late 1943 until the end of the war in Europe.

SS: *Schutzstafel*, the elite organization of the National Socialist Party headed by Heinrich Himmler. Originally a special bodyguard for Hitler, it became police organization in the Third Reich.

Waffen-SS: special SS units that operated as elite military units on both the eastern and western fronts.

V-2: Vengeance Weapons, the V-2 and its buzz bomb predecessor, the V-1, were rockets developed by the Germans and launched against targets in Britain during the last year of the war.

Biographical Notes

Chamberlain, Neville (1869–1940). Last prewar prime minister of Great Britain. Associated with the policy of appeasement and the Munich Conference.

Chiang Kai-shek (1887–1975). Leader of the Chinese Kuomintang and head of state of Nationalist China.

Churchill, Winston (1874–1965) Wartime leader of Great Britain. Churchill became prime minister on May 10, 1940, the day Germany launched its invasion of Western Europe. He was an inspiring orator whose leadership during Britain's dark days of 1940 and 1941 held the nation together. He worked tirelessly to create and maintain the anti-Nazi alliance and cemented a particularly close relationship with the United States. More than FDR, Churchill remained wary of Stalin's postwar intentions.

De Gaulle, Charles (1890–1970). Tank commander in the French Army and cabinet minister in the French government in 1940. In exile he became leader of the Free French Forces.

Eisenhower, Dwight (1890–1969). American and Allied Supreme Commander in North Africa, Sicily and northwest Europe. He was in charge of Operation Overlord and commanded the Allied military forces in Europe. Known mainly for his remarkable personal political skills, desperately needed in managing a coalition military force. Eisenhower determined the overall military strategy during the western drive into Germany, advocating a broad-front approach rather than a dash for Berlin.

Goering, Hermann (1893–1946). Head of the four-year plan in prewar Germany; commander of the German Air Force (*Luftwaffe*); and officially second in command of the Third Reich.

Guderian, Heinz (1888–1953). Tank commander and architect of the *Blitzkrieg*; commanded German armored forces in France and Russia.

Halsey, William (1882–1959). Fleet Admiral "Bull" Halsey played a key role in U.S. naval operations against the Japanese in the Central Pacific. He commanded the U.S. Central Pacific Fleet at the crucial Battle of Leyte Gulf in October 1944.

Harris, Arthur (1892–1984). Air Chief Marshal, Bomber Harris was commander of the Royal Air Force's Bomber Command from 1942 until the end of the war; he was associated with the policy of nighttime area bombing of Germany.

Heydrich, Reinhard (1904–1942). Head of the Reich Main Security Office, Heydrich took charge of the SS extermination squads (*Einsatzgruppen*) on the Eastern Front in 1941. Heydrich was responsible for drafting the "Final Solution of the Jewish Question" and presided over the Wannsee Conference in January 1942.

Himmler, Heinrich (1900–1945). Head of the SS (Reichsfuhrer SS) throughout the Third Reich. Himmler was the primary architect of Nazi extermination policy in Europe and was the second most powerful figure of the Nazi regime.

Hirohito (1901–1987). Emperor of Japan, Hirohito officially presided over Japanese policy throughout the war but was largely a figurehead. In the war's final days, he intervened to press the military leadership to terminate hostilities.

Hitler, Adolf (1889–1945). Führer of the Third Reich who came to power in 1933. Hitler directed every aspect of German policy and increasingly intervened directly in military decisions. More than any other individual, he bears responsibility for the Second World War and its horrors.

King, Ernest (1878–1956) Appointed Commander in Chief of U.S. Naval Forces at war's outbreak, he assumed duties as Chief of Naval Operations and became the leading figure in the U.S. Navy during the war. In Allied councils he consistently pressed for greater attention to the Pacific Theater.

MacArthur, Douglas (1880–1964). Dominant American military figure in the Pacific Theater, MacArthur survived the Japanese assault on the Philippines in 1941, vowing "I shall return." He did so in January 1945. While Nimitz directed American forces in the Central Pacific, MacArthur led the advance through the southwest. At war's end he accepted Japanese surrender on Halsey's flagship, the U.S.S. *Missouri*.

Marshall, George (1880–1959). Army Chief of Staff at war's outbreak, Marshall presided over the creation of the U.S. Army, which in 1939 possessed fewer than 200,000 troops. He became chairman of the Joint Chiefs of Staff and FDR's most trusted military advisor.

Molotov, Vyacheslav (1890–1970). Served as Soviet foreign minister throughout the war. He began his career with the Nazi-Soviet Pact in August 1939 and continued as Stalin's foreign representative with the Allies after Germany's invasion of the Soviet Union in 1941.

Montgomery, Bernard (1887–1976). Field Marshal Montgomery was the leading British military figure of the Second World War. He played a major role in the Allied victories in North Africa, Sicily, and Italy, and under Eisenhower's command he planned Operation Overlord. On D-Day Montgomery was ground commander of Allied forces under Eisenhower's supreme command and directed an Allied army group until the end of the war.

Mussolini, Benito (1883–1945). Fascist dictator of Italy from 1922 to 1943. Mussolini embarked on an expansionist policy in Ethiopia in 1935 and supported Franco in Spain in 1936. He entered the Second World War as Hitler's junior partner, invading France only after the Germans had smashed the French Army, and he mounted a disastrous campaign against Greece in November 1940, only to be bailed out by Hitler. Defeated in North Africa, he was deposed in July 1943 and was again rescued by Hitler to rule a German puppet state in northern Italy. He was captured and executed by partisans in April 1945.

Nagumo, Chuichi (1887–1944). Vice-Admiral Nagumo was the commander of the Japanese First Carrier Fleet. He directed the Japanese assault on Pearl Harbor in December 1941 and at the Battle of Midway in 1942. He fought unsuccessful naval engagements off Guadalcanal and later at Saipan, and he committed suicide in July 1944.

Nimitz, Chester (1885–1966). Nimitz commanded the U.S. Pacific Fleet from just after Pearl Harbor until the end of the war. In 1942 he assumed command of the Central Pacific Theater and directed the island-hopping drive through the Gilberts, Marshalls, and Marianas toward the Japanese home islands.

Patton, George (1885–1945). Easily the most flamboyant American general, Patton was a vocal advocate of armored warfare. He commanded a corps in Operation Torch, directed the 7th Army in the invasion of Sicily, and led the spectacular Allied breakout from Normandy as commander of the U.S. 3rd Army. His intervention during the Battle of the Bulge was a decisive factor in the Allied victory.

Petain, Henri-Philippe (1856–1951). French hero of the First World War, Petain entered the government of Paul Reynaud in 1940 during the German invasion. Rather than bolstering French morale, Petain advocated an armistice, undermining those, such as de Gaulle, who wished to fight on. He assumed power and offered the Germans an armistice on June 22, 1940. He served as head of the new collaborationist Vichy regime until its collapse, was tried after the war and sentenced to death, but de Gaulle commuted his sentence to life in prison.

von Ribbentrop, Joachim (1893–1946). Became Hitler's foreign minister in 1938 and negotiated the Nazi-Soviet Non-Aggression Pact in August 1939. His influence waned during the war. Tried at Nuremberg, he was hanged in 1946.

Rommel, Erwin (1891–1944). Excellent German commander chosen by Hitler to lead the Afrika Korps where he established his reputation as "the Desert Fox." He was placed in charge of preparing German defenses for the anticipated Allied landing in northwest Europe. Wounded after D-Day, he was implicated in the plot to overthrow Hitler on July 20, 1944, and was offered the choice of suicide or standing trial. Hitler gave him a hero's funeral, claiming that he had died of his combat wounds.

Roosevelt, Franklin D. (1882–1945). President of the United States since 1933, FDR was a towering figure in the alliance against Hitler and Japan. He struggled against American isolationism until the Japanese attack on Pearl Harbor threw the United States into the war, and he sent aid to Britain and the Soviet Union under "Lend-Lease." Agreeing with Churchill that defeat of Germany was the first priority, he presided over American policy, both military and diplomatic, until his death in April 1945. He held out great hopes for the United Nations, an organization that he inspired and founded.

von Rundstedt, Gerd (1875–1953). Rundstedt came out of retirement in 1939 and led an army group in the invasions of Poland and France. His troops executed the breakthrough that stranded British and French forces in Belgium, but Rundstedt halted his forces before Dunkirk, allowing British and some French troops to be evacuated. In 1941 he commanded German forces in the Ukraine and in 1942 was named commander in chief of the West, a post he held until July 1, 1944. He planned the Ardennes offensive of December 1944 but retired after its failure in March 1945.

Spaatz, Carl (1891–1974). Spaatz commanded U.S. air forces in Europe and then in the Pacific. An advocate of daylight strategic bombing, Spaatz led the 8th Air Force in England, the principal American instrument in the strategic air campaign against Germany. Later he directed U.S. air forces in North Africa, and in 1944 he assumed the position of commanding general of the strategic air force in Europe. In the spring of 1945 he took up the same post in the Pacific Theater, where he directed the final air assault on Japan.

Speer, Albert (1905–1981). Hitler's architect, who in 1942 became the mastermind of Germany's economic mobilization for war. As minister of armaments and munitions, Speer managed to increase German war production, despite massive Allied bombing, until September 1944.

Stalin, Joseph (1879–1953). Dictatorial leader of the Soviet Union and its armed forces. Mistrustful of the West, Stalin entered into a non-aggression pact with Hitler in 1939 and faithfully fulfilled its terms until the German invasion in June 1941. His purge of the Red Army in 1938 had seriously weakened the armed forces but Stalin presided over their revival and made shrewd military appointments, especially the selection of Georgi Zhukov. Stalin never really overcame his mistrust of the West, and tensions between the Soviet Union and the United States grew during the last year of the war.

Tojo, Heideki (1884–1948). A military man who became prime minister of Japan in 1941, Tojo directed the Japanese war effort until the summer of 1944. He held two addition positions—war minister and chief of army staff—and was the central figure in Japan's conduct of the war. He resigned after the fall of the Marianas in July 1944. After the war he was one of the seven Japanese to be hanged as a war criminal by the Allies.

Truman, Harry (1884–1972). A senator from Missouri at the war's outbreak, Truman was elected vice president in 1944 and became president upon FDR's death on April 12, 1945. He continued FDR's policies, though he would find himself on a collision course with Stalin at the Potsdam conference and afterward. He remained in office until 1953, playing a leading role in shaping the contours of the cold war.

Yamamoto, Isoroku (1884–1943). Japan's leading naval strategist and an early advocate of carrier-based aircraft in naval operations. As minister of the navy and subsequently commander of the 1st Fleet, Yamamoto oversaw the buildup of the Imperial Navy and its air power. Although he was convinced that Japan could not prevail in a protracted war with the United States, he devised the daring plan of attack on Pearl Harbor which he hoped would cripple American naval power in the Pacific. He was also responsible for planning the ill-fated naval attack on Midway. He was killed in April 1943 when American aircraft shot down an plane in which he was traveling to inspect the Western Solomons.

Zhukov, Georgi (1896–1974). Deputy supreme commander and chief of the Red Army during virtually all of the Second World War, Zhukov earned his reputation with a successful action against the Japanese in Mongolia during 1939. After the German invasion of the Soviet Union, he held a series of important command positions in defense of Smolensk, Leningrad, and finally Moscow in the fall of 1941. The "Savior of Moscow," he went on to become the "Savior of Stalingrad" as well, commanding the Soviet defense and counterattack against Paulus's 6th Army. Zhukov would lead the great Russian sweep into the Ukraine, Poland, and finally Germany. His troops entered Berlin on May 2, and the Germans surrendered to him on May 8, 1945.

Bibliography

* Denotes Essential Reading

I. General Works

Gilbert, Martin. *The Second World War*. Among the most extensive and useful of the single-volume histories of the war.

*Keegan, John. *The Second World War*. New York: Penguin Books, 1989. The best synthetic treatment of the war by the most respected military historian today. The book offers not only the essential storyline of the war but an incisive interpretation.

*Overy, Richard. *Why the Allies Won*. New York: Norton, 1996. An insightful and probing examination of the factors that led to the Allied victory. The best interpretive treatment of these issues in the literature today.

Weinberg, Gerhard. *A World at Arms: A Global History of World War II*. Cambridge: Cambridge University Press, 1994. An encyclopedic analysis of the war that is particularly strong on the diplomacy of the conflict.

II. The Diplomatic Origins of the Second World War

*Iriye, Akira. *The Origins of the Second World War: Asia and the Pacific*. London: Longman, 1987. A brief but probing analysis of the diplomatic origins of the conflict in Asia and the South Pacific by the leading expert in the field.

Kitchen, Martin. *Europe Between the Wars: A Political History*. London: Longman, 1988. A very useful account of the diplomacy of the inter-war period from Versailles in 1919 to the outbreak of war in 1939.

Rich, Norman. *Hitler's War Aims: Ideology , the Nazi State, and the Course of Expansion*. New York: Norton, 1973. Still the best treatment of Hitler's foreign policy and war aims in English.

*Taylor, A. J. P. *The Origins of the Second World War*. New York: Athenaeum, 1961. A highly controversial but at times brilliant analysis of the coming of the war. Taylor's treatment of German foreign policy is questionable but his explanation of appeasement and the dilemmas of British and French policy in the inter-war years is compelling.

III. The Air War

Crane, Conrad. *Bombs, Cities, and Civilians: American Air Power Strategy in World War II*. Lawrence, Kansas: University of Kansas Press, 1993. A very useful examination of American bombing which emphasizes the differences between American and British policy.

Hastings, Max. *Bomber Command*. London: Pan Books, 1981. A very readable account of the RAF's Bomber Command.

Murray, Williamson. *Luftwaffe*. Baltimore: The Nautical and Aviation Publishing Co., 1985. The best analysis of the German air force in World War II. Excellent evaluation of the Luftwaffe's strengths and weaknesses and the effects of Allied bombing.

Overy, R. J. *The Air War, 1939–1945*. Chelsea, MI: Scarborough House, 1991. The best overall treatment of the air war in Europe and Asia, examining the policies of all the major combatants.

Perret, Geoffrey. *Winged Victory: The Army Air Forces in World War II*. New York: Random House, 1993. A very readable volume that deals with American air operations around the globe.

Schaffer, Ronald. *Wings of Judgement: American Bombing in World War II*. New York: Oxford University Press, 1985. A provocative and enlightening examination of the development, evolution, and execution of American strategy during World War II.

Terraine, John. *A Time for Courage: The Royal Air Force in World War II*. New York: Macmillan, 1985. A useful companion volume to Hastings's work.

IV. The War at Sea

Boyne, Walter. *Clash of Titans: World War II at Sea*. New York, Touchstone Books, 1995. A highly readable one-volume account of naval combat around the globe.

Miller, Nathan. *War at Sea: A Naval History of World War II*. New York: Oxford University Press, 1995. More detailed and analytic than Boyne's fine book, a good companion to Boyne and Morison.

*Morison, S. E. *The Two-Ocean War: A Short History of the United States Navy in the Second World War*. New York: Little Brown and Co., 1963. An excellent condensation of Morison's multi-volume history of the American navy during the war. Morison's work remains at the top of the list.

Padfield, Peter. *War Beneath the Sea: Submarine Conflict During World War II*. New York: John Wiley & Son, 1995. The standard work on submarine warfare around the globe.

V. The War in Asia and the South Pacific

Alperovitz, Gar. *The Decision to Use the Atomic Bomb*. New York: Vintage, 1995. A revisionist analysis of Truman's decision to employ the atomic bomb in 1945.

Bergerud, Eric. *Touched with Fire: The Land War in the South Pacific*. New York: Penguin Books, 1996. An important examination of how the land war in the South Pacific was fought, dealing not only with the formulation of strategy but with the actual conditions on the ground.

Costello, John. *The Pacific War*. New York: Quill, 1982. A very useful single-volume history of the war.

Dower, John. *War Without Mercy: Race and Power in the Pacific War*. New York: Pantheon Books, 1986. Offers a controversial interpretation of the confrontation between Americans and Japanese, arguing that race was the dominant feature of the Pacific war.

Feis, Herbert. *The Atomic Bomb and the End of World War II*. Princeton: Princeton University Press, 1966. Feis argues that Truman's decision to use the bomb was based largely on his determination to bring the war to a speedy end and stop the slaughter. A useful counterpoint to Alperovitz's revisionist argument.

Ienaga, Saburo. *The Pacific War 1931–1945*. New York: Pantheon Books, 1978. A provocative interpretation of the war from a Japanese perspective—one highly critical of Japanese policy and motives.

*Lord, Walter. *Incredible Victory: The Battle of Midway*. New York, Harper-Collins, 1967. Riveting account of perhaps the most important naval battle in the Pacific war.

*Prangle, Gordon W. *At Dawn We Slept: The Untold Story of Pearl Harbor*. New York: McGraw-Hill, 1981. An excellent depiction of the attack on Pearl Harbor and the controversy surrounding it.

Ross, Bill D. *Iwo Jima: Legacy of Valor*. New York: Vintage, 1988. A powerful analysis of this important battle, this book is among the very best narrative accounts of the slaughter on Iwo Jima.

*Spector, Ronald H. *Eagle Against the Sun: The American War with Japan*. New York: Free Press, 1985. The most comprehensive and probably the best single-volume history of the war in the Pacific.

Weintraub, Stanley. *The Last Great Victory: The End of World War II, July/August 1945*. New York: Penguin, 1995. An important analysis of the last months of the war, especially the decision to drop the atomic bomb on Japan.

VI. The War in Europe

Ambrose, Stephen E. *D-Day, June 6, 1944: The Climactic Battle of World War II*. New York: Simon and Schuster, 1994. A detailed, moving , and highly readable account of the Allied invasion of Normandy.

Clark, Alan. *Barbarossa: The Russian-German Conflict, 1941–1945*. New York: Quill, 1985. A very lively one-volume account of the colossal conflict between these two ideological adversaries.

D'Este, Carlo. *Decision in Normandy*. New York: E.P. Dutton, 1983. A probing analysis of the Allied strategic conflicts and their resolution during the Normandy campaign.

———. *World War II in the Mediterranean 1942–1945*. Chapel Hill, N.C.: Algonquin Books: 1990. The best overall treatment of the different campaigns in the Mediterranean theater.

Erickson, John. *The Road to Berlin: Stalin's War with Germany*. Boulder, Colo: Westview Press, 1983. Among the best treatments of the Red Army's relentless drive into Germany, as the Russians went onto the offensive in 1943–1945.

*———. *The Road to Stalingrad*. New York: Harper & Row, 1975. An important account of the German offensives in the Soviet Union from 1941 to the defeat at Stalingrad in 1943.

Grahm, Dominick, and Shelford Bidwell. *Tug of War: The Battle for Italy, 1943–1945*. New York: St. Martin's Press, 1986.

*Keegan, John. *Six Armies in Normandy: From D-Day to the Liberation of Paris*. New York: Penguin Books, 1983. A brilliant analysis of D-Day invasion and the strategic differences between Britain and the United States prior to—and after—D-Day.

VII. The Experience of Combat

Ambrose, Stephen E. *Band of Brothers: E Company, 506th Regiment, 101st Airborne from Normandy to Hitler's Eagle's Nest*. New York: Simon and Schuster, 1992. Follows the experiences of a 101st Airborne company from training, through Normandy, Operation Market Garden, and into Germany.

*————. *Citizen Soldiers: The U.S. Army from the Normandy Beaches to the Bulge to the Surrender of Germany, June 7, 1944-May 7, 1945*. New York: Simon and Schuster, 1997. An excellent treatment of the American war effort, from top to bottom, in northern Europe.

Astor, Gerald. A Blood-Dimmed Tide: The Battle of the Bulge by the Men Who Fought It. New York: Dell Publishing, 1992.

*Bartov, Omer. *The Eastern Front, 1941–1945: German Troops and the Barbarization of Warfare*. New York: St. Martin's, 1985. A searing account of Germany's war without rules against the Red Army.

*Childers, Thomas. *Wings of Morning: The Story of the Last American Bomber Shot Down Over Germany in World War II*. Reading, MA: Addison Wesley, 1995) The tragic story an American air crew and their families.

Ellis, John. On the Front Lines: The Experience of War Through the Eyes of the Allied Soldiers in World War II. New York: John Wiley & Sons, 1990.

Fahey, James J. *Pacific War Diary 1942–1945: The Secret Diary of an American Sailor*. Boston: Houghton-Mifflin, 1963.

Hynes, Samuel. *Reflections of a World War II Aviator*. New York: Pocket Books, 1989. A beautifully written account of an American aviator's training and war in the Pacific.

Linderman, Gerald. *The World Within War: America's Combat Experience in World War II*. New York: The Free Press, 1997. An analysis of the experience of combat in Europe and the Pacific. It deals largely with American experiences, but also examines those of the Japanese, Germans, and Russians.

*Sledge, Eugene. *With the Old Breed: At Peleliu and Okinawa*. New York: Oxford University Press. The most powerful memoir of the war in the Pacific. An unforgettable, haunting book that captures the horrors of combat in two of the most memorable campaigns of the war.

VIII. America at War: The Homefront

*Blum, John M. *V Was For Victory: Politics and American Culture During World War II*. New York: Harcourt Brace-Jovanovich, 1976. Perhaps the standard work on life in the United States during the war.

Fussel, Paul. *Wartime: Understanding and Behavior in the Second World War*. New York: Oxford University Press, 1989. A provocative and biting examination of wartime attitudes on both the homefront and the front lines. The author contrasts the "high-mindedness" of the homefront with the brutal realities of war.

Milward, Alan S. *War, Economy and Society 1939–1945*. Berkeley, CA: University of California Press, 1977. A comparative analysis of the major combatants' mobilization for war and the social consequences thereof.

Noakes, Jeremy, ed. *The Civilian in War: The Home Front in Europe, Japan, and the USA in World War II*. Exeter, 1992. An informative collection of articles dealing with various aspects of social and cultural life in the major powers during the war.

*O'Neil, William. *A Democracy At War: America's Fight at Home and Abroad in World War II*. New York: Free Press, 1993. A very useful treatment of life on the homefront in the United States, examining race relations, the changing role of women, popular entertainment, and sexual mores.

*Reynolds, David. *Rich Relations: The American Occupation of Britain, 1942–1945*. New York: Random House, 1995. An exceptional book that deals not only with Anglo-American relations at the highest levels but provides a very revealing portrait of both British and American societies as the collided when American troops arrived in Britain in 1942.

IX. The Holocaust

Bauer, Yehuda. *A History of the Holocaust*. New York: Doubleday, 1982. An excellent overall treatment of the evolution of Nazi racial policies.

*Browning, Christopher. *Ordinary Men: Police Battalion 101 and the Final Solution in Poland*. New York: Harper-Collins, 1992. An extremely powerful and well argued examination of the opening phase of Nazi genocide in Poland by one of the leading historians of the Holocaust.

*Friedlander, Henry. *The Origins of Nazi Genocide: From Euthanasia to the Final Solution*. Chapel Hill, N.C.: University of North Carolina Press, 1997. The best of the many comprehensive studies of the Holocaust.

Hilberg, Raul. *The Destruction of the European Jews*. New York: Holmes & Meier, 1985. Hilberg's work remains the starting point for any reading about the Holocaust.

X. Biographies/Memoirs of the Major Wartime Leaders

Ambrose, Stephen E. *Eisenhower: Soldier, General of the Army, President Elect, 1890–1952*. New York: Simon and Schuster, 1983. Comprehensive treatment of Eisenhower's career by his definitive biographer.

*Bullock, Alan. *Hitler: A Study in Tyranny*. London: Odhams Press, 1952. Bullock's classic biography remains, despite numerous newer works, the essential one volume treatment of Hitler and his rule.

*Churchill, Winston. *The Second World War*. Six volumes. London, 1948–1955. A classic memoir/history of the war years by Britain's wartime prime minister. Still electrifying reading.

*D'Este, Carlo. *Patton: A Genius for War*. New York: Harper-Collins, 1995. A very readable book that breaks down many of the myths about America's most colorful general.

Doolittle, James H. *I Could Never Be This Lucky Again*. New York: Bantam, 1991. General Doolittle relates his experiences, from his prewar career to his famous 1942 raid on Tokyo to his leadership of the Eighth Air Force.

*Eisenhower, Dwight D. *Crusade in Europe*. New York: Doubleday, 1948. The Allied commanding general's account of the defeat of Nazi Germany. A remarkable memoir/analysis.

Hamilton, Nigel. *Monty: Master of the Battlefield, 1942–1944*. London: Hamish Hamilton, 1983. A detailed and spirited account of General Bernard Montgomery's role in the war, from the campaign in North Africa to the D-Day invasion.

———. *Monty: The Field Marshal, 1944–1976*. London: Hamish Hamilton, 1986. Hamilton continues the story with the invasion of northern Europe in 1944 and traces Field Marshal Montgomery's contribution to the Allied victory as well as his evaluation of subsequent events.

Notes

Notes